Tropes

Tropes

Properties, Objects, and Mental Causation

Douglas Ehring

UNIVERSITY PRESS

UNIVERSITY PRESS

Great Clarendon Street, Oxford, OX2 6DP,

Oxford University Press is a department of the University of Oxford.
It furthers the University's objective of excellence in research, scholarship,
and education by publishing worldwide. Oxford is a registered trade mark of
Oxford University Press in the UK and in certain other countries

© Douglas Ehring 2011

The moral rights of the author have been asserted

First published 2011
First published in paperback 2014

All rights reserved. No part of this publication may be reproduced, stored in
a retrieval system, or transmitted, in any form or by any means, without the
prior permission in writing of Oxford University Press, or as expressly permitted
by law, by licence, or under terms agreed with the appropriate reprographics
rights organization. Enquiries concerning reproduction outside the scope of the
above should be sent to the Rights Department, Oxford University Press, at the
address above

You must not circulate this work in any other form
and you must impose this same condition on any acquirer

Published in the United States of America by Oxford University Press
198 Madison Avenue, New York, NY 10016, United States of America

British Library Cataloguing in Publication Data
Data available

Library of Congress Cataloging in Publication Data
Data available

ISBN 978–0–19–960853–9 (Hbk)
ISBN 978–0–19–870303–7 (Pbk)

To my wonderful wife, Ann Saucer, and to the two best girls in the whole wide world, Bella and Sophia.

Contents

Acknowledgments	viii
Introduction: Properties and concrete particulars	1

Part I: Tropes

1. Distinguishing particulars from universals	19
2. Why believe in tropes?	46
3. The individuation of tropes	76
4. Bundle Theory	98
5. Tropes and mental causation	136

Part II: Natural Class Trope Nominalism

6. Why Natural Class Tropes?	175
7. The classic objections to Natural Class Trope Nominalism	203
8. The determination objections	227
Bibliography	242
Index	247

Acknowledgments

In the process of writing this work, I have greatly benefited from the writings of David Armstrong, Keith Campbell, and David Lewis, among others. I benefited from the comments and conversations of my colleagues at Southern Methodist University in Dallas, including Eric Barnes, David Hausman, Steve Sverdlik, Philippe Chuard, Luke Robinson, Soraya Gollop, and Steven Hiltz. I am indebted to Brad Thompson and Justin Fisher for their insightful comments on various chapters and, especially, to Robert Howell who read and commented extensively and discerningly on the entire manuscript. I am also indebted to David Papineau and Scott Sturgeon for earlier conversations that influenced this work. I particularly want to thank Mark Heller for his help with this manuscript and for many years of highly stimulating metaphysical conversations. I am also grateful for the remarkably thorough and useful comments of referees, which I am sure prevented many errors from entering into the final manuscript. Above all, I want to thank Jessica Wilson for her extremely penetrating and comprehensive comments on this work, which played a pivotal role both in the details of this work and its organization. I am most grateful to my wife, Ann, for her unflinching support and encouragement. I am indebted to SMU for a sabbatical and a Gerald J. Ford Fellowship while working on this manuscript.

This book incorporates material from several published articles, listed below. Permission of the original publishers (Wiley Blackwell, Oxford University Press, Taylor & Francis, and Springer) is gratefully acknowledged.

"Mental Causation, Determinables and Property Instances." *Nous* 30 (1996): 461–80.
"Lewis, Temporary Intrinsics, and Momentary Tropes." *Analysis* 57 (1997): 254–8.
"Trope Persistence and Temporary External Relations." *The Australasian Journal of Philosophy* 76 (1998): 473–9.
"Tropeless in Seattle: The Cure for Insomnia." *Analysis* 59 (1999): 19–24.
"Temporal Parts and Bundle Theory." *Philosophical Studies* 104 (2001): 163–8.
"Spatial Relations Between Universals." *The Australasian Journal of Philosophy* 80 (2002): 17–23.
"The Causal Argument Against Natural Class Trope Nominalism." *Philosophical Studies* 107 (2002): 179–90.
"Part-Whole Physicalism and Mental Causation." *Synthese* 136 (2003): 359–88.
"Property Counterparts and Natural Class Trope Nominalism." *The Australasian Journal of Philosophy* 82 (2004): 436–54.
"Distinguishing Universals From Particulars." *Analysis* 64 (2004): 326–32.

Introduction
Properties and concrete particulars

Properties and objects are present the world over. We cannot take a step without bumping into them. We cannot construct a theory in science without referencing them. We eat, sleep, and drink them. Given their ubiquitous character, one might *think* that there would be a standard metaphysical account of properties and objects since part of the business of metaphysics includes dealing with various things that are everywhere. But there is no such account, only widely divergent takes on these fundamental categories, including their rejection. Properties and objects remain a philosophical mystery. The main goal of this work is to provide a metaphysical account of properties and of how they are related to concrete particulars.

On the broadest level, this work is meant to be a defense of tropes and of Trope Bundle Theory as the best accounts of properties and objects, and a defense of a specific brand of Trope Nominalism, Natural Class Trope Nominalism. Each of these tasks is pursued separately, with the first part of this work acting as a general introduction and defense of tropes and Trope Bundle Theory, and the second part acting as the more specific defense of Natural Class Trope Nominalism. I try to demonstrate in Part 1 that there are tropes and indicate some of the things that tropes can do for us metaphysically, including helping to solve the problems of mental causation, while remaining neutral between different theories of tropes. Only in the second part do we get the full picture of what a trope is.

Why think, at the outset, that Trope Theory is worth pursuing? The reason is that Trope Nominalism, if successful, would yield a bonanza of metaphysically significant results. For example, given Trope Nominalism:

- There are no universals, a category of things that many philosophers have found to be mysterious.
- There are no substrata or bare particulars, also thought to be problematic.
- We have a one-category ontology, which is more parsimonious than the typical universals-based two-category ontology.
- We can account for resemblance between objects and between properties.
- We can account for property persistence (more on this in a moment).

- We can account for the metaphysical character of concrete particulars.
- We can account for the ontology of causal relata and the nature of the causal relation.
- We can solve the problems of mental causation.

So tropes can potentially do a lot of metaphysical work, but that still leaves open the question of why one should pursue Natural Class Trope Nominalism in particular, a far-from-orthodox version of Trope Theory that is generally considered a non-starter. The reason is clear-cut. There is a *big* problem with what I will call the Standard Trope Theory of Campbell and Williams. The problem is that the conception of tropes embedded in this version of Trope Theory is not stable. Standard Theory tropes collapse either into exemplifications of universals or some non-Standard conception of tropes. The time has come to pursue an alternative conception. The best alternative, surprisingly, I will suggest, is found in Natural Class Trope Nominalism.

1. Sparse properties, problems, and theories of properties

I will now provide some stage setting, with a brief description of the philosophical background concerning properties. My goal in this section is twofold: (1) to spell out the main, but not the only problems that a theory of properties is meant to solve; and (2) to situate Trope Nominalism—and the specific version of that theory I defend, Natural Class Trope Nominalism—into the matrix of available metaphysical accounts of properties. First, I will indicate the kind of properties that are at issue in this work, "sparse properties," by reference to the distinctive roles such properties play. Second, I will describe the two main issues a theory of sparse properties should address, including the traditional problem of "one over many," but also including a nontraditional problem concerning property persistence. The latter has *not* been discussed much in the literature, but I take it to be central to a theory of properties. Third, I will briefly outline the main candidates for what a sparse property is. Fourth, I will outline the main claims of this work about sparse properties. In the next section, I will discuss concrete particulars.

1.1 Sparse properties

Following Lewis and others, sparse properties can be distinguished from abundant properties. For every meaningful predicate there is an abundant property, but not so for sparse properties. Abundant properties serve as the semantic values of meaningful predicates, but abundant properties are not limited to the semantic values of the actual predicates or even to those of predicates we could possibly possess. There is an abundant property for "any condition we could write down, even if we could write at infinite length and even if we could name all those things that must remain nameless because they fall outside our acquaintance" (Lewis 1986b: 59–60). (For

Lewis, abundant properties are sets of possible objects: every such set is an abundant property, but not every such set is a sparse/natural property.) Sparse properties, on the other hand, are picked out, primarily, by reference to their role in accounting for similarity among concrete particulars and accounting for the causal powers of concrete particulars. Not every abundant property guarantees similarity or bestows causal powers.

How should these two characteristics of sparse properties be understood? I will understand the role of grounding objective similarities as follows: objects a and b resemble each other in some respect just in case there is a sparse property P that characterizes a and b or there are similar sparse properties P and P', such that P characterizes a and P' characterizes b. The second disjunct is meant to allow for the possibility that sparse properties are tropes. I take "characterization" here to be whatever relation or non-relational "tie" that exists between an object and a property P that makes it true that "a is P." How one understands "a is characterized by P" will depend on one's account of what it is for an object to have property. (For example, depending on one's theory, "a is characterized by P" might be understood as "a instantiates P," "a includes P as a non-spatio-temporal part" (in the case of tropes), "a is a member of P" (in the case of Natural Class Object Nominalism) or "a resembles all the members of P" (in the case of Resemblance Object Nominalism).) As for causal powers, the idea is that for every causal power of an object there is a sparse property or properties that account for that causal power, and for every sparse property there is a set of causal powers that property bestows, leaving open the question of whether those causal powers are essential to that property.

More doubtful is a third characteristic, minimality, that Lewis attributes to sparse properties. According to Lewis, sparse properties are restricted to properties from physics upon which all other properties supervene.[1] There are no supervening, redundant sparse properties. "There are only just enough of them to characterize things completely and without redundancy" (Lewis 1986b: 60). On closer inspection, however, minimality appears *not* to be a necessary feature of sparse properties. In an infinitely complex universe, which may be our world, there would be no fundamental properties, but there would be sparse properties—no bottom-level sparse properties, but sparse properties nonetheless that asymmetrically supervene on lower-level properties (Schaffer 2004: 99).[2] Thus, I will *not* assume that sparse properties are confined to a minimal base.[3] One consequence of this rejection of minimality is that a theory of

---

[1] Alternately, one might suggest, as a referee does suggest, a characterization of minimality in terms of whatever the fundamental properties happen to be, avoiding the assumption that the only fundamental properties are physical.

[2] He also argues that fundamental properties would not be suited to account for all macro-level similarities and causal powers (Schaffer 2004: 94–5).

[3] Schaffer replaces "minimality" with "primacy": "sparse properties serve as the ontological base for linguistic truths" (2004: 100). Lewis lists three other characteristics of sparse properties: "they are intrinsic, they are highly specific, the sets of their instances are *ipso facto* not entirely miscellaneous..." (1986b: 60). I will follow Schaffer here, again, and treat these characteristics as somewhat secondary, as characteristics that

properties must also take into account higher-level properties. Since the latter properties will likely include mental properties, I will also show how Trope Theory can be applied to mental properties, especially with respect to their causal powers, a requirement for being a sparse property, demonstrating that Trope Theory provides a solution to the problem(s) of mental causation, which seems to exclude the causal powers of mental properties.

I will not present an argument for the existence of sparse properties or review various philosophical arguments for sparse properties that appeal to conceptual analysis, considerations of ontological commitment or truthmakers, and will assume that there are sparse properties. What I will do is argue that sparse properties are tropes.

1.2 Two problems of properties

1.2.1 One Over Many The first task of a theory of sparse properties/relations is to provide a metaphysical account of the phenomenon of sameness of type across different tokens, the problem of *One Over Many*. A theory of sparse properties must account for the fact that distinct objects can have the "same property type," specifying what makes for "sameness of type." The standard way of setting up this problem involves different objects at the same time so that the issue concerns "oneness" at the level of types across objects at the same time: for example, two electrons of the same charge at the same time. However, this problem is not restricted to sameness of type across different objects at the same time. It includes sameness of type across different objects at different times or the same object at different times. For example, a theory of sparse properties must account for the fact that the ball at t and the same ball at a later time are of the same type, say, of the "red" type. At one extreme is a theory of sparse properties as universals that are literally shared across objects, a view according to which properties are not reducible to concrete objects in any way. Toward the other end of the spectrum is the view that makes sameness of type a matter of object–object resemblances: two objects are the same type in virtue of being members of a class of mutually resembling objects. Alternately, one can think of this as a problem about similarity in some respect. What accounts for the fact that the balls are similar with respect to color? A theory of sparse properties must metaphysically account for similarity in a certain respect between concrete particulars.[4]

1.2.2 One Over Many Times There is a second problem that a theory of sparse properties must also solve, the problem of property persistence: one property over many times, or, for short, the problem of *One Over Many Times*. The problem I have in

---

sparse properties have in virtue of having the similarity-grounding and causal-power-generating characteristics (Schaffer 2004: 94).

[4] Another problem is to account metaphysically for the fact that the same concrete particular can be a token of more than one type. A theory of sparse properties will account metaphysically for this fact, guaranteeing that a's being P does not collapse into a's being Q for any pair of distinct properties, P and Q. Rodriguez-Pereyra calls this the problem of "many over one" (2002: 46).

mind has not been widely discussed in philosophy. What is property persistence in the sense I have in mind? I do not mean the problem of accounting for sameness of property type over time. Using red as an example, *property type persistence* is a matter of exactly similar shades of red being exemplified by, say, a ball at t and a ball at t'. This is an instance of the issue of "sameness of type" mentioned earlier and not a distinct issue. Property type persistence is compatible with the destruction of the ball followed by its replacement with an exactly similar, but non-identical ball in the same location. In the latter case, however, one form of property persistence is missing. The property instance of red that characterizes a ball that is *not* replaced persists in a way that we do not find in the object replacement case. I will call this "property persistence," or, alternately, "property instance persistence." The difference between property persistence and mere property type persistence is not just a matter of the difference between one object and two different objects exemplifying the same fully determinate property type at different times. There can be mere property type persistence even in a single object across time. This point becomes clear when property persistence is contrasted with "immaculate property replacement." Suppose that there is a machine that eliminates all electrical charge from objects without a trace and with no other effect on the object, and a second machine instantly generates electrical charges in the same object. Each machine is directed, say, at the same particle, set to destroy/create an electrical charge of the same magnitude. As a result, there is no apparent shift in electrical charge in the particle from t to t'. There is a difference between this case and property persistence in which the particle undergoes no transformation by way of any machines, but retains its electrical charge over this same time period. The first case involves the replacement of one property by another, albeit an exactly similar property. The particle's electrical charge *changes* in immaculate property replacement in some sense, although imperceptibly. I call that kind of property change "nonsalient qualitative change." The second case does not involve property change. In the case that involves no intervention, the particle's electrical charge *persists*. Property persistence is not simply a matter of the same object exemplifying the same fully determinate property type at different times. Something else is involved. A theory of sparse properties must give a metaphysical account of property persistence.

1.3 Theories of properties

I will now describe the main candidates for sparse properties, followed by a sketch of the main claims I will make about sparse properties.[5]

---

[5] I am leaving out of the discussion Predicate/Concept/Mereological Nominalism/Ostrich Nominalism. For the Predicate Nominalist, a concrete object has a property F in virtue of the fact that the predicate "F" applies to that object. For the Concept Nominalist, a is F in virtue of the fact that a falls under the concept of F. Two objects share a property F just in case both objects are such that the predicate "F" applies to them (Predicate Nominalist)/both objects fall under the concept of F (Concept Nominalist). Under the Mereological Nominalism, which is closer to Resemblance Object Nominalism and Natural Class Object Nominalism than to Predicate/Concept Nominalism, properties are sums, not classes, of particulars. The property

1.3.1 Resemblance Object Nominalism For the Resemblance Object Nominalist, what makes it true that a concrete object *o* has the properties it has is *o*'s overall resemblance to other objects. This electron has a certain charge because it overall resembles other electrons.[6] What makes *a F* is that it overall resembles all actual (and, if modal realism is true, merely possible) *F* things, along with other conditions.[7] Overall resemblance between concrete objects is not further reducible to or explainable in terms of the properties of objects, the possession of shared universals or resembling tropes, or by being co-members of a natural class (Rodriguez-Pereyra 2002: 6). Two objects, *a* and *b*, resemble each other in a certain respect, say, redness, just in case each object overall resembles all the objects in a class of red things (Rodriguez-Pereyra 2002: 64).[8] Properties are classes of suitably resembling actual objects (and, in addition, merely possible concrete particulars, if modal realism is true).

1.3.2 Natural Class Object Nominalism For the Natural Class Object Nominalist, what makes *a F* is that *a* is a member of a certain natural class of *F* things. For a thing to be

---

of being red is the mereological sum of all and only red things. A particular is red just in case it is a part of the property redness. I reject Predicate and Concept Nominalism because of widely accepted objections. Properties could have existed even had there been no language or concepts (Armstrong 1989a: 11). Mereological Nominalism is also objectionable: "what makes something square cannot be that it is a part of the sum of square particulars, for many such parts are not square, for example, any sum of two squares is not a square" (Rodriguez-Pereyra 2002: 222). "Ostrich Nominalism" is the view that sentences such as "*a is F*" commit us to the existence of a particular object, *a*, but not to a property of being *F*. This is supposed to follow from Quine's semantic theory that says that "*a is F*" is true just in case there is an *x*, such that "*a*" designates *x* and "*F*" applies to *x* (Rodriguez-Pereyra 2002: 43).

[6] According to the "aristocratic" version of Resemblance Object Nominalism, the property of *F*-ness is a class of concrete particulars organized around certain exemplar *F* objects, such that each member of the *F* property class resembles each member of that exemplar group at least as closely as those exemplars resemble each other (Price 1953: 20–2; for an alternate formulation, see (Manley 2002: 78)). On the "democratic" version, *a* is *F* in virtue of resembling all the *F* objects, along with other conditions, and properties are *maximal* classes of certain resembling concrete particulars. (But see (Rodriguez-Pereyra 2002: 61) for a Resemblance Object Nominalist who rejects this identification of properties with such classes.) A class of resembling particulars is maximal just in case for any pair of members of the class, *a* and *b*, *a* and *b* resemble each other and nothing outside the class resembles every member of the class.

[7] Some of the objections to Resemblance Object Nominalism include the following. (1) *The Resemblance Regress Objection* Russell and others argue that the Resemblance Nominalist faces either a vicious infinite regress of resemblance relations or must make resemblance a universal. See (Campbell 1990: 38) for a discussion and defense against this objection. (2) *The Causal Objection* Resemblance Object Nominalism, Armstrong argues, is not compatible with the fact that when an object acts causally it does not do so in virtue of things other than itself, since this view implies that the object acts in virtue of the entire class of *F* things (1989a: 49–50). (3) *Type-Level Truths About Properties* It has been claimed that Resemblance Object Nominalists cannot provide an analysis of sentences such as "red resembles orange more than it resembles blue" and "redness is a color" (Armstrong 1978a: 59–61. See (Rodriguez-Pereyra 2002: 91–2) for a possible reply).

[8] Other objections to this view include the following. (1) *Imperfect Community* There could exist a class of particulars such that every two of them resemble each other, but it is not the case that they all share some property in common. (See Rodriguez-Pereyra 2002 for a full treatment.) (2) *Companionship* Suppose that all the red objects are square, but not all of the square objects are red. In that case, every square object resembles every red object, but there are some square objects that are not red. (Again, see Rodriguez-Pereyra 2002 for a full treatment.)

white is for it to be a member of the natural class of actual, white objects (Armstrong 1989a: 18). Properties are natural classes of concrete objects, but being a natural class is not reducible further. Resemblance-in-a-respect is a matter of co-membership in a natural class. (An object *o* is *R*-related to object *o'* just in case the ordered pair <*o,o'*> is a member of a certain natural class of ordered pairs.) Although not reducible, naturalness comes in degrees, with both a maximum—perfectly natural classes—and a minimum—classes that are not natural to any degree. Exact resemblance between concrete particulars is a matter of co-membership in a perfectly natural class.[9] If Natural Class Object Nominalism is combined with modal realism, sparse properties are natural classes of actual and possible objects.[10]

1.3.3 Universalism According to Universalism (Armstrong's version), properties and relations are universals, and universals are capable of being wholly present at more than one location at the same time. The charge of this electron and the exactly similar charge of that electron are literally identical, and that very same charge universal is wholly present where the first electron is present and wholly present where the second electron is present.[11] Exact similarity-in-a-certain-respect between objects is grounded

---

[9] Some of the most important objections to Natural Class Object Nominalism include the following. (1) *The Modal Objection* Natural Class Object Nominalism seems to imply wrongly that *a* would *not* have been *F* had that *F* class not existed because, say, one of its non-*a* members had not existed (Armstrong 1989a: 27; Wolterstorff 1970: Chap. 8). (2) *The Order of Explanation Objection* Contrary to Natural Class Object Nominalism, since membership in a natural class of objects is determined by an object's properties, those memberships cannot account for what properties an object has (Armstrong 1989a: 28). (3) *The Causal Objection* Natural Class Object Nominalism, Armstrong argues, is not compatible with the fact that when an object acts causally it does not do so in virtue of things other than itself, since this view implies that the object acts in virtue of the entire class of *F*, membership in which is what it is for *a* to be *F*. (4) *Type-Level Truths About Properties* This view, it has been argued, has difficulty with generating nominalistically acceptable paraphrases of higher-order truths about properties such as "redness is more similar to orangeness than to blueness" and "redness is a color." Some of these problems are solved on Lewis's Natural Class Object theory (1986b: 50–69).

[10] The most defensible versions of Resemblance Object Nominalism and Natural Class Object Nominalism seem to require a commitment to modal realism in order to handle the following objections. (1) *The Contingently Coextensive Property Objection* There are or could be cases of contingently coextensive but distinct properties, *F*-ness and *G*-ness. Actualist versions of these theories imply in those cases that *F*-ness and *G*-ness are identical. (2) *The One Instance Objection* It is possible that there is only one object in the world or only one *F* object in the world, none of the parts of which are also *F*, but that object would still be *F*, even though there are no other *F* objects it resembles or there is no multi-membered natural class of *F* objects of which it is a member (Rodriguez-Pereyra 2002: 90). These two objections fail against the modal realist versions of these theories because, in that case, *F*-ness and *G*-ness will be instantiated by differing sets of actual objects plus merely possible objects and there will be more than one instance of *F*, even if there is only one actual instance. This apparent need for modal realism gives us a reason to set these accounts aside and look for alternatives. Modal realism is generally rejected by philosophers with some exceptions, and there are intuitions, that I share, that run against modal realism, actualist intuitions to the effect that the only things that are real are the things of the actual world (van Inwagen 1986: 198).

[11] Armstrong, at one point, says that this is a crude way of talking about the locations of universals and offers an alternative, but this is the most widely held view of universals (1989a: 99).

in the sharing of an identical universal.[12] Inexact resemblance between concrete particulars is sometimes a matter of possessing universals that inexactly resemble each other, where inexact resemblance between universals is a matter of the partial identity of those universals (Armstrong 1997: 47–68).[13] In addition, universals bestow causal powers, different powers for different universals. And, for every causal power of a thing there is some universal or group of universals that accounts for that power (Armstrong 1989a: 82).

1.3.4 Standard Trope Theory For the trope theorist, properties are not universals, but particulars. The charge property of electron *e* is numerically distinct from the exactly similar charge property of electron *e'*. What makes an individual object white is possession of a particular whiteness trope. Objects *a* and *b* are similar with respect to whiteness in virtue of being characterized by similar but non-identical whiteness tropes. Fully determinate property types are maximal classes of exactly resembling tropes, such that the trope members of that class exactly resemble each other and there are no tropes outside that set that exactly resemble those tropes. On what I will call *Standard Trope Theory*, best represented by Campbell, the nature of a trope is *not* determined by its resemblance relations with other tropes or by its membership in natural classes of tropes.[14] A trope's nature determines its relations of resemblance to other tropes and its membership in natural classes.[15] Resemblance between tropes is an internal relation grounded in the nature of those tropes.[16] In addition, a trope is not reducible to an exemplification of a universal by a particular. Exemplifications are complex, including both a property component and a non-property component,

---

[12] For Armstrong, it is not the case that there is a predicate for every universal, and the existence of a meaningful predicate does not guarantee the existence of a corresponding universal. For example, there are no (1) universals corresponding to predicates that make an essential reference to a particular (1978b: 14–15), (2) universals corresponding to predicates that necessarily apply only to a limited number of things (1978b: 14–15), (3) universals corresponding to "being identical with itself" and similar predicates (1978b: 47), and (4) universals corresponding to empty predicates.

[13] Inexact property–property resemblance, thus, requires at least one complex property. Inexact resemblance at the property level transfers down to the object level. A 10-foot thing is similar to an 8-foot thing because being 10 feet is inexactly similar to being 8 feet, and the latter is true because being 10 feet and being 8 feet are partly identical.

[14] "What is it *about charge* in virtue of which it is charge? Its being what it is" (Campbell 1990: 30).

[15] Campbell holds that "there is no one-to-one correspondence between significant predicates and tropes." Campbell also holds the following. (1) Tropes are not individuated spatio-temporally, but primitively (1999: 25). (2) Tropes ordinarily occur in conjunction with other tropes (1990: 3). (3) The redness of an object may occupy the same location as its shape, although no two tropes "of the same kind" can occupy the same location at the same time (1999: 55). (4) Tropes are the causal relata (1990: 22). (5) Concrete particulars are bundles of tropes (1990: 21). (6) Predication consists of asserting that a trope of a certain kind is compresent with the complex of tropes referred to by the subject term (1990: 41). (7) Free-floating tropes are possible (1990: 59). (8) Campbell is tentatively committed to an actualist theory of possibility in the form of combinatorialism (1990: 94).

[16] Resemblance is objective for basic tropes.

whereas (basic) Campbellian tropes are simple. A trope's nature and its particularity are identical.[17]

1.3.5 Resemblance Trope Nominalism Resemblance Trope Nominalists hold that the nature of a trope *is* determined by its resemblance relations to other tropes. Resemblance among tropes is not reducible to or determined by the nature of the resembling tropes. Similarity-in-a-certain-respect between concrete particulars is explained by reference to the similarity of non-identical tropes that each object possesses. A fully determinate property type of F-ness is the maximal class of exactly resembling F-tropes. A less-than-fully determinate property type, G-ness, is a maximal class of inexactly resembling G-tropes.

1.3.6 Natural Class Trope Nominalism For the Natural Class Trope Nominalist, the nature of a trope is determined by its memberships in natural classes of tropes. What is it about a charge trope in virtue of which it is a *charge* trope? It is its membership in a certain natural class of charge tropes. The naturalness of a class of tropes is not reducible, but it comes in degrees. A fully determinate property type, F-ness, is the maximal and perfectly natural class of F-tropes. A less-than-fully determinate property type of G-ness is a maximal but imperfectly natural class of G-tropes. Resemblance among tropes is reducible to co-membership in a natural class. Tropes t and t' are similar in virtue of being co-members of at least one natural class of tropes. The members of a fully determinate property type resemble each other exactly. The same trope is both an F trope and a G trope just in case t is a member of the natural class of F tropes and the natural class of G tropes. Objects a and b are similar in some respect just in case a has a trope t and b has a trope t' such that t and t' are members of a common natural class. Property types F and G resemble each other just in case F and G overlap or are subclasses of a common natural class.[18]

1.4 The main claims about properties

1.4.1 The universal–particular distinction The first major claim of this work concerns the distinction between particulars and universals. In light of various difficulties, I reject the main contemporary approaches to the characterization of this distinction, including

---

[17] Tropes are not a "union of distinct elements, one particularizing and the other furnishing a nature" (Campbell 1990: 20).

[18] Trope theories are immune to any pressure to adopt modal realism based on the traditional cases involving contingently coextensive properties or properties that have only a single instance. For the Natural Class Trope Nominalist, different property types, P and P', that are contingently coextensive are still not identical since each such property type is constituted by a different class of actual tropes. (However, I will consider a different "coextensive properties" objection against Trope Theory later, but will suggest that it fails.) And, in a single instance case, the Natural Class Trope Nominalist can appeal to that trope's membership in the singleton class that includes that trope as grounding its nature. The Resemblance Trope Nominalist is also not forced to move in the direction of modal realism by either case, nor is the Standard Trope Nominalist.

the most popular approach in terms of the capacity for being wholly present in more than one location at the same time (universals). I defend the Williams characterization: there can be exact duplicates of a particular, but not of a universal. More informally, I defend the thesis that no one could build a copy machine for universals, unlike particulars. One novel aspect of my argument in favor of this view is my critique of a position I call "Categorical Primitivism," according to which simple universals of the same -adicity are merely numerically different. If correct, that would mean that universals generally not only could have but *do* have exact duplicates, violating the Williams's characterization of the universal–particular distinction.

1.4.2 In favor of the existence of tropes The second main claim is that there are tropes. What is special about my argument for tropes is my claim that there is a kind of phenomenon, property persistence, largely overlooked by philosophers, that is best accounted for by reference to enduring tropes. As indicated earlier, property persistence is distinct from the traditionally discussed datum of "one over many," and cannot be accounted for if properties are universals. Property persistence, or more specifically in this work, persisting properties *in motion*, are enduring tropes. A moving instance of redness, a spinning charge property, a sinking mass property: all of these are enduring tropes.

1.4.3 Tropes and mental causation The third main claim is that a trope ontology is key to solving the problems of mental causation. There are two aspects to this claim: a token-level identity thesis; and a type-level part–whole thesis. First, mental causes are tropes that are identical to physical tropes. Second, mental property types are classes of tropes and the physical types that realize mental types are subclasses or parts of those mental types. The latter part–whole relation at the type-level leaves room for the causal relevancy of the mental types. In short, the apparently problematic nature of mental causation falls away once one combines the thesis that causal relata are tropes (and mental tropes are identical to physical tropes) with an understanding of property types as classes of tropes, which opens up the prospect of a type-type part–whole theory of the relationship between mental and physical types, in contrast to a 1950s-style type-type identity theory.

1.4.4 Against Standard Trope Nominalism The fourth main claim is that the Standard account of tropes is not coherent. Campbellian tropes collapse either into exemplifications of universals or into one of the alternate conceptions of tropes. Under the Standard conception, a basic trope lacks constituents that are not tropes, and certainly lacks a distinct nature-giving constituent and a particularity-given constituent. I charge, following others, that the tropes of Standard Theory must have distinct particularity-given and nature-giving components, which will mean that they collapse either into exemplifications of universals or tropes of some non-Standard character.

1.4.5 In favor of Natural Class Trope Nominalism The fifth main claim is that Natural Class Trope Nominalism provides us with the most plausible conception of tropes. This claim in itself is novel relative to contemporary metaphysics. Natural Class Trope

Nominalism is commonly believed to be out of the running given the broad agreement among metaphysicians that this theory is subject to fatal counterarguments.[19] I try to show that those counterarguments are overrated. What is most novel in my response to these well-entrenched objections is my use of property counterpart theory (without modal realism). The basic idea is that once it is recognized that the modality of properties conforms to the dictates of counterpart theory—once Natural Class Trope Nominalism is combined with this account of the modality of properties—the classic objections lose their force.

2. Objects

I will now provide some background about concrete particulars, describing the main candidates for concrete particulars, followed by a sketch of the main claim I will make about them.

2.1 Blob Theory

Resemblance Object Nominalism and Natural Class Object Nominalism require that objects not be built up from properties either as bundles of properties or as complexes made up of properties and some non-property component. Given either of these theories of properties, properties are logically posterior to concrete objects, and objects must be understood as unstructured *blobs*. A Blob Theory is inconsistent with properties as tropes or universals. If properties are tropes or universals, then either an object is just a bundle of properties or an object includes as constituents both properties and a non-property substrate that is itself a particular.

2.2 Substance-Attribute Theory

On Substance-Attribute theories, if properties are universals, then the attributes of concrete objects are universals, which inhere in the substrate, and if properties are tropes, the attributes are tropes.[20] For Armstrong, the non-property component of an object, a "thin particular," is a concrete particular taken apart from its properties, and "thick particulars" are concrete particulars taken along with all or some of their properties.[21] The thin particular instantiates the concrete object's universals.[22]

---

[19] Stout was the first to propose this type of theory (1921–3, 1923). There have been no sustained defenses of this position since Stout.

[20] When a thin particular instantiates a universal, for Armstrong, the result is a state of affairs, the mode of composition of which is non-mereological (1989a: 88).

[21] One function of a thin particular is to provide a basis for individuating objects if properties are universals, even in the most extreme case of indiscernibility. This function is unnecessary if properties are tropes. A second function is as a unifier: some but not other properties belong to object a in virtue of the fact that those properties inhere in the substrate of a. A third function, for Armstrong, is to provide a basis for the existence of the various universals that exist (since universals must be instantiated). A fourth, possible function is to provide a basis for object persistence despite changes in properties.

[22] One objection to this conception of a concrete object is that it leads to an infinite regress:

Suppose that a instantiates F and that a is a particular and instantiation and F are universals. What makes it the case that a is characterized by F rather than, say, by G is that F stands in this instantiation relation to

2.3 Bundle Theory

On a Bundle Theory, there is no substratum/thin particular. Each concrete object is a bundle of its properties.[23] "The thing stands to one of its properties as a whole stands to a mere part..." (Armstrong 1989a: 62). The properties of the same object are mutually compresent. They do not inhere in a non-property substratum. Compresence is interpreted as either the relation of being in the same place at the same time or as primitive and non-reducible, typically the latter. On a universals-based Bundle Theory, a concrete object is a bundle of compresent universals. For the Trope Bundle theorist, a concrete object is a bundle of tropes without any substratum.[24] The bundles that constitute concrete particulars are not *sets* of properties since that would make concrete objects abstract. Concrete particulars are mereological wholes of properties, but not every sum of properties is a concrete particular. The constituent tropes of a bundle must be connected by a relation of compresence. A concrete particular is a mereological sum of tropes that are mutually compresent, but only if that sum is maximal or complete[25] (Oliver 1996: 36). Traditionally, compresence is taken to be a two-place relation (although more recently it has been suggested that this relation is of variable-adicity).[26] In addition, compresence is generally understood not to be an internal relation, but an external relation.[27] The tropes/universals of the bundle do not necessitate that those tropes/universals stand to each other in a relation of compresence.[28]

---

a but G does not stand in that relation to *a*. But then what makes it the case that that instantiation relation holds between *a* and *F* but does not hold between *a* and G? "Must we not take the constituents and the tie and then put them together by another relation? But then we have the constituents, the tie and the 'putting together', another tie, and the old Bradleian regress proceeds" (Armstrong 1997: 118). For Armstrong's response, see (1997: 118–19).

[23] I reject the substrate–attribute view in favor of the bundle view because Bundle Theory is more parsimonious.

[24] Tropes are "the very alphabet of being, the simple, basic, and primal items from which all else is built or derives" (Campbell 1990: xi).

[25] A bundle of mutually compresent properties is complete if and only if any further property that might be added to it would fail to be compresent with at least one property in the bundle.

[26] If properties are universals and compresence is two-placed, the compresence relation is symmetrical, but not transitive (whereas U_1 and U_2 might characterize object *a* such that they are mutually compresent, and U_2 and U_3 might characterize a different object *b* such that they are mutually compresent, U_1 and U_3 might fail to be mutually compresent or characterize together any object).

[27] The tropes/universals could, for example, continue to exist and enter into new compresence relations (whether they could be transferred to a new object or continue to exist without standing in any compresence relation to anything else are different issues).

[28] On an "egalitarian" Bundle Theory, the properties of the bundle are not divided into essential and accidental properties. An alternative to Egalitarian Bundle Theory is Simons' *Nucleus Trope Theory*, a theory that is meant to avoid making all of an object's properties essential to it and avoid making change impossible (Simons 1994). A thing consists of an inner core or nucleus of essential properties and an outer band of accidental properties. The nucleus includes all the tropes that must co-occur together but are not part of each other. The tropes of the outer shell depend on the individual tropes of the kernel, but the tropes in the outer shell may be replaced without the nucleus ceasing to exist (1994: 567–8). The nucleus requires supplementation by further tropes of certain determinable kinds, but not by any specific individual tropes (1994: 568). According to Simons, however, a concrete object might lack an accidental outer shell or lack a nucleus of essential properties (1994: 568).

2.4 The main claim about concrete particulars

2.4.1 Trope Bundle Theory The sixth main claim of this work is that concrete objects are trope bundles. Concrete objects are maximal bundles of mutually compresent tropes. They are tropes all the way down. A big part of what is novel about my treatment of Trope Bundle Theory is how I handle a key objection to it, the Regress Objection. According to this objection, Trope Bundle Theory is either uneconomical or gives rise to a vicious infinite regress. The idea is that if compresence is itself a trope, then there is an infinite regress, at least if compresence tropes are themselves compresent with the other tropes in the bundle between which it obtains.[29] I argue that this regress can be stopped once it is recognized that compresence is a self-relating relation, a relation that can take itself as a relatum. The supposed infinite regress for the bundle theorist involves an unending series of compresence tropes, $c_1, c_2, \ldots$, and c_n, but the series, $c_1, c_2, \ldots$, and c_n is taken to be infinite because it is assumed that each "additional" compresence trope is *not* identical to the immediately preceding compresence trope in the series. However, if compresence is a "self-relating" relation, this assumption may be false and there is no infinite series of distinct compresence tropes.

3. Chapter outline

3.1 Part 1 Trope Nominalism

In Chapter 1, I focus on the distinction between universals and particulars. I begin by examining attempts to characterize this distinction that center on the notion of instantiation or exemplification, arguing that these instantiation-based attempts fail. I, then, consider the widely held "Aristotelian" formulation of the distinction, which makes universals, but not particulars, capable of multiple simultaneous locations. I suggest that necessary amendments to the Aristotelian formulation—to deal with counterexamples—naturally lead to a very different formulation, according to which universals are those entities for which exact inherent similarity is sufficient for identity and particulars are those entities for which it is not sufficient.

In Chapter 2, I argue for the existence of tropes. I begin with a brief catalogue of previous arguments for tropes and then launch into a new argument for their existence. I argue that property motion—such as the redness of a ball moving through space—requires enduring tropes and, hence, tropes. Universals and exemplifications and causal chains of exemplifications of universals are insufficient to make sense of this phenomenon. In the second part of this chapter, I take up an objection to the possibility of enduring tropes, which is analogous to Lewis's "temporary intrinsics" objection to enduring objects.

---

[29] A universals-based Bundle Theory does not face this same regress objection, since if properties and relations are universals and compresence is a genuine relation, compresence is a universal and there cannot be more than one compresence relation (although there may be a regress of states of affairs).

In Chapter 3, I consider trope individuation. I argue that trope individuation is a primitive, lacking any further reduction or analysis. I present a number of reasons for rejecting the principle that tropes are individuated spatio-temporally, including the fact that that principle is incompatible with enduring tropes, the possibility of time traveling enduring tropes and extended simple tropes. I also criticize an argument in favor of the Spatio-Temporal Principle of individuation, to the effect that that Principle is required by Trope Theory in order to block the "no-property-swapping" objection to Trope Theory. According to the latter objection, Trope Theory wrongly entails the possibility that exactly similar properties could have been swapped. I also consider a broader question of what kinds of tropes might exist. In particular, I respond to arguments from Campbell that are meant to rule out the possibility of "manifest," medium-sized tropes.

In Chapter 4, I defend Trope Bundle Theory. More specifically, I defend the Bundle Theory thesis that concrete particulars or substantial particulars, such as tables and chairs, are wholly constituted by and are identical to complete bundles of compresent properties. Along the way, I defend the claim that the bundled properties are tropes, not universals. I take bundles to be mereological sums of properties, the constituents of which are parts of the bundle, with the trope parts of the bundle restricted to those tropes that are mutually compresent. I try to show some of the advantages of a trope-based Bundle Theory over a universals-based Bundle Theory. I also propose refinements to the theory in response to various objections, especially to the objections that Bundle Theory makes all of the properties of an object essential to it, is incompatible with change and leads to an infinite regress. I propose that Bundle Theory is best coupled with Temporal Parts Theory or Stage Theory in order to handle the first two of these objections. I also suggest that the regress does not arise since compresence is a "self-relating" relation.

In Chapter 5, I will argue that if properties are tropes, then we can help solve the two main problems of mental causation. The first problem of mental causation that I consider concerns the possibility of mental causes of physical events in a causally closed physical world, and the second concerns the possibility of mental causes being efficacious in virtue of their mental properties in such a world. If mental property types are identical to physical property types, then a "token identity" response to the first problem of mental causation property is immediately available, but this type-type identity claim about mental and physical property types is not generally considered to be viable, since this type-level identity thesis is inconsistent with the widely accepted principle that the same mental property can be realized by the instantiation of disparate physical properties or types. I argue that a widely discussed alternative account of the relation between mental and physical property types, according to which mental property types are determinables of the physical property types that realize them, fails. I propose my own account of that relationship: mental tropes that have physical effects are themselves physical tropes, and the physical types that realize mental types are subclasses or parts of those mental types. The latter part–whole relation at the type-level leaves room for the causal relevancy of the mental types under which mental causes fall, despite the causal relevancy of the physical types under which they also fall. Causal powers of a property type are to be understood in terms of the causal powers of its member tropes. The causal powers of property types that stand to each other in the part–whole relation *overlap*, opening up the way to a solution to the problem of mental causation.

3.2 Part 2 Natural Class Trope Nominalism

In Chapter 6, I turn to the task of picking a conception of tropes among the three main rival trope theories, Campbell's well-known Trope Theory, Natural Class Trope Nominalism and Resemblance Trope Theory. I argue that the tropes of Natural Class Trope Nominalism are superior to Campbellian tropes. Campbellian tropes collapse into exemplifications of universals or into one of the alternate conceptions of tropes. I, then, argue that Natural Class Trope Nominalism is superior to Resemblance Trope Nominalism with respect to the tasks of accounting for property–property resemblance and explaining the logical characteristics of resemblance. I also respond to the following two "collapse" objections directed against Natural Class Tropes: (a) Natural Class Tropes are indistinguishable from bare particulars; and (b) Natural Class Tropes are indistinguishable from objects.

In Chapter 7, I take up certain key objections to Natural Class Trope Nominalism that have made this position extremely unpopular. The first objection is the "One-Over-Fewer" objection. The basic worry is that this form of nominalism seems to rule out the genuine possibility that a property might have had fewer instances than it has. This objection has been pivotal in the rejection of Natural Class Trope Nominalism. The second objection, the "One Over More" objection, is that Natural Class Trope Nominalism also seems to exclude the genuine possibility that there could have been one more, for example, red trope. The third objection, the "Causation" objection, is that Natural Class Trope Nominalism seems to make all properties causally irrelevant by requiring the causal relevancy of non-local tropes for the causal relevancy of any tropes local to a causal sequence. All three of these objections can be answered, I will argue, by adopting a counterpart theory of properties without adopting modal realism.

In Chapter 8, I consider the question of whether or not Natural Class Trope Nominalism is consistent with the fact that some properties stand to each other in the determination relation. There is a *prima facie* case to be made that Natural Class Trope Nominalism is *not* consistent with some of the main features of the determination relation. As it will turn out, I argue, Natural Class Trope Nominalism can answer this objection, if it is combined with property counterpart theory.

PART I

Tropes

1

Distinguishing particulars from universals

Trope Nominalism requires a viable distinction between universals and particulars. Otherwise, its claim that there are properties but they are particulars, not universals, will have no substance. Some philosophers, however, reject the distinction between universals and particulars, and, by implication, between universals and tropes. MacBride, for example, claims that this distinction is an unsupported dogma of metaphysics (2005: 566).[1] Rejecting the universal–particular distinction naturally gives rise to the worry that Trope Nominalism rests on a false dualism. In this chapter, I will try to specify an acceptable distinction between universals and particulars, and one between universals and tropes. I will consider the main attempts to characterize the distinction between universals and particulars, beginning in (1) with three attempts that center on the notion of instantiation or exemplification. These three proposals fail to distinguish adequately between universals and particulars because they assume that properties are restricted to universals and that whatever distinguishes properties from concrete particular objects also distinguishes universals from particulars. If there are or could be tropes, then these three proposals must fail. In (2), I turn to the traditional, "Aristotelian" formulation, which makes universals, but not particulars, capable of multiple simultaneous locations. I will suggest that necessary amendments to the Aristotelian formulation naturally lead to a very different formulation from D. C. Williams. According to the latter, universals are those entities for which exact inherent similarity is sufficient for identity and particulars are those entities for which it is not sufficient. I develop the Williams formulation further in (3) and argue for its superiority to the Aristotelian view in (4).

1. Three instantiation-based accounts

Instantiation-based accounts focus on some putative difference between universals and particulars with respect to instantiation, either with respect to the products of that

---

[1] MacBride says, "the distinction is often affirmed in the absence of compelling grounds" as is the assumption that "*if* there are particulars and universals *then* they must belong to radically different kinds" (2005: 566).

relation or with respect to the relation itself. In discussing these three accounts, I will operate under the following methodological principle: an account of the distinction should leave room for the possibility of tropes. The idea is that an account of the distinction itself should not automatically rule out the possibility of properties that are particulars. This methodological principle, however, is itself revisable. If, for example, it can independently be shown that tropes are not possible, then we can revisit the question of how to account for the distinction between universals and particulars without having to consider the possibility of tropes. However, since I believe that tropes are possible, and, in fact, I argue for their existence in Chapter 2, I do not see the need to revise this methodological principle.

1.1 The numerical account

Some philosophers, mostly notably Russell and Armstrong, claim that particulars and universals set different numerical constraints on the internal constituents of the products of instantiation, "facts" or "states of affairs." The universal "is tall" can only appear in atomic states of affairs with precisely two constituents, the universal itself and another entity, such as "Obama is tall" (or three constituents, if instantiation is a relation and also a constituent of atomic states of affairs), but the particular, Barack Obama, can appear in atomic states of affairs with varying numbers of constituents, such as "Barack Obama is in his forties" and "Barack Obama is married to Michelle Obama" (MacBride 2005: 587).[2] States of affairs such as "Obama and Jones are tall" are not counterexamples because they are not atomic states of affairs. The possession of -adicity sets the divide "between what a particular is *qua* particular and a universal *qua* universal" (Armstrong 1997: 168). "Universals... may be characterized as entities that can only ever occur with n constituents. By contrast, particulars... may be characterized as entities that can occur in fact with any number of constituents" (MacBride 2005: 569). Universals are "unigrade," but particulars are "multigrade" (2005: 569). Numerical constraints or a lack thereof are what makes something a universal or a particular.[3]

The claim that particulars are multigrade is plausible for concrete particulars.[4] The Empire State Building can figure in atomic states of affairs with varying numbers of

---

[2] A referee suggested the point about "instantiation" as possibly a third constituent.

[3] MacBride also usefully distinguishes another version of this account of the universal–particular distinction according to which each universal has a fixed number of argument places, even if a different number of individuals may occupy each such place on different occasions for some universals. There are no "varigrade" universals, even if there are some multigrade universals, whereas particulars are varigrade. However, he argues that even this view is defective. There are collective predicates that seem to be associated with universals that are not only multigrade but varigrade, such that there is variation in the number of argument places each such universal has from one occasion to another. MacBride gives the following examples: the relation of belief and the instantiation relation.

[4] See (MacBride 2005) for worries, however.

constituents, but this claim does not generalize to all particulars. If there are or could be tropes, it is plausible that some of them could be unigrade.[5] There is nothing to rule out a one-place redness trope or a two-place next-to relation trope unless there is some reason also to exclude a one-place redness universal or a two-place next-to universal. In fact, we will be convinced that universals are unigrade only if we are convinced that properties must be unigrade and think that properties are universals. But the conviction that properties are unigrade is compatible with properties being tropes *or* universals. It remains an open question whether or not P is a particular or a universal even after we have established that P has a definite -adicity. If there is a close connection between -adicity and propertihood, that connection does not illuminate the universal–particular distinction unless properties are restricted to universals.[6] For the numerical account to work, then, it must be demonstrated that tropes are impossible, and if it can be shown that properties are tropes, which I think can be shown, then this formulation of the distinction between universals and particulars is not adequate.[7]

1.2 The completeness account

A second instantiation-based proposal consists in the claim that universals, but not particulars, are incomplete. An "incomplete" entity has "a gap waiting to be filled by a complete entity" (MacBride 2005: 604). If that gap is not filled, then that entity will not be instantiated, but the same is not true of complete entities for which there is no gap-filling requirement for instantiation. Universals are "gappy." The universal "is red" has a gap that can be filled by an object such as this ball. Particulars are not "gappy." This ball does not have a gap that can be filled by redness. A particular

---

[5] Or, if there is something problematic about unigrade tropes, say, because all properties can figure as constituents in higher-order properties, then there is probably something problematic about unigrade universals too.

[6] In addition, as MacBride argues, at least some universals appear to be multigrade, if there are universals. There are true sentences involving collective predicates, such as "forming a circle," that seem to be made true by states of affairs with multigrade universals as constituents (2005: 571–2). Further, as MacBride also points out, a universal, such as "yellowness," may be a constituent of a state of affairs with only one more constituent, such as "yellow's being a color," or two more constituents, such as "yellow's being brighter than black." Perhaps all universals, then, can serve as arguments in higher-order universals of varying numbers of constituents, making all universals multigrade. For possible defenses against these objections, see (2005).

[7] Strictly speaking, as a referee points out, all that needs to be shown is that some properties are tropes even if there are also universals. Note also that the unigrade/multigrade distinction might still be useful to the trope nominalist by providing a basis for making distinctions *within the domain of particulars*. The idea would be that whereas tropes are unigrade, concrete objects (and perhaps classes of tropes) are multigrade. A red trope, say, red_1, for example, is a one-place property and, as such, cannot serve as the "constituent" trope of a state of affairs with more than two constituents, but a concrete particular, such as George Bush, can be a constituent of states of affairs with varying numbers of constituents. We could still accommodate multigrade "properties" even if all tropes are unigrade since the trope theorist distinguishes between particular properties (tropes) and property types (classes of tropes). "Collective predicates" correspond to property types, classes of tropes, within which there is -adicity variation. The members of the property class of "carrying a boat" vary in -adicity, but no specific "carrying a boat" trope does. This use for the unigrade–multigrade distinction, however, would require some response to the objection from higher-order properties/relations, which if cogent would seem to exclude many or all unigrade tropes.

instantiates a universal when that particular object, a complete entity, fills this gap and saturates the universal, an incomplete entity (MacBride 2005: 604).[8] Furthermore, an incomplete entity cannot fill the gap in another incomplete entity.[9] If universals are unigrade, as dictated by the numerical account, then that fact will presumably be explained on this account by including the requirement that each "gappy" entity has a definite number of gaps, but this account sets up no numerical constraints on universals.

According to the "completeness account," tropes must be complete, not gappy, since they are particulars. That means that they need not be combined with "complete" entities in order to exist. One implication is that if there are tropes, they must be capable of existing without characterizing anything. A red trope must be able to exist even it does not characterize an object. This is a substantial and debatable thesis about tropes, and it is a thesis that should not follow just on the basis of the particularity of tropes. There is nothing in the notion of a trope *qua* particular that requires this capacity. Demonstrating that there could be free-floating tropes would require some further argument. Furthermore, even if this point is rejected on the grounds that particularity does carry the implication of the capacity for independent existence, the proponent of this view will still have trouble with tropes. That is because part of the reasoning, I would suggest, that supports an "incomplete" account of universals will also support an "incomplete" account of tropes. We will be convinced that universals are incomplete only if we are convinced that properties must be incomplete, but the thesis that properties are incomplete would mean that tropes, if they exist, are incomplete since they are properties.[10] Thus, if there are tropes, then the proponent of this view should treat them as gappy and, hence, abandon the claim that gappy entities are restricted to universals. In short, one must avoid taking a possible feature of properties, their gappiness, as a feature restricted to universals, but not particulars. Once it is recognized that properties might be particulars—indeed that there are tropes as we shall see—the completeness account of the universal–particular distinction loses its appeal.

---

[8] The main objection to this view is that concrete objects seem no less incomplete than universals. "Neither particulars nor universals are capable of being instantiated in isolation. They all seem incomplete, demanding the presence of other items with which to enter into instantiation" (MacBride 2005: 606; also see Ramsey 1925: 17). Moreover, there does not seem to be any basis for claiming that while both universals and particulars are incomplete, universals are *especially* incomplete as compared to particulars. In addition, as MacBride points out, this view cannot account for the instantiation of higher-order universals by lower-order universals, since under this conception, instantiation requires the saturation of an incomplete entity by a complete entity but both higher- and lower-order universals are incomplete (MacBride 2005: 607).

[9] "Identify the distinction between particulars and universals with the distinction between *complete* and *incomplete* entities. Instantiation then results from complete particulars *saturating* incomplete universals" (MacBride 2005: 604).

[10] It might be suggested that there is an additional reason for thinking universals are gappy: the same universal can be instantiated by multiple objects. This reason, however, really brings into play another way of characterizing the distinction, the Aristotelian formulation, which I will discuss shortly. One of the advantages of the "completeness" account is that it does not presume that universals, but not particulars, can be multiply instantiated.

1.3 The exemplification account

The "numerical account" focuses on a putative numerical difference between universals and particulars with respect to states of affairs. The "completeness account" focuses on a putative difference in dependence between universals and particulars with respect to the exemplification relation. The "exemplification" account focuses on a supposed asymmetry associated with the relata of the exemplification relation. Only certain kinds of things can play the role of "exemplifiers" and other kinds of things can play the role of "exemplified." Universals get exemplified, but particulars do not. Particulars are those things that exemplify (or could exemplify), but are not exemplified, and universals are those things that get exemplified (or could get exemplified), but do not exemplify. "Particulars are entities that figure in the first argument position of the relation; universals are entities that figure in the second" (MacBride 2005: 595). The universal, "being red," is exemplified by balls, for example, but balls are not exemplified by anything. Or, if there are higher-order universals that are exemplified by lower-level universals, universals are those things that both exemplify and are exemplified whereas particulars only exemplify.[11] The universal "redness" may both be exemplified by a ball and exemplify "being a color," but the ball is not exemplified by anything.

The "exemplification" account also runs into trouble with tropes. The main argument for this proposal rests on a premise about an asymmetry between properties and individuals: "Properties are properties *of* individuals. Relations are relations *holding between* individuals. But individuals are not individuals *of* their properties. Nor do individuals hold between the relations which relate them" (Armstrong 1989b: 44). From this premise, it is inferred that universals exemplify, but particulars do not. In fact, there is a missing step in this argument. Even if there is this asymmetry between properties and individuals, it does not follow that that asymmetry tracks the universal–particular distinction. That only follows if properties are universals, not tropes. If properties are tropes, this asymmetry might still hold, but it would not capture the universal–particular distinction. The argument, at best, provides a basis for distinguishing between properties and individuals, leaving open the question of whether that

---

[11] If exemplification were symmetric, it could not be used to make this distinction in this way. But what warrants the assumption that exemplification is not symmetric? MacBride suggests that in so far as the warrant for the assumption that exemplification is asymmetric is connected to the main function of the exemplification relation—of binding together the constituents of a fact when they are instantiated so as to distinguish that fact from a mere collection—this assumption is not justified (2005: 598). However, there does seem to be a warrant for the assumption that exemplification is not symmetric. Suppose that exemplification is symmetric. Now, if a exemplifies U and b exemplifies U, then U is wholly present where a is located and wholly present where b is located. When we apply this "location" assumption to the case in which o exemplifies a multiply located U, supposing that exemplification is symmetric, then it will follow that o is itself multiply located (at the same time). But no particular can be wholly present at two different locations at the same time. Hence, exemplification is not symmetric. But that brings us to the Aristotelian characterization of the distinction. If the latter account of the distinction is required to warrant some of the assumptions of the exemplification account, then one has reason to set the latter aside and focus on the former.

distinction also corresponds to the distinction between universals and particulars, including particularized properties.

Furthermore, if this account were applied to tropes, it would have the implication that tropes could not be "exemplified" since they are particulars, whereas it is not so clear that tropes could not play the role of "exemplified" or something very close to that role. If there were tropes, certainly tropes could be had by objects, but "being had by" and "being exemplified by," in this context, closely parallel each other, especially given that "exemplification" is not precisely specified under the exemplification account. Both of these relations are supposed to be asymmetrical relations. And both function to bind together the constituents of a fact when they are instantiated so as to distinguish that fact from a mere collection. Objects can have/exemplify, but cannot be had by/be exemplified by other things. Without further specification of "exemplification," the exemplification account provides, at best, only a way of distinguishing objects and properties, not particulars and universals. This point can be made more vivid by reference to a particular specification of "instantiation" or "exemplification," according to which for an object to instantiate a universal U is for that universal to be a non-spatial-temporal part of that object. There is nothing to prevent application of that "being a part of" notion of instantiation to tropes and objects. Without further specification of "exemplification," we should not grant that the exemplification relation can provide a basis for distinguishing between universals and particulars.[12]

1.4 The general problem with instantiation accounts

These three approaches assume that all and only properties are universals, and that whatever distinguishes properties from concrete particulars will be what distinguishes universals from particulars, either the unigrade–multigrade distinction, the incomplete–complete distinction, or the exemplified–exemplifying distinction. Each approach begins with a reasonable claim about what distinguishes properties from concrete particulars while tacitly assuming that all and only properties are universals and that the only particulars are concrete particulars. Within each account it is then inferred that what distinguishes properties and concrete particulars distinguishes universals and particulars. It is implicitly assumed that tropes are not the kinds of things that can play any of these roles. However, being unigrade, being incomplete, and being exemplified, arguably, might all be characteristics of tropes. It should not be built into the debate about what distinguishes universals from particulars that there could not be particularized properties. Tropes can play any of the roles that are legitimately played by properties.

---

[12] MacBride argues that it is not clear that "the constituents of a fact require the assistance of any relation or tie (asymmetric or otherwise) to be bound together. It may be that the constituents of a fact are connected immediately" (2005: 598).

2. The Aristotelian formulation

The "Aristotelian" way of drawing the distinction between universals and particulars focuses on a supposed difference in how universals and particulars are located in space and time. Universals, but not particulars, can be in more than one place at the same time. Universals, but not particulars, can have multiple, simultaneous spatial locations. This formulation, however, does not mean that particulars can in no sense be present in more than one place at the same time nor that universals always have or even sometimes have multiple locations. Particulars can be present in more than one location at the same time in the sense that they can have proper spatial parts that are present in different locations simultaneously. What particulars cannot do under this formulation is be wholly present simultaneously in multiple locations. On the other hand, a universal might be instantiated only once at any time it is instantiated at all, but that would not be inconsistent with the Aristotelian approach, which requires only the capacity for simultaneous multiple locations. The idea is that a chair cannot be wholly present in two places at the same time, but its chairness—understood as a universal—can. Universals and tropes are said to differ in this same way. The universal redness can be in two places at the same time, but a redness trope cannot be multiply located.

Putative counterexamples directed at this formulation of the universal–particular distinction involve either particulars that can be multiply located or universals that cannot be multiply located. In particular, (1) it has been argued that there can be multiply located particulars and it can be similarly argued that there can be multiply located tropes, and (2) it has been argued that there can be necessarily singly located universals, in which case there is nothing to distinguish such universals from tropes. Consider two proposed counterexamples to the particular side of the spatial formulation.

Case 1: Spatially extended, but spatially partless particulars

It is possible for there to exist spatially extended simple particulars that lack all manner of parts. Each such object would be multiply located, present at each location it occupied, but not be so present by way of a spatial (proper) part. Although the region occupied by this object would have proper parts, the object itself would not have any proper parts. These are "extended simple" objects.

At this point, it is important to distinguish between extended simples that are multi-located ("multi-locaters") and those that are "spanners" (McDaniel 2007: 134). Extended simple particulars that are spanners do not constitute a counterexample to the Aristotelian formulation. An extended simple that is a multi-locater both occupies an extended spatio-temporal region R as well as all the spatial points in that extended spatio-temporal region.[13] Since extended simples have no parts, extended simples that are multi-locators do not have proper parts that occupy proper parts of the region occupied by that extended simple. The extended simple itself, not proper parts of itself, occupies R as well as occupying proper parts of R. Extended simples that are multi-locators bear the occupation relation to more than one extended space-time region.[14] A spanner, on the other hand, occupies exactly one extended spatial region, but does not occupy any proper part of that extended region.[15] Neither a multi-locater nor a spanner have proper parts that occupy proper parts of the extended region occupied by the object. However, a multi-locater, but not a spanner, occupies each of those proper parts of the extended region.[16] Since spanners have a unique location in space-time they are not counterexamples to the Aristotelian formulation.

Arguments for the *possibility* of extended simples include arguments from reasonable principles of modality. Sider, for example, argues for the possibility of extended simples from the assumption that location is a fundamental relation, and the principle of modality that any pattern of instantiation of a fundamental relation is possible. "These principles imply the possibility of the location relation's holding in a one-many pattern between a mereologically simple object and points of space—an extended simple ... everyone should admit *some* combinatorial element to possibility, and it seems likely that that element will be enough for extended simples" (Sider 2007: 52). But there are also arguments based on science for the *existence* of extended simples. (1) Parsons argues that since all objects are mereological sums of simples and that there are only finitely many simples (an empirical claim grounded in part in the discovery of Avogadro's number, the number of hydrogen atoms in a gram of hydrogen), some simples have extension. The idea is that otherwise, no such object would be extended, since anything composed solely of finitely many extensionless things would also be extensionless. Parsons speculates that the extended simples are the most fundamental objects of physics, leptons, and quarks (2000). (2) Simons suggests that modern physics supports extended simples: "the evidence from physics appears to be that the

---

[13] Following McDaniel, assume that material objects and space-time are united by a fundamental relation, occupation, which is itself a primitive relation. Objects occupy specific regions of space-time and, at least typically, if x occupies a space-time region r, every part of x occupies some part of r, and also, typically, x does not occupy a proper part of r, but a proper part of x does. Also following McDaniel, say that x uniquely occupies R just in case x occupies R and no other regions, and that x is multi-located if and only if x occupies R and occupies R', where R and R' are not identical. "According to this conception, an extended simple bears the occupation relation to continuum many spacetime points, the fusion of which is an extended spatiotemporal region" (McDaniel 2007: 134).

[14] Note that under this characterization of a multi-locator, simple objects that endure will be temporal multi-locators, but these sorts of objects do not constitute a counterexample to the Aristotelian formulation, but spatial multi-locators do.

[15] Spanners are not multi-located; they uniquely occupy a single extended region of spacetime (McDaniel 2007: 134).

[16] McDaniel offers as a possible example of a spanner a singleton set, which might be interpreted as a simple that is located just where its member is without having proper or improper parts that occupy different sub-regions of its location.

leptons and quarks which compose matter, and which are either physically ultimate or close to being physically ultimate, have no proper parts" (Simons 2004: 376). (3) Braddon-Mitchell and Miller argue that Planck squares (two-dimensional squares that are Planck length by Planck length), the smallest regions of space that plausibly compose our world, lack parts but are extended (2006: 222–6). In short, there are a number of plausible reasons to take seriously the possibility of extended simples, so it is reasonable to find a place for extended simples *qua* particulars within a characterization of the universal–particular distinction.

Case 2: Time-traveling, but temporally partless (enduring) particulars

It is possible for there to exist time-traveling particulars, without temporal parts. Since persistence for such particulars is not a matter of relations between temporal parts, it would be possible for a particular to be multiply located (wholly present at different locations) at some time *t*. That would be the case if a particular traveled backward in time to meet its earlier self. In particular, suppose that Tommy The Time Traveler is an enduring particular who travels back in time to meet himself. At that earlier time of the meeting, Tommy is wholly present in two different locations. Call these "enduring time-travelers."

According to this second problem case, the possibility of endurance combined with time travel gives rise to the possibility of particulars that behave like universals. This case will require, however, that there are no convincing reasons to exclude either the possibility of enduring particulars, or the logical or metaphysical possibility of time travel. There is an extensive literature on both of these topics which I will not try to canvass here. The admission of either Case 1 or Case 2 would violate the traditional way of drawing the distinction between universals and particulars, since the particulars involved in these cases satisfy the characterization of *universals*. Extended simple objects, of the "multi-located" variety, occupy more than one location at the same time, as do self-meeting enduring time travelers. These difficulties spill over to the trope–universal distinction if there are similar cases that can be generated for tropes.

Case 3: Partless but extended trope

Suppose that the partless but extended object of Case 2 is characterized by a trope, say a whiteness trope, "Whitey." If the object is white throughout, then Whitey will also be multiply located in the sense of being wholly present at each location at which that object is wholly present. Or, consider a property of a fundamental, mereologically simple particle, for example, possibly a quark. That property will be multi-located if that particle is multi-located.

Case 4: Enduring time-traveling tropes

Suppose that there are enduring tropes, tropes that are persistent over time in the sense of being wholly present at more than one moment (I argue in Chapter 2 for enduring tropes). If Tommy The Time Traveler possesses such an enduring trope, say, an enduring mass trope, that trope will be wholly present in more than one place at the same time when Tommy encounters himself. Tommy's massness meets Tommy's massness.

2.1 Modifications of the Aristotelian formulation

I will now consider some efforts to modify the Aristotelian way of drawing the universal–particular distinction in response to these supposed counterexamples. I will argue that these modifications naturally lead to an alternative, non-Aristotelian formulation of the distinction. I have in mind two such modifications, modifications that I will suggest should not be understood independently from each other, but under a more general reformulation. Although the general reformulation that I will propose of the Aristotelian view handles these supposed counterexamples, it is still unsatisfactory, as we shall see. The shortcoming of the forthcoming modified spatial formulation is that it makes the distinction between particulars and universals mysterious. I will argue for a more fundamental characterization of the difference between universals and particulars that explains the modified spatial formulation and clears up any mystery generated by the latter. Here are the proposed modifications to the spatial formulation.

MODIFICATION 1

The idea for this first modification is based on the apparent fact that the possibility of partless but extended particulars is limited in a certain specific way. The following restriction seems to apply to partless but extended objects (which do not time travel). A single object of that type cannot be spatially scattered. More precisely, there cannot be a partless but extended particular that occupies *disjoint* spatial locations *l* and *l'* at the same time, such that there is no series of spatially contiguous locations linking *l* and *l'* where that particular also (wholly) occupies those locations.[17] A partless extended particular could not, say, for example, be such that it included only two non-contiguous regions, each sitting at two ends of a warehouse. Whatever might motivate positing an extended (non-time-traveling) spatially partless particular will never be enough to motivate positing one that is scattered. So the first modification is as follows:

> Universals can have multiple, simultaneous spatial locations disjoint or otherwise, but (non-time-traveling) particulars cannot have multiple, simultaneous *scattered* spatial locations.

---

[17] For whilst, supposedly, indivisible shaped atoms can, like universals, be wholly present at more than one place at a time, they can only be wholly present in *contiguous* places at the same time. Universals... are capable of being present at many spatially discontinuous locations at a time (MacBride 1998: 221).

This modification is consistent with the possibility of a non-scattered, partless, extended particular.

MODIFICATION 2
The first modification does not help with Case 2 since enduring time travelers may occupy disjoint locations at the same time.[18] There is, however, a further modification that will help. Time-traveling self-meeting particulars are causally linked, but "self-meeting" universals need not be. As Cody Gilmore suggests,

> one possible "way to distinguish universals from particulars is to note that a universal can be wholly present in distinct spacetime regions R and R★ *even if there is no causal relation holding between the contents of these regions*, whereas this does not seem to be the case for particulars" (Gilmore 2003: 427).

This formulation is certainly compatible with our time-travel case since the self-meeting, simultaneous incarnations of the particular are, arguably, causally connected by way of their later incarnations. On the other hand, two simultaneous, spatially separated instantiations of a universal, say chairness, need not be causally connected. A particular that is wholly present at different locations, l and l', at the same time, such that there is no series of spatially contiguous locations linking l and l' where that particular also (wholly or partly) occupies those locations, must be such that the l and l' incarnations of that particular are causally connected. This covers the enduring time-traveler case.

In fact, we can bring these two modifications together through a more general line of modification. These cases have in common the fact that there is some external relation holding between the multiply located particulars—a different one in each case—without which we would not posit a single, multiply located particular. A multiply located particular, x at l and x at l', must either occupy (wholly) spatially contiguous locations, or x at l and x at l' must be causally connected.[19] On the other hand, universal U at l at t and U at l' at t may be identical even if they are not spatially contiguous or causally connected, or, more generally, *independently of any external relations between them*. This gives us a modified spatial formulation:

---

[18] MacBride discusses this kind of case and notes a different restriction: "So whilst time travel cases show how one particular can be wholly present at two places at the same external time, what these cases do not show is how one particular can be wholly present at two places at the same personal time. There seems no reason however that universals could not be capable of this latter feat" (1998: 223). My misgiving about this observation is that I am unsure that the concept of personal time applies to universals, since they do not endure in the sense that particulars do. In any case, he suggests a refinement to the "spatial" formulation: the capacity for particulars to be wholly present in distinct places at the same time "is restricted, by contrast to universals, to moments of external time."

[19] I put this as a disjunction because the causal condition may not be satisfied by the particulars of Case 1. In that case, we cannot presume that the "sides" of the object are causally connected.

something is a universal just in case it has a capacity for multiple location that is independent of external relations and a particular otherwise.[20]

Universals can be identical, but particulars cannot, across different locations *independently of any external relations that may or may not hold between them/their instantiations*.

The difficulty is that this modified formulation makes the distinction between particulars and universals mysterious. Why do particulars not have, but universals do have, an unrestricted capacity for multiple locations? If particulars could not under any conditions have simultaneous multiple locations then there would be no such mystery. However, if the examples above are credible, a particular (remember Tommy) can be in two places at the same time, like a universal, but not without some external relation. This difference might turn out to be a brute difference between universals and particulars, but if it can be explained, that explanation will provide a significant insight into the distinction itself. I will now suggest that there is a more fundamental difference.

3. Similarity accounts

To see that there really is a more fundamental difference, consider first that this revised spatial account seems to imply that there are conditions sufficient for the identity of universals, but not particulars, across different locations that are *independent of any external relations between them/their instantiations*. There are conditions which, if satisfied, guarantee that universals, U_1 and U_2, with different locations at the same time, are identical, conditions that have nothing to do with the spatial or causal relations of these instantiations of U_1 and U_2 to each other. It is, then, natural to speculate that these sufficient conditions involve *internal relations* between universals across different locations. In what might these internal relations consist? I will suggest that the sufficient condition we seek has something to do with the different roles similarity plays with respect to the identity conditions for universals and particulars.

3.1 Inexact similarity and partial identity

As a first pass at such an account, I will begin with the relation of inexact similarity. I want to consider a "similarity/identity" formulation of the difference between universals and particulars that makes that difference a matter of a connection between inexact similarity and partial identity. To set the stage for this formulation, recall Armstrong's treatment of inexact similarity between universals. According to Armstrong, some universals have other universals as constituents. The 10 grams mass universal includes constituent universals such as the 6 grams mass and the 5 grams mass universals. Inexactly similar universals, U_1 and U_2, are partially identical in that

---

[20] In neither Case 1 nor Case 2 do we find a particular that is multiply located in a spatially disjoint, causally unconnected fashion.

these universals share universal parts. The 10 grams mass universal inexactly resembles the 9 grams mass universal because they are partly identical, since both have as a constituent the 1 gram mass universal. Two universals that do not have in common any constituent universals will not resemble each other to any degree. Armstrong speculates that what appear to be relations of inexact resemblance between simple universals that lack constituents—such as the universals of being red and being orange—will eventually yield to physicalist reductions that will show those universals to have constituents, some of which are shared. The greater the degree of similarity between universals, the greater the degree of partial identity, with the limiting case of exact similarity being identity. So, for example, if this view is right, the overlap between red and orange is greater than the overlap between red and yellow. Suppose for the sake of discussion that this is the right way to analyze inexact similarity among universals. Based on that analysis, here is a possible characterization of the universal–particular distinction:

> particular entities are those which do not conform to the principle that inexact similarity is sufficient for partial identity and universal entities are those which conform to that principle.

Redness is a universal because the inexact similarity of redness and orangeness is sufficient for their partial identity, but this red ball is a particular since the inexact resemblance of this red ball and any other object is not sufficient for their partial identity. Redness and orangeness are partially identical, but a red ball and an orange ball do not share any parts. Is this formulation of the universal–particular distinction adequate?

There are two reasons to reject this formulation of the universal–particular distinction. The first is that Armstrong's account of inexactly resembling universals, even if universals exist, may not pan out. For Armstrong's account to be successful, it must not be the case that there are inexactly resembling simple universals. For example, if it turns out that colors are simple, which Armstrong denies, but colors are universals, then this account will not be right. Given this uncertainty, a characterization of the universal–particular distinction should not be closely tied to this specific view of inexactly resembling universals. Second, even if we grant Armstrong his analysis of inexactly similar universals, this formulation is inadequate. The difficulty is that there is a similar connection between inexact similarity and partial identity in the case of concrete particulars if properties are universals. Suppose that two balls are inexactly similar, differing in their dimensions and various other ways, but exactly resembling each other in color. The realist says that those two balls then share the same universal. On one plausible interpretation, whether concrete particulars are bundles or include a substratum, that means that these balls are partially identical since there is a non-spatio-temporal part or constituent that they share in common. (For the realist who accepts this interpretation, inexact similarity between particulars is, at best, not sufficient for partial identity of spatial parts.) The point is that even if there is a close connection between inexact resemblance and partial identity for universals, that same connection might also be found among concrete particulars, if properties are universals. (Notice also on the Armstrongian account of inexact resemblance among universals, objects that resemble each other inexactly in virtue of possessing inexactly resembling universals will also overlap.) And, we don't want to presume that properties are not universals in setting up the distinction between universals and particulars, any more than we should presume that properties are universals, not tropes. However, there is an alternative formulation of a similarity/identity account, which does not make any reference to partial identity, that does not presume that properties are not universals, nor does it presuppose any particular account of inexact resemblance among universals.

3.2 Exact similarity and identity

The account I have in mind was proposed by D. C. Williams and others. The idea is that universals but not particulars conform to the Identity of Indiscernibles Principle—*a* and *b* are identical if they share all their inherent properties (inherent properties being those a thing has no matter what the rest of the world is like).

"Particular entities are those which do not conform to the principle of the identity of indiscernibles, which is that identity of kind entails identity of case; that is, particulars are entities which may be exactly similar and yet not only distinct but discrete" (Williams 1986: 3).

Call the claim that universals but not particulars conform to the Identity of Indiscernibles, the Exact Similarity Formulation.[21] Consider two spatially distant instances of red that are exactly alike. According to the Exact Similarity Formulation, the rednesses that are instantiated are universals just in case they are identical. On the other hand, if these rednesses are not identical, although exactly similar, then they are not universals, but particulars. The potential for having a wholly distinct duplicate is what makes something a particular and the absence of that capacity makes something a universal. God could not make a Xerox machine for any universal, but he could make one that worked for all particulars. God could run off a perfect copy of Peter the Particular, but not of Humanness the Universal.

Notice that Williams's formulation will turn out to be *false*, if it is not possible for any pair of particulars to be indiscernible with respect to their inherent (for now, read "non-relational") properties, but numerically distinct. Fortunately, there seems to be convincing reasons for thinking that the Principle of the Identity of Indiscernibles, or one which makes reference to "inherent"/"non-relational" properties, is not a

---

[21] As Keith Campbell puts Williams's point, "where particulars are concerned, matching of inherent properties is not sufficient for identity... universals' identity is guaranteed by inherent matching" (1990: 44). See also (Armstrong 1989a: 105–6): "If we consider ordinary, first-order particulars, then, ... two things, while remaining two, can resemble exactly. At least exact resemblance is possible (assuming that the Identity of Indiscernibles is not a necessary truth). In the limit, resemblance of particulars does not give identity. But now consider the resemblance of universals. As resemblance of properties gets closer and closer, we arrive in the limit at identity. Two becomes one."

necessary truth for particulars.[22] As Armstrong argues, it seems to be possible for two particulars, say two ball bearings or two electrons, to be indistinguishable with respect to all their non-relational properties. There does not appear to be any reason for excluding the possibility of distinct particulars that are inherent duplicates. In addition, it is likely that this version of the Principle of the Identity of Indiscernibles is not even contingently true of particulars. Since it seems to be physically possible for two particles to be non-relationally indistinguishable, there would seem to be a decent chance that this principle is not true (in fact, a high probability given the enormous number of particles in the world) (Armstrong 1978a: 94). Furthermore, it seems that for *any* particular x, it is metaphysically possible for there to exist an inherent duplicate of x.

3.2.1 "Being identical with x" Still, it might be objected that this version of the Principle of the Identity of Indiscernibles *must* be true for particulars since no two particulars could ever be exactly similar. It might be argued that there are non-empirical considerations that guarantee that the strong version of the principle is true. The idea is that every particular x must differ inherently from every other particular, in that x will have the property of "being identical with x" lacking in these other particulars. I think that the proper response in this context to this objection requires that we examine more closely what "inherent" is supposed to mean in the Williams formulation. I would suggest that "inherent" means "intrinsic." The idea is that entities for which being intrinsically exactly similar is sufficient for identity are universals and entities for which that is not true are particulars. But, as the literature on "intrinsic properties" makes clear, there are different notions of "intrinsic" so we need to indicate which notion is operative in this formulation. Three different notions of "intrinsic" have been identified in the literature on "intrinsic" properties.

The three notions of intrinsic properties are non-relational-intrinsic, qualitative-intrinsic, and interior-intrinsic. The first notion of an intrinsic property is that of a non-relational property. Roughly, x's having a relational property consists in x's standing in some relation R to y. The property of "being 5 feet from a barn" is a relational property. This notion should be further narrowed to those that involve x's standing in some relation to y where x and y are wholly distinct (Dunn 1990; Humberstone 1996; Sider 1993).[23] The second notion of an intrinsic property is a qualitative property. Intrinsic properties are all and only those properties which do not differ between duplicate objects (where a duplicate of x might be merely possible). Finally, there is the notion of an intrinsic property as an "interior" property. As Dunn describes this notion, "metaphysically, an intrinsic property of an object is a property that an object has by virtue of itself, depending on no other object" (1990: 178). This is the

---

[22] Whether or not entities are exactly similar in the context of Williams's formulation should not depend on whether they resemble each other with respect to their relational properties (or, more strictly, their relational properties that involve relations to wholly distinct entities).

[23] This restriction allows the inclusion of "having two parts of equal weight" as intrinsic.

sense of "intrinsic" Moore has in mind when he says, "it is obvious that there is a sense in which, when two things are exactly like, they must be 'intrinsically different' and have different intrinsic properties, merely because they are two ... the mere fact that they are *numerically* different does in a sense constitute an intrinsic difference between them, and each will have at least one intrinsic property which the other has not got – namely that of being identical with itself" (1922b).

The sense of "inherent" operative in Williams's formulation is best captured by reference to the notion "qualitative-intrinsic properties." If we think of "inherent" in terms of qualitative-intrinsic properties, the form of the Principle of the Identity of Indiscernibles discussed above will not necessarily be true for particulars. Different particular objects might still be *relevantly* indiscernible since it will not be relevant that x will have the property of "being identical with x" lacking in these other particulars. Differences with respect to "being identical with x" at best show that different particular objects must differ in their interior-intrinsic properties, not their qualitative-intrinsic properties. By emphasizing qualitative-intrinsic properties, we will also exclude properties that correspond to predicates such as "the property of being distinct from everything that is not identical to x" that are logical constructions from the property of "being identical to x/y," since such properties cannot be shared by duplicates.

Furthermore, there is a convincing reason to reject "being identical with x" as a sparse property. The idea is that for something to be a property it must be possible for it to contribute to similarity across objects. P is a property only if it is possible for two objects to be exactly similar with respect to P. P must provide a basis for "many" to be exactly similar in a certain respect. If properties are universals, this capacity is just the capacity to be "one over many."[24] If properties are tropes, that is not so, but tropes still provide a basis for similarity. In any case, whether or not properties are universals or tropes, since "being identical with x" cannot serve as a basis for exact similarity in a certain respect across non-identical objects, "being identical with x" is not a property.[25] Also note that "being identical to x" is not needed to provide a truthmaker for "Socrates is identical to Socrates." The truthmaker for this statement is just the individual Socrates, just as "Socrates exists" is made true by Socrates (Rodriguez-Pereyra 2002: 36).

So now we can restate Williams's formulation:

---

[24] Armstrong says that "being identical with x" is not a property on the assumption that all properties are universals. He says that since it lacks "a necessary mark of universals, the logical possibility that the class of particulars which have this property be an infinite class. Universals are potential ones over many" (1978a: 93).

[25] At this point, it might be suggested that this anti-property argument against "identical with x" also works against "being the tallest man," since the latter can only apply to one individual. In fact, we can guarantee that "being the tallest man" is a property because it is equivalent to "being uniquely P" and P is a property. We don't want to rule out "being uniquely P" as a property. The propertihood of "being the tallest man" is parasitic on the propertihood of "being one of the tallest men." Notice also that if the Bundle Theory of concrete objects is a necessary truth, then "being identical with x" could not be a property (Armstrong 1978a: 93).

x is a particular just in case it is possible that there exists a y such that x and y are non-identical but exactly similar independently of their non-intrinsic properties, and x is a universal just in case it is not possible that there exists a y such that x and y are non-identical but exactly similar independently of their non-intrinsic properties.

If x is an object, this will mean that x is a particular just in case it is possible that there exists a y, such that x and y are intrinsically exactly similar but x and y are not identical. For objects, exact inherent similarity depends on the properties that characterize each object.

3.2.2 Property individuation and the Williams formulation For properties, exact inherent similarity is determined not in terms of the inherent higher-order properties of the similar properties. Since properties are natures, they can be exactly inherently similar to each other in virtue of themselves/their natures, depending on what these properties are like "in themselves," which is a matter of what those properties are rather than what properties they have.[26] In order to apply this formulation of the universal–particular distinction to properties, I must briefly describe a debate about the issue of how properties are individuated: by reference to their categorical natures, if any, or by reference only to their causal or nomic roles, or by reference to both their categorical natures and their causal/nomic roles. According to monistic views of property individuation, only one of these options holds for all properties. Non-monistic views allow for more than one depending on the specific property. I will focus here on monistic views.

Although it is generally agreed that properties bestow causal powers on the objects that they characterize, or that they fill certain nomic roles, there is disagreement about the connection between such powers/roles and properties. On one variation of the monistic casual/nomic role view, a specific nomic role—as specified by a "Ramsey Lawbook"—is necessary and sufficient for each property.

"The essence of a property, on this view, is its place in the Ramsified lawbook. To derive the Ramsified lawbook, conjoin the law statements, uniformly replace each property name by a variable, and prefix the result with a unique-existential quantifier ∃! for each variable. To find the place of a given property, delete its associated quantifier. The resulting open sentence describes the essence of this property. To be that property is to satisfy that sentence" (Schaffer 2005: 2).

On another variation of the monistic causal/nomic role view, certain causal powers are necessary and sufficient for each property.

"The essence of a property, on this view, is its potential causes and effects. The potential causes and effects of a property are given by a cause-function from circumstances and potential causes to the property in question, together with an effect-function from the property in question

---

[26] If x is a property, then x is a particular just in case it is possible that there exists a y such that x and y are exactly similar independently of their non-intrinsic properties.

and circumstances to potential effects. To be that property is to fulfill that function" (Schaffer 2005: 2–3).

For those who think that a property's nature is categorical, in contrast to a monistic causal/nomic role view, each property is individuated independently of its nomic or causal role. (A "mixed" monistic view takes each property to be individuated both by its nomic or causal role and by the "categorical" nature of the property.) For some proponents of "categorical" individuation, the categorical nature of a property is a "quiddity," an inner non-dispositional qualitative nature, such that each property is not only numerically different than other properties (even of the same -adicity), but different qualitatively.[27]

How should the Williams formulation be applied to properties depending on which of these views is adopted? If a property's nature is its nomic role or its causal powers, this formulation will dictate that property P is a universal just in case there could not exist a property P' that had an exactly similar causal/nomic role to P, but was not identical to P. If properties are categorical, only bestowing specific causal powers accidentally, then the Williams formulation will dictate that property P is a universal just in case there could not exist a property P' that had an exactly similar categorical nature, but was not identical to P. On the mixed view, the Williams formulation dictates that a property P is a universal just in case there could not exist a property P' that had an exactly similar causal/nomic role to P and an exactly similar categorical nature, but was not identical to P.

There is, however, a version of the categorical view that may not be consistent with the Williams formulation of the universal–particular distinction, since it implies that some pairs of universals violate the Identity of Indiscernibles Principle, if there are universals. According to this version of categoricalism, simple universals of the same -adicity are exactly similar, but numerically distinct.

"One would say that every universal that had the same -adicity...was, if simple, merely numerically different from every other universal of that same -adicity. The -adicity could not be conjured away. It would be essential to the universal... But within an -adicity equivalence class... the difference between universals would be no more than the difference between different particulars considered merely as particulars" (Armstrong 1997: 168).

Hence, when you grasp the "nature" of one universal within an -adicity equivalence class, then you have grasped the nature of all the universals within that same class (Armstrong 1997: 168). It is not the case that within an -adicity equivalence class "each of them has its own nature, its whatness or *quidditas*, so that to have encountered one is emphatically not to have encountered all" (1997: 168). On this view, the Identity of Indiscernibles would not be true of universals that fall within an -adicity equivalence class of simple universals. For example, on this view, if crimsonness and

---

[27] For discussions of these and related views, see, for example, Armstrong (2005); Ellis, (2001); Harre and Madden (1975); Hawthorne (2001); Heil (2003); Martin (1993); and Shoemaker (1984b).

1-gram-massness are both simple and one-place universals, then they differ only numerically and not in their natures since each universal is not and does not have its own nature. Universals can have exact duplicates, just like particulars. If this view is correct, then there do exist exactly similar but numerically different simple universals: "To uphold this view is to reject the Principle of the Identity of Indiscernibles with respect to properties. Properties can be just different in the same way that ... particulars can just be different although having all their features in common" (Armstrong 1983: 160).[28] What motivates Armstrong to propose this "deflationary" account of the quiddity of universals? He suggests that a stronger conception of the quiddity of universals will give them an "inner nature" that would "elude the resources of natural science to deal with ... so much the worse for ... strong quiddity" (Armstrong 1997: 169). Notwithstanding this epistemological motivation, I will suggest that this view—which I will call Categorical Primitivism—is not an option open to the Universalist. Categorical Primitivism is not consistent with the existence of universals or with the fundamental principles that apply to universals. So whether or not a stronger notion of a universal's "quiddity" is epistemologically viable, Categorical Primitivism must be taken off the table.

According to realism, universals play a certain role grounding similarity between objects. In particular, if objects *a* and *b* are exactly similar, then *a* and *b* share all their universals. Thus, if objects *a* and *b* are duplicates, then for every universal *U* possessed by *a* *U* is possessed by *b* and for every universal *U'* possessed by *b* *U'* is possessed by *a*. However, if Categorical Primitivism is accepted, then the mutual possession of the same universals is *not* a necessary condition for exact similarity between objects. To see this, suppose that *a* and *b* possess the same number of universals of each -adicity, but that *a* and *b* share no universals in common. Simplifying a great deal, suppose that *a* and *b* each possess only one one-place universal, but these universals are wholly distinct from each other, and *a* and *b* each possess only one two-place universal, but these universals are wholly distinct from each other, and so on. *a* and *b* certainly fail to meet the necessary condition for being duplicates of sharing all their universals. However, given Categorical Primitivism, *a* and *b* are duplicates, since for each universal possessed by *a* there is an exactly similar but numerically distinct universal possessed by *b*, and for every universal possessed by *b* there is an exactly similar but numerically distinct universal possessed by *a*. For example, consider the one one-place universal possessed by *a*, say *U*, and the one one-place universal possessed by *b*, say *U'*. Although *U* and *U'* are numerically distinct, *U* and *U'* are exactly similar given Categorical Primitivism. In fact, if Categorical Primitivism is true, then *U* is no more similar to itself than *U* is to *U'*. Hence, objects *a* and *b* resemble each other to the same degree—exactly—that *a* resembles itself. The fact that *a* and *a* share all their universals does not make for a greater degree of qualitative similarity than found in the *a*/*b* pair given Categorical

---

[28] Armstrong makes this comment about the view that the identity of universals is primitive, but it seems to apply also to Categorical Primitivism.

Primitivism. Categorical Primitivism is inconsistent with a fundamental principle of realism that objects that share no universals are neither similar nor exactly similar.

Furthermore, Categorical Primitivism is not consistent with various possible universals-based accounts of inexact similarity among universals. Consider two very different accounts. On the first, at least some cases of inexact resemblance between simple universals, including those of the same -adicity, involve primitive relations of inexact resemblance. On the second, in all cases of inexact resemblance among universals, at least one of the universals is not simple and resemblance is a matter of partial identity. U and U' are inexactly similar just in case they are partially identical. Neither of these accounts of inexact resemblance between universals is consistent with Categorical Primitivism.

Consider the first view according to which there are pairs of simple universals of the same -adicity that are inexactly similar. In particular, suppose that the orangeness universal and the redness universal are of the same -adicity and each is simple. This possibility is inconsistent with Categorical Primitivism. According to the latter, although simple universals of the same -adicity resemble each other, they do so exactly, not inexactly. Hence, Categorical Primitivism is not consistent with the possibility of inexactly resembling simple universals of the same -adicity.[29]

According to the second view, inexactly resembling universals, U and U', are such that either or both are not simple and U and U' only partially overlap. For example, although it might appear to be the case that redness and orangeness are simple universals, one or both is complex and they are partially identical: they share some constituent universal and at least one of them has a constituent universal that is not a constituent of the other. Universals U and U' are inexactly similar just in case U and U' are only partially identical. But, mere partial identity between universals is not sufficient for mere inexact resemblance given Categorical Primitivism. To see this, consider two conjunctive universals, U and U'. The conjunct universals of each are simple, where all the conjunct universals are of the same -adicity: U is P & Q and U' is P & R. Q and R are not identical universals but they have the same -adicity. U and U' are only partially identical. But are they inexactly similar? To answer this question, notice that a sufficient condition for the exact similarity of two conjunctive universals consisting, say, of X & Y and W & Z is that X and W are exactly similar and Y and Z are exactly similar. In the case at hand of U and U', the first conjuncts of U and U' are exactly similar since they are identical. So there is partial overlap. Hence, there should be only inexact similarity between U and U'. But where does the inexact resemblance come from? It cannot come from P, the first conjunct in each universal. So it must come from Q and R. So it better *not* turn out that Q and R resemble each other exactly since if they do then since P resembles itself exactly then the conjunctive properties

---

[29] This means that Armstrong's backup position to the partial identity view—if we find out that some inexactly resembling universals are simples—in and of itself refutes the strong quiddities view, since on that view there can be no simple universals of the same -adicity that resemble inexactly: they all resemble exactly.

resemble exactly. But, according to Categorical Primitivism, since Q and R are simple universals of the same -adicity, they are exactly similar. Hence, U and U' are exactly similar despite the fact that they are only partially identical.

Second, given Categorical Primitivism, partial identity is not even a necessary condition for inexact resemblance among universals. Consider two universals. U is a simple universal. U' is the conjunctive universal, P & Q. P is a simple universal that is distinct from U, but of the same -adicity. In that case, U and P are exactly similar given Categorical Primitivism. U and Q are of different -adicities. But if a conjunctive universal U' is such that one, but only one, of its conjuncts is exactly similar to a simple universal U, then U' and U are inexactly similar. But in this case there is no partial identity. Hence, Categorical Primitivism is not consistent with the assumption that partial identity is a necessary condition for inexact resemblance between universals.

Categorical Primitivism is not consistent with the inexact resemblance among simple universals of the same -adicity or with the claim that simple universals are never inexactly similar, but complex universals are inexactly similar just in case those universals are partially identical. The realist must reject Categorical Primitivism if he is to provide an account of inexact resemblance between universals and an account of the exact similarity of concrete particulars, which he must. So the fact that Categorical Primitivism is inconsistent with the Williams formulation of the universal–particular distinction does not matter.

At this point, it might be suggested, in defense of Categorical Primitivism, that resemblance between properties, and resemblance between objects as derivative on resemblance between universals, depends also on the specific nomic roles filled by/causal powers bestowed by universals. In the case of simple universals, it might be suggested that each of two simple universals must have different causal/nomic roles. In that case, they will not be exactly similar. This view, even if it helps account for the inexact similarity of simple universals of the same -adicity, excludes cases of two simple universals of the same -adicity being exactly similar. There will, then, be no cases of exactly similar but distinct simple universals, and, hence, no violation of the Williams formulation. On the other hand, if we drop the claim that distinct universals must have distinct causal/nomic roles, we will be back with some of the objections already mentioned. (1) Consider pairs of distinct simple universals of the same -adicity: U and U' of n-adicity, U'' and U''' of $n+1$-adicity, and so on. Suppose that universals within a pair share the same causal/nomic role. Now consider two objects a and b such that a is U and b is U' and a is U'' and b is U''', and so on. a and b share no universals, but are duplicates. Hence, these "universals" do not play the role assigned to them by the realist. (2) This view is also not consistent with the realist assumption that partial identity between universals is sufficient for inexact similarity between those universals. Consider two conjunctive universals, U and U'. The conjunct universals of each are simple: U is P & Q and U' is P & R. Q and R are not identical universals. U and U' are only partially identical, but are they inexactly similar? U and U' will be exactly similar if Q and R resemble each other exactly. But, according to our modified Categorical

Primitivism, since Q and R are simple universals of the same -adicity, they are exactly similar if they also share all their causal powers. So suppose that they do. Hence, U and U' are exactly similar despite the fact that they are only partially identical.[30]

4. Compared to the Aristotelian formulation

The Exact Similarity Formulation is superior to the revised Aristotelian formulation for two reasons. Recall the two formulations.

> *The Revised Aristotelian Formulation*: something is a universal just in case it has a capacity for multiple location that is independent of external relations and a particular otherwise.
>
> *The Exact Similarity Formulation*: x is a particular just in case it is possible that there exists a y such that x and y are non-identical but exactly similar independently of their non-intrinsic properties, and x is a universal just in case it is not possible that there exists a y such that x and y are non-identical but exactly similar independently of their non-intrinsic properties.

First, the latter can be read as making the former more precise. Recall that the revised spatial formulation seems to point to unspecified internal relations that are sufficient for identity for universals, but not for particulars. The Exact Similarity Formulation specifies those internal relations sufficient for the identity of universals, but not particulars. The relevant internal relation is exact inherent similarity. In that sense, the Exact Similarity Formulation is more precise than the revised Aristotelian formulation. Second, the Exact Similarity Formulation dispels any mystery generated by the revised spatial formulation. Recall that under the revised Aristotelian formulation, universals and particulars both have the capacity of simultaneous multiple locations, but this capacity in particulars is limited in a way that it is not in universals, but no further difference between particulars and universals is incorporated into the revised Aristotelian formulation that might explain that difference. The Exact Similarity Formulation explains why it is that universals have a capacity for multiple locations unrestricted by external relations.[31] Differences in the capacity for multiple locations are grounded in differences in the role of exact similarity vis-à-vis identity. Inherently

---

[30] On this view, partial identity is still not a necessary condition for inexact resemblance among universals. Consider two universals. U is a simple universal. U' is the conjunctive universal, P & Q. P is a simple universal that is distinct from U, but of the same -adicity. Suppose that U and P have the same causal powers. In that case, U and P are exactly similar given modified Categorical Primitivism. U and Q are of different -adicities. But if a conjunctive universal U' is such that one, but only one, of its conjuncts is exactly similar to a simple universal U, then U' and U are inexactly similar. But in this case there is no partial identity. Hence, modified Categorical Primitivism is not consistent with the assumption that partial identity is a necessary condition for inexact resemblance between universals.

[31] It also explains why universals lack the capacity not to be located where their exact duplicates are located. In addition, since particulars have the capacity *not* to be identical to indiscernibles, they have the capacity not to be located where exactly similar things are located.

exactly similar universals are identical *no matter how they are related spatially or causally (or temporally)*. They need not be spatially continuous or causally connected. Since inherent exact similarity can hold independently of any particular external relations, unrestricted multiple locations are possible for universals. Objects (and properties) that are particulars do not satisfy this same identity condition. Exact inherent similarity is not sufficient for identity for particulars. Hence, objects (and tropes) cannot claim a capacity for multiple locations, unrestricted by external relations, on the basis of this identity condition, as can universals. And, particulars, both objects and tropes, do not satisfy some *other* identity condition that would supply an independent grounding for a capacity for multiple locations unrestricted by external relations. There is no longer a mystery as to why universals and particulars differ in this capacity for multiple locations.

One additional advantage of the "similarity" formulation over an Aristotelian characterization of the distinction is that the former, but not the latter, leaves open the possibility of particulars that are not located in space. Suppose, for example, that there are mental particulars that exist outside of space. Their particularity would be a matter not of being able to exist wholly in two places at the same time, but in the capacity for having distinct duplicates. The same point applies to mental properties if they exist outside of space.

4.1 Extended simples and time travelers

With the Exact Similarity Formulation in hand, let's now return to the problem cases involving partless but extended particulars and time-traveling enduring particulars. As indicated, the Aristotelian way of distinguishing particulars from universals cannot distinguish partless-but-extended and enduring-time-traveling particular objects from universals. In both cases, there are particulars that are wholly present at more than one location at the same time, which gives the wrong result under the unrevised Aristotelian formulation. On the other hand, the Exact Similarity Formulation gives the result that a self-meeting time-traveling enduring object is *not* a universal, though it is multiply located. The time-traveling object is a particular because it could fail to be identical to something that was inherently exactly like it. There *could be* an exactly similar object at that same time that was *not* identical to that time-traveling object. For example, in addition to the self-meeting Tommy The Time Traveler at *t*, there could have been an exactly similar person nearby that was not identical to Tommy, a Tommy duplicate. The capacity for having a duplicate is a capacity that Tommy possesses, and it is that capacity that marks Tommy off as a particular. The same thing explains why the spatially partless but extended object is a particular, not a universal. There *could be* an exactly similar object at that same time that was *not* identical to that object. For example, suppose that some distance away from the partless but extended object *a* is an exact duplicate, object *b*. If *a* were a universal, *b* would not be a duplicate but would be *a* itself. Similar points apply to Cases 3 and 4 involving tropes. The Exact Similarity Formulation classifies a self-meeting time-traveling enduring trope *not* as a universal. The time-traveling trope is a particular because it could fail to be identical to something that was exactly like it. The same thing explains why the spatially partless trope is a particular, not a universal.

4.2 Necessarily singly located universals

As indicated, there is another kind of purported counterexample directed at the standard way of distinguishing particulars from tropes: necessarily singly located universals. If there are such universals, then the standard assumption that universals have the capacity for simultaneous multiple locations must be false. For the sake of discussion I will suppose that there could be necessarily singly located universals, such as "being the funniest man," a far from uncontroversial assumption.[32] For the supposed universal "being the funniest man" to constitute a counterexample to the Exact Similarity Formulation, it must be possible for there to exist an individual who has a property *P* exactly similar to but not identical with the property of "being the funniest man." That, however, does not seem possible. Clearly, if Don Knotts is the funniest man, Don Knotts cannot be that individual: he cannot both have the property of "being the funniest man" and another exactly similar property that is not that property. For any other individual, either that person will be funnier than or equally funny as Don Knotts, in which case Don Knotts is not the funniest man, or he will be less funny, in which case he does not have a property that is exactly similar to the property of "being the funniest man" possessed by Don Knotts. For universals like "being the funniest man" it will not be possible to find cases that violate the exact similarity principle, cases in which exactly similar properties are non-identical. Such properties vacuously satisfy the universals side of this formulation. Since there can be no duplicates of this property (there can be only one instantiation), there can be no non-identical duplicates.

The matter cannot be left here. We need to deal with the possibility of tropes that necessarily cannot have distinct duplicates. Suppose, for example, that there are properties such as "being the funniest man," but they are tropes rather than universals. (I do not want to assume either that there are no such properties or that they are universals, not tropes.) The particular side of our formulation will not be satisfied. Satisfaction of the particular side of that distinction requires that there could exist a non-identical duplicate of that property. But in this case, as we have just seen, there can be no such distinct duplicate of the property of "being the funniest man." That means that this property, if we suppose it to be a trope and, hence, a particular, does not come out as a particular by this characterization of the distinction. This property vacuously satisfies the universal side of our formulation and comes out as a universal not a trope, but it

---

[32] To guarantee that this property can only be instantiated in one location at a time we must also assume, for the sake of argument, that no man can be in two places at once (contrary to the time travel possibility). MacBride mentions this point (1998: 214).

may not be a universal, or at least we should leave the possibility open in formulating the distinction between universals and tropes.

In response, I would suggest what I think is a minor modification of the Williams formulation to accommodate the possibility of singly instantiated properties like "being the funniest man." To set the groundwork for this modification, notice that the property "being the funniest man" is identical to the property "uniquely being one of the funniest men." What I would, then, suggest is that in determining whether or not *this* property is a particular or a universal, we should consider whether the property "being one of the funniest men" is a universal or a particular. If and only if the latter property is a universal or a particular so is the former property. The idea is that "uniquely being *P*" is a universal or a trope in a derivative sense just in case "being *P*" is a universal or a trope. If "being one of the funniest men" is a universal/trope, so is "uniquely being one of the funniest men" (and so is "being the funniest man" since that property is the same as "uniquely being one of the funniest men"). There is no need to decide whether or not "uniquely being one of the funniest men" is, in fact, a universal or a trope at this point. What is important is to specify what it would mean for that property to be one or the other. (Notice that this modification can also be formulated so as to save the spatial formulation from this counterexample by supposing that the universality of "being the funniest man" is inherited from the universality of "being one of the funniest men," if it is a universal.) Finally, it is worth noting that even if this modification were unsuccessful, "being the funniest man" is not a likely candidate for a sparse property in any case.[33]

5. Summary and more on similarity

We have been discussing the charge that there is no defensible basis for distinguishing particulars from universals and, hence, no viable distinction between universals and tropes. After dismissing three instantiation-based characterizations of the universal–particular distinction, we turned to the Aristotelian characterization and to a number of possible counterexamples to that characterization. After exploring a modification to the Aristotelian view, we shifted to the exact similarity characterization. The Exact Similarity Formulation can handle partless but extended objects and enduring time travelers, and it dispels any mystery generated by the revised spatial formulation, making it superior to the latter. In addition, the Exact Similarity Formulation can

---

[33] Alternately, as a referee suggests, one might argue that universals such as "being the funniest man" do not pose a problem for the similarity-based account, even if they do for the spatial account. Under the spatial account, it must be possible for a universal to be multiply instantiated in a single space-time—at different places in the same world. But if similarity is what is at stake, there does not seem to be any reason to restrict our condition to instantiations/duplicates at a world. In that case, there could be multiple instantiations of the universal "being the funniest man" or multiple duplicates of the trope "being the funniest man" across worlds. If this suggestion is right, there will be no need to hitch the status of "being the funniest man" as a universal or a trope to status of "being one of the funniest men."

handle necessarily singly located properties. In what follows, I will assume an exact similarity characterization of the universal–particular distinction.[34] Applied to properties, that means that a property is a universal if and only if exact inherent similarity is sufficient for identity, otherwise it is a trope.[35] A particular-only ontology should be understood as follows: nothing exists for which exact inherent similarity is sufficient for identity. That is what it means to say that there are no universals.

Now let's consider the following objection.[36]

> If similarity enters into distinguishing universals from particulars, then that means that similarity is a fundamental notion—or at least, more fundamental than set membership, which grounds similarity according to Natural Class Trope Nominalism. In particular, if universals may be similar *without* belonging to a set, this suggests that Natural Class Trope Nominalism has the order of explanation backwards so far as whether similarity or set membership is more fundamental.

In short, the Exact Similarity Formulation is not compatible with one component of Natural Class Trope Nominalism, the position I eventually defend.

This objection might be read in two ways. The first runs: if similarity enters into distinguishing universals from particulars, then similarity is fundamental, not being further reducible, contrary to Natural Class Trope Nominalism. This version of the objection is not convincing. Consider an analogy involving causation. Suppose that the notion of causation enters into distinguishing between X and Y, say, intentional and unintentional actions. Clearly, that use of causation does not have the implication that causation itself is not reducible. The second reading runs: if similarity enters into distinguishing universals from particulars, then similarity is more fundamental than set membership, contrary to Natural Class Trope Nominalism, and that is because if similarity grounds the universal–particular distinction, universals may be similar without belonging to a set. This version of the objection also fails to be compelling. There is no account of similarity, even between universals, that is built into the Exact Similarity Formulation. Not only does the Exact Similarity Formulation not imply that similarity is not reducible at all, it leaves it open *how* similarity is to be reduced, if reducible. In particular, even if similarity grounds the universal–particular distinction, that does not

---

[34] The Natural Class Trope Nominalist should accept the Williams formulation (suitably modified) over the traditional spatial formulation, given the possibility of enduring time-traveling tropes, say, belonging to a self-meeting time-traveling object, and, perhaps, the possibility of tropes of spatially partless objects (a spatially partless object that is uniformly white, for example, will possess a white trope that is also wholly present at each of that object's locations). If either of these possibilities is genuine, then universals, but not tropes, will have the capacity for simultaneous multiple locations unrestricted by external relations. In that event, the trope theorist will be faced with the question of what explains this difference in capacity, leading us by way of an answer to the Williams formulation. Hence, I would suggest that the universal–trope distinction should be drawn in terms of the Williams formulation as modified by the Natural Class Trope Nominalist. Specifically, a property is a universal if and only if membership in the same perfectly natural class is sufficient for identity, otherwise it is a trope.

[35] If it turns out that there are properties of the form "uniquely being P" we will have to modify this formulation as described earlier, although I doubt that this is a sparse property.

[36] I owe this objection to a referee.

automatically mean that universals may be similar without belonging to a set. There is *no* implication on this issue one way or the other. Indeed, as far as the Exact Similarity Formulation goes, similarity between universals *might* be a matter of co-membership in a natural class. The Exact Similarity Formulation for distinguishing between universals and particulars is neutral on this question. The idea is that no matter how similarity gets cashed out, the distinction between universals and particulars follows the Exact Similarity Formulation. The only implication here is that a deeper understanding of the distinction between universals and particulars awaits an account of similarity, but that is not a problem for this formulation. The Exact Similarity Formulation of the distinction between universals and particulars makes use of the relation of similarity without attempting to give an account of similarity in setting up the distinction, and this is how it should be if the distinction is not to depend on any particular account of the "problem of universals," which will have consequences for how to understand resemblance between objects and between properties. One can view a successful account of the "problem of universals"—or, more precisely, an account of similarity associated with such an account—as providing the basis for a deeper understanding of the distinction between universals and particulars, since such an account will supply a fuller understanding of resemblance.

6. What's next?

On the assumption that there is a viable distinction between universals and particulars, I will turn in the next chapter to the topic of tropes directly, or more specifically, to the question of "Why believe in tropes?" Although various arguments have been offered in the literature, I believe the strongest argument for tropes can be made around the phenomenon of qualitative persistence over time. I will suggest that there is a form of qualitative persistence that has been overlooked, a kind of persistence that can only be accounted for if there are tropes. In particular, I will claim that this phenomenon is possible only if there are enduring tropes, tropes that can be wholly present at more than one moment over time. If properties are universals, not tropes, qualitative persistence in all its manifestations is not possible. However, as we shall see, for this argument to be sustained, it must not turn out that enduring tropes are not possible. I will develop and respond to an argument, "the argument from temporary external relations," that has just that implication. I will attempt to show that this objection can be overcome by a proper understanding of the temporally bounded nature of tropes, both properties and relations.

2
Why believe in tropes?

In this chapter, I present an argument for the existence of tropes. More specifically, I argue for the existence of enduring tropes, tropes that exist wholly at each moment of their existence. I will argue that properties can move, but that that requires enduring tropes. Universals, exemplifications of universals, and even causally connected chains of exemplifications won't do. Neither will causally connected chains of momentary tropes. In the second part of this chapter, I will take up an objection to the possibility of enduring tropes, an objection that is analogous to Lewis's "temporary intrinsics" objection to enduring objects.

1. Preliminary: A grab bag of earlier arguments for tropes

There are a number of philosophical arguments for the existence of tropes in the literature. I will briefly describe the main ones before launching into a new argument for tropes. If any one of these arguments is sound, then one already has good reason to believe in tropes.

1.1 *Trope Nominalism is Superior to its Rivals* One line of argument for tropes, put forward by Campbell, consists of the claim that Trope Nominalism is superior to its two- and one-category rivals. Campbell argues that the main two-category alternative to Trope Nominalism—with an ontology that posits both concrete particulars and universals—faces difficulties not faced by Trope Nominalism, including misgivings about universals—"there must be *something* dubious about items that can be simultaneously completely present in indefinitely many objects" (1990: 12), objections to the substratum or bare particular component of concrete particulars, as well as objections to the relation of instantiation that is supposed to bind the items from the two categories together in concrete particulars. In addition, even if Trope Nominalism were not superior to its two-category rival in these various ways, Campbell claims that Trope Nominalism would still be preferable to a two-category ontology given Occam's Razor, all other things being equal (1990: 17). Campbell also tries to show that the main one-category alternatives to Trope Nominalism, including Resemblance Object Nominalism and a one-category Universalism, face insurmountable objections not faced by Trope Nominalism.

1.2. *The Explanatory Power of Tropes* Proponents of the existence of tropes often appeal to the explanatory power of tropes in accounting metaphysically for a number of different phenomena.

A. *Resemblance and Shared Properties* One line of argument for tropes, put forward by Campbell, Williams, and other proponents of tropes, consists in the claim that tropes can serve as a basis for accounting for resemblance between objects and the "common nature" of certain objects. Each of two objects that are exactly alike in some respect, say, blueness, although seeming to share a property, includes a numerically distinct, but exactly similar blue trope. "To the question: what is it for the two objects to share a common property? the reply must be: there is no such sharing, except for joint membership in a natural kind, which is not a universal but a collection of tropes" (Campbell 1990: 32). Classes of exactly similar tropes ground the relation of exact-similarity-in-certain-respects between objects.

B. *Concrete Particulars* Tropes can also provide a basis for an account of concrete particulars as bundles of properties. "The trope theory of diamonds is a bundle theory. This diamond is a compresent bundle of tropes, i.e. of particular cases of qualities. It combines in a compresent collection hardness, transparency, brilliance, many-facetedness, a carbon constitution...and so on" (Campbell 1990: 20). One advantage of a Bundle Theory is that it dispenses with the need for a substratum—and the need for an "inherence" relation between an object's properties and its substratum—and one advantage of a Trope Bundle Theory of objects over a universals-based Bundle Theory is that it is compatible with the possibility of qualitatively indiscernible but numerically distinct objects. I defend a trope-based Bundle Theory of concrete objects in Chapter 4.

C. *Causal Relata* Another line of argument for tropes consists in the claim that they can account for the metaphysics of causes and effects: "when we say that the sunlight caused the blackening of the film we assert a connection between two tropes..." (Williams 1953b: 172). Tropes are the right sorts of things to be causes and effects: "accommodation of the ontology of causes into the trope scheme is so smooth because what is required is an element that combines particularity with a very restricted qualitative nature, since causes are always features...and every particular cause is a particular feature..." (Campbell 1990: 23). Or, again, "it is the heat of this stove, here and now, that burns you, on the finger, here and now...It is not the stove, the whole stove, that burns you; not even the whole stove here now...It is the *temperature* that does the damage. Moreover, it is not any temperature, or temperature in general, but *this* particular case of temperature..." (1990: 22–3). I have also argued that causal relata are best read as tropes given the various features of the causal relation, including the (perhaps limited) transitivity of that relation (Ehring 1997a and 2009).

D. *The Causal Relation* In my (1997a), I argued that a theory of causation should posit a physical connection between causes and their direct effects. The general idea is that causes and their direct effects are physically connected by something that persists.[1] The nature of the persistence involved cannot just be a matter of spatio-temporal or nomological relations among temporal stages of that persisting "entity," but must be a matter of that entity being wholly present at each moment that it exists. Otherwise, the theory of causation will fail to handle preemptions in all its variations. I suggested that the physical connection component of causation should be understood in terms of enduring tropes. The "glue" of causation consists in enduring tropes.[2]

E. *Property Persistence* In (1997a: 91–115), I also presented an argument for enduring tropes based on the requirements of a non-circular analysis of property persistence. The main competitor account—universals-based—of property persistence involves causally connected chains of exemplification of the same universal over time, but such an analysis, in all likelihood, is ultimately circular.[3] How can we specify the right kinds of causal chains for property persistence except by reference to those causal chains that are "appropriate to property persistence"?[4] On the other hand, an account of property persistence as trope endurance is not circular. (This earlier argument from property persistence turned on the contention that enduring tropes are required to give an analysis of property persistence as contrasted with nonsalient qualitative change, whereas the argument to be developed in detail in this chapter revolves around the claim that enduring tropes are required to account for the difference between two cases of property

---

[1] Only such a theory can handle preemption in all its variations.

[2] Wilson (2009b: footnote 30) claims that a trope-persistence account of causation faces certain difficulties and that many of its advantages can be gained by positing resembling universals or tropes rather than strictly identical tropes. Notwithstanding any difficulties facing a trope-persistence account of causation, an appeal to comings-to-be of resemblances will face its own difficulties, in particular, the presence of such comings-to-be along the *preempted* line in certain cases of preemption, something that motivates an appeal to enduring tropes.

[3] In cases of nonsalient property change the causal chain between exemplifications of the same universal is missing or somehow not appropriate, but not so in cases of genuine property persistence. I argued that various substantial attempts to specify the *kinds* of causal chains between exemplifications of the same universal that are appropriate for property persistence fail to distinguish all forms of property persistence from nonsalient qualitative change. The proponent of a universals-based causal account of property persistence would eventually be driven to a circular analysis because such an account will need to appeal to "*appropriate*" causal chains, where "appropriate" must mean something like "typical of or compatible with property persistence."

[4] This charge of circularity will apply both to a Worm-type theory of property persistence or a counterpart-theoretic Stage-type theory of property persistence.

persistence, one of which involves a stationary property and the other of which involves a moving property.)
- F. *Events* Campbell argues that events are best accounted for in terms of tropes. "When we view the characteristics of objects as distinct entities... we move to a situation extremely favourable for the treatment of several otherwise intractable problems. Take *events*, for example. Events are particulars... Yet events are inherently qualitative and/or relational... Now on the trope scheme, events fit in without difficulty. Since the tropes are themselves particulars, a succession of tropes at a place will itself be a particular occasion. And since tropes have natures, trope succession, will involve that transformation of quality or relation which every event consists in" (1990: 22).
- G. *Structural Properties* Campbell argues that structural properties—properties with parts that stand to each other in specific arrangements—are best treated as structures of tropes, not universals. The idea is that properties such as being a methane molecule (CH_4) and being a butane molecule (C_4H_{10}) cannot be easily distinguished if properties are universals since they would have the same universal constituents, but can be distinguished if properties are tropes. "There cannot be... four *being an atom of hydrogens* present in each instance of *being a methane molecule*... the way to allow that a property can have four, or ten, different hydrogen constituents is to allow them particularity... the property of *being methane* occurs... with four particular hydrogen tropes as constituents" (1990: 46).
- H. *Perceptual Argument* Williams argues that tropes, rather than universals or even concrete particulars, are the primary objects of perception: "a little observation of a baby, or of oneself in a babyish mood, will convince the candid and qualified that the object of such absorption is not the abstract universal... and certainly not the concrete particular... but is in sooth the abstract or trope, this redness, this roundness, and so forth" (1953a: 16–17).
- I. *Linguistic Argument* Wolterstorff argues that certain uses of expressions such as "the green in the lower-left-hand corner of Cezanne's *L'Estaque*" must be read as referring to tropes rather than to universals (1960: 187).
- J. *Mental Causation Argument* Robb (1997) argues that if properties are tropes, then various threats to the possibility of mental causation (based on the completeness of physical causation and the absence of widespread overdetermination) can be defeated. I support a trope-based solution to the problem(s) of mental causation in Chapter 5.

In what follows I will present a further argument for tropes. However, even if this argument fails, there appears to be a sufficient basis in the literature for positing tropes. Also, as indicated, one can take Chapter 4, which develops and defends a trope-based

Bundle Theory of concrete particulars, and Chapter 5, which develops and defends a trope-based treatment of mental causation, as further arguments for the existence of tropes based on their explanatory power.

2. An argument for enduring tropes from property motion and the spinning sphere[5]

I begin with the phenomenon of qualitative or property persistence. Consider a passing car outside your window. The car persists and moves along the road. But so do its various spatial parts such as its seats and steering wheel. How else would the car persist and move? In addition, as the car passes, one also notices that so does the car's color and the car's mass. One can see the car's properties persist and move as much as one can see the car persist and move. How else could the car persist and move? Object persistence and motion are closely connected to property persistence and motion. Now consider an unchanging red ball. We readily attribute persistence to the ball itself. In addition, we recognize, at least implicitly, that the color of the ball also persists. And, we recognize that there is more to the persistence of the ball's color than the fact that exactly similar shades of red are exemplified by, say, a ball at t and a ball at t'. If one red ball is destroyed and replaced with a ball of the "same" color, for example, although the same property type is instantiated at t and at t' (whether property types turn out to be universals or classes of tropes), one form of property persistence is absent. There is something more going on in the case in which the red ball persists unchanged in color. The property instance of red that characterizes a ball that is not replaced persists in a way that we do not find in the replacement case. I will call the phenomenon found in the replacement case "mere property type persistence," and the second "property persistence," or, alternately, "property instance persistence."

The difference between property persistence and mere property type persistence is not just a matter of the difference between one object and two different objects exemplifying the same fully determinate property type at different times. There can be mere property type persistence even in a single object across time. This point becomes clear when property persistence is contrasted with "immaculate property replacement." Consider the following two situations:

Immaculate Property Replacement There is a machine that eliminates all electrical charge from objects without a trace with no other effect on the object. A second machine instantly generates electrical charges in objects. Suppose that these two machines, directed at the same particle, are set to activate at just the same moment t'. The second machine is set to generate an electrical charge in the particle of exactly

---

[5] An argument that is similar to the argument of this section is presented in my (1997a) to show that not all forms of property persistence can be accounted for on the basis of causally connected momentary tropes.

the same magnitude that the particle previously exhibited. As a result, there is no apparent shift in electrical charge in the particle from t to t'.[6]

Property Persistence The particle undergoes no transformation by way of any machines, but retains its electrical charge over this same time period.

The first case involves the replacement of one property by another, albeit an exactly similar property. The particle's electrical charge *changes* in Immaculate Property Replacement in some sense. The change, however, is imperceptible. Call this "nonsalient qualitative change." The second case does not involve property change. In property persistence, the particle's electrical charge *persists*. Property persistence is not simply a matter of the same object exemplifying the same fully determinate property type at different times. Something else is involved and the argument I will develop in the following sections for enduring tropes will trade on just what that something else is. More specifically, it is the phenomenon of property persistence—as that phenomenon is related to property movement—that will provide the basis for my argument for the existence of enduring tropes.[7]

At this point, it might be objected there is really no such thing as nonsalient qualitative change. In particular, it might be claimed that in Immaculate Property Replacement, what happens is that the two machines simply cancel each other out, with no net effect. For example, suppose that both machines act by sending out a "ray" and that these rays cross paths and simply cancel each other out before reaching the particle, with the consequence that there is no nonsalient qualitative change. In response to this worry, I would suggest that although there are ways in which this case could be developed that do not involve nonsalient qualitative change, there are other versions of the case and other cases in which it is not reasonable to posit

---

[6] Since thought experiment plays a role in my case for tropes, it is worth pointing out that not everyone agrees that thought experiments in philosophy are legitimate. There seem to be at least two kinds of critiques. The first line of attack is associated with "experimental philosophy." The idea, in part, is to discredit the use of armchair intuitions in philosophy by attacking the assumption that there will be widespread agreement with respect to intuitions about such cases. This assumption is challenged by reference to empirical surveys that seem to reveal extensive disagreements or by reference to experiments that seem to show that intuitions about such cases may vary according to the order in which various thought experiments are presented. For a discussion of this line of attack, see (Sosa 2007). I tend to agree with Sosa's defense of thought experiments against this line of attack. The second line of attack is directed at the move from conceivability to metaphysical possibility. For a discussion, see the essays in (Gendler and Hawthorne 2002). This involves many difficult and complex issues. Space does not permit a detailed treatment. Suffice it to say that I think the thought experiments I propose do reveal genuine possibilities.

[7] A referee entertains the following objection to this argument for tropes. If nothing much hangs on accommodating the possibility of persisting properties in motion—no dire consequences follow from not doing so—then this is a fairly weak argument in favor of tropes. In fact, there are at least two dire consequences in not accommodating property motion. First, and most directly, there is such a thing as persisting properties in motion and a metaphysical theory should be consistent with this phenomenon. Second, property persistence, including persisting properties in motion, is fundamental to causation, either playing a role in all causal sequences or at least playing a crucial role in the distinction between a causal and a non-causal process.

"canceling out." (1) Because of how the machines operate in other circumstances we may have good reason to reject the "canceling out" hypothesis. Suppose, for example, that in another case the creator is set to generate a charge double in magnitude as that which the particle currently possesses and the destroyer machine is set to eliminate a charge equal in magnitude to that which the particle currently exhibits. Suppose also that charges are not physically divisible or addable. If when both machines operate at the same time, directed to the same particle, there is a doubling, rather than no change, in the charge of the particle, we will have reason to reject "canceling out." Even if the destroyer machine in the canceling-out process halved the effectiveness of the creator machine, we could not assume that the doubled charge of the particle was the result of "addition" since the laws exclude that possibility. Finally, in the case in which both machines are set to the same magnitude, if the machines operate in the same way as in the doubling case, we would then have reason to think that in Immaculate Property Replacement there is no canceling out. (2) Consider another case in which a creator machine doubles the charge of a particle and sometime later a destroyer machine halves the charge of that same particle. Suppose that there is a law that prevents division of a minimum charge quantum and that any particle with twice the charge of the minimum possesses two different charges. Assume that on some occasions the destroyer machine destroys the original charge, but on others it destroys the new charge generated by the creator machine. In the first case, the charge after halving is not identical to the original charge, but in the second case, it is identical. Even though these particles match perfectly over time at the level of charge universals, there is a change in the first case at the properties level that is missing in the second case, but there is no room for canceling out since the machines operate at different times. The canceling out worry cannot get a grip on this variation on nonsalient qualitative change. (3) Finally, a more indirect response to the canceling-out worry is to note that in the literature on physical-object identity, cases of immaculate object replacement—in which an object is destroyed by a destroyer machine and immediately replaced by an indistinguishable object by a creator machine—are widely accepted as involving object replacement, nonsalient object change, rather than canceling-out. But notice that immaculate object replacement involves immaculate property replacement and nonsalient qualitative change at least relative to a location. Since these cases are generally accepted as possible, so ought purer cases of nonsalient qualitative change be accepted.[8]

---

[8] A referee suggests that given the intimate relation between objects and properties—the idea being that properties are modifications of objects—it is not clear that immaculate property replacement makes sense. In response, I would make two points. First, if this objection involves the assumption that necessarily properties are modifications of objects, I would reject that assumption. Here, I agree with Schaffer (2003) that such clustering of properties is merely a contingent fact. One can, as a consequence, consider a case of object-free, immaculate replacement that completely avoids this worry. Second, the case we have considered does not involve any free-floating properties in any case. On the other hand, one might take this objection to rely on a different assumption that the same property could not have been possessed by any other object—property swapping is not possible. However, even if we grant as much that does not exclude immaculate replacement.

2.1 Approaches to persistence

There are two broad approaches to persistence, three-dimensionalism and four-dimensionalism. A three-dimensionalist says that a persisting object endures—existing for more than one moment and existing wholly at each moment of its existence. On this view, a ball that persists from t to t' is wholly present at both times. The four-dimensionalist, either in the form of a Worm theorist or a Stage theorist, on the other hand, denies that objects can endure (Sider 2001).[9] On a Worm view, ordinary persisting objects are space-time worms with temporal parts that are appropriately related, "R-related." An object that persists from t to t' has temporal parts at t and at t' that are R-related. On Stage Theory, ordinary continuants are instantaneous stages, not space-time worms. The red ball is identical with an object stage, say, at t. What makes it true that that red ball persists until t' is that there exists an instantaneous red ball stage s' at t' that is a counterpart to s. The relevant counterpart relation is the R-relation. The distinction between three-dimensionalism and four-dimensionalism can also be applied to what I am calling "property persistence." For a three-dimensionalist, property persistence will be a matter of property endurance, but not so for a four-dimensionalist. For the latter, either Worm Theory and Stage Theory will be true of persisting properties. Persisting properties will either be space-time worms with temporal parts that are "R-related" or identical to instantaneous stages that have counterparts at other times.

I will defend a trope-based three-dimensionalist approach to property persistence. I begin by indicating why a proponent of universals (2.2) is not in a position to take a three-dimensionalist approach to property persistence, followed by a critique (2.3) of an exemplification-based four-dimensionalist approach to property persistence—in light of the distinction between property motion and property stasis—as that view might be developed by a proponent of universals.

2.2 Universals and three-dimensionalist accounts of property persistence

There are two possible forms a universals-based three-dimensionalist account of "property persistence" might take. The first emphasizes that universals are capable of "endurance" in the sense that the same universal can be wholly present at different times. The universal "red" can be wholly present on Monday and yet again on Tuesday. Property persistence might, then, just be understood as universal endurance, but such an account of property persistence, based solely on universals, will not work,

---

The latter does not require that a property could have been possessed by a different object, nor does it require the possibility of property transfer across objects.

[9] It is usually assumed that whichever view, endurantism or perdurantism, is true is necessarily true and that deciding between these views is an *a priori* matter. But it should be pointed out that some philosophers hold that this debate should be decided on a posteriori grounds, and that it is open to the three-dimensionalist/four-dimensionalist to hold that three-dimensionalism/four-dimensionalism is contingently true (or that the debate is a posteriori, but that whichever view is true is necessarily true) (Jackson 1994).

at least as that phenomenon is contrasted with mere property type persistence. Both in the case of Immaculate Property Replacement and in the sister case of Property Persistence, the same charge universal is instantiated at and after t, if there are universals. Property persistence collapses into mere property type persistence if we are restricted to universals. Even if there are universals, property persistence is not just a matter of "universal endurance." Something in addition to enduring universals must be brought into play to make sense of this contrast in three-dimensionalist terms.

The second form of a universals-based three-dimensionalist treatment of property persistence involves the notion of an enduring exemplification of a universal. Property instance persistence is a matter of the endurance of an exemplification of a universal. A red property instance persists from t to t' just in case there is exemplification of the universal red at t that exists wholly at t and wholly at t'. There are problems with this suggestion. First, it does not appear to be consistent with the typical way of understanding the exemplification of a universal by an object at a time. Under this conception, the exemplification of a universal by an object at a time has a time as a constituent and it is partly individuated by its constituent time. If the constituent times are instantaneous, then, the exemplification of universal U at t is not identical to the exemplification of U at t' if t is not identical to t'. The exemplification of the redness universal at 2 p.m. by this ball is not identical to the exemplification of the same redness universal by this ball at 3 p.m., no matter how intimately they are connected. On the other hand, if the constituent times in some cases involve extended periods in time, say "t through t'," (perhaps in the case of property instance persistence but not in the case of nonsalient property change), that will not generate an *enduring* exemplification of a universal, but a temporally extended exemplification with temporal parts. Under this conception, the exemplification of redness from t to t' is not wholly present at t, bringing us to a four-dimensionalist approach to property persistence. (I will discuss four-dimensionalist treatments of property persistence in the next section.)

Still, one might take the phenomenon of property persistence to motivate an alternative account of exemplification individuation, allowing exemplifications to endure through time, an account that guarantees that it is not the case that new exemplifications of a seemingly persisting property are constantly coming into and going out of existence with every tick of the clock or that exemplifications have temporal parts. In fact, whatever form this alternative characterization of enduring exemplification takes, either it will not help to distinguish property persistence from nonsalient property change, or if it does, that is only because something very much like enduring tropes are posited. Consider that an exemplification has various "components," including the exemplification relation—if it is a relation—(a universal on this view), the object, and the constituent universal. In order to distinguish Property Persistence from Immaculate Property Replacement, some difference must be found at the level of these "components." The difficulty is that in each case these components remain—except the time—constant over the relevant time period. There is no new object, new universal, or a new exemplification relation (if it is a universal) that comes into existence during that period. Since there is no basis for thinking that these cases, Property Persistence and Immaculate Property Replacement, differ in any way with respect to objects and universals, there is no room for finding an enduring exemplification in one case but not in the other. On the other hand, if the exemplification relation is *not* a universal, then perhaps the distinction at issue could be accommodated after all. Why couldn't exemplifications of universals provide a basis for distinguishing property persistence (those are the exemplifications of universals by object that include an enduring exemplification relation) from nonsalient property change (those are the exemplifications of universals by object that do not include an enduring exemplification relation)? If the appeal to an enduring exemplification is going to provide a basis for distinguishing the two cases, an enduring exemplification of a universal by an object will include something very much like an enduring trope: a particularized exemplification relation capable of enduring in a temporal fashion or of being switched out. Hence, it would seem that the only way for the Universalist—who adopts an enduring exemplification approach to property persistence—to make the distinction at issue is to accept enduring tropes (since it is hard to see what would distinguish these from enduring tropes).[10]

2.3 Universals and four-dimensionalist accounts of property persistence

The proponent of universals will need to shift to a four-dimensionalist approach to property persistence. How might that go? If Worm Theory is applied to property persistence, then instantaneous exemplifications of a universal at a time will serve as the temporal parts of a persisting property (or if Stage Theory is applied, the property instance will be identical to an instantaneous exemplification of a universal stage with a counterpart relation determining its persistence). On a Worm Theory, property persistence is a matter of a series of momentary exemplifications related in the right way. What is the right way? Spatio-temporal continuity might be required, but that will not guarantee property persistence. In both Immaculate Property Replacement and Property Persistence we find spatio-temporal continuity, but only in one case is there property persistence. Another possibility is to appeal *both* to spatio-temporal continuity and similarity (in the form of qualitative similarity). The idea, then, is that the right relation is largely similarity-based.[11] However, adding qualitative similarity to the mix will not be enough. In both Immaculate Property Replacement and Property

---

[10] Thanks to a referee for suggesting this way of putting the point.
[11] It might be suggested that the right relation should be read as a similarity-based counterpart relation without a causal component. A referee suggests that treating the relation this way would fit with the usual extension of counterpart-theoretic relations to stages or slices. But, in fact, the usual development of Stage Theory does bring into play causal relations between stages. Consider, for example, what Sider (2000: 84) says when discussing Stage Theory: "the temporal counterpart relation is the same as the 'genidentity' or 'unity' relation used by the worm theorist to unify the successive stages of continuing space-time worms." But the "genidentity" relation used by the Worm theorist is typically thought to have such a causal component. And there is good reason for this inclusion, since without it, Stage Theory will give the wrong results in cases of object immaculate replacement.

Persistence, we find the same degree of qualitative similarity over time, but only in one case is there property persistence. Causation must be added to the mix.[12] It might be said that, in cases of property persistence, but not in cases of immaculate property replacement, there is an appropriate causal connection or causal chain between the exemplifications of the relevant universal at different times.

2.3.1 The sphere case Unfortunately, a causal-exemplifications-based four-dimensionalist account will fail for some cases of property persistence.[13] In order to make this point, I need to bring into our discussion the "spinning sphere" case from the literature on physical-object persistence. Although the original purpose of this example was to test various accounts of object persistence, it can also be used to test an exemplification-based four-dimensionalist account of property persistence. I will argue that an indeterministic form of this case demonstrates the inadequacy of any causal-exemplification theory of property persistence, at least given certain background assumptions about causation.

The Sphere Case: consider two perfectly homogeneous, qualitatively indistinguishable spheres, made of non-particulate, non-atomistic matter in exactly similar surroundings.[14] One sphere is spinning and the other is stationary. At any moment in its history, however, each sphere's intrinsic properties (understood as universals or property types) and its relations to other objects at that time, do not vary whether or not it is rotating. (Let's suppose for purposes of simplification, that in the case of the spinning sphere the property moves from time t_1 to time t_2 from the NW region of the sphere to the SW region, whereas in the other sphere it remains in the NW region from t_1 to t_2.)[15]

---

[12] A referee suggests the possibility of treating the R-relation as a primitive relation. While this is a possibility, it should only be adopted as a last resort since that would mean positing a wholly new kind of non-supervening relation with only one function, whereas positing enduring tropes is less extravagant and gives us a basis for accounting for a wide range of phenomena, including, for example, object–object resemblance and the nature of objects (by way of a Trope-Bundle Theory of objects).

[13] If the best account of causation involves enduring tropes, then that would provide another reason to reject the causal 4-D Universalist account of property persistence—namely, that the appeal to causal connection between exemplifications tacitly assumes that there are enduring tropes.

[14] (Armstrong 1980a). See also (Kripke) for a similar example.

[15] The spinning sphere case and similar cases have recently come under fire. Maudlin (2007), in particular, argues that at present we have no good grounds for thinking that the sphere case is metaphysically possible. There are no actual cases of such spheres and we have no grounds for thinking that homogeneous matter is physically possible. "We therefore do not have the usual grounds that we have for thinking that a non-actual state is metaphysically possible" (2007: 186). Maudlin also rejects any effort to argue that, although we have no reason to believe that the sphere case is physically possible, we still have reason to think it metaphysically possible on the grounds that "it is metaphysically possible that physics might have been different from what it is..." (2007: 187). If there is no actual homogeneous matter and perfectly homogeneous matter is not physically possible—or, at least we have no reason for thinking it is physically possible—he suggests that we have no reason to think such matter is metaphysically possible. "We simply think it is possible because we have produced a description and decided to nominate it a metaphysically possibility. The latter approach simply fails to make any contact with reality..." (2007: 188). It is not enough to show that a description of the spin case is logically non-contradictory, since something that is logically possible may still be metaphysically impossible. I do not find this line of skepticism convincing. First, we do not generally apply such stringent requirements to knowledge claims about what is metaphysically possible. For example, although

Consider the color of the NW quadrant of the sphere at t_1. In both spheres, there is property persistence and, in particular, the color property instance of the NW quadrant persists. That color instance persists from t_1 to t_2 in both spheres in my sense of "property persistence." However, in only one sphere does that color instance move. Our question is whether the exemplification-based four-dimensionalist account can provide a basis for reading off that difference in property instance motion between the two spheres. Before answering that question, I will introduce an indeterministic twist on the sphere case.

The Indeterministic Sphere Case: Consider two perfectly homogeneous, qualitatively indistinguishable spheres, made of non-particulate, non-atomistic matter in exactly similar surroundings. In the case of both spheres, the laws dictate that there is a 50% chance that the color property in the NW quadrant at t_1 will relocate to the SW location at t_2, and there is a 50% chance that the NW color property at t_1 will remain at the NW location at t_2. But as in the sphere case, one sphere spins but the other remains stationary. At any moment in its history, however, each sphere's intrinsic properties (understood as universals or property types) and its relations to other objects at that time do not vary whether or not it is rotating.

In this version of the case, the movement of the color property is a probabilistic matter. A causal theory of property persistence based around causally connected exemplifications of universals must distinguish between the following two scenarios:

(1) the color property that characterizes the NW region of the sphere at t_1 moves to the SW region occupied by the sphere at t_2; and
(2) the color property that characterizes the NW region of the sphere at t_1 remains in the NW region occupied by the sphere at t_2.

The causal-exemplification theorist will need to show that these two scenarios are distinguishable as follows:

(3) the exemplification of the color universal by the portion of the sphere that occupies the NW region at t_1 is causally connected to the exemplification of the color universal by the portion of the sphere that occupies the SW region at t_2, and

---

there is no actual thing that accelerates from less than the speed of light to greater than the speed of light, and although this pattern of acceleration is not physically possible, we are not tempted to think that we don't know that this pattern of acceleration is metaphysically possible. Second, we may have reason to think something is metaphysically but not physically possible if we have reason to think something similar is physically possible. For example, we have reason to think that it is metaphysically possible for something to accelerate from less than the speed of light to greater than the speed of light because it is physically possible for something to accelerate from much-less-than the speed of light to near the speed of light. Hence, given that we have reason to think that a nearly perfectly homogenous sphere is physically possible, that gives us some reason to think that a perfectly homogeneous sphere is metaphysically possible. Third, even if we concede that we do not *know* that the spin case is metaphysically possible, we may know enough to *presume* that it is possible, say, based in part on intuitions, a presumption that can be overturned if contrary evidence appears. Maudlin says that we should place no weight on such intuitions, but he does not provide a compelling reason for not trusting our intuitions in this matter.

(4) the exemplification of the color universal by the portion of the sphere that occupies the NW region at t_1 is causally connected to the exemplification of the color universal by the portion of the sphere that occupies the NW region at t_2.

Can a causal difference be established between the two cases?

The answer depends on what we assume about causation. I will assume that causal facts supervene on non-causal facts (for a response to arguments in favor of the non-supervenience of the causal on the non-causal, see my (1997a: 61–8)). In 2.3.2, I will argue, first, that if causation satisfies the doctrine of Humean Supervenience (which I will describe in a moment) the causal-exemplification account of property persistence will fail for some versions of the Indeterministic Sphere Case. The idea is that if causation satisfies the HS thesis, as a number of philosophers hold, there will be pairs of spheres that differ between (1) and (2) but do not differ between (3) and (4). That leaves no room for a causal-exemplification account of property movement/stasis in all sphere cases that is compatible with the doctrine of the Humean Supervenience of causation. In 2.3.3, I turn to reductionist theories of causation that may or may not satisfy the HS thesis, but which do not include enduring tropes in the reduction base. I will argue that the relevant causal difference—that between (3) or (4)—cannot be demonstrated between our spinning and stationary spheres.[16] In Section 2.3.5, I will show how enduring tropes provide a basis for distinguishing between the color movement and color stasis in the Indeterministic Sphere Case.

2.3.2 Causation and Humean Supervenience Suppose that causal facts supervene on non-causal facts such that there can be no causal difference without a non-causal difference. That supposition is made more precise by assuming that causation satisfies the doctrine of the Humean Supervenience such that the supervenience base for causation includes only the instantiation of fundamental properties and spatio-temporal relations between particular things (Lewis 1994: 473). The fundamental properties are "local," "perfectly natural intrinsic properties of points, or of point-sized occupants of points" (1994: 474). Leave open whether these fundamental properties are universals or classes of tropes. Humean Supervenience sets up fairly strict conditions on the supervenience

---

[16] A referee worries about my assumption that causal facts supervene on non-causal facts, pointing out that "many" reject this assumption. In response I would suggest that among philosophers of causation, reductionism remains the dominant position with only a minority disagreeing. In addition, I do not find the main arguments against the broad thesis that the causal supervenes on the non-causal to be compelling (see my (1997a: 61–8)). The referee also worries about that part of my argument that involves the supposition that causation satisfies a Humean Supervenience thesis, given that many philosophers reject the latter thesis. In fact, I am not making my argument for tropes dependent on that thesis (although I try to show what difficulties ensue for a causal-exemplification view of property persistence for those who do accept the Humean Supervenience of causation). My main goal is to show that a reductionist about causation (who does not appeal to enduring tropes) will not be able to sustain a causal-exemplification view of property persistence. I include the more extreme form of reductionism about causation according to which causation does satisfy a Humean Supervenience thesis for the sake of completeness.

base for causation.[17] Causation supervenes on the "spatio-temporal arrangement of local qualities." The supervenience base does not include facts about identity over time, except perhaps facts about universals, including facts about persisting objects or persisting tropes.[18] On the assumption of Humean Supervenience, there must be differences in the spatio-temporal arrangement of fundamental properties in Cases 3 and 4 if there are causal differences between (3) and (4). If not, then on the assumption that causation satisfies the doctrine of Humean Supervenience, we must conclude that the causal-exemplification account of the difference between (1) and (2) fails.[19]

There are two main proposals for HS-acceptable, non-causal differences that *must* show up between the spinning and stationary sphere, non-causal differences that will determine of which sphere, (3) or (4) holds, if the causal-exemplification account of property persistence is right. I will suggest that neither purported non-causal difference between the spinning and stationary spheres is guaranteed to accompany the difference in motion in the spheres.

Intrinsic instantaneous velocity

Instantaneous velocity is not traditionally understood to be a "local" property, and, as such, it cannot be in the Humean Supervenience base for causation. Velocity has typically been treated as a property that derives from the positions that a thing has at different times, but no facts about persisting objects can appear in the base.[20] Tooley, however, has offered an alternative conception of instantaneous velocity that makes it compatible with Humean Supervenience. According to Tooley, instantaneous velocity

---

[17] Humean Supervenience is the thesis that "all there is to the world is a vast mosaic of local matters of particular fact, just one little thing after another" (Lewis 1986b: ix–x).

[18] Lewis says that the persistence of universals does not violate HS (1986b: xiii).

[19] A referee worries that the two-spheres-only world would not contain probabilistic laws. If the laws supervene on the local, Hume-intrinsic spatio-temporal facts and, on the usual Best System understanding, the laws supervene in being the strongest, simplest axiomatization of these facts, then there would be no probabilistic laws in such a simple world. On the other hand, if the world is sufficiently complex as to sustain probabilistic laws as part of the Best System, then there is no barrier to the Best System also including facts about whether certain objects or properties are enduring or not. First, I am not convinced that the two-spheres-only world will not contain probabilistic laws, even given the Humean Supervenience of laws. But, second, even if we must consider the laws of more complex worlds, and even if these laws include some reference to the endurance of objects/properties that will not undermine the case, such probabilistic laws will not determine the relevant facts of endurance highlighted in the case. Even if the laws dictate, for example, that the color property of the NW quadrant will endure, it will not dictate where that property will end up. For each sphere, the laws dictate a 50% chance that the color property in the NW quadrant at t_1 will relocate to the SW location at t_2, and a 50% chance that the NW color property at t_1 will remain at the NW location at t_2. The laws will not determine whether or not the property moves, since those motion facts are supposed to be indeterministic. Furthermore, although in this discussion I am assuming that there is some way to accommodate probabilistic laws given Humean Supervenience, in the event that that is not so—which is probably right—then we will need to consider *broader* reductionist views of causation, not tied to Humean Supervenience. I do that in Section 2.3.3.

[20] On this conception, "the velocity of an object at any time necessarily involves reference to the positions of that object at neighboring times" (Tooley 1988: 227). Velocity consists in the first derivative of a function specifying the object's positions at various times that fall on a continuous curve that is differentiable at every point.

does not supervene on the positions of an object over time. Instead, it is an intrinsic property, a theoretical property that explains change in position. Velocity is "whatever plays the role of velocity accorded to velocity by the laws of nature" (Hawley 2001: 79).[21] If instantaneous velocity is an intrinsic property, then it could be argued that the spheres, or their parts and the properties of their parts, must differ at various times in velocity and that such differences will be causally responsible for the difference between the spheres in the positions of the parts and properties of those parts at later times. It might then be argued that there must be such differences in "Tooleyan" velocity between the spinning and stationary spheres. If there must be such differences, then those differences may help the causal-exemplification theorist distinguish between (3) the color exemplification by the NW quadrant at t_1 being causally connected to the color exemplification by the SW quadrant at t_2 and (4) the color exemplification by the NW quadrant at t_1 being causally connected to the color exemplification by the NW quadrant at t_2 in a way that is compatible with the Humean Supervenience of causation doctrine. Without HS-acceptable differences such as these, the causal-exemplification theorist who holds the doctrine of the Humean Supervenience of causation cannot claim that in the case of one sphere (3) is true but in the case of the other sphere (4) is true. Unfortunately, even granting that instantaneous velocity is an intrinsic property—a claim that is challenged by Zimmerman (1998) and Hawley (2001)—and even granting that the spheres (including the parts and property instances) in the probabilistic case have such velocities, we cannot assume that there will be a difference in instantaneous velocity at t_1 (or any time) of the spheres, their quadrants or their color instances corresponding to the difference in motion in the spheres: our spinning and stationary spheres (or their color property instances) may share the same instantaneous velocities at t_1 in particular.[22] To see this, recall that in the Indeterministic Sphere Case, the relevant laws of motion are probabilistic. That means, in part, that

---

[21] Velocity is a theoretical, intrinsic property implicitly defined by the laws of motion, but which can be explicitly defined by "Ramsifying" the laws of motion à la David Lewis's method (Zimmerman 1998: 275). In fact, as Zimmerman argues, "Tooleyian" velocity does not appear to be an intrinsic/local property: "It is, then, part of the definition of instantaneous velocity that it be the property of an object which is such that its possession at each instance of an interval, together with its location at the beginning of that interval and the length of the interval, determines where *that very same object* will be at the end of the interval... It is simply in the nature of laws of motion that they describe how earlier states of motion of a given object help to determine subsequent states of motion of *the same object*" (1998: 282). Hawley makes a similar point. Hawley argues that velocity grounds counterfactual conditionals which concern what goes on at other times: "To attribute instantaneous velocity to the present stage is to say something partial and conditional about certain future stages and not about others. It is to say something about how future stages of a persisting object will vary according to the forces which apply" (2001: 79).

[22] Another problem is that by Tooley's own account of velocity, such spheres must lack instantaneous velocities. According to Tooley, if the position of an object is determined only probabilistically, then that object does not possess instantaneous velocity at any time. Such sequences "would not have a velocity at any time, even if all its positions happened to fall along a curve describable by some continuous, differentiable function." That is so since whatever velocity is, it must be causally relevant to its positions at later times on Tooley's account, but there is no such causal relevancy for the "instantaneous velocity" in such case; only the object's position at a time (probabilistically) causally matters to its later positions. What that means is that neither the NW portion of our sphere nor the NW property has Tooleyan instantaneous velocity. The

even if the instantaneous velocities of the color instances of the NW quadrants at t_1 are specified and those velocities are the same in both spheres, those velocities even in combination with the laws/forces will not necessarily determine the same later, relative positions of the color instances. For the same intrinsic velocity at t_1, the laws may assign some probability to the NW quadrant not changing locations at t_2 or changing locations to the SW area. If the laws of motion are probabilistic, then even if instantaneous velocity is intrinsic, the two spheres may agree on all their HS-base properties at t_1. In short, we cannot assume that the difference between property instance motion and stasis in our pair of spheres in the Indeterministic Sphere can be accounted for on a causal-exemplification theory of property persistence that is consistent with the Humean Supervenience of causation, even given the assumption that instantaneous velocity is an intrinsic property.

ROBINSON'S QUASI-QUALITIES

The second proposal for HS-acceptable differences in non-causal properties can be found in Robinson (1989). Robinson argues that the difference between a stationary sphere and a rotating sphere is a difference with respect to certain "second-order quasi-qualities having the quality of vectors." These second-order properties are causally responsible for the propagation of the sphere's first-order properties, and, hence, for the velocity of the sphere. They are responsible for the law-governed propagation of the sphere's material properties in a certain direction, different directions in the rotating and stationary spheres. These second-order properties, although causally responsible for the sphere's velocity, are not identical to those velocities. But these second-order properties are intrinsic/local and may thus serve as a basis for distinguishing between a rotating and a stationary sphere. By extension, one might suggest that a vector determines the movement (or lack of movement) of the NW color at t_1, a different one if that color is moving than if it is not. Unfortunately, this proposal will not help in the Indeterministic Sphere Case. Robinson's second-order properties are causally responsible for the direction of propagation of the sphere's first-order material properties. However, in the Indeterministic Sphere Case, we must suppose that these lines of causal influence from these second-order properties to the direction of propagation of the first-order properties are probabilistic. That means that two spheres might agree on all their Robinsonian second-order properties but differ as to whether they are spinning. Even if the second-order properties probabilistically favor it, motion at the same velocity would not be guaranteed. Nor does it guarantee motion of the color property of the NW quadrant at t_1. These spheres may, then, agree on all their intrinsic properties at each time, including their second-order properties, but differ with respect to the positions of their quadrants/colors at different times.

---

causal-exemplification theorist cannot, then, appeal to differences in such velocities across the two sphere cases to ground a difference in causal relations.

2.3.3 Broader reductionist theories of causation Although there are other possible candidates for HS-acceptable non-causal differences between the rotating and stationary spheres, none seems promising. At this point, I will set the HS thesis aside and consider how a causal-exemplification account of the difference between property motion and property stasis might go, if the causal-exemplification theorist is not committed to the Humean Supervenience of causation, although still committed to the supervenience of the causal on the non-causal. More specifically, I will now consider the causal-exemplification account of property persistence in the context of various reductionist theories of causation that may or may not strictly satisfy that Humean Supervenience thesis. (Recall that a 4-D *non-causal* exemplification account of property persistence that is similarity-based is bound to fail to provide a basis for distinguishing between Property Persistence and Immaculate Property Replacement.) I will focus on reductionist theories of causation that make the causal supervene on the non-causal even if not on the non-causal supervenience base posited by the Humean Supervenience thesis. For example, I will consider the relevance of a probabilistic theory of causation to the Indeterministic Sphere Case. A probabilistic theory might very well make causation supervene on the non-causal, but if chances do not satisfy Humean Supervenience, then that theory will not satisfy the Humean Supervenience thesis about causation. The possible failure of Humean Supervenience will not concern us.

Either a reductive theory of causation will include enduring tropes in the reduction base or it will not. If it does, simply by bringing causation into an account of property persistence will bring into play enduring tropes. Since such theories give the game away immediately to the trope theorist, I will set them aside. If it does not, I will argue that the causal-exemplification approach to property motion in the Indeterministic Sphere Case fails.

There are a variety of contemporary reductive accounts of causation that do not involve reference to enduring tropes. Here, I want to suggest that whichever of the most prominent accounts of this type is plugged into the causal-exemplification account of property movement/stasis, the result is the same: there is no basis for distinguishing between the two scenarios. I conclude that, barring the development of a new reductive account of causation, the universals-based four-dimensionalist approach to distinguishing between these scenarios fails. What follows is a brief run-through of the predominant contemporary reductionist accounts of causation applied to the Indeterministic Sphere Case by way of the causal-exemplification account.

THE NEO-HUMEAN VIEW
Consider the combination of a causal-exemplification account of property persistence with a neo-Humean or regularity theory of causation (see Mackie 1974 and Davidson 1980). On the latter theory, roughly, c and e are causally connected just in case they are connected by a law—the pair is an instance of a lawful regularity. Given this combination, the difference between (3) and (4) is the difference between

(3') there is a lawful connection between NW color exemplification at t_1 and t_2 and the SW color exemplifications at t_2, and

(4') there is a lawful connection between the NW color exemplification at t_1 and the NW color exemplifications at t_2.

However, in the probabilistic case, the laws in combination with the initial conditions at t_1 do not discriminate between these two possibilities. Alternately stated, given a causal-exemplification theory of property persistence and a neo-Humean theory of causation, although the indeterministic law that governs this case guarantees that the color will either be at the NW or SW quadrant at t_2, it does not determine movement or stasis of that color. There is a probabilistic law connection between the NW color exemplification at t_1 and the NW color exemplification at t_2 (the former increases the probability of the latter under the relevant law), *and* between the NW color exemplification at t_1 and the SW color exemplification at t_2 (the former increases the probability of the latter under the relevant law). The key is that the laws are indeterministic, allowing for a lawful connection between the earlier state and both of the later states. If the laws were deterministic, this argument would not work. The relevant laws given the non-causal facts determine merely that that property will continue to exist in one location or the other, but no more.[23] Hence, on the basis of this law—combined with a neo-Humean theory of causation and a causal-exemplification account of the difference between the scenarios—whether or not the color property is moving is not determined.[24]

COUNTERFACTUAL THEORY

Counterfactual theories of causation, typically, state that an effect is counterfactually dependent on its immediate cause.[25] Indirectly causally connected events are

---

[23] A referee worries that my concern about the neo-Humean-based causal-exemplification account of property persistence is an epistemological, not a metaphysical concern. The referee says that even if the states of affairs at time t_1 plus the probabilistic laws won't in themselves provide a basis for distinguishing whether the pattern at the later time resulted from property movement or not, that is an epistemological matter. At the later time, the laws will have operated in one way or another, even if we are not in position to know which way they operated. From a metaphysical point of view, however, in the relevant sense of "distinguish," the neo-Humean can distinguish property movement from non-movement as reflecting which disjunct of the probabilistic law(s) eventuated, as a matter of fact, on the occasion in question. In response, I would suggest that the main point of the argument is not epistemological. The question is whether the laws plus all the relevant facts, including facts about what happens after t_1, but not including facts about persistence over time (facts about which way the coin flipped, so to speak), *determine* facts of persistence. The issue is not that we cannot predict what will happen after t_1, but that even after the sequence has unfolded we cannot read off certain facts of persistence (property movement or non-movement) from the laws—even given that the laws "operated"—and the other relevant facts, including some facts about what happens after t_1. The point is that "how" the law operated—which disjunct eventuated—is determined by the facts of persistence, not the other way around. The mere fact that the law operated does not determine the facts of persistence. But if the neo-Humean reductionist account of causation is combined with a causal-exemplification account of property persistence, those facts *should* determine property movement or non-movement. The causal facts are supposed to supervene on the non-causal facts—not including facts about endurance—plus the laws, but in this case that supervenience relation fails.

[24] This argument is adopted from (Tooley 1987: 199).

[25] See, for example, (Lewis 1986a).

connected by a chain of events such that each member of the chain is counterfactually dependent upon its immediate predecessor. Applied to the case at hand (assuming that the earlier color exemplification is an immediate cause of either the t_2-NW or t_2-SW color exemplification), a counterfactual-causal theory will say that the NW color property exemplification is stationary/moving during the time period if and only if it

> had the NW color property before t_1 not existed, the NW color property/SW color property at t_2 would not have existed.

Under the probabilistic conditions of our case, however, *it will not be true* that had an earlier color exemplification trope not been realized, the t_2-NW color exemplification would not have been realized. And, *it will not be true* that had an earlier color exemplification not been realized, the t_2-SW color exemplification/momentary trope would not have been realized. In the absence of the exemplification of the color property by the NW quadrant at t_1, either the NW quadrant or the SW quadrant would have failed to exemplify that color property at t_2, but we cannot be more definite. It is not true that in all the closest worlds in which the NW quadrant at t_1 lacks that color property at t_1, the NW quadrant lacks it at t_2. Similarly, it is not true that in all those worlds, the SW quadrant lacks that color property at t_2. In some of the closest worlds in which the NW quadrant lacks that color property at t_1, the NW quadrant lacks that color property at t_2, but in some of the closest worlds in which the NW quadrant lacks that property at t_1, the SW quadrant lacks it at t_2. Hence, a counterfactual theory of causation combined with a causal-exemplification account of the difference between the scenarios will not provide a basis for determining which scenario is operative.

PROBABILISTIC THEORY

Probabilistic theories of causation come in either a non-counterfactual form or a counterfactual form. The basic idea behind non-counterfactual probabilistic theories of causation is that causes increase the probability of their effects understood in terms of conditional probabilities. The basic idea of a probabilistic counterfactual theory is that the cause is such that had it not occurred the probability of the (immediate) effect would have been different. In neither case do our prospects for determining whether or not the color property of the NW quadrant is moving improve. On the assumption that none of these probabilities are 1 or 0, we will not be able to infer that the color property is stationary or that it is moving on either version of a probabilistic theory. All we can determine is that there is some probability that the color property is moving and some probability that it is stationary. Consider, for example, the counterfactual version. Suppose that the NW trope at t_1 had not been realized, but that things had otherwise been as much like the actual world up to t_1 as possible. Would the probability of an absence of color at the NW location at t_2 have been increased? The answer is that it would have been, since at t_1 there was a certain probability that the sphere would remain stationary. However, it is also true that the introduction of an absence of color at the NW location at t_1 would have meant that the chance of an absence of color at the SW location at t_2 would have been greater. This is so since at t_1 there is some chance that the sphere will rotate. Hence, a causal-exemplification account of property motion in combination with a probabilistic theory of causation will not determine in this case whether or not the color property in the NW quadrant is rotating.

I conclude that a causal-exemplification theory of property persistence fails. I would also suggest that a similar theory in terms of causally connected momentary tropes will also fail. On such a theory, the colors in our case are tropes, but momentary tropes, and the difference between property motion and stasis is a matter of whether the appropriate momentary tropes are causally connected. This kind of account will not work in our Indeterministic Sphere Case for the same reasons that the causal-exemplification theory does not work.[26]

2.3.4 Property persistence secondary to object persistence? One other option that must be considered is that property persistence is secondary to object persistence, and that once the object persistence facts are determined, the property persistence facts will follow, including whether or not there is property movement. Suppose, for example, that the NW quadrant at t_1 is identical to the NW quadrant at t_2. Will that be sufficient for the conclusion that the NW color at t_2 is identical to the NW color at t_2? Suppose that object persistence is best understood in terms of four-dimensionalism and that between the temporal parts/stages, the NW quadrant at t_1 and the NW quadrant at t_2, there must be a causal connection. Now we are back to the original purpose of the sphere case, testing accounts of object persistence. Here, I would suggest that such a theory will require a determination of the causal relations between property instances. Why think that? Objects and even temporal parts/stages are not *themselves* causal relata, at least non-derivatively. The causal relations between object stages are derivatively causally related in virtue of causal relations between property instances of those stages, which returns us to the issue of determining which of the likes of (3) and (4) are true. On the other hand, if object persistence is object endurance, then I would suggest that even if it is true, for example, that the NW quadrant of the sphere is wholly present in the NW region of the sphere at t_1 and, again, at t_2, it does not follow that the color of the NW quadrant of the sphere has persisted in the NW location. Object endurance does not guarantee property identity. In our case of "Immaculate Property Replacement" we have a failure of property persistence despite no failure in object persistence. What else is required, beyond object persistence, to determine whether or not the color of the NW region of the sphere changes location or not? It must be determined which exemplification of color at t_2 is caused by the exemplification of color by the NW quadrant at t_1. But we have already seen that on theories that make causation supervene on the non-causal—excluding theories that include in causation's reduction

---

[26] For a full statement of this argument, see my (1997a: 104–14).

base facts about trope endurance—it will not be determined which t_1-exemplification causes which later t_2-exemplification.

2.3.5 Enduring tropes At this point, I will suggest that the only viable account of property persistence, in light of the Indeterministic Sphere Case, is in terms of enduring tropes. We can account for the difference between a moving color property and a stationary color property in the Indeterministic Sphere Case as follows. The color property is stationary if and only if the color trope that is wholly present at t_1 in the NW region of the sphere is wholly present at t_2 in the NW region of the sphere. Under the assumptions of our example, the color property is moving from t_1 to t_2 if and only if the color trope that is wholly present at t_1 in the NW region of the sphere is wholly present at t_2 in the SW region of the sphere. In short, in order to account for property persistence in all its manifestations, there must be enduring tropes. In particular, persisting moving properties, as highlighted by the spinning sphere case, are only possible if enduring tropes are possible. Furthermore, since the phenomenon of property motion is also readily found in the actual world, I also conclude that there actually are enduring tropes.

Enduring tropes also neatly account for Immaculate Property Replacement *versus* Property Persistence. Recall that in the former case there is a machine that eliminates the electrical charge of a particle without a trace, while a second machine instantly generates an electrical charge of the same magnitude in that particle. Whereas an enduring charge trope characterizes the particle in Property Persistence, one charge trope is replaced by a numerically different but exactly similar charge trope in Immaculate Property Replacement.[27]

2.4 A digression: The sphere case as test of accounts of object persistence

I will now briefly turn to the original purpose of the sphere case as a test of four-dimensionalist theories of object persistence. According to four-dimensionalist theories, object persistence is a matter of having temporal parts at t_1 and t_2 (or, if the object is the momentary stage at t_1 à la Stage Theory, having a temporal counterpart at t_2). For the four-dimensionalist, either the Worm theorist or Stage theorist, temporal parts of an object or the stage that is the object and its temporal counterpart must be causally connected. In our Indeterministic Sphere Case, the sphere is spinning if and only if the temporal part/stage of the NW region of the sphere at t_1 is causally connected to the temporal part/stage of the SW region of the sphere at t_2, but not causally connected to the t_2 NW temporal part. Stages of the same object are causally connected in virtue

---

[27] With respect to the overall choice between Armstrongian Universalism and Trope Theory, we can, start with Armstrong's asssessment that the theories are very close to being tied, but I would suggest there is a tie-breaker: Trope Theory is better suited than Universalism to handle property persistence and property change. Once we have tropes, it is hard to see the need for universals. In short, the "end game" should be played around property persistence.

of the causal connections between the property instances of those stages. However, as we have seen, it is far from clear what those causal connections supervene on. Suppose that the supervenience base is HS-acceptable or at least acceptable given the standard reductionist theories of causation which do not posit enduring tropes. In that event, it will not be possible to differentiate between the moving and stationary spheres—on the reasonable assumption that causation supervenes on the non-causal. However, I would suggest that if the non-causal supervenience base includes enduring tropes, then there is a basis for a four-dimensionalist causal account of object persistence either in the form of Worm Theory or Stage Theory. Those causal connections supervene on or are reducible to enduring tropes (plus other non-causal facts). A four-dimensionalist account of object persistence can give an account of the spinning sphere case if causation supervenes on/reduces in part to enduring tropes. The idea is that the stages, the NW quadrant at t_1 and the SW quadrant at t_2, are causally connected just in case their property instances are causally connected and that their property instances, which are tropes at a time, are causally connected just in case these tropes are identical or partially identical, as well as satisfying the other conditions of a theory of causation. (I give a reductive account of causation built around enduring tropes in (1997a).)[28]

Hawley offers the position closest to this kind of account of object persistence in the literature. Her view is a causation-based four-dimensionalist account of object persistence. However, she posits "special" causal relations between earlier and later stages of a persisting object that are grounded, in part, in non-spatio-temporal, non-supervenient relations between those stages (2001: 85).[29] She intends her view to be consistent with the doctrine that there can be no causal difference without a non-causal difference, although not with the Lewisian version of the Humean Supervenience of causation (2001: 89). The relations that ground the persistence of ordinary things are non-supervenient, "which is to say that whether two stages are suitably related is not entirely determined by the intrinsic properties of those stages, or even by those intrinsic properties plus spatio-temporal relations between those stages" (2001: 71). How do

---

[28] What this means is that, contrary to what has been argued in the literature, the following three doctrines are mutually compatible: (1) objects persist either by having different temporal parts at different times or by having counterpart stages; (2) the temporal parts/stages of a persisting thing must be causally connected in an appropriate way; and (3) causation is supervenient or reducible to non-causal facts such that causation supervenes on the non-causal. There is no such incompatibility once it is understood that the supervenience base for causation includes enduring tropes. On the other hand, there is an analogous set of doctrines concerning property persistence that *are* incompatible. (1') properties persist either by having different temporal parts at different times or by having counterpart stages; (2') the temporal parts/stages of a persisting property must be causally connected in an appropriate way; and (3') causation is supervenient or reducible to non-causal facts. I have argued that the Indeterminist Sphere Case shows that if causation supervenes on the non-causal, then properties do not persist by way of causally connected temporal parts/stages. And I have suggested that this incompatibility should be resolved by replacing a four-dimensionalist view of property persistence with an enduring trope account.

[29] A causation-based four-dimensionalist account based on various standard theories of causation, such as regularity and counterfactual theories that do not bring into play such non-supervenient relations as part of the reduction base for causation, will fail.

our views compare? First, I also hold a causation-based four-dimensionalist view of object persistence, and I also hold that causation supervenes on the non-causal, including what Hawley would call certain non-supervenient relations. However, whereas she does not specify what these relations are, I do. On my view, the supervenience base for causation in general, not just the causal relations between stages of a persisting object, includes enduring tropes. And, since such relations of endurance across time do not themselves supervene on intrinsic properties and spatio-temporal relations, causation is grounded, in part, in what Hawley calls "non-supervenient" relations. The advantage of my view is that there is no mystery about what these non-supervenient relations are. They are simply relations of endurance for tropes.

3. Objection: The argument from temporary external relations against enduring tropes

I have argued for the existence of tropes by arguing for the existence of enduring tropes. My argument, however, is incomplete since I have not yet addressed an objection which, if cogent, entails that enduring tropes are not possible. The argument that I have in mind is somewhat analogous to the "argument from temporary intrinsics," which Lewis directs against enduring concrete objects. According to Lewis, if object o is wholly present at distinct times and o has P at one of these times, but Q at the other, where Q is incompatible with P, then o is both P and Q. For example, if this chair is wholly present today and yesterday, but it is blue today and red yesterday, then it would seem that it is both blue and red. But nothing can be both blue and red (all over), so there are no enduring concrete objects. Although the argument from temporary intrinsics does not apply to enduring tropes—since tropes lack intrinsic properties that change over time—there is a similar argument which does not involve changing intrinsic properties. Cross-temporal trope identity faces the problem of temporary external relations:

If trope A and trope B are wholly present at distinct times, t and t', and A stands at distance D from B at t, but A stands at distance D' from B at t', where D is incompatible with D', then A and B stand to each other in incompatible relations.

For example, suppose this redness trope is 5 feet from this blueness trope now, but these same tropes yesterday were 4 feet apart. If the redness trope today and yesterday are identical and the blueness trope today and yesterday are identical, then this redness trope is both 4 feet from and 5 feet from this blueness trope. But no two things can be both 4 feet apart and 5 feet apart from each other. Hence, there are no enduring tropes.

How might we respond to this objection? I believe that the best approach involves something similar to the relativization-to-a-time strategy that is most familiar in the context of the problem of temporary intrinsics. However, before getting to that solution, I will briefly discuss an analogous trope solution to the problem of temporary intrinsics for the three-dimensionalist view of object persistence.

3.1 The trope solution to the problem of temporary intrinsics

A "three-dimensionalist" takes object persistence to be a matter of an object being wholly present at more than one moment. The problem of temporary intrinsics for three-dimensionalism concerns intrinsic properties. Intrinsic properties hold of an object independently of what is the case elsewhere and elsewhen, independently of facts about other regions that have no causal influence on the object. A *temporary intrinsic* is an intrinsic property that characterizes an object during only part of the object's history. The problem of temporary intrinsics for the three-dimensionalist is just this: if object o is wholly present at both t and t' (o at t is identical with o at t'), and o has P (an intrinsic property) at t, but o has property Q at t', where Q is incompatible with P, then o is both P and Q, given the indiscernibility of identicals. One proposal for disabling this objection is to reinterpret "at t, o has P, but Q at t'" in terms of relations to a time: o stands in the P-at relation to t and Q-at relation to t', where standing in the P-at to one time is not incompatible with standing in Q-at to a different time. Thus, the "relation to a time" reply takes it that if Lewis is bent at t and straight at t', then Lewis stands in the bent-at relation to t and the straight-at relation to t'. One relation to a time is affirmed and another relation to a different time is denied of Lewis.[30] David Lewis has objected that this "relation to a time" proposal unacceptably turns intrinsic properties into relations: "this is simply incredible ... If we know what shape is, we know that it is a property, not a relation" (Lewis 1986b: 204). Lewis's objection is that "bent" is metaphysically misread as a relation on the "relation to a time" view. Here I would like to argue that we can maintain something like the "relation to a time" reply to the problem of temporary intrinsics if properties are tropes and avoid Lewis's objection. However, this solution to the problem of temporary intrinsics is not open to the Universalist since it assumes that properties are tropes. This solution, if successful, thus, supplies a further reason for preferring tropes to universals.

Suppose that tropes are momentary, and, thus, not able to be wholly present at more than one wholly distinct time. On this view, the charge of this electron at t is non-identical to the charge of this electron at any distinct time t'. One consequence of the momentary trope view that is directly relevant to the goal of distinguishing "time-indexed" properties from relations to a time is that this makes tropes analogous to the temporal parts of concrete objects, if there are such. Recall that the temporal parts proponent claims that objects have temporal parts, as well as spatial parts, and that persistence is a matter of an object having different parts present at different time periods. Just as some temporal parts of objects are or may be momentary particulars,

---

[30] It is not enough that the property is replaced by a relation. There would still be a problem if Lewis bore incompatible relations to the same time. But here there is no contradiction since these relations *differ* with respect to their time-relata.

tropes will be momentary (abstract) particulars. The significance of this analogy is found in the fact that just as a temporal part of an object o would be time-indexed without being a relation of object o to a time, a momentary trope would be time-indexed without being a relation to a time—at least in the case of momentary *intrinsic* tropes.[31] "Bent-at-t," when it applies to a particular object, will under the (momentary) trope view pick out a specific momentary, non-relational trope. In short, no more reason exists for treating momentary tropes as relations than for treating temporal parts of objects as relations.[32] What this means is that Lewis's objection to the "time-indexed-property" view will not go through if properties are momentary tropes, since momentary intrinsic tropes are not relations to a time.

But now suppose that intrinsic properties are enduring tropes. Can the problem of temporary intrinsics still be resolved under the assumption that intrinsic properties are enduring tropes? A "time-indexed" response to the problem is still available. The incompatibility problem is resolved as follows under the assumption that P and Q are enduring tropes. Since P and Q have temporal boundaries, they can do the work that a "relation to a time" would do in dispelling any apparent incompatibility. There is no incompatibility in ascribing P and Q to o, since P and Q, although enduring, exist in non-overlapping time periods. To make this point clear, let's return to the temporal parts response to the problem of temporary intrinsics. The problem is that if o is wholly present at both t and t', then the same object has incompatible intrinsic properties, P and Q, if o is P at t and o is Q at t'. The temporal parts theorist resolves this apparent incompatibility by denying that o is wholly present at both t and t'. Rather P and Q hold of distinct parts of o: the t-temporal part o is non-derivatively P and the t'-temporal part of o is Q. But notice this solution still works if the "t" temporal part of o is itself an *enduring* entity that wholly exists at more than one moment and the "t'" temporal part of o' is an enduring entity that wholly exists at more than one moment, as long as these two entities are non-identical and do not overlap in time. What is important to the solution is the non-identity of the "t-part" and the "t'-part" and the fact that these parts do not overlap, even if those parts are themselves enduring entities. Similarly, the trope solution to the problem of temporary intrinsics goes through even if the relevant tropes endure, as long as they are not identical and do not overlap in time.

---

[31] Time-indexing does not necessarily generate a relational view even though it does if properties are universals. Times can, in a sense, be built into tropes because tropes are particulars, like the temporal parts of objects, not universals. We do not face the difficulty we did with universals—where time-indexing meant an additional argument place for times, turning the universal into a relation.

[32] Exemplifications may also be temporally bounded without being relations/relational properties. Why not, then, take intrinsic properties to be "exemplifications of universals," not universals? This is not viable since that would mean that the object that has an intrinsic property *has an exemplification* of a universal: the object exemplifies an exemplification rather than a property.

3.2 The trope solution to the problem of temporary external relations

Now let's return to the problem of temporary external relations for enduring tropes. If we treated distance as a three-place relation with an argument place for times—distance is a three-place relation among, in this case, *A*, *B* and a time, *t*, or as two-place relations with times built in, then we can solve this problem. If *D* and *D'* are thus relativized to different times in either way, then any appearance of incompatibility is eliminated. The difficulty with temporal relativization is that it conflicts with our sense that distance is a *two-place* relation (or with our sense that it is a two-place relation that does not include a time as a component).[33] The temporal relativization proposal would seem unacceptably to turn two-place relations into three-place relations (or into two-place relations with times built in, "time-relational" two-place relations such as "_ and _being at a distance *d* at *t*").[34]

The incompatibility problem and Lewis's criticism of the "relation to a time" view can both be resolved at once *if* talking about "time-indexed" properties is reinterpreted as *not* just another way of talking about relations to a time or time-relational relations. This reinterpretation depends on remodeling the "relation to a time" view in terms of *time-located tropes*, properties that are particulars which exist in time, without being relations to a time or without including a time as a component. In fact, once we take seriously the proposal that relations are tropes, this alternate interpretation is quite natural. In short, the situation is entirely different if relations are tropes rather than universals.[35] In that case, there is room for a "time-indexed" response to the incompatibility problem that avoids treating the distance relation, for example, as a three-place relation or as a two-place relation with a time as a component. In order to demonstrate as much, I will first consider the view that trope–trope temporary external relations are momentary tropes and, then, the view that such relations, in some cases, are persisting tropes that are wholly present at each moment of their existence. For the "time-indexed" response to work, it does not matter which of these views is ultimately adopted.

---

[33] Lewis objects to taking distance as a three-place relation with an argument place for worlds as follows: "their distance, it seems, is a relation of *A* and *B* and nothing else—it is not really a three-place relation of *A*, *B*, and this or that world" (1986b: 206, footnote 6).

[34] If relations are universals, then this objection will hold. Time-indexing of *universals* means turning them into relations to a time or into impure time-relational two-place relations. Time-indexing the universal "_ and _ being at a distance *d*" *must* mean positing a universal relation "_ and _being at a distance *d* at _" with *three* argument places for particulars, including one for times, or as a two-place relation that is an "impure universal" with a particular time as a component, "_ and _being at a distance *d* at *t*." This is so because universals as such do not have temporal boundaries, either momentary or otherwise, unlike spatio-temporal particulars. Since universals as such are not dated, any conception of time-indexed universals must involve treating them as relations with a place for times or treating distance as an impure time-relational two-place relation.

[35] For a critique of the view that relations are tropes, see (Hochberg 1988), and for a reply to that critique, see (Campbell 1990: 58–65 and Chapter 5).

3.3 Momentary distance tropes and relativization

If external relations (among persisting tropes) are themselves momentary tropes, then there is a way to reinterpret the "relation to a time" reply so as to avert a three-place relationalist reading of the distance relation or a reading of the distance relation as including a time as a component.[36] If relations between tropes are momentary, then these relations cannot be wholly present at more than one distinct time. To see that such time-indexing does not by its very nature generate a three-place view or a time-relational view, consider again, the straightforward analogy between momentary tropes and the temporal parts view of physical objects. According to the latter view, objects not only have spatial parts but temporal parts: at any given moment in the history of a persisting object only a part of that object is present. The temporal parts of objects, if there are such, are necessarily temporally bounded—they are time-indexed. However, what is perfectly clear is that temporal parts of objects are not relations to a time, but simply short-lived objects of a sort. Analogously, momentary tropes are short-lived particularized properties and relations, and, as such, are not relations to a time. Momentary tropes have a temporal location just in the same sense that temporal parts of physical objects do. A momentary trope is time-indexed without being a relation to a time or including a time as a component, and, as a consequence, we do not face the difficulty that we did with universals—where time-indexing means an additional argument place for times, turning all such universals into relations to times, or including a time as a component. In short, there is no more reason for treating momentary relation-tropes as relations to a time or as time-relational than for treating momentary objects as relations to a time. Hence, this worry about "relations to a time" cannot get off the ground.

To understand better how the momentary trope view—as applied to trope–trope relations—resolves the apparent incompatibility brought on by temporary external relations between persisting simple tropes, consider a further analogy, this time between the momentary trope response to that problem and the temporal parts response to the analogous problem of temporary external relations for physical objects. Suppose that objects o and o' stand in D (say, 5 feet apart) at t, but at D' (say, 6 feet apart) at t'. The objection goes that if o and o' are wholly present at both t and t', then the same objects bear incompatible relations to each other. The temporal parts theorist resolves this apparent incompatibility by denying that o and o' are wholly present at both t and t'. Rather D and D' hold of distinct pairs of objects: the t-temporal parts of o and o' stand in D and the t'-temporal parts of o and o' stand in D'. External relations are non-derivatively attributed to the (temporal) parts of larger wholes (the objects) and that which is attributed may be read without contradiction as wholly present to each thing (part) to which it is attributed. What is important to notice is that the momentary

---

[36] If time is discrete, a "moment" will be the smallest unit of time, but if time is continuous then some other way of defining "moment" and "at one time" will have to be found. What is basic, however, on the momentary view is that where t and t' are non-overlapping temporal spans or points, then any trope that occupies t is non-identical, in whole and in part, to any trope that occupies t'.

trope view of trope–trope external relations, when combined with a three-dimensionalist view of persisting non-relational tropes, mimics this approach in reverse, so to speak. One member of the class of the 5-feet-apart tropes, D, (a t-member) characterizes A and B, but no other members of *that class* characterize A and B, just as on the temporal parts view the t-temporal parts of o and o' may be characterized by D even if no other temporal parts of o and o' are so characterized.[37]

3.4 Enduring distance tropes and relativization

Now consider the second view that some temporary external relations *endure* over time. Again, suppose that A and B are enduring simple tropes and that A and B are related by D (being 5 feet apart) during one time period (t through t') and by D' (being 4 feet apart) during a different time period (t'' through t'''), where D and D' are apparently incompatible. Also assume that D endures and that D's endurance is a matter of being wholly present at each moment of its existence. Can the incompatibility problem still be resolved under this different assumption—that D is an enduring trope rather than a momentary trope? A "time-indexed" response to the problem of incompatibility is still available. The incompatibility problem is resolved as follows under the assumption that D and D' are enduring tropes. Since D and D' have temporal boundaries, they can do the work that a "relation to a time" would do in dispelling any apparent incompatibility. There is no incompatibility in ascribing D and D' to A and B, since D and D', although enduring, exist in non-overlapping time periods. Just as there is no incompatibility on the "relation to a time" view in bearing the relation D-at to t but the D'-at relation to t' (and thus not the D-at relation to t'), there is no incompatibility in standing in D and D'. This compatibility is possible in part because our 5-feet-apart trope relation that endures from t to t' is not identical to any 5-feet-apart trope relation realized from t'' to t'''.[38]

This response to the incompatibility problem also successfully avoids treating D as a three-place relation or as a time-relational relation. To see this we need to follow our analogy with the three-dimensionalist view of object persistence a bit further. Consider that, on the view under discussion, an enduring trope relation will exist for a certain period of time and as such will have temporal boundaries, but still be an enduring

---

[37] Here I am not necessarily making spatial relations into spatial entities, a proposal that has serious difficulties (see Hochberg 1988: 192), but I am "temporalizing," so to speak, spatial relations.

[38] This lack of incompatibility continues to hold in the case of objects o and o' even if these objects fail to have their times essentially or if these times fail to be components of these objects. The same points apply to the "time-indexed" solution to our incompatibility problem that is supplied by time-located tropes. In addition, it is worth pointing out that there is no incompatibility between saying that "A and B stand in D at t" but "A and B do not stand in D at t'" even though A and B are wholly present at both t and t', because the sentence that attributes D can be thought of as making two claims: (1) that there is some relation-trope D from a certain class of tropes that A and B stand in; and (2) that D exists during a period that includes t. To deny that A and B, which also are wholly present at t', stand in D at t' is to assert that it is not true that there is a relation-trope D from a certain class of tropes that A and B stand in such that D exists during a period that includes t'.

particular—one that is wholly present at each moment of its existence. Nothing in this conception makes such relations "relations to a time" or as time-relational relations, as the analogous view of physical objects demonstrates. The three-dimensionalist view of objects, which parallels the view of persisting relations under review, takes the persistence of an object to be a matter of the object being wholly present at each moment of its existence. This view does not reduce objects to "relations to a time" or make them time-relational. On the three-dimensionalist view, physical objects exist in time, are generally non-momentary and lack temporal parts, but are certainly not relations to a time. Similarly, there is no reason to think that if there are enduring trope relations they must consist in relations with at least one place for times or as including a time as a component. If D is understood to be an enduring trope relation, there is nothing in this account of D that makes D out to be a three-place relation to a time or as time-relational.

This appeal to enduring distance relations involves the reasonable presupposition that when two tropes or objects cease to stand to each other in a particular trope relation, say a specific 5-feet-apart trope relation, that that trope relation ceases to exist. In particular, this response presupposes that that trope relation does not go on to hold between a different pair of tropes or objects. This assumption about the dependence of trope-relations on their relata strikes me as quite plausible.[39]

3.5 An objection to the time-bound character of trope relations

Finally, I need to consider an objection to my response to the argument from temporary external relations against the possibility of enduring tropes. Most trope proponents seek to account for what it is for two objects to be tokens of the same type in terms of exact resemblance among tropes. If objects o and o' are 5 feet apart and o'' and o''' are 5 feet apart, then these pairs are tokens of the same type in virtue of the fact that the members of the first pair stand to each other in a certain relation-trope D and the members of the second pair stand in D', where D and D' are non-identical but exactly resembling tropes.[40] This account of type identity is not supposed to vary even if D and D' are realized at *different* times, t and t'. However, on the time-bound account of relational tropes, it would appear that if o and o' stand in D at time t but o'' and o''' stand in D' at t', D and D' do not intrinsically resemble each other exactly, since D is located at t and D' at t'. In short, on this objection, even if my response to the argument from temporary external relations works, a new problem is created for this more general trope program.

This objection focuses attention on what it is for a trope to be temporally located. There are, indeed, interpretations of being temporally located that would give this objection weight, for example, on an interpretation according to which a trope's being temporally located means that a trope's time of realization is "built in" in the

---

[39] I came to see this dependence in refereeing a paper on my work.
[40] See, for example, (Campbell 1990: 30–2).

sense that the time is a part of or a component of the trope. In that case, cross-temporal intrinsic exact resemblance is jeopardized. If A and B's being related by D at t means that built into D as a component is t, then D would not resemble exactly any other trope realized at a different time t'. But time-located tropes need not be understood in this way. Just as concrete objects are dated particulars without the time at which they exist being components of those objects, the same point holds for tropes. Tropes have temporal boundaries in the same sense that concrete objects do—they have a temporal location, either momentary or otherwise. And, just as a concrete object may exist during a period t without t being a component of the object, the same point applies to tropes. Furthermore, in the same sense that this point continues to hold of the temporal parts of objects and of enduring objects that lack temporal parts, it also holds of tropes whether they are momentary or not.[41] Finally, tropes at different times may be exactly similar in the sense that their natures can be exactly similar, since those natures do not include a temporal component.

4. Summary and what's next

I have argued that the phenomenon of property persistence, especially in the form of property motion, provides the basis for an argument for the existence of enduring tropes. I have also considered in detail a certain line of objection to enduring tropes that parallels the "temporary intrinsic" objection to enduring objects. I argued that once tropes are understood to be temporally bounded entities, this objection can be answered.

Now that we have settled on the existence of tropes, we must consider the question of how tropes are individuated. What are the necessary and sufficient conditions for tropes t_1 and t_2 in the same world being identical? In the next chapter, I will look at two answers found in the literature: (1) the primitivist approach, according to which there is no further reduction of trope individuation; and (2) the spatio-temporal approach, according to which exactly similar tropes are not identical if and only if they stand to each other in some spatio-temporal distance relation greater than zero. I will defend the primitivist approach. I will also address a related issue concerning a possible size limit for tropes to the effect that there can be no medium-sized tropes such as the red trope of this shirt. I will show that certain arguments meant to rule out medium-sized tropes fail.

---

[41] More generally, the time-located character of tropes mirrors that of concrete objects and this should not be surprising, since tropes, as abstract particulars, are typically non-spatial parts of concrete objects.

3
The individuation of tropes

What are the necessary and sufficient conditions for tropes *x* and *y* being identical? This is the question of how to individuate tropes, and it is a question that is not automatically answered by opting for one of the three rival trope theories, including Natural Class Trope Nominalism.[1] I turn to this question in this chapter and argue that trope individuation is a primitive, lacking any further reduction or analysis. Also, in this chapter, I will address the possibility of "manifest" or medium-sized tropes, such as the redness of this shirt. A principle of individuation does not settle the possibility of medium-sized, ordinary tropes, and, in fact, Campbell has presented a series of arguments against the possibility of such tropes. I will show that Campbell's arguments are ineffective.

1. Trope individuation

There are a number of principles of trope individuation on offer. I will discuss two such principles, the Primitivist Principle and the Spatio-Temporal Principle. The *Primitivist Principle* is that tropes *x* and *y* are numerically distinct tropes if and only if they are numerically distinct.[2] For the Primitivist, there is no analysis or reduction of trope individuation. Whether or not tropes *x* and *y* are identical is not reducible to some set of facts that does not involve trope identity, including facts about the locations or spatio-temporal relations of *x* and *y*. (This is not to say that the Primitivist Principle is not compatible with informative sufficient conditions for non-identity such as: if *x* and *y* are not intrinsically exactly alike, say, one is a squareness trope and the other a redness trope, they are not identical.) The *Spatio-Temporal Principle* individuates intrinsically exactly similar tropes in terms of spatio-temporal distance: a non-zero spatio-temporal distance between intrinsically exactly similar tropes *x* and *y* is necessary and sufficient for their non-identity. Tropes *x* and *y* are distinct if and only if *x* and *y* are either not intrinsically exactly alike or they are some spatio-temporal distance apart from each

---

[1] Campbell, at one point, held a spatio-temporal view, but later switched to a primitivist account of individuation without generating any inconsistency with the rest of his Trope Theory.

[2] Schaffer states this principle as follows: "x and y are distinct tropes iff they are primitively quantitatively distinct" (2001: 248). Campbell describes this view as follows: "... *individuation is basic and unanalysable* ... what is it about one F trope that makes it the F trope that it is and not some other F trope? ... just being that F trope rather than any other" (1990: 69).

other.³ This principle does not exclude coincident tropes that are not intrinsically exactly alike.⁴

There is a third principle of individuation that I will not discuss in detail. The *Object Principle* says that exactly similar tropes are distinct just in case they characterize wholly distinct objects. The redness trope of object x is identical to the exactly similar redness trope of object y if and only if objects x and y are identical. I will immediately dismiss the Object Principle. This principle is independent of the other two principles if objects have substrata, since in that case this principle individuates exactly similar tropes by reference to the substrata in which they inhere. But if objects are bundles of properties, without substrata, as I will assume, the individuation of an object will, in part, depend on the prior individuation of the elements, tropes, of that bundle. If, for example, objects that are wholly constituted by bundles of tropes may not be distinct if their constitutive tropes are not distinct, then it is clear that the Object Principle is not independent of the other two principles. In addition, even if trope bundles may be distinct if they share all their constituent tropes, the Object Principle will still not be independent of these other two principles on a Bundle Theory. Given the Bundle Theory, the individuation of bundles will at least in part depend on the prior individuation of tropes. Suppose, for example, that there are two bundles with exactly similar tropes. If these tropes are *not* identical, then those bundles are *not* identical (even if having all the same constitutive tropes does not guarantee the identity of these bundles). Hence, since bundle individuation depends in part on trope individuation, we can set this principle aside. Furthermore, I see nothing to rule out the possibility of object-free or free floating tropes (Schaffer 2003).

1.1 Rejecting the Spatio-Temporal Principle

I have four reasons for rejecting the Spatio-Temporal Principle. First, stationary enduring tropes constitute a counterexample to this principle, since if tropes are individuated spatio-temporally, stationary enduring tropes would not be possible.⁵ If there could be such tropes then even if there is a temporal distance between tropes t and t'—but, say, no spatial distance between them—that is not sufficient for the non-identity of t and t'. The argument of Chapter 2, if sound, establishes the existence of stationary tropes that endure. Second, there are moving enduring tropes, but that is not consistent with the Spatio-Temporal Principle according to which not sharing a

---

³ "x and y are distinct tropes iff they are either not exactly resembling, or at distant locations" (Schaffer 2001: 249).

⁴ This principle does *not* explain the mutual exclusion of same-level determinates. A crimson trope and a blueness trope cannot have the same spatio-temporal location, but that kind of exclusion, relative to a spatio-temporal location, is not explained by the Spatio-Temporal Principle.

⁵ One might argue, in response, that enduring tropes are limited to "temporal spanners." By a mere temporal spanner, I mean an entity that occupies a temporal region, r, greater than a temporal point, but does not wholly or partly occupy any sub-period of r. Only "temporal multi-locators" tropes are inconsistent with this Principle, not temporal spanners, since the latter have only *one* temporal location. In reply, I refer the reader back to Chapter 2 for an argument for temporal multi-locator tropes.

location is sufficient for non-identity. Even if there is a temporal distance *and* a spatial distance between tropes *t* and *t'*, that is not sufficient for the non-identity of *t* and *t'*.[6] Third, time-traveling enduring tropes are possible. A time-traveling enduring trope that meets itself would be wholly present at two locations at the same time, which is incompatible with the Spatio-Temporal Principle of trope individuation.[7] The fourth reason is the possibility of extended simple tropes of the "multi-locator" variety. An extended simple, multiply located trope would be wholly present at more than one location.[8]

1.2 Against an argument for the Spatio-Temporal Principle

Nevertheless, there is an argument in favor of the Spatio-Temporal Principle that must be considered. The idea developed in this argument is that the Spatio-Temporal Principle in combination with Trope Theory (plus a counterpart theory) can provide a basis for blocking the "no-property-swapping" objection to Trope Theory, whereas the same is not true of the combination of the Primitivist Principle with Trope Theory. According to the no-property-swapping objection, Trope Theory wrongly entails the possibility that exactly similar properties can be swapped. According to Schaffer, Trope Theory with the Primitivist Principle does not exclude this "empty possibility"—where an "empty" possibility is *not* a possibility—but Trope Theory in combination with the Spatio-Temporal Principle (along with counterpart theory) does exclude property swapping.

In one version of the no-property-swapping argument against Trope Theory, the "swapping" is relative to spatial positions and in the second, relative to objects.

> *Swapping Across Locations (positional swapping)* If the redness here is exactly similar to but numerically distinct from the redness there, then the redness that is located here could have been located there and vice versa. But these are not, it is claimed, genuinely different possible situations. So, if properties are particulars, then property swapping relative to spatial locations should be possible, but it is not. Therefore, properties are not particulars. On the other hand, if properties are universals, positional swapping of properties is not possible since nothing could have been swapped with itself.[9]

---

[6] The first and second reasons for rejecting the Spatio-Temporal Principle under discussion do not support the rejection of a broader principle that takes the location of a trope as its history through space and time. Why reject this broader view? This broader view should be rejected because of the genuine possibility of "trope piling." Trope piling consists in the presence of at least two exactly similar tropes in the same location at the same time. If the piling of two momentary tropes is possible, then this broader view must be rejected. I argue for the possibility of trope piling in 1.3.2.

[7] This possibility was given as one reason for rejecting the "Aristotelian" account of the distinction between universals and particulars.

[8] A fifth possible reason for rejecting the Spatio-Temporal Principle is the possibility of non-spatial temporal tropes. For a defense against this reason, see (Schaffer 2001: 251–2).

[9] If properties are particulars, then one case of some property *F* is a different item from each other case, no matter how closely they resemble. Hence, where there are two different but exactly resembling cases, call

Swapping Across Objects If the redness of this rose is exactly similar to but numerically distinct from the redness of that rose, then the redness of this rose could have been the redness of that rose and vice versa. But this is an empty possibility and, thus, properties are not tropes.[10]

Positional property swapping, if it were possible, would not require property swapping across objects. For example, if positional property swapping were possible, then the swapping of indiscernible objects would bring with it positional property swapping.[11] Also, property swapping across objects, if possible, would not require positional property swapping if objects could swap locations *and* swap properties. I will focus on the positional version of the no-swapping argument, as it is a bit stronger, not being open to the possible rejoinder that no trope could have characterized any other object than the object that it actually characterizes.[12]

1.2.1 A first approximation of the no-swapping argument for the Spatio-Temporal Principle A first approximation of the "no-swapping" argument runs as follows:

> The Spatio-Temporal Principle blocks the possibility of cross-location trope swapping since that Principle makes the identity of a trope, t, depend on its location so that t could not have had a different location.[13] On the other hand, the Primitivist Principle does not have this implication.

This first approximation, however, as Schaffer shows, fails. The Spatio-Temporal Principle determines trope identity in the same world, not across worlds, but the possibility of swapping is an inter-world, not intra-world, phenomenon. Furthermore, this principle should *not* be extended across worlds. The same property could have

---

them F_1 and F_2, there are two possible situations: F_1 is at place P_1 and F_2 is at place P_2, and the other way around, F_1 is at P_2 while F_2 is at P_1.

[10] Suppose . . . we are dealing with property tropes, and that the two tropes involved, P' and P'', resemble exactly. Since the two tropes are wholly distinct particulars, it appears to make sense that instead of *a* having P' and *b* having P'', the two tropes should have been swapped (Armstrong 1989a: 132).

[11] Notice that even if our Trope Theory entails the possibility in some sense of both kinds of swapping, the objector would need to show that swapping is not possible in the relevant sense. But what kind of possibility is at issue? If it is logical possibility, then one can reply that swapping is not logically impossible since no logical contradiction can be derived from swapping. If it is physical possibility that is at issue, one can reply that swapping has not been shown to be inconsistent with the laws of physics. Finally, if metaphysical possibility is at stake, then it can be pointed out that neither Schaffer nor Armstrong have argued for the claim that swapping is metaphysically impossible. I owe these points to a referee.

[12] Even if object–object trope swapping is impossible, still positional trope swapping is not ruled out if indiscernible objects could have swapped positions.

[13] But the presumption in favor of trope swapping is not excluded by the Primitivist Principle of trope individuation. According to Schaffer, "Trope theory with QI rules that the result of the swap is an ontologically distinct situation" (2001: 250).

been located somewhere else—Schaffer calls this "trope sliding," even if trope swapping is impossible. But a crossworld version of the Spatio-Temporal Principle would rule out the genuine possibility of "trope sliding."[14]

1.2.2 Schaffer's improved no-swapping argument for the Spatio-Temporal Principle A more promising version of this argument is offered by Schaffer. The idea is that combining a counterpart theory of modality and the Spatio-Temporal Principle will block the possibility of trope swapping.

It is not possible that *this* redness of this rose and *that* exactly resembling redness of another could have been swapped because "the nearest relative of the redness of the rose which is *here* at our world would be the redness still *here* 'post-swap'" (Schaffer 2001: 253). "The redness which would be here has exactly the same inter- and intraworld resemblance relations as the redness which actually is here, and the same distance relations, and hence it is a better counterpart than the redness which would be *there*" (2001: 253). Trope swapping is impossible since it would require that the counterpart of the redness that is actually here is the redness that would be there.[15]

An immediate worry about this line of argument is that it excludes too much, not only trope swapping, but also the possibility that a trope could have been located somewhere other than its actual location, trope sliding. Schaffer, however, argues that this combination of Trope Theory, the Spatio-Temporal Principle and a counterpart theory, does not rule out trope sliding. In particular, this combination does not rule out that "the redness of the rose could have been *there* rather than *here* had the wind blown differently" (2001: 251).

The redness of this rose could have been there rather than here is true because there is a world in which there is a redness "which is in perfectly isomorphic resemblance relations to its worldmates as the actual one to its worldmates, with just a slight difference in distance with respect to, e.g., the roundness of the moon."

He concludes, "thus counterpart theory allows for sliding, because the nearest relative of the redness of the rose which is here at our world, is the redness of a rose which is there at the wind-shifted world(s) in question" (2001: 253).[16]

---

[14] Schaffer's point applies also to the Primitivist Principle of individuation, a principle that does not imply either the possibility or impossibility of trope swapping. More generally, no principle of individuation of this type alone will determine that swapping is possible or not possible.

[15] For a counterpart theorist, it is possible that *a* is *F* just in case there is a possible world with a counterpart to *a*, which is not identical to *a*, that is *F*. Being a counterpart is determined by similarities. For tropes, the relevant aspects of similarity are combinations of relations of resemblance and distance according to Schaffer (2001: 252).

[16] Note that if properties are universals, then some property sliding is possible: a universal instantiated at *L* could have been instantiated at *L'* where that universal is in fact not instantiated.

1.2.2.1 THE PRIMITIVIST CAN BORROW SCHAFFER'S REASONING

Suppose, for the moment, that the Spatio-Temporal Principle combined with a counterpart theory of modality does exclude trope swapping while allowing trope sliding. Does that mean that the Spatio-Temporal Principle is superior to the Primitivist Principle? It does not, since a proponent of the latter can adopt that same strategy. The Primitivist Principle can *also* be combined with a counterfactual theory of modality, in which case the same counterfactual-based reasoning is available to the Primitivist. To see this, first notice that the Primitivist Principle, like the Spatio-Temporal Principle, is set up to apply within worlds, not across worlds. Second, the Primitivist could also deny crossworld trope identity and hold a counterpart theory for tropes. He can, then, follow Schaffer and claim that the closest counterpart to the redness actually here in Schaffer's would-be swapping case is the redness that would be here "post-swap" on the grounds that the redness that would be here has exactly the same resemblance relations and distance relations as the redness which actually is here. So even if Schaffer is right about the benefit of combining the Spatio-Temporal Principle with a counterpart theory of modality, the same benefit can be generated by combining the Primitivist Principle with a counterpart theory for tropes.[17]

1.2.2.2 SLIDING LEADS TO SWAPPING

Unfortunately, the goal of accommodating trope sliding while rejecting *all* forms of trope swapping is *not* really a viable option for either the proponent of the Spatio-Temporal Principle or the Primitivist Principle. The possibility of trope sliding brings

---

[17] A referee worries that the Primitivist cannot borrow Schaffer's response. The thought is that if one accepts that trope individuation within a world is primitive, one is *required* to accept crossworld trope identity. In fact, I don't think there is any such requirement. First, one's principle of trope individuation *within* a world—whether it is the Spatio-Temporal Principle or the Primitivist Principle—leaves open the question of crossworld trope identity or the lack thereof. Second, one might have *good reasons* for rejecting crossworld trope identity; for example, if one is a modal realist, one might have reasons analogous to those some modal realists endorse for rejecting crossworld object identity. The same referee suggests the further point that if the Primitivist does not think that resemblance or spatio-temporal relations at a world are determinative of the identity or non-identity of tropes *x* and *y* at a world, he should not think that resemblance or spatio-temporal relations at a different world isomorphic to actual resemblance or spatio-temporal relations would be determinative of trope counterpart relations, which after all are supposed to play the role identity plays in modal deliberations. This objection would certainly hold some weight if an *analogous* use were made of spatial and temporal relations between tropes in different worlds, say, between *x* at *w* and *y* at *w'*, as partly determinative of the counterpart relation. But no such appeal is made in light of the fact that there are no spatial and temporal relations between tropes in different worlds. The spatial and temporal relations involved are intra-world relations, combined with resemblance relations between those relations. The latter are relevant to the counterpart relation across worlds and that is compatible with the denial that intra-world spatial and temporal relations are determinative of identity within a world. If we did make an appeal to spatial and temporal relations across worlds, *that* would create a tension if those same types of relations within a world were rejected as determinative of identity (but of course there would be a worse problem: there are not inter-world spatial and temporal relations). *Those* relations, if there were any, would be analogous to the relations we are rejecting as determinative of intra-world trope identity. I see no such tension between rejecting the spatio-temporal account of trope individuation within a world and bringing into play similarities across worlds with respect to spatial and temporal trope relations within worlds as playing a role in the counterpart relation.

with it, I will now suggest, the possibility of positional trope swapping. And, since a Trope Theory *should* accept the possibility of trope sliding (Schaffer is right about this point), he must accept the possibility of at least some forms of positional trope swapping.

Why think that once the possibility of trope sliding is admitted, then the possibility of positional trope swapping must also be admitted? Consider a series of cases.

> *Case 1*: a circular pane of red glass is affixed to a tree. The redness trope of the top left quarter, as well as of the other three quarters, of the pane would have been rotated 1 degree clockwise if the wind had blown differently—say at velocity v_1—than it actually did.
>
> *Case 2*: a circular pane of red glass is affixed to a tree. The redness trope of the top left quarter, as well as of the other three quarters, of the pane would have been rotated 2 degrees clockwise if the wind had blown differently—say at velocity v_1—than it actually did.
>
> . . .
>
> *Case 179*: a circular pane of red glass is affixed to a tree. The redness trope of the top left quarter, as well as of the other three quarters, of the pane would have been rotated 179 degrees clockwise if the wind had blown differently—say at velocity v_1—than it actually did.
>
> *Case 180*: a circular pane of red glass is affixed to a tree. The redness trope of the top left quarter, as well as of the other three quarters, of the pane would have been rotated 180 degrees clockwise if the wind had blown differently—say at velocity v_1—than it actually did.

Cases 1 through 179 are cases of trope sliding, not cases of trope swapping, but Case 180 is not only a case of trope sliding but also a case of (positional) trope swapping.[18] It is a case of trope swapping, since one difference between the actual world and the counterfactual world is that the redness trope of the top left quarter and the exactly similar redness trope of the bottom right quarter have exchanged locations (along with other differences including a difference in the locations of the sections of the pane). As a trope theorist, we should and do grant that each of the cases, 1 through 179, is possible and that each is a case of trope sliding. Furthermore, since it is possible that had the wind blown differently then the circular pane of glass could have rotated 179 degrees,

---

[18] Or, the series can be set up using roses with the first and last cases as follows:

> *Case 1*: two exactly similar red roses are respectively in the "12 o'clock" and "6 o'clock" positions. Had the wind blown differently, the first rose and its redness trope would have been rotated slightly clockwise to the "12 o'clock plus 1 second" position and the second rose would have been in the "6 o'clock plus 1 second" position.
>
> *Swapping*: two exactly similar red roses are respectively in the "12 o'clock" and "6 o'clock" positions. Had the wind blown differently, the first rose and its redness trope would have been rotated clockwise to the position of the second rose and the second rose would have been located where the first rose is located.

then we should grant that it is possible that if the wind had blown differently then the pane of glass could also have rotated 180 degrees. But in Case 180, there is trope swapping, if there are tropes. Hence, if trope sliding in the form of Case 179 is possible, so is (positional) trope swapping. For the trope theorist, positional trope swapping is just a double case of trope sliding in which each sliding trope "ends up" in the location of the other sliding trope. Although, this example does not show that the swapping of tropes across objects—as we saw in Schaffer's rose case—with no other differences, is possible, it does show that positional trope swapping is possible, if trope sliding is possible. (Notice, also, that we can suppose that the laws of motion are such that the motion of each quarter of the pane is discontinuous, not occupying any of the intermediate positions between its initial position and its final position as a result of the gust of wind. Notice also that I do not intend this argument to be a Sorites argument. I am not appealing to the small difference between Case 1 and Case 2 to argue that since Case 1 is possible, then Case 2 is possible, and to the small difference between Case 2 and Case 3 to argue that since Case 2 is possible, then Case 3 is possible, and so on. Rather I am appealing to the independently evident possibility of each of the cases, 1 through 179 (and to the small difference between just Case 179 and Case 180), to argue for the possibility of Case 180.)

One possible response would be to reject Case 179 as a case of trope sliding (and all of the other cases in the series as cases of trope sliding) even if it involves the genuinely distinct possibility that the top left quarter of the pane had been located 179 degrees in the clockwise direction. One might argue as follows:

> Consider the redness trope of the top left quarter in the actual world. There are a number of candidates for counterparts to that redness trope in the wind-shifted world of Case 179, including the redness of the top left quarter of the counterpart pane. According to Schaffer, the relevant aspects of similarity are some combination of fundamental relations of resemblance and distance, but that means that the nearest relative of the redness trope of the top left quarter from the actual world is the redness trope of the top left quarter of the pane in the "post-wind" world, since the latter redness trope has exactly the same inter- and intra-world resemblance relations as the former redness trope. Hence, Case 179 as understood as a case of trope sliding is not possible.[19] Case 179, at best, involves only a difference in the locations of the sections of the pane, not the tropes of the pane.

---

[19] One might respond by trying to factor in the difference in wind between the actual world and the wind-swept world in determining counterparts. So let's assume that there is some way to do that with the result that the counterpart to the redness of the top left quarter is the redness of the top right quarter in the wind-shifted world(s). The difficulty is that factoring in the wind in this way will also require an adjustment of the assessment of the *Swapping* case. In that case, there is also a wind involved. So if the involvement of a wind dictates a different assessment of the similarity of crossworld redness trope in this case, we can expect the same in the *Swapping* case. So I don't think Schaffer can use the Spatio-Temporal Principle in combination with counterpart theory to show that trope sliding is possible while trope swapping is not possible.

In fact, there is an independent reason to accept the possibility of Case 179 as a case of trope sliding if one posits tropes. Consider the following series of cases:

One Quarter Red: a circular pane of glass is affixed to a tree, but only the top left quarter is red, the rest of the pane being white. The redness trope of that quarter circle would have been rotated 179 degrees clockwise had the wind blown differently.

A Little More Red: a circular pane of glass is affixed to a tree. Only the top left quarter plus a little bit more is red, but the rest of the pane is white. The redness trope of the top left quarter would have been rotated 179 degrees clockwise had the wind blown differently.

. . .

Almost All Red: a circular pane of glass is affixed to a tree. All but a little sliver of the pane is red. The redness trope of the top left quarter circle would have been rotated 179 degrees clockwise had the wind blown differently.

All Red (Case 179): a circular pane of glass is affixed to a tree. The pane is red all over. The redness trope of the top left quarter of the pane would have been rotated 179 degrees clockwise had the wind blown differently.

Certainly, for the trope theorist, One Quarter Red is possible and it involves trope sliding. A Little More Red is also possible and it too involves trope sliding. The same is true for all of the cases up to and including Almost All Red. I suggest that if Almost All Red involves trope sliding, then so does All Red (Case 179). (Again, this is not a Sorites argument since I am appealing to the evident possibility of each case from One Quarter Red to Almost All Red rather than arguing that since One Quarter Red is possible, A Little More Red must be possible since there is only a small difference between these cases and since A Little More Red is possible so must, say, Still More Red be possible since there is only a small difference between these cases and so on up the line of cases.)

In short, the possibility of trope sliding brings with it the possibility of positional trope swapping. So the trope theorist must accept at least positional trope swapping since he should accept trope sliding.

The Universalist must reject Case 180 as a case of property swapping, and he must reject all the other cases as involving property sliding. The Universalist will deny that Case 180 is a case of property swapping since properties are universals, and universals cannot be swapped. Still, the Universalist can admit that Case 180 involves a genuine possibility since it involves the swapping of *sections* of the pane. The sections are swapped, but not the universals. The trope theorist can also accept that the sections are swapped, but he does *not* have the option of denying there is any property swapping in Case 180 on the grounds that properties are universals.[20] The Universalist can also

---

[20] Might he say that the sections are swapped but not the tropes? That does not seem right, since that would mean that each of two objects—the relevant sections of the pane—could have been located where the other object is located but with the result that the tropes of each object would have been exchanged.

admit that the other cases involve *section* sliding, but deny that those cases involve universal sliding. Hence, there is no corresponding argument to show that the possibility of universal sliding brings with it the possibility of universal swapping, since Cases 1 through 179 do not involve universal sliding.[21]

Thus, I am suggesting that the trope theorist must accept the possibility of trope swapping, at least of the positional variety. But if the Trope Theory also adopts a counterpart theory for individual tropes, then we need to say how that possibility can be accommodated given Schaffer's claim that a counterpart theory in combination with Trope Theory excludes the possibility of trope swapping. How can the trope theorist accommodate positional trope swapping given a counterpart theory? What we need to do is admit that there are contexts in which the positional trope swapping of Case 180 is a genuine possibility. This requires that the counterpart relation be context-relative. Given that assumption, one can hold that in contexts in which the possibility of swapping is genuine, the relevant counterpart relation, or rather the similarity relations that ground that relation, is such that the redness trope in the lower right quadrant in the relevant non-actual world is the best candidate for a counterpart to the redness trope in the upper left quadrant in the actual world. In those "swapping is possible" contexts, the redness trope in the upper left quadrant in the relevant non-actual world is *not* a counterpart to the redness trope in the upper left quadrant. This requires dropping the requirement that x's counterpart must resemble x more closely than do the other things in that world, no matter what counterpart relation is at stake. The relevant context requires *less than exact similarity* for the relevant counterpart relation in this context. Such contexts will also open up the possibility of trope swapping across objects in which the only difference from the actual world is the exchange of exactly similar tropes across objects.

1.2.3 Swapping is not a special problem for Trope Theory So let's suppose that the trope theorist cannot avoid trope swapping in some form without rejecting trope sliding, but that he ought to accept the possibility of trope sliding. Does accepting the possibility of trope swapping really put Trope Theory at a big comparative disadvantage? Not with respect to any account of properties that accepts the possibility of exactly similar, but wholly distinct particulars, whose spatial locations are not essential to them. Any such theory must deal with the presumption of the possibility of swapping vis-à-vis locations with respect to such particulars. For example, the Armstrongian realist who can reject property swapping still admits "thin particulars," opening up the possibility of thin particular swapping.[22] Indeed, Armstrong admits that the "swapping" of thin

---

[21] Indeed, the Universalist will argue that the trope theorist must posit a form of property sliding in Cases 1–179, but that although these cases differ in the position of various sections of the pane, they do not differ in the positions of the redness property. For example, according to the Universalist, although Cases 1 and 45 differ in the position of sections of the pane, they do not differ with respect to the position of the redness property that is instantiated.

[22] Schaffer: "all substrates are swappable" (2001: 250, footnote 8).

particulars is possible (1997: 107–8). Armstrong considers a world consisting of only two simple individuals, *a* and *b*, with the former having simple property *F* and the latter having simple property *G*. In this world there are two atomic states of affairs:

(1) *Fa* & *Gb*.

However, he also accepts that the following represents a world distinct from (1):

(2) *Ga* & *Fb*.

The only difference between these two worlds, however, is that the thin particulars, *a* and *b*, have been swapped, a non-empirical difference without causal consequences.[23] The tropist and the realist who accept thin particulars are equally committed to some form of "empty" swapping. There is no special problem for the trope theorist as compared with Armstrongian realism. And isn't it reasonable to think that there could be numerically distinct but intrinsically exactly similar particulars of some sort? If so, that opens up the possibility of swapping.

Finally, notice that the trope theorist should probably reject in any case—and much earlier in the discussion—the assumption that trope swapping should be ruled out. The possibility of the "immaculate replacement" of one property by an exactly similar property is a close cousin of the alleged possibility of trope swapping, the former of which motivates enduring tropes. Hence, the trope theorist's *first thought* on hearing about the no-property-swapping argument should be: why think that trope swapping should be ruled out since that possibility is closely related to the possibility of "immaculate replacement?"

1.3 The trope piling argument against the Primitivist Principle and for the Spatio-Temporal Principle

There is a second "empty possibility" argument against the Primitivist Principle and for the Spatio-Temporal Principle based on the idea of trope piling. Trope piling consists in the presence of at least two exactly similar tropes in the same location at the same time. To see how this argument works, however, we must distinguish between two forms of trope piling, what Schaffer calls "trope stacking" and "trope pyramiding."[24]

---

[23] And, there are other examples of thin particular swapping. Consider a world in which there are two atomic states of affairs:

(3) *Fa* and *Fb*, where *a* is at P_1 and *b* is at P_2.

The thin particular *a* is located at P_1 and the thin particular *b* is located at P_2. But it would seem that the realist must accept that the following represents a distinct world, not the same as (3):

(4) *Fa* and *Fb*, where *a* is at P_2 and *b* is at P_1.

[24] "Call the first type of alleged pile, whose multiplicity is hidden, a *stack*, and the second type of alleged pile, whose multiplicity is discernible, a *pyramid*, (viewed from above, only the top of a stack is visible, but the entire surface of a pyramid is)" (Schaffer 2001: 254, footnote 11).

Trope Stacking: *a* and *b* are roses that are indiscernible with respect to redness (one does not have a more saturated redness than the other), but a, and not b, has a pile of two exactly resembling rednesses (Armstrong 1978a: 86).
Trope Pyramiding: there are two point-sized particles, *a* and *b*. *a* has a pile of exactly resembling massiveness tropes and *b* has one massiveness trope that exactly resembles each of the piled tropes of *a*, but the "piled" particle, *a*, is discernibly more massive than the un-piled particle, *b* (Schaffer 2001: 254, footnote 11).

Trope stacking involves an "empty possibility," not a genuine possibility, according to Schaffer. The argument is that the Primitivist Principle, but not the Spatio-Temporal Principle, is compatible with the possibility of trope stacking, which is a point in favor of the Spatio-Temporal Principle over the Primitivist Principle.[25] The Spatio-Temporal Principle automatically rules out all forms of trope piling, since under this principle there cannot be numerically distinct tropes that are intrinsically exactly similar but occupy the same spatio-temporal location. The Primitivist Principle has no such implication.

1.3.1 Intensive differences One possible response available to the Primitivist is to try to turn this trope piling objection around on the Spatio-Temporal Principle by pointing out that the Spatio-Temporal Principle is not, but the Primitivist Principle is, compatible with trope pyramiding, which is not only not an empty possibility but is, in fact, required to account for certain phenomena.[26] The Spatio-Temporal Principle excludes the possibility of more than one exactly similar trope sharing the same location, whether that involves trope stacking or trope pyramiding. More specifically, the Primitivist might suggest that the rejection of trope pyramiding should count quite heavily against the Spatio-Temporal Principle since there is a phenomenon that can be coherently explained by trope pyramiding and for which there is no acceptable alternative explanation: the phenomenon of "purely intensive differences." Here is an example of a purely intensive difference. Two partless point particles, *a* and *b*, differ in massiveness, say, *a* is twice as massive as *b*. A "trope pyramiding" explanation of this difference might run as follows: there are two 1-unit massiveness tropes in *a* but just

---

[25] The "empty" possibility of trope stacking, then, appears to be compatible with the Primitivist Principle, but not with the Spatio-Temporal Principle, which is an apparent advantage of the latter principle over the former. However, there may be a way to weaken this blow against the Primitivist Principle. One might argue that although there is this difference between the principles as to what is possible, proponents of both principles could agree that we could never have a good reason for thinking that there are any cases of trope stacking. This follows automatically under the Spatio-Temporal Principle simply from the fact that that principle rules that trope stacking is not possible. But notice that the Primitivist can take the view that although trope stacking is possible, no one would ever have a good reason to think that that possibility has been actualized. Positing trope stacking would always be unmotivated. If there is no discernible difference between a case of trope stacking and case where there is only a single trope—the former case would involve the same powers, etc., as the latter—there would be no reason to posit more than one trope, even if one holds the Primitivist Principle of individuation. This point is related to a point made by a referee.

[26] Since trope pyramiding involves distinct but exactly similar tropes that stand to each other at a non-spatial temporal distance, it is something that is excluded by the Spatio-Temporal Principle.

one in *b*. This explanation is not available on the Spatio-Temporal Principle, but it is on the Primitivist Principle.

1.3.1.1 SCHAFFER'S RESPONSE TO THE INTENSIVE DIFFERENCES ARGUMENT FOR TROPE PYRAMIDING

Schaffer, a proponent of the Spatio-Temporal Principle, argues, however, that (1) the trope pyramiding explanation of purely intensive differences faces a serious difficulty with respect to the theory of predication and that (2) there is an alternative non-piling explanation of purely intensive differences that does not face that same serious difficulty: the massiveness tropes of *a* and *b* are inexactly similar, and neither involves a trope pile.[27] If Schaffer is right, the advocate of spatio-temporal individuation gets the right result in excluding "empty" trope stacking, while still providing an alternative, non-pyramidal understanding of purely intensive differences, a phenomenon which the Primitivist fails to explain adequately (2001: 254, footnote 11).

Let's start with Schaffer's claim that a trope pyramiding explanation of purely intensive differences will lead to problems with the theory of predication. Schaffer argues that the piling explanation of purely intensive differences is inconsistent with any plausible theory of predication. Here is what he has in mind. Suppose that a point particle with 5g mass is analyzed as a five-high pile of 1g masses. That means that that particle has a 1g mass.

Since the object has 1g mass, it follows that it can be truly said that 'the object is 1'... But of course the object is 5g, not 1g (2001: 254).

In other words, the pyramiding explanation of purely intensive differences commits us to false predications derived from the "component" tropes that make up the pyramid. Schaffer also argues that any attempt to complicate the theory of predication to accommodate piling will be such that the theoretical gains of allowing for piling will be "dissipated in the newfound complications of predication" (2001: 254). The resulting theory of predication will be too complicated. In fact, as I will now suggest, Schaffer is wrong to think that the Spatio-Temporal Principle is at a comparative advantage with respect to the theory of predication.

First, one can grant that it is in fact true of a 5g object that it is 1g, but allow that it is pragmatically odd to assert as much, since we usually assume that predications of

---

[27] A further reason that is considered by Schaffer to allow for trope piling (keeping in mind that trope piling is excluded by the Spatio-Temporal Principle) is to account for the fact that more than one indiscernible boson can occupy the same place at the same time. "The piling of bosonic tropes seems to be not just a conceptual possibility, but an empirical reality" (2001: 254). In response, Schaffer suggests that his account of purely intensive differences should be extended to "boson piles," thereby avoiding the need for trope piles to handle "boson piles." Without going into the details of Schaffer's proposed way of handling "boson piles," it can be pointed out, as noted by a referee, that his approach seems to require that fundamental physics come down a certain way, which is at least a cost of his approach.

number and quantity are maximal unless otherwise specified.[28] For example, it is strictly true though pragmatically odd to say that I have a brother when I in fact have two brothers. Second, even if this true-but-odd response is rejected, it is not clear that trope piling requires significant complications in the theory of predication. Third, even if trope piling does lead to burdensome complications in the theory of predication for the Primitivist, it can be argued that those same complications will be required by the proponent of the Spatio-Temporal Principle for a different, but related reason.

As to the second point, let's focus on a specific, trope-based account of predication mentioned by Schaffer, that of D. C. Williams, and let's consider how one might complicate Williams's account of predication. On Williams's account, *a* is *F* if and only if the bundle of compresent tropes in *a* and the set of exactly resembling tropes in *F* overlap.[29] This account will fail in cases of trope pyramiding, but not if we add one clause:

> *a* is *F* if and only if the bundle of compresent tropes in *a* and the set of exactly resembling tropes in *F* overlap *with respect to a unique trope*.

Under this revision, we cannot say truly that *a* is 1g because there is no *unique* trope in the bundle of tropes (remember there is a five-high pile of 1g tropes) that is also in the set of exactly resembling 1g tropes. The object is 5g, on the other hand, since there is a unique 5g conjunctive trope that is both in the *a*-bundle and the set of exactly resembling 5g tropes.

But suppose that things are not so simple and that further, burdensome complications are necessary by the piling explanation of intensive differences. Would that mean the Spatio-Temporal Principle is better suited to the requirements of a theory of predication? Only if the trope theorist who holds the Spatio-Temporal Principle of trope individuation does not also require similar complications in the theory of predication independently of the possibility of trope piling. To see that the proponent of the Spatio-Temporal Principle is not better off with respect to the theory of predication—he will also be forced to complicate that theory—consider a phenomenon similar to trope piling, which I will call "imperfect trope piling." Here is an example. Suppose that massiveness tropes come in different varieties: 1g; 2g; and 3g. The 2g trope (and the 3g trope) does not include 1g tropes as constituents. Consider, then, a "pile" of such massiveness tropes made up of a 1g trope, a 2g trope, and a 3g trope (call this an "imperfect" trope pile). Object *a*, then, is 6g. The revision I have proposed entails wrongly that *a* is also 1g since *a* has a unique 1g trope. So more revisions are required, and it starts to look like Schaffer is right about the need to couple

---

[28] What Schaffer claims is ascribed to "any plausible theory of predication" is better read as a matter of the pragmatics of predication. What has been implicated is false, but not what has been predicated. I owe this point to a referee.
[29] In general, I would suggest that the theory of properties should drive the theory of predication, rather than the other way around. However, I will set that point aside and focus on Schaffer's comparative claim about predication.

the Primitivist Principle with significant complications to the theory of predication. But notice that this point will carry weight against the Primitivist Principle and for the Spatio-Temporal Principle only if the latter need not be paired with similar complications to the theory of predication. In fact, the Spatio-Temporal Principle will need to be so paired since the latter principle does not exclude "imperfect" trope piles. Imperfect piles are not piles of exactly similar tropes, and the Spatio-Temporal Principle rules out only "perfect" piles. What that means is that the proponent of the Spatio-Temporal Principle will also need to complicate the theory of predication, since he does not exclude imperfect piling.[30]

So let's suppose that proponents of these two principles of individuation face similar difficulties with respect to the theory of predication and that neither theory is favored by this issue (or that neither theory need worry about Schaffer's objection since it is strictly true though pragmatically odd to say a 5g object is 1g). Still, it might seem that the proponent of the Spatio-Temporal Principle need not allow for pyramiding since he has Schaffer's alternative, non-piling explanation of intensive differences. Even if it cannot be shown that there is anything especially defective in the pyramiding explanation of intensive differences or that there is any defect that does not also show up in the spatio-temporal camp, still one might opt for the non-pyramiding explanation of intensive differences and simply reject pyramiding. I will now suggest that given that the Spatio-Temporal Principle allows for the possibility of imperfect piling, it should allow for pyramiding.

1.3.2 Imperfect piling is not that different than pyramiding Imperfect "piling," the possibility of which is compatible with the Spatio-Temporal Principle, is so close to trope pyramiding as to make it untenable to accept the former but reject the latter. Consider a continuum of imperfect trope piling cases beginning with a 1g trope coinciding with a 2g trope, followed by a case in which a 1g trope coincides with a 1.999g trope and so on until just before we reach the potential case of trope pyramiding involving two 1g tropes. None of these cases, except the 1g-1g pyramid case, is excluded by the Spatio-Temporal Principle and there are empirical differences between all of these cases. Now consider a case on the "other side" of the 1g-1g case: a 1g trope coincides, say, with a .999g trope. Again, the Spatio-Temporal Principle does not rule this out. However, the 1g-1g case in this continuum is ruled out. Why rule out this one case? Not because

---

[30] Some complication like the following will be required: a is F iff the bundle of compresent tropes in a and the set of exactly resembling tropes in F overlap and for any trope, t, that is in that overlap area, t is not part of a trope in the bundle that is also a G trope where G is a determinable of F. Another possibility might be to argue that imperfect piling is already excluded by the principle that determinates of the same level exclude each other. That might rule out the a-bundle including both a 1g mass trope and a 2g mass trope. But there are two difficulties with this approach. First, the exclusion principle should be read as applying to the "total mass" in this case. No object can have a total mass of 1g and a total mass of 2g. The principle does not apply to the components of a trope pile. Second, if the principle does apply to the components of an imperfect pile, then it can be extended to the components of a perfect pile. Since the principle is not given any deeper explanation, there would seem to be no reason to limit it to imperfect piles.

there are no empirical differences between this case and the others. There are. The Spatio-Temporal Principle's rejection of the possibility of pyramiding is arbitrary given its compatibility with the possibility of imperfect trope piling. A principle of individuation either should exclude all of these cases or none. The Spatio-Temporal Principle allows for imperfect trope piling but not for trope pyramiding, but trope pyramiding is a limiting case of imperfect trope piling. There is something arbitrary about allowing for the latter but not the former.

1.4 Schaffer's multiple location objection to primitive individuation

There is one more argument outlined by Schaffer in favor of the Spatio-Temporal Principle that I want to consider. The idea is that this principle is better suited to one of the main rationales for Trope Theory: the avoidance of repeatable entities. Since the Spatio-Temporal Principle bans the possibility of the same trope at a spatial distance from itself at the same time, that principle fits nicely with this rationale.[31] However, it should be noted that this rationale follows from another rationale for Trope Theory, the avoidance of universals, given a traditional understanding of universals. The "no repeatable entities" motivation is interchangeable with the "no-universals" motivation, given the traditional, Aristotelian characterization of the universal–particular distinction, according to which particulars are not repeatable. But, as argued in Chapter 1, this Aristotelian view of particulars is wrong. Particulars have a limited capacity for repetition. What the trope theorist cares about is an ontology without universals. A Primitivist Principle of trope individuation *and* a Spatio-Temporal Principle of trope individuation combined with a Trope Theory will give that result, but the former has an advantage over the latter: the Spatio-Temporal Principle goes too far in ruling out limited repeatability for tropes whereas the Primitivist Principle does not.[32]

2. Campbell's arguments against medium-sized tropes

A principle of trope individuation still leaves open important questions about how Trope Theory maps onto the world. In particular, Campbell has raised a series of arguments, independently of his own preferred principle of trope individuation, against the possibility of "manifest," medium-sized tropes. If his arguments are sound, many of our ordinarily recognized properties must be rejected. In this section, I want to suggest that the trope theorist need not follow Campbell to this conclusion.

---

[31] The Spatio-Temporal Principle rules out the repeatability of tropes ("the redness of the rose is distinguished from the redness of the sunset by location"), but "it is at least nonobvious whether QI succeeds in this regard" (Schaffer 2001: 249).

[32] What Schaffer takes to be a disadvantage of the Primitivist Principle, that it is compatible with time-traveling enduring tropes, should, in fact, be treated as an advantage of the Primitivist Principle over the Spatio-Temporal Principle.

2.1 Campbell's first objection to spatially medium-sized tropes

Suppose that R is a continuous, medium-sized region, and that R is red throughout. Either there is just one red trope occupying that region or there are many red tropes in that region. Campbell argues that there are absurdities with either option. Under the *first option*, there is one red trope occupying R, but no red tropes that occupy any sub-region, r, of R. Take one such sub-region, r, a region that is sufficiently extended to be a red region. r does not include a redness trope, but it would have included a redness trope if the non-r areas of R had not been red, say, because we painted those areas blue. But then a mere Cambridge change would have resulted in the r region going from being a region that did not include a red trope to being a region that did, but no mere Cambridge change should bring a trope into existence[33] (Campbell 1990: 136). Hence, the first option must be rejected. The *second option* is to take R to include a redness trope that is the union of many distinct redness tropes (1990: 137). One possibility is that the redness trope of region R is a union of point-sized redness tropes. This possibility, however, is inconsistent with Campbell's assumption that colors have minimal spatial requirements. The other possibility is that the R-sized, homogeneous redness trope is the union of a specific number of trope minima. According to Campbell, the total number of trope minima, N, under this option, is determined by dividing the total area of R by the area occupied by a minimal red trope.[34] The difficulty is that there will be no determinate breakdown of that total area into minimal redness tropes, but many different ways of exhaustively dividing up the total area into N minimal-trope size units. It will, then, be arbitrary or interest-determined what the basic tropes of that type are in that area, but basic tropes are neither arbitrary nor interest-determined. Hence, since these are the only options of reading R as including a R-sized redness trope, there is no such trope. More generally, there are no medium-sized tropes, composed or not composed of trope minima, which are larger than points.

2.1.1 Dismissing the first horn

From the assumption alone that R includes only one red trope, it does not follow that each sub-region of R includes no red tropes. This will not be true in cases in which the medium-sized trope is an extended simple. To see this, suppose that that one R-sized red trope is an *extended simple*, which is also a multi-locator that wholly occupies each minimally-sized-for-red sub-region. In that case, one red trope would occupy both R and wholly occupy the relevant sub-region, r. Consider an analogy with universals. Suppose that there is just one red universal instantiated throughout R. That same redness universal may also occupy r. That is certainly possible for a universal. If so, painting the non-r regions of R red would not

---

[33] "*Being a trope* cannot have any genuine foundational status if it can be gained or lost by items that retain their identity throughout the transformation" (Campbell 1990: 136).

[34] The specific minimal area associated with a type of trope, if any, will vary across types.

bring a red universal into existence in r, since r would have already included that redness universal. But, the same point applies if the red trope that occupies R is an extended simple that is a multi-locator. In that case, it operates like a universal in R. Campbell has not established the first horn. (Campbell cannot respond that by taking the R-sized red property to be a multi-locator we are taking it to be a universal, not a trope. It will still qualify as a particular if exact similarity is not sufficient for identity for this property.) So Campbell has not shown that on the assumption that R includes only one red trope that each sub-region of R includes no red tropes. Still, this does not show that his first horn does not apply to cases in which the relevant medium-sized trope is not an extended simple.[35] So suppose that we concede that in those cases the relevant medium-sized trope is composed of distinct, smaller tropes of the same type. Let's even suppose that most medium-sized property instances are not extended simples. We must consider the second horn to address those cases.

2.1.2 Dismissing the second horn There are two possible ways to show that the second horn of the "dilemma" fails.

Possibility 1. According to the second horn, if a medium-sized trope occupying a region R were composed of smaller, minimally sized tropes, then the ratio of the total area R to the area of a minimally sized trope would determine the number of tropes of that type in R. But, it will then turn out that it is arbitrary or interest-relative which of multiple ways of dividing up R into areas of that minimal extension is selected. In response, one can challenge the assumption that we must pick just one such division. To see this, suppose that minimally sized red tropes are *extended simples*, which can spatially overlap.[36] Also suppose that the total area R forms a circle and that the area of a minimal trope is one half of the area of such a circle. Consider two different ways of dividing up the circle into halves, one based on an imaginary line from the top point to the bottom point and the other on an imaginary line straight across the circle. These divisions give us two different answers as to what the two minimal tropes are. My suggestion is to accept both divisions as picking out genuine tropes, abandoning the Campbellian assumption that there are only two minimal tropes in that area. Further, since there is an indefinite number of such divisions, given other ways to divide the circle in two, there is an indefinite number of minimal tropes in the circle. The idea is that instead of claiming that only one such division is correct we allow that all such possible divisions give us a genuine breakdown into basic minimally sized red tropes,

---

[35] A referee suggests that tropes might be individuated in part by shape. How might that help with the first horn? If their shapes—including their borders—individuate tropes, one might argue that changing the boundaries of the redness trope that occupies R destroys that trope but brings into existence a new redness trope that is r-shaped. That involves a genuine change in the r region rather than a mere Cambridge change relative to that region by way of a change in what holds true of its borders. However, I would suggest that some enduring tropes can survive at least some changes in their shapes.

[36] With extended simples, spatial overlap cannot also involve mereological overlap. The area of overlap between two extended simples cannot include a proper part of either extended simple since each lacks proper parts.

with the consequence that there are an indefinite number of spatially overlapping minimal red tropes.

It might be objected that this leads to "trope piling," the presence of more than one exactly similar trope in the same location.[37] More specifically, it might be objected that for any sub-region of R, say x, that is smaller than the minimum required for a red trope and is an area of overlap between two or more minimally sized red tropes, an indefinite number of red tropes "cross" x under this proposal. We, then, have a red trope pile at x. In fact, there is no trope piling with respect to x since, strictly speaking, x is not occupied by any red trope since such occupancy requires an area greater than x.[38]

Possibility 2. But now suppose that there are no such extended, minimally sized, but simple tropes either in all cases or in some cases so that "possibility 1" cannot be relied upon in all cases. Campbell assumes that there are just two options with respect to the minimal size of the relevant tropes: either they are point-sized or all of them have the same specific, greater-than-a-point size. But there is another possibility. Minimum redness tropes must be greater than point-sized, but there is no specific size they must be. Each redness trope is further divisible into redness tropes, but there is no number N such that for an area A, N is the number of minimal redness tropes present in that area. Each part of each redness trope is extended and further divisible into smaller redness tropes. Why would this help with the second horn? Because we don't end up with any minimally sized tropes of that type and, hence, the problem of selecting among different possible candidates for those minimally sized tropes does not arise. There is no need to select among different possible ways of dividing up the medium-sized trope into such minimally sized tropes. Hence, there is no basis for Campbell's worry that admitting "divisible" medium-sized tropes of this sort requires that the basic tropes are arbitrary or interest-relative.

Hence, there are a number of ways in which there could exist medium-sized tropes that would not be subject to Campbell's first dilemma argument.

---

[37] Armstrong and others have claimed that property piling is not a genuine possibility (as it is not if properties are universals), and that an adequate account of properties should not allow for this empty possibility (Armstrong 1978a: 86).

[38] If we also suppose that each of the extended simple red tropes is a "multi-locator," wholly occupying not only a region the size of a minimal red trope, but being wholly present at each sub-region in that region, including r, we get trope piling at r. In fact, we should not suppose that these minimal red tropes are multi-locators. The key is to see that extended minimally sized tropes are not multi-locators, but spanners. How would that eliminate trope piling? If minimal red trope x is a spanner, it occupies only one region and it has no parts. There is no trope piling with respect to any point or sub-region of any minimal region in the circle since, strictly speaking, no such sub-region is occupied by any red trope if minimal red tropes are spanners, and, thus, no minimal region or sub-minimal region will be occupied by more than one exactly similar red trope. But why think that minimal red tropes are spanners? The reason is that if minimal red tropes were multi-locators with respect to each minimal space that they occupied, then that region would not be the *minimal size* for tropes of that type. There would be a sub-region of it that was also occupied by that red trope.

2.2 Campbell's second objection

Campbell also argues against medium-sized tropes on the basis of spectrums.[39] Consider the following color spectrum. There is an apparently continuous variation in color from one side to the other and an apparently continuous variation in saturation from top to bottom, with the top being the least saturated. He argues that every attempt to divide up objectively such spectrums into minimal color tropes will lead to difficulties. Either we end up with point-sized color tropes, contrary to the assumption that color tropes cannot be point-sized, or arbitrary/interest-relative units. If there is color variation across each minimal, greater-than-a-point sized color trope, then decisions about how much variation is compatible with a given trope will be arbitrary or interest-relative.[40] If no variation is allowed, then we are back to point-sized color tropes.

2.2.1 Response to Campbell Imagine a grid that divides up an expanse of uniform color into regions of minimally sized color squares (assume that the minimal extension of a color is square shaped for sake of argument), say, m-sized adjacent squares, associated with color properties. Now imagine placing this grid over our color spectrum. There are two possibilities not covered by Campbell's analysis.

The *first possibility* is that each m-sized square gives us a uniform color trope—not a smaller spectrum—when placed across the spectrum in one way, and that placed across the same spectrum at, say, another angle we end up with a different division into uniform m-sized color squares. I would suggest that, in that case, each grid divides up the spectrum into fully objective color tropes. There will be many alternative ways of dividing up the spectrum into m-sized adjacent squares depending on the many different ways of fitting a m-based grid across the spectrum.[41] The situation is similar to that of the uniform red expanse, discussed above, that can be divided up in many diverse ways of minimal red tropes. In this case, however, differently angled grids divide up the spectrum into tropes of different colors, each angle generating a pattern of colors. Each such square on each grid represents a minimal color trope. Overlapping m-sized squares from these two grids represent color tropes that overlap (without trope piling since each square is minimally sized for colors). We are not required to select arbitrarily one of these grids as giving the only acceptable breakdown into minimal colors. The *second possibility* is that each grid square generates a smaller spectrum, assuming no minimal spatial requirements on colors other than being greater than a point. Each part of the color spectrum, no matter how small, is extended and further

---

[39] The question about how to individuate properties in a color spectrum also arises for universals.
[40] And because the transitions are smooth, there is no natural break between one of these atoms and its neighbors (Campbell 1990: 139).
[41] Each such square includes an extended simple color trope.

divisible into smaller spectrums.[42] We don't end up with any minimally sized color tropes, so there is no need to decide arbitrarily how much variation is acceptable for each minimally sized color trope.

2.3 Campbell's objection to temporally extended tropes of medium duration

Campbell also has a dilemma argument against temporally extended tropes, say, a redness trope of medium duration, D. There are two ways to divide up temporally such tropes, both of which produce difficulties. According to the first, a trope of medium duration does not have tropes of that same type as temporal parts.[43] The difficulty, argues Campbell, for this first possibility, is that had we painted R black, say, after the first half of that period, then there would have been a redness trope in R during the first half of that period, but that would mean that a mere Cambridge "change" would have made it the case that during the earlier half-period a red trope existed and occupied R. But mere Cambridge "changes" cannot bring a trope into existence. The other possibility is that tropes of medium duration break down into tropes of minimal duration. We, then, count forward from the first moment of the trope's existence by units of that minimal length to determine the specific minimal tropes of which that longer-lived trope is composed. Here, Campbell argues that given the indeterminacy as to when a certain "manifest" trope came into existence, "it will be indeterminate where each succeeding minimal . . . trope ends and the next begins" (1990: 141). He uses the example of "solidity." When a wall, say, one made out of wet cement, is being built, at what point does it become solid? It will, then, be arbitrary or interest-relative how that trope of longer duration breaks down into tropes of minimal duration, since it will be arbitrary/interest-relative at what point in the building of the wall that we declare it to be solid.

Response to Campbell In response to the *first horn*, the trope theorist should affirm that there can be enduring red tropes. In the case at hand, there are, then, two possibilities. The first is that the redness trope that is wholly present during the entire period is also wholly present during that first half. In that case, had we painted R black during the second half of that period, that same redness trope would still have existed during the first half. The second is that the entire period is of minimal duration for a redness trope. In that case, painting the R region black during the second half would not have generated a redness trope during the first half.[44] The *second horn* is also ineffective.

---

[42] Josh Parsons discusses a similar case involving a "gunky" cloth that embodies such a spectrum: "every extended part of the cloth contains a subtle gradient between two colours... So no part of the cloth has a uniform colour distribution. So the non-uniform colour distribution of the whole cloth is not equivalent to some property that specifies the spatial arrangement of uniformly coloured parts of the cloth" (2004: 178).

[43] Suppose that we say that red trope r persists from t to t' in region R and that for any temporal period shorter than t to t' there is no red trope in that region.

[44] And, for periods less than the minimal required for that property, both the proponent of universals and the proponent of enduring tropes should deny that during that sub-minimal period there would have been a red trope/universal in existence at that location had we made any Cambridge change relative to that period.

Campbell argues that since it is indeterminate when the "manifest" trope came into existence, it will be indeterminate at what point each succeeding minimal trope of that same type ends and the next begins. In fact, although it may be indeterminate (and, hence, arbitrary or interest-determined) at which point we can begin to apply our term, to use Campbell's example, "solid," that is a function either of the limitations of our language or of our knowledge, not the world. The trope itself is fully determinate and that trope either endures or it does not, whatever the difficulties of classifying it, given our limited linguistic resources or our limited epistemic situation.

3. What's next?

In the next chapter, I will defend a Trope Bundle Theory of concrete particulars. Some of the advantages of a trope-based Bundle Theory over a universals-based Bundle Theory will be demonstrated. I will also pursue refinements to the theory in response to objections that Bundle Theory makes all of the properties of an object essential to it, is incompatible with change and leads to an infinite regress. Bundle Theory is best combined with four-dimensionalism in order to handle the first two of these objections. The regress objection will be handled by treating compresence as a "self-relating" relation.

4
Bundle Theory

In this chapter, I will defend the Bundle Theory thesis that concrete particulars or substantial particulars, such as tables and chairs, are wholly constituted by complete bundles of compresent properties. Although a bundle theorist might hold this constitutional claim without the further claim that concrete particulars are identical to bundles of properties, I will also endorse that identity claim. In addition, I defend the claim that the bundled properties are tropes, not universals. In turn, I take bundles to be mereological sums of properties, the constituents of which are parts of the bundle.[1] Bundles are not sets or Armstrongian states of affairs that embody a mode of composition that is not mereological. However, since not just any mereological sum of tropes is a concrete particular, the trope-parts of the bundle are restricted to those tropes that are mutually compresent. What is compresence? It is not spatial coincidence at a time since it is not necessarily true that all concrete objects have spatial locations. Non-physical objects are possible, so spatial coincidence is not a requirement of compresence. And, coincidence is not sufficient for compresence. Campbell offers two cases to demonstrate non-sufficiency: (1) a portion of the earth's magnetic field is where a pea pod is; and (2) non-identical objects coinciding for a short period (Campbell 1990: 175, footnote 5). I will opt for the view that compresence is non-reducible. My defense of a Trope Bundle Theory will consist in showing some of the advantages of a trope-based Bundle Theory over a universals-based Bundle Theory, as well as suggesting refinements to the theory in response to various objections that have been raised. I will not pursue a comparison between bundle theories and non-bundle theories. However, it is worth pointing out that a Substrate–Attribute Theory is not as parsimonious as Bundle Theory. I will proceed by considering the main objections to Bundle Theory.

1. Objections to Bundle Theory as such

Some objections to Bundle Theory do not depend on whether the bundled properties are tropes or universals, whereas other objections do so depend. I will begin with two objections that are independent of whether the properties that are bundled are tropes or universals, the problem of essential properties and the problem of changing bundles.

[1] For a nice defense of Bundle Theory against the charge that properties cannot be parts of objects, see (Robb 2005).

In the case of the second of these objections, I will argue that the best response works only if the bundled properties are tropes rather than universals. This amounts to an indirect argument for Trope Bundle Theory over universals-based Bundle Theory.

1.1 The problem of essential properties

The first objection is that Bundle Theory makes all of an object's properties essential:

> Bundles have all of their constituent properties essentially. If objects are bundles of their properties, then all of an object's properties are essential to it. However, ordinary objects generally do not have all of their properties essentially, and, hence, a Bundle Theory of objects must be wrong.

This objection does not depend on whether bundles are sums, sets, or states of affairs or on whether the bundled properties are universals or tropes. If bundles are mereological sums of properties, then since a mereological sum could not have differed with respect to its parts, it will follow that ordinary objects have all of their properties essentially.[2] Similarly, if bundles are sets of properties, since sets have their members essentially, objects will have all of their properties essentially (van Cleve 1985: 96). And, even if bundles are Armstrongian states of affairs (which are not sums of their constituents or sets), it is reasonable to think the same objection will arise. Can this problem be solved? It can be solved, as O'Leary-Hawthorne and Cover suggest, if Bundle Theory is combined with a counterpart semantic theory for statements about ordinary particulars. According to a counterpart theory, modal statements about an object o are made true or false "not by how o itself (that very thing) is in some possible world, rather in virtue of facts about how things that are similar to o in the relevant ways are in other possible worlds" (O'Leary-Hawthorne and Cover 1998: 209). The relevant respects of similarity are determined by the context which selects a counterpart relation, different counterpart relations being selected by different contexts in some cases. What makes it true that a particular object o could have had different properties is that a non-identical counterpart to o in another possible world has different properties than does o. Even if x is a mereological sum or set of properties, say, including property P and lacking Q, o could have lacked P or possessed Q, so long as there is a possible world in which there is a bundle-sum/set of properties, n, which is not identical to o, but is a counterpart to o (under a counterpart relation that does not require a sum/set with the same constituents/members), such that n lacks P or possesses Q.[3] In short, although mereological sums have their constituents essentially and sets have their members essentially, even if bundles are sums or sets, the apparent implication of

---

[2] As O'Leary-Hawthorne and Cover point out: "... mereological sums have their constitutents essentially. But ordinary things do not have all of their properties essentially. Doesn't it follow that ordinary things are not identical with bundles of properties?" (1998: 209).

[3] "According to Bundle Theory, those counterparts will not, strictly speaking, be identical with the actual individual (the standard move for the counterpart theorist), but rather will be similar in the contextually relevant way to the mereological sum" (1998: 209).

Bundle Theory that all of an object's properties are essential to that object can be avoided by adopting counterpart semantics for talk about ordinary objects.

1.2 Bundles and the problem of change

A second problem, that of change, also does not depend on the differences between a universals-based and a trope-based Bundle Theory.

> Since bundles cannot change, but concrete objects can and do, concrete objects are not bundles. The same bundle complex cannot at one time be composed of one set of property-parts, but a different set at a different time. Change means replacement, not persistence for bundles of properties. But if bundles cannot change, neither can objects if objects are bundles. However, some concrete objects can survive at least some changes in their properties. Bob The Bundle cannot, but Bob The Person can change.

This objection is independent of whether properties are universals or tropes. And this objection seems to hold even if bundles are not mereological sums, but sets or states of affairs.

Various philosophers have suggested that Bundle Theory can be made compatible with object change if Bundle Theory is combined with four-dimensionalism. This is the strategy I will defend here. This combination can be worked out in one of two ways, depending on which version of four-dimensionalism, Worm Theory or Stage Theory, is adopted. On Worm Theory, ordinary persisting objects are space-time worms with temporal parts that are appropriately related, "R-related," and object persistence is a matter of the same space-time worm having temporal parts at more than one moment.[4] If Bundle Theory is combined with Worm Theory, the bundles in the combined theory do *not*, strictly speaking, correspond to ordinary objects. Ordinary objects turn out to be space-time worms whose instantaneous temporal parts are complete bundles of compresent tropes. The two components of a Worm-Bundle Theory are as follows:

(1) an *instantaneous object stage* is a complete bundle of compresent properties (Casullo 1988: 128); and
(2) an *ordinary continuant* is a series of R-related instantaneous stages (1988: 127).

Only instantaneous stages are bundles of compresent properties, but instantaneous stages are not ordinary objects. The problem of change is then solved. Although *bundles* of compresent properties cannot change, objects are not bundles of compresent properties. An object is a space-time worm consisting of a series of non-identical

---

[4] The object does not exist wholly at each moment that it exists; only part of it exists at that time, a temporal part. For an alternative approach that is meant to be compatible with an endurantist Trope Bundle Theory, see (Wilson 2008).

bundles that are *R*-related.[5] The effect is to abandon a strict Bundle Theory of objects since properties from different time slices of an object will generally fail to be mutually compresent. On Stage Theory, ordinary continuants are instantaneous stages, not space-time worms, and object persistence is understood in terms of counterpart theory. An object *o*, which is identical to an instantaneous stage *s* at *t*, will exist at a later time *t'* just in case there exists an instantaneous stage *s'* at *t'* that is a counterpart to *s*. The relevant counterpart relation is the *R*-relation. If Bundle Theory is combined with Stage Theory, then the former says that each stage-object is a complete bundle of compresent tropes. Change is compatible with Bundle Theory if objects are instantaneous stages that are trope bundles, and object persistence is a matter of standing in a counterpart relation to non-identical stages at some later time. This solution allows that bundles cannot survive changes in their parts. However, what makes it true that objects—which are momentary bundles—can survive change is that they can stand in an appropriate counterpart relation to non-identical bundles at a later point in time.

At this point, I will suggest that combining Bundle Theory with four-dimensionalism favors a trope-based rather than a universals-based Bundle Theory. Here is why. Suppose that properties are universals, and consider Worm-Bundle Theory. We get asymmetrical results for changing and unchanging objects. If object *x changes* continuously from *t* to *t'*, then the *t*-bundle will not be identical to the *t'*-bundle since their component universals will differ. No bundle at a moment in the range from *t* to *t'* is identical to any bundle in that range from another moment, and *x*'s persistence will be determined by clause (2) during this period. On the other hand, if there is no change during that period, the bundles at each instance in that series will be identical to each other since their component universals are the same. Clause (2) will, then, *not* apply. The *R*-relation will require that its relata are not identical. The *R*-relation applies only to "a series of momentary things." We, then, have a temporal parts account for changing objects and a non-temporal parts account otherwise. This is objectionable. An account of the persistence of complex objects should not vary depending on whether the object happens to be changing or not. A similar difficulty arises for Stage Theory. Again, suppose that the components of the bundle are universals, and consider an unchanging bundle during a certain time period. The bundles at each instance in this period will be identical to each other. But in that case, the object's persistence during this time period will be a matter of endurance, not counterpart relations. It might be suggested that the bundle theorist should reject any requirement of symmetry and accept a "mixed" account of object persistence: a non-four-dimensionalist theory of the persistence of objects during periods of intrinsic unchange and a four-dimensionalist theory of the persistence of objects during periods of intrinsic change. The difficulty with this conception is that it conflicts with our intuition that

---

[5] On this interpretation, "if the complex FGH...stands in relation R to the complex FGK then one and the same *enduring* thing has changed its properties. It is, of course, *also* true that we have replacement of one *momentary* thing by a different *momentary* thing" (Casullo 1988: 129).

whatever accounts for object persistence does not vary across unchanging and changing objects.

Symmetry between changing and unchanging objects will be established if we replace universals with *momentary* tropes. Momentary tropes are not and cannot be wholly present at more than one moment. If the members of each bundle are momentary, then the bundles will be. Even if the object does not change with respect to the property types under which its tropes fall or with respect to the number of tropes it contains—even if the bundles are exactly similar—they will be non-identical, since no member of one bundle is identical with any member of the other. Under this assumption, a four-dimensionalist theory is then equally applicable to changing and unchanging objects alike. On Worm Theory, a persisting, unchanging object in all cases will, then, consist of R-related bundles of non-identical momentary tropes as will a persisting, changing object. On Stage Theory, an unchanging/changing object *o* at *t* persists if and only if there is a later counterpart of *o*.

Still, this solution is available only if we are willing to tie Bundle Theory to the assumption that all tropes are momentary.[6] But, in fact, some tropes may violate this assumption and be wholly present at more than one moment, as I argued in Chapter 2.[7] That seems to open up the possibility of bundles of *only* enduring tropes and we are back to our asymmetry problem. Suppose that object *x* is a complex of enduring tropes that does not change from *t* to *t'*. In that case, the *t*-complex is identical to the *t'*-complex. It is wholly present at both times, with the consequence that *x* has no temporal parts at those times. Temporal Parts Theory can be made consistent with unchanging objects and Bundle Theory only with a guarantee of temporally distinct bundles. In short, if a bundle of only enduring tropes endures over time without any change in the enduring tropes that make up the bundle, then there is no series of momentary stages, clause (2) does not apply, and we will have a non-temporal-parts account of its persistence. We will end up with different accounts of persistence in the case of changing and unchanging objects.

Here I want to suggest a solution to the asymmetry problem brought on by enduring tropes, which is not available if properties are universals. To set the groundwork for restoring symmetry, consider a mixed case. Suppose *x* consists of the sequence *FGH* followed by *FGH'*, where *H* and *H'* are non-identical but exactly similar momentary tropes, and *F* and *G* are enduring tropes. Since the members differ, so do *FGH* and *FGH'*. These bundles may be treated as momentary stages and *x*'s persistence may then be analyzed by way of Stage Theory or Worm Theory. As long as each such bundle has at least one momentary trope there will be no asymmetry in how persisting changing objects and persisting unchanging objects are analyzed. Bundle Theory is compatible

---

[6] This solution is not available if properties are universals, since universals in general are not momentary. They can exist wholly at different times.

[7] See also my (1997a: Chapters 4 and 5).

with a four-dimensionalist theory and enduring tropes if each (complete) bundle includes a momentary trope.

Is there any reason to think that each (complete) bundle includes a momentary trope? There is. The key is to include the compresence relation, *C*, itself in the bundle.

> A *momentary* thing is a complete complex of properties which all stand in the relation of compresence to one another and the compresence relation that relates those properties.

This formulation leaves open two possibilities: either being in the bundle is sufficient for being compresent with the other components of the bundle, or it is not sufficient. Alternative formulations would assume either that *C* itself is compresent with each of the other members of the bundle or that it definitely is not, but that *C* is still in the bundle. (In the next section, I will consider the objection that the first alternative leads to a vicious regress. I will suggest that it does not.) In any case, *if C* itself is a momentary trope, then temporally distinct bundles will be distinguishable, even if they share all their other members, since *C* is included in the bundle. Do we have a reason to think that every compresence trope is momentary? Here are three reasons.

(1) One function of each instance of the compresence relation in a Bundle Theory is to determine one and only one time at which the bundled properties are compresent. Thus each instance of the compresence relation, in a complete bundle, should be dated and that date should change depending on the moment at which the bundle exists. The latter is not possible if each *C* is an enduring trope because each *C* would not mark out one moment in time, but a series of moments. The fact that properties stand to each other in a particular instance of the compresence relation would not determine one and only one time at which these properties were compresent by way of that compresence trope (which is compatible with those same tropes being compresent at a different time in virtue of a different instance of the compresence relation).

(2) The second reason to think that each compresence trope is momentary has to do with a further characteristic or role of this relation. According to Bundle Theory, the compresence relation is supposed to be an "equivalence relation," a relation that divides up the relevant domain of properties into exclusive bundles. Only if compresence is symmetrical and transitive can it accomplish this purpose. However, as it turns out, compresence will fail to be transitive if properties are universals. Even if universal *U* is compresent with universal *V* (both are instantiated by object *a*) and *V* is compresent with universal *Z* (both are instantiated by object *b*), *U* and *Z* may fail to be compresent if no object instantiates both *U* and *Z*. One of the advantages claimed for trope-based Bundle Theory is that compresence comes out as transitive. The idea is that if *U*, *V,* and *Z* are tropes in our example, then objects *a* and *b* must be identical and *U* and *Z* must be compresent:

Suppose we are dealing with tropes... Compresence could then be symmetrical and *transitive* because properties would, as it were, not stray outside the bundle (Armstrong 1989a: 71).

In fact, tropes will guarantee the transitivity of the compresence relation only under certain further assumptions about tropes. If all tropes are momentary, compresence will be transitive. However, if some tropes endure, transitivity may fail. Suppose that V is not a momentary trope, but an enduring trope that exists from t to t'. U is a momentary trope existing at t and Z is a momentary trope existing at t'. Also suppose that the object, a, that is characterized by U and V at t ceases to exist after t, although V, the enduring trope, survives the destruction of a, characterizing a different object, b, at t', which is also characterized by Z. In that case, although U is compresent with V and V with Z, U is not compresent with Z. Transitivity fails.

There are two ways to fix this problem. The first is to ban enduring tropes. I reject that option because I think there are compelling reasons, as indicated, to posit enduring tropes. The second is to modify our conception of the compresence relation, or perhaps simply clarify it. Transitivity can be guaranteed if compresence relations are themselves momentary tropes. For example, transitivity will not be violated in our example if compresence is a momentary trope. In that case, although U is t-compresent with V, V is not t-compresent with Z (although it is t'-compresent with Z). Hence, to guarantee the transitivity of each compresence trope, given the possibility of enduring tropes, we should assume that each such trope is momentary.

(3) A third reason for assuming that compresence tropes are momentary is to guarantee a further characteristic of the compresence relation: mutually compresent properties belong to a single object. Consider a series of three short-lived objects, x, y, and z, such that one is replaced by the next at t, t', and t''. x is characterized by tropes U and V, y is characterized by tropes V and Z, and z by U and Z. Hence, U and V are compresent, V and Z are compresent, and U and Z are compresent. (U, V, and Z endure.) Furthermore, suppose that the compresence trope in each case is the same, an enduring compresence trope, C. U, V, and Z, then, form a complete complex of compresence even though no object corresponds to that complex. In order to exclude this possibility, it is advisable to assume that compresence tropes are momentary. Given the latter assumption, we could not attribute the same compresence trope to these three objects at these different times.

Does the proponent of a Universals-Bundle Theory have a similar option of including the compresence relation in the bundle as a basis for solving the problem of change for Bundle Theory? Suppose that C is the compresence universal. If C is included in the FGH bundle at t and the FGH bundle at t', the result is a $FGHC$ bundle at one time and a $FGHC$ bundle at the other time. Since C is a universal relation relating the same universals in each bundle, we still have not distinguished the bundles. Alternately, we might think of C as a relation that takes both universals and times as its relata. C would then relate F, G, and H to t in one instance and to t' in the other. That might mean that C is included in each bundle, but one of its relata, the time, is not included in the bundle. But then the bundles at t and at t' would not be distinguishable by their members. Or, it might mean that along with C, the time is also a constituent of the bundle. Each bundle would include F, G, H, and C, and as a constituent of C, a particular time, *t* in one case and *t'* in the other, making these bundles distinguishable from one another. This interpretation abandons Bundle Theory since Bundle Theory makes momentary objects bundles of properties, not bundles of properties and other sorts of things, such as times.[8]

It might be suggested that the instantiation of *C* (the compresence universal) at a time, if that instantiation is momentary, distinguishes the bundles, even if *C* itself does not do so. In fact, this suggestion will not help. If instantiation or exemplification is a genuine entity that qualifies as a particular, the Universals-Bundle Theory cannot include it as a constituent in the bundle since those constituents are limited to universals. And, if it is a universal, it is not clear how this helps.

At this point, we need to say more about what it is for a trope to be momentary so as to demonstrate that the inclusion of a momentary compresence trope in the bundle does not require inclusion of a non-property component, a time, in the bundle. What is it for a trope to be momentary? If a momentary trope is read as a relation to a time, then, the time itself would have to be included as a constituent of *C*, and, hence, of the bundle. Fortunately, there is another interpretation. A momentary trope is time-indexed, but it is not a relation to a time nor does it include a time as a constituent. A momentary trope exists for only a moment and cannot be wholly present at more than one moment, but being momentary in this sense is compatible with not being a relation to a time or including a time as a constituent. A momentary trope may be momentary just in the sense that instantaneous temporal stages are momentary on a temporal parts account of object persistence. An object's instantaneous temporal stages, if there are any, are necessarily momentary. But they are not relations to a time and do not include times as constituents. They are simply necessarily short-lived objects.[9] I propose that we adopt this second conception of momentary tropes along with the claim that compresence is a momentary trope and each complete bundle includes a compresence trope. That will guarantee that Bundle Theory is compatible with four-dimensionalism even in the case of unchanging persisting objects.

But that leaves the question of choosing between Worm and Stage Theory. There is a reason to prefer a Stage Theory version of Bundle Theory. The bundle component of Worm-Bundle Theory is a theory of instantaneous stages, which are merely proper parts of objects. The effect is to abandon a strict Bundle Theory of objects and substitute a Bundle Theory of something else, instantaneous object stages and then go from there to

---

[8] It might seem that there is a third possibility. Each *C* (in each bundle) is a "time-indexed" universal without including a time as a constituent, analogous to our conception of a momentary trope. The challenge for this proposal is in giving an interpretation of "time-indexed" universals that distinguishes temporally distinct bundles, but does not include times in the bundles. No such interpretation is reasonable if properties are universals. Either the time is included in each *C* and we abandon Bundle Theory, or the time is not included and we cannot distinguish the bundles. The root of this dilemma is that universals as such are not dated and the only way to generate a dated "universal" that distinguishes exactly similar universals except for their time of instantiation is by inclusion of the time.

[9] Under this second conception, momentary tropes are short-lived particularized properties and relations that have a temporal location just in the same sense that the temporal parts of objects do.

a theory of objects. Stage Theory does not have this limitation. Although a Stage-Bundle Theory makes bundles instantaneous stages—and not space-time worms—it also makes these stages ordinary continuants, objects.

1.2.1 A possible objection I have argued that in order to restore symmetry in a bundle-theoretic four-dimensionalist account of object persistence, compresence should be viewed as a momentary trope. My argument assumes that bundles that have the same constituents are identical (call that the "constituency principle"), but that principle might very well be false. If that principle is false, it does not follow from the fact that two bundles share all of their constituents, that those bundles are identical. For example, if that principle is false, it might turn out that bundles at different times that are wholly constituted by the same tropes (or universals) are, nonetheless, not identical.

This principle is *not* false if trope bundles are mereological sums of their constituent tropes since the "constituency principle" applies to mereological sums. Hence, the proponent of this possible objection must also reject the claim that bundles are mereological sums of properties and suggest some alternative conception of bundles. So let's consider some alternative, non-mereological conceptions to see whether any of them guarantee that the constituency principle fails for bundles and fails in the *right* way.

Suppose that bundles are sets, not mereological sums. Will this help? If bundles are sets, the constituency principle will apply given that the members of a set are its sole constituents. Sets, although not mereological sums of their members, are the same if and only if they have the same members. So failing to be a mereological sum of its constituents *in this way* would not establish that a bundle did not satisfy a constituency principle.

Suppose that bundles are Armstrongian states of affairs, which operate under a principle of composition that violates the constituency principle such that states of affairs with the same constituents may fail to be identical: the state of affairs of Bob's loving Sally appears not to be identical to the state of affairs of Sally's loving Bob, even though they have the same constituents (Bob, Sally, and loves). If bundles are Armstrongian states of affairs, then they will not satisfy the constituency principle. Does this mean that bundles at distinct times will not be identical? No. To see why not, notice that states of affairs will violate the constituency principle only if they differ internally, even if not with respect to their constituents. "Bob's loving Sally" differs from "Sally's loving Bob" with respect to the internal ordering of their constituents. There is no reason to think that states of affairs at different times with the same constituents must differ internally. In short, even if bundles are states of affairs, they would still conform to a modified "constituency principle": states of affairs are identical if and only if they share all their constituents and are internally ordered in the same way. We can then suppose that in our persistence case, the enduring tropes/universals that are the shared constituents of the bundles at t and t' are internally arranged in the same way at those different times.

Alternatively, it might be argued that any non-zero temporal distance between bundles, even if those bundles share all their constituents and those constituents are arranged internally in the same way, is sufficient for the non-identity of those bundles. The difficulty is that a non-zero temporal distance is not sufficient for the non-identity of tropes/universals, the constituents of bundles, and it is reasonable to presume that the same is true for bundles unless some non-question-begging reason is given to think otherwise.

2. Problems for universals-based Bundle Theory

Although the problems of essential properties and change for Bundle Theory do not depend on whether the bundle properties are tropes or universals, some objections to Bundle Theory do so depend. I will now consider two objections to Bundle Theory on the assumption that properties are universals. The universals-based Bundle Theory I have in mind does not allow for any irreducible particulars: "irreducible particulars have no place in a perspicuous description of the world" (O'Leary-Hawthorne and Cover 1998: 205). The second of these objections, the Duplication Objection, is especially important since it provides a reason for a bundle theorist to adopt Trope Bundle Theory.

(A) COMPLEX OF COMPRESENT UNIVERSALS BUT NO OBJECT

The first objection is that the constituent universals of a complex of compresent universals may fail to characterize jointly any one object. There can be complexes of compresent universals that do not correspond to any one object (Armstrong 1989a: 71).

> Suppose that universals P and Q are compresent in object a, universal Q and R are compresent in object b, and universals R and P are compresent in object c, but nothing, including any of these objects, has all three of these properties. Since these properties are pairwise compresent, universals P, Q, and R form a complex of compresence without constituting an object.

Furthermore, it will not help to bring in the requirement that such complexes be complete, including all and only the properties that are compresent with all of the properties in the bundle. We can simply stipulate that no other property is compresent with all three of these properties, P, Q, and R. Can this problem be solved for a universals-based Bundle Theory? O'Leary-Hawthorne and Cover suggest that it can be by modifying what is generally assumed about the compresence relation, that it is a two-place relation. O'Leary-Hawthorne and Cover suggest that this assumption is optional and should be replaced. Compresence is better thought of as either a variable-polyadic relation or as various $2+n$-adic relations. n universals form a bundle only if there is "some n-adic bundling relation or compresence relation they stand in" (1998: 219, footnote 8). Under this proposal, it will be denied that P, Q, and R in our example stand to each other in a three-place compresence relation, which they must if they are to characterize a single object. Since I myself will postulate that compresence is a variable-polyadic relation or that there are various 2+n-adic compresence relations as part of my response to infinite regress objections to Trope Bundle Theory, I will not dispute this response to this objection.

Note that Trope Theory is generally thought to be exempt from this objection on the grounds that if properties are tropes, then since, for instance, the Q property of a is not identical to the Q property of b, the tropes involved will not form a complex of compresence even if compresence is invariably a dyadic relation. However, as indicated in 1.2, Trope Bundle Theory will face a similar problem unless compresence tropes are momentary.

(B) THE DUPLICATION PROBLEM

The second objection to a universals-based Bundle Theory, the duplication objection, comes in two versions, depending on the scope of a universals-based Bundle Theory. Bundle Theory may either be thought of as a claim about the actual world or about all possible worlds (O'Leary-Hawthorne and Cover 1998). According to the first version, the universals-based Bundle Theory claims that in the actual world substances are constituted out of universals. On the second version, Bundle Theory makes that same claim about all possible substances and all possible worlds: every possible world is wholly constituted out of universals and every particular object in every world is a sum of universals. The "duplication" objection is, as directed to the second version, that Universals-Bundle Theory wrongly makes the principle of the Identity of Indiscernibles necessarily true.

> Necessarily, bundles of universals are identical if they include all the same universals, so if all possible particular objects are bundles of universals, necessarily, objects are identical if they share all their properties. But, the Identity of Indiscernibles Principle is not necessarily true.

If the properties referred to in this principle are restricted to non-relational properties, this principle entails that, necessarily, objects that are indiscernible with respect to their *non-relational* properties are identical, but pairs of non-identical objects sharing all their non-relational universals are certainly possible.[10] If the properties referred to in the Principle include relational properties, then the Principle says that, necessarily, objects that are indiscernible with respect to their non-relational and their (pure) relational universals are identical. But, non-identical objects that are indiscernible in this way are also possible.[11] For example, in "Black's World," there are two qualitatively identical

---

[10] Armstrong excludes "properties" such as "being identical with a" as admissible non-relational properties on the grounds that they are not universals and, second, because "this 'property' involves the very thing which the theory seeks to analyze: the particular a itself" (1978a: 93).

[11] An example of an impure relational property is "being a cousin of John Kerry." An example of a pure relational property is "being a cousin of someone." Since the theory reduces ordinary particulars to bundles of universals, impure relational properties cannot be included in the bundles (1978a: 94).

spheres in a relational space. These spheres are the same size and mass as well as color, but at a non-zero spatial distance from each other.[12] Although numerically distinct, these spheres are indiscernible with respect to their non-relational and their (pure) relational properties (Black 1952; see also Armstrong 1978a: 95–6 and Ayer 1954: 34).[13]

A similar objection can be directed against the actual-world restricted version of Bundle Theory according to which the particulars objects of the actual world are wholly constituted out of universals as are any other actual particulars, including locations. (The "actual" version of Bundle Theory is compatible with there being some particular object in some merely possible world that is not wholly constituted out of properties, say, because it includes a bare particular, a possibility, if genuine, that would make the Identity of Indiscernibles Principle not necessarily true.)

> For at least some actual concrete particular, x, it is possible that there is a duplicate of x, but for any bundle of universals, y, it is not possible that there is a duplicate of y (a bundle of universals with all and only the universals as y that is numerically distinct from y).

O'Leary-Hawthorne and Cover present this objection as follows:

Consider some electron e. Couldn't there be entities that are intrinsic duplicates of e but which are nevertheless distinct from e? It seems so. Consider a mereological sum of universals. Could there be a mereological sum s of universals that is qualitatively identical but numerically distinct from s? It seems not. In short, the principle of the Identity of Indiscernibles appears to be true of mereological sums of universals, but not of ordinary individuals. And so it seems that ordinary individuals are not mereological sums of universals (1998: 211).[14]

---

[12] In response to cases meant to demonstrate the possibility of non-identical but qualitatively indistinguishable objects in a symmetrical universe, Hacking (1975) has argued that all such cases can be redescribed as involving only one object in a non-absolute space. "It is vain to contemplate possible spatiotemporal words to refute or establish the identity of indiscernibles" (1975: 249). As a counter to such skepticism, Adams (1979: 17–19) argues that since it is possible for there to exist non-identical objects that are only slightly different qualitatively from each other, then there could also exist a case of two objects that are exactly similar qualitatively (a limiting cases as the objects become more and more alike). Rodriguez-Pereyra (2004: 74) gives a similar argument with which I concur: "But Black's world *is* possible. For there is a possible world with two almost indiscernible spheres. That is, there is a possible world like Black's except that the spheres differ infinitesimally in temperature. No one should deny the possibility of such worlds, and certainly there is nothing in them that a bundle theorist cannot accept. That world contains *two* particular spheres, a and b. But if a has a temperature T and a different particular b of the same kind as a has a temperature T★ infinitesimally different from T, then it is possible for a to have T★. Thus if the world with the almost indiscernible spheres is possible, so is another world in which the spheres are completely indiscernible. So Black's world, which contains two indiscernible particulars, is possible."

[13] Another argument against the Universals-Bundle Theory is the following: one particular might have only properties of another particular but lack some of those properties such that the properties of the first are a sub-set of those of the second and, hence, not a complete complex of compresent properties (Armstrong 1978a: 97).

[14] The idea is that since e is a sum wholly constituted out of its properties and necessarily e is such a sum (e could not have included in addition to its properties, say, a bare particular), then necessarily any indiscernible bundle is identical to e. So any world in which there is a sum identical to e, there is only one such sum in that world. If so, then e could not have had a duplicate. But, the objection goes, e could have had

How might the Universals-Bundle theorist respond to this version of the duplication objection?

One response brings into play relations and relational properties by supposing that bundles include both relations and relational properties: even if we grant the possibility that *e* could have existed in a world with an intrinsically indiscernible duplicate, the electrons that make up that pair will be discernible relationally (after all, they would exist at different locations). There is no possible world with numerically distinct electrons that are indiscernible when relations and relational properties are counted as relevant to discernibility.[15] Even though universals-based Bundle Theory has the implication that *e* could not have had a duplicate—there could not have been indiscernible but numerically distinct electrons just like *e*—that is not really a problem for Bundle Theory since *e* could not have had an intrinsic and relational duplicate.[16] O'Leary-Hawthorne and Cover rightly dismiss this response. Electron *e* could have existed in a symmetrical world, a Black world, in which there existed also a duplicate of that electron that duplicated not only its non-relational universals but its (pure) relations and relational properties.[17] "In such a world there would seem to be no differences between the electrons, not even relational differences. Assume that the ontological nature of ordinary electrons to be as the bundle theorist depicts it to be, and this symmetrical universe looks to be ruled out. But that is to rule out as impossible what is clearly possible" (O'Leary-Hawthorne and Cover 1998: 211).

2.1 The "Bi-Located Electron" reply

The most interesting response to the duplication objection, in either version, is the one suggested by O'Leary-Hawthorne and Cover.

According to the theory of immanent universals, it is routinely true that universals can be fully present in many places—that is, at some distance from themselves. It is thus of a piece with the Bundle Theory that a bundle of universals can be fully present at many places at once (1998: 212).

It is possible that the electron, since it is a bundle of universals, could have been 5 feet from itself, wholly present in two places at once, a single bundle some distance from

---

a duplicate. Notice that this objection also applies to a Universals-Bundle Theory that claims application to all possible worlds. Also notice that this objection does not require that there exist an actual individual with an actual intrinsic duplicate, but only that there is at least one actual individual, the electron *e*, that could have had a duplicate.

[15] So even if there could not be a mereological sum *s* of universals that is qualitatively identical but numerically distinct from *s*, and even if electron *e* is a mereological sum of universals, there is no "duplication" problem for Bundle Theory, since electron *e* could not really have had an intrinsic and relational duplicate.

[16] Electron *e* could have had such a duplicate only if there is a world in which there are two electrons that are numerically distinct but indiscernible, including relationally, but, according to this response, there is no such world.

[17] In particular, there is a possible world in which a pair of electrons exist in a symmetrical universe, and, hence, do not differ in terms of their (pure) relations and relational properties.

itself. Although there is some sense in which the objector is right—that it is possible that there could have been intrinsic and relational duplicates of the electron—strictly speaking, the possibility envisioned is misdescribed as "duplication." What could have been the case is that that *one* electron could have been in two places at the same time. Actual substantial particulars, being bundles of universals, have the capacity for multiple locations at the same time, because their sole constituents, universals, do. Call this the "Bi-Located Electron" response.

2.1.1 What's wrong with the Bi-Located Electron response in a world of universals I want to suggest that this is not a coherent response, at least given Pure Universalism, a view defended by O'Leary-Hawthorne and Cover. *Pure Universalism* is the view that there are no irreducible particulars.[18] Here is an argument against the Bi-Located Response.

> The Argument from Local External Relations: Suppose that object-bundle *a* at location *L* is 2 feet from bundle *c* at *L"* and bundle *b* at *L'*, is *not* 2 feet from bundle *c*. Suppose that bundle *a* and bundle *b* are identical, bi-located bundles. It follows that bundle *a* is 2 feet from bundle *c* and bundle *a* is not 2 feet from bundle *c* since *a* and *b* are identical. But that is contradictory.

How might one respond to this argument? Let's begin with the assumption that the spatial relations and failures of spatial relations between bundles are somehow derivative on the spatial relations—or failures of spatial relations—among the universals that wholly constitute those bundles. Also assume that the spatial relations and failures thereof between the universals that constitute the relevant bundles are not derivative on spatial relations or failures of spatial relations among anything else, including between spatial points. In particular, suppose that the truth of "bundle *a* at *L* is 2 feet from bundle *c* at *L"* " derives from the fact that every universal that is a constituent of *a* is 2 feet from each universal that is a constituent of *c*. For example, the fact that *a* is 2 feet from *c* derives, in part, from the fact that universal, *U*, instantiated by *a* and a universal, *V*, instantiated by *c* are such that *U* at *L* is 2 feet from *V* at *L"*. And assume that the truth of "bundle *b* at *L'* is *not* 2 feet from bundle *c*" similarly derives from the fact that each universal instantiated by *b* is *not* 2 feet from each universal instantiated by *c*. In particular, suppose that the fact that *b* is not 2 feet from *c* derives, in part, from the fact that there is a universal *U'* instantiated by *b* and a universal instantiated by *c*, *V*, such that *U'* at *L'* is not 2 feet from *V* at *L"*. So now let's focus in on those non-derivative spatial relations and failures thereof between universals to determine if this will provide a way around the argument from local external relations against the Bi-Located Response.

In fact, making the spatial relations and failures thereof among bundles derivative in this way will not provide any real help since we can simply repeat the "argument from local external relations" at the level of these universals, recalling that *a* and *b* are

---

[18] My objection may or may not hold against the view that concrete particulars such as tables and chairs are bundles of universals, but there are some irreducible particulars, for example, locations.

indistinguishable with respect to their constituent universals. So suppose that U and U' are identical in this case. U at L is 2 feet from V at L'' and U' at L' is not 2 feet from V at L''. But since U at L is identical to U' at L' we have a contradiction: U is 2 feet from V and U is not 2 feet from V. So it would appear that making the spatial relations and failures thereof of bundles of universals derivative on the spatial relations and failures thereof of their constituent universals does not avoid contradiction.

However, before fully endorsing this application of the argument from local external relations to universals, we need to consider possible ways around the argument from local relations as it is applies to universals.

(A) CATEGORY MISTAKE

The first counter-response is modeled on a defense of universals against a related charge. The charge is that the same universal could be wholly present in more than one location at the same time, but nothing can do that. One response to *this* charge is to claim that it encodes a category mistake.[19] A universal can be in more than one place at the same time because it is a universal, but particulars cannot and there is no further explanation for this difference. A similar category defense might be applied to the argument from local external relations.

> Two particulars cannot be 2 feet and not 2 feet apart from each other, but two universals can be.

This is a category-based difference between universals and particulars, a difference that has no further metaphysical explanation. As it stands, this defense amounts to a flat denial that it is contradictory for U to be both 2 feet and not 2 feet from V at the same time. But this is unpersuasive, since it is not possible for x to both have and not have a specific relation R to y no matter under which category x and y might fall.

> What is really needed is some way to block the argument from
> "U at L is 2 feet from V and U at L' is not 2 feet from V"

to

> "U is 2 feet from and not 2 feet from V."

For example, one might find some genuine basis for challenging the identity claim or argue that the premise, when properly interpreted, does not entail the conclusion. I will explore a number of possible reasons.

(B) LOCALISM

Consider an argument analogous to the argument from local external relations as applied to enduring particulars.

---

[19] "The supposition that it is absurd for a quality to be in two places at once comes from confusing qualities with particulars... The question is answered first by specifying the category or ontological type... and then point out that certain things are or fail to be true of it just because it belongs to that type" (Landesman 1971: 6).

The Argument from Temporary External Relations: if enduring objects *a* and *b* are each wholly present at distinct times *t* and *t'* and *a* is 2 feet from *b* at *t*, but *a* is not 2 feet from *b* at *t'*, then *a* is both 2 feet from *b* and *a* is not 2 feet from *b*. But the same object can't be both 2 feet and not 2 feet from another object.

The presentist rejects this argument on the grounds that there are no times except for the present and, hence, no (contradictory) relations between the enduring particulars holding at different times.[20] A spatial analogue would be the following. Only one spatial region in our example (of the two), either that occupied by *a* and *c* or by *b* and *c*, is real. Hence, there are no (contradictory) spatial relations holding across *both* of those regions.[21] Presentism may or may not be wildly implausible, but localism as described certainly is. We can move on.

(c) TROPE RESPONSE

A second possible response is modeled on a response to the problem of temporary external relations that treats spatial relations as momentary tropes not capable of being wholly present at more than one distinct time. According to the latter, in our example of temporary spatial relations between *a* and *b*, one and only one member of the *t*-class of distance relations (a 2-foot-apart trope) relates *a* and *b*, and one and only one member of the *t'*-class of distance relations (a non-2-foot-apart trope) relates *a* and *b*. These momentary trope relations from different times are compatible. A similar response is available to the problem of temporary intrinsics (see Chapter 2). The spatial analogue treats external relations as necessarily local tropes. External relations are tropes not capable of being wholly present at more than one distinct location. One and only one member of the location-*X* class of distance relations (a 2-foot-apart trope) relates *U* and *V*, and no *Y*-class 2-foot-apart trope relates *U* and *V*. *X* includes the locations of *a* and *b*, and *Y* includes the locations of *a* and *c*. These attributions are compatible.[22] This response, however, is not available to the defender of non-derivative spatial relations between universals who will certainly not want to treat distance relations as tropes.[23]

---

[20] For a discussion of the related problem of temporary intrinsics and responses to that problem that parallel the responses described below (except for the Trope view), see (Lewis 1986b: 202–5).

[21] Localism rejects the premise that *U* at *L* is 2 feet from *V* and *U* at *L'* is not 2 feet (but some other distance) from *V*. One or the other of these conjuncts is false, since one of these spatial regions doesn't exist.

[22] The inference from "*U* at *L* is 2 feet from *V* and *U* at *L'* is not 2 feet from *V*" to "*U* is 2 feet from and not 2 feet from *V*" does not hold up. The premise should be read as affirming a certain 2-foot-apart trope of *U* and *V* but as denying any 2-foot-apart trope from a different class of tropes. The conclusion, which affirms and denies the same 2-foot-apart relation, does not follow. See my (1997b: 254–8).

[23] An alternative might be to treat distance relations of some universals as somehow derivative on the distance relations of universals such as "being at *L*." But if "*L*" refers to a location, understood to be an irreducible particular, not a universal, this is not an option under Pure Universalism. On the other hand, it might be suggested that even if locations are not irreducible particulars, these location universals, such as "being at *L*," act like particulars—in not being instanced at multiple locations—providing a basis for getting around the Argument from Local External Relations. In fact, I don't see why "being at *L*" would act like a particular if "*L*" does not pick out a location understood to be an irreducible particular.

(D) SPATIAL PARTS

Another strategy can be derived from the temporal parts response to the problem of temporary external relations: two simultaneous temporal parts of a and b are 2 feet apart and a *different* pair of simultaneous temporal parts of a and b are not 2 feet apart. The spatial analogue posits spatial parts of universals U and V. The L-located U is a distinct spatial part of a larger (scattered) whole that includes the *distinct* L'-located U, also a spatial part. As such, the L-located U may be 2 feet from V even if the L'-located U is not 2 feet from V.[24] This response, like the trope view, is not available to the defender of universals. If properties are universals, then exactly similar properties are identical, and we cannot divide up U spatially and retain the view that U is a universal. U is wholly present—not merely partially present—at each location of instantiation.

(E) SPACE INDEXING

This last response relativizes the distance relation, understood as a universal, to a third place for location (or the having relation to a further place for location). This response is analogous to the "time-indexing" response to the problem of temporary external relations: every distance relation universal has a third argument place for times, and as a consequence, a, b, and t, in our example, stand in the 2-foot-apart-at relation and, compatible with this, a, b, and t' (a different set of relata) do not stand in the 2-foot-apart-at relation. The spatial analogue runs as follows. Distance relations have an additional place for spatial location (and maybe a fourth place for times).[25]

> Where X includes the locations of a and b and Y includes the locations of a and c, U is 2-feet-relative-to-*location* X from V, but U is not 2-feet-relative-to-*location* Y from V. There is no contradiction since there is a difference in one argument place.[26]

---

[24] U-at-L and U-at-L' are not identical, and thus the inference from "U at L is 2 feet from V and U at L' is not 2 feet from V" to "U is 2 feet from and not 2 feet from V" is blocked.

[25] The key to this strategy is that two universals may both bear and not bear to each other the same distance relation if there is difference in the third place for locations. It is not just that the relation is three-placed. If the relata are held constant, then the contradiction would remain. But in our example we do find a suitable variation in this third place.

[26] However, the *Distance-as-Three-Placed* strategy does not even ostensibly work for all variations of the problem of local external relations. Consider a new case:

> U and V are each instantiated twice at t, once each at the North and South Pole, perfectly overlapping at each Pole. U at the North Pole is north of V at the South Pole and U at the South Pole is not north of V at the North Pole. The apparent contradiction then is this: U is both north and not north of V.

To apply the *Distance-as-Three-Placed* view successfully, we need to show that U stands north-of V relative-to-X, but U does not stand north-of V relative-to-Y, where X and Y are *different* locations. Is there any choice for X and Y that will make this work? If X is the North Pole alone, then since the North Pole instantiation of U is not north of the North Pole instantiation of V, it is false that U stands north-of-at the North Pole to V. The same point applies if X and Y are the South Pole. We need X (and Y) to include both the North Pole and the South Pole. So suppose that X and Y are each "the North and South Pole." In that case, X and Y include exactly the same locations, and the apparent contradiction is not dispelled. X and Y must be different. But there are no viable candidates for different values. However, there may be more complicated variants of the "relativization to a location" strategy that will handle this case, at least if Pure Universalism is not assumed to be true (see Gilmore 2003).

The contradiction is then eliminated since no claim is made that the same relation with the same relata both holds and does not hold. How are we to understand this response? The space indexing response will either be combined with Space-Time Relationalism or with Space-Time Absolutism. In discussing this response, we need to keep in mind that locations are not irreducible particulars, given Pure Universalism, the thesis that the actual world (or all possible worlds) and its contents are constituted solely out of universals.

Consider the Space-Time Relationalism option. On this view, there are no spatial relations among locations that are independent of the spatial relations among the occupants of space, in this case universals and bundles of universals. The relativizing strategy works only if there is some distance between location X and location Y (or at least between a part of X and a part of Y), otherwise X and Y are not different and then we still have a contradiction since the relativizing strategy eliminates the contradiction only if there is a difference in the location relata. So what makes it true that there is a distance between X and Y? On the relationist view, that is grounded on the spatial relations of the contents of space: here universals and bundles of universals. But positing non-derivative truths about relations and the failure thereof among universals or between bundles of universals, given Pure Universalism and the Bi-Located Response, leads to contradictions (or, so says the argument from local external relations). So the proponent of the space indexing option, which is aimed at helping us avoid contradictory spatial relations between universals, cannot appeal to non-derivative spatial relations/failures of spatial relations between universals or between bundles of universals at this point.

Now consider the Space-Time Absolutism option. On this view, locations stand to each other in spatial relations that are independent of the spatial relations among the occupants of space. But now notice that we cannot assume that points are non-reducible particulars. So assume that there is just one Pointhood universal with many instances. The first problem is that for the relativization approach to work there must be more than one point, because the relativization strategy requires at least some universals to be paired with different points, but if there is just one Pointhood universal it is hard to see how that can be. Second, the Space-Time Absolutism option will work only if spatial points can non-derivatively stand in/fail to stand in spatial relations to each other. But if there is only one universal, Pointhood, the Argument from Local External Relations applies to it:

> *The Argument from Local External Relations Applied to Pointhood*: Assume that the universal Pointhood has spatial relations non-derivatively to itself. Suppose that Pointhood of one instantiation, I, is 2 feet from Pointhood of a different instantiation, I'. Pointhood, then, is 2 feet from Pointhood. But now consider another instance I'' of Pointhood. Pointhood of instance I'' is not 2 feet from Pointhood of instance, I. The Pointhood of instantiation I is 2 feet from Pointhood of instantiation I' and not 2 feet from Pointhood of instantiation I''. Since the Pointhood of I is

identical to the Pointhood of *l'* and the Pointhood of *l"*, all of which are identical to Pointhood, Pointhood is 2 feet from Pointhood and Pointhood is not 2 feet from Pointhood. But that is contradictory.

This argument also shows why we cannot make the spatial relations and failures of spatial relations among bundles derivative on the spatial relations and failures of spatial relations among spatial points given Pure Universalism.

There is one further line of response worth considering. The Argument from Local External Relations that is being directed against universals-based Bundle Theory in the context of Pure Universalism involves the claim that, in our example, bundle *b* at *L'* is *not* 2 feet from bundle *c*. In response, it might be suggested that in the situation described that is not true, since that same bundle is bi-located: given its *L* location, it is not true that bundle *b* is not 2 feet from *c*. The difficulty with this response is that we will then fail to account for the fact that *object b* is not 2 feet from object *c*. Given this response, we cannot derive this fact (or related facts) from any of the bundle-theoretic facts. This line of response is not compatible, for example, with the fact that something traveling from object *b* to object *c* would *not* travel a total of 2 feet. That amounts to a *reductio ad absurdum* of the claim that it is not the case that bundle *b* at *L'* is not 2 feet from bundle *c*.

2.2 Rodriguez-Pereyra's response

Another response to the duplication objection, proposed by Rodriguez-Pereyra, is to suggest that substantial particulars are not identical to bundles of universals, but are identical to instances of bundles of universals. A concrete object is wholly constituted by all of the universals it exemplifies, but that concrete object is not identical to the bundle of those universals. In addition, bundles of universals can be in two places at the same time, but not concrete particulars since concrete particulars, although constituted by universals which can be bi-located, are not identical to bundles of universals, but are identical to instances of bundles of universals, which cannot be bi-located.

"When a bundle is in a place, there is also another entity there, namely an instance of the bundle... the instance and the bundle are two distinct entities. Unlike the bundle itself, an instance of a bundle cannot be in more than one place at once. So a bundle that is in more than one place at once has more than one instance, one in each place in which it is... Thus this bundle of universals wholly located here is the same bundle as that bundle of universals wholly located there, but this instance hereof the bundle in question is not the same as that instance thereof the same bundle" (Rodriguez-Pereyra 2004: 78).

So electron *e* can have an indiscernible duplicate, *e'*, indiscernible both non-relationally and relationally in a Black world, such that *e* and *e'* are constituted by the same bundle of universals, but *e* and *e'* are not identical since each is a distinct instance of that bundle.

For this response to be convincing the constituency principle must be rejected and it is rejected by Rodriguez-Pereyra.[27] More specifically, he rejects the following principle:

(PCI) Necessarily, for all complex objects x and y and for every entity z, if z is a constituent of x if and only if z is a constituent of y, then x is numerically identical to y (Rodriguez-Pereyra 2004: 76).

If this principle is true then if x and y share all their constituents, then x and y are identical. So if this principle is true then if an instance of a bundle is wholly constituted by the bundle, then Rodriguez-Pereyra cannot be right in positing numerically distinct instances of the same bundle of universals. But Rodriguez-Pereyra argues that this principle is not, in fact, true for all modes of composition. For example, this principle fails to be true of the mode of compositions supposedly operative in Armstrongian states of affairs, for which possessing all their constituents in common is not sufficient for identity (Bob's loving Sally has the same constituents as Sally's loving Bob but is not identical to Sally's loving Bob). Still, his response will not work if the following weaker principle, which excludes states of affairs, applies to concrete particulars:

(PCI★) Necessarily, for all particulars x and y and for every entity z, if z is a constituent of x if and only if z is a constituent of y, then x is numerically identical to y (Rodriguez-Pereyra 2004: 77).

But Rodriguez-Pereyra rejects even this weaker principle since, he suggests, we have no positive reason for thinking that this weaker principle applies to concrete particulars. What would such a positive reason look like? A positive reason for thinking this principle applies to concrete particulars would be that the mode of composition that applies to concrete particulars obeys this principle. However, the most obvious ways of making it true of concrete objects—by treating concrete objects as mereological sums or sets of the universals that they exemplify—fails according to Rodriguez-Pereyra. It fails, he thinks, since all of the universals exemplified by a concrete object might exist (and hence that sum and set might exist) even if the object itself failed to exist. For example, although the universals U and V might exist and compose a sum and be members of a set, there may still be no object that is characterized by those universals. So concrete objects are not sums or sets of universals, according to Rodriguez-Pereyra. Since, Rodriguez-Pereyra asserts, there are no other such candidates for a mode of composition for concrete particulars—other than the set-theoretic or mereological modes of composition—that would obey PCI★, he concludes that there is no reason to adopt the weaker principle.

[27] Why does Rodriguez-Pereyra not include a time/place-bound instantiation/exemplification—understood as not a universal—in each bundle so that some bundles might differ in that way alone? If he did, Rodriguez-Pereyra would not have to abandon the constituency principle. Although this may be an option, the result would no longer be a version of Bundle Theory according to which concrete particulars are wholly constituted by universals (whether or not they are identical to such bundles). But Rodriguez-Pereyra wants to defend Bundle Theory, not abandon it.

What are we to make of this defense of Bundle Theory (modified to identify concrete particulars with instances of bundles rather than bundles *per se*)? The difficulty is that even if we reject (PCI*), that does not establish that differently located instances are numerically distinct. Even if sharing the same constituents is not sufficient for identity, it does not follow that a non-zero distance between instances *is* sufficient for their non-identity. The issue is whether or not there is any reason to think *instances of universals* always obey the principle that a non-zero distance is sufficient for their non-identity even though *universals* (and bundles of universals) themselves do *not* obey that principle.

One possible reason, which is not available to Rodriguez-Pereyra, is that instances but not bundles of universals include locations as constituents where locations are irreducible particulars. This reason is not available because it violates the assumption that bundles and instances are both wholly constituted out of universals.[28]

Another possible reason for thinking bundles of universals and instances of bundles of universals differ in this way might be that instances of bundles, but not bundles, are *states of affairs*. So let's suppose that instances of bundles are states of affairs. Now there certainly are examples, familiar from Armstrong, designed to show that states of affairs do not satisfy this principle. The difficulty is that none of the standard examples used to show that states of affairs violate PCI—such as our Bob–Sally case mentioned earlier—suggest that for states of affairs a non-zero distance between them is sufficient for non-identity. For example, in the Bob–Sally case, PCI is violated, if it is, not because of a difference in constituents, but only because the states of affairs involved—Bob's loving Sally and Sally's loving Bob—differ in the internal order of the constituents and certainly not because of a non-zero distance between these states of affairs.

A further option is to suggest that instances of universals/instances of bundles of universals and universals/bundles of universals just differ in this way without any further metaphysical explanation: instances of universals are numerically distinct if there is a non-zero distance between them. The difficulty with this response is that it presupposes that in general the distinction between instances of universals and universals is exclusive, but it is not. If instances of universals themselves may be universals and a non-zero distance between universals is not sufficient for their identity, then the mere postulation that concrete particulars are instances of universals will not guarantee that they are not universals, and, hence, that they fail to operate like universals in this respect. Might not an instance of a universal itself—for example, the instantiation of a universal *U* by another universal *U'*, which is an instance of *U*—be a universal? If so, an instance of a universal

---

[28] A referee makes the suggestion that even if locations are not irreducible particulars, perhaps singly instanced location universals—such as "being at L_1"—act like particulars. How might this help? Suppose that bundle *b* does not include any such "location universal," but that bundle *b* has the property of being at L_1. Different instantiations of bundle *b* will differ in this way, and that is the reason to think that *instances of universals* obey the principle that a non-zero distance is sufficient for their non-identity even though bundles of universals themselves do *not* obey that principle. The difficulty is that either "L_1" refers to irreducible particular or it does not. If it does, then the Pure Universalist cannot adopt this approach. But suppose that it refers to a particular that is wholly constituted by a bundle of universals. In that case, it is not clear that a non-zero-distance guarantees non-identity for such entities.

may be a universal and operate like a universal. If so, being an instance of a universal is not sufficient for not being universal. As a possible example of an instance that is also a universal consider Armstrong's view of laws. If it is a law that F's are G's where F and G are universals, that is a matter of a relation of necessitation, also a universal, holding between F-ness and G-ness. The state of affairs of F-ness necessitating G-ness, an instance of the relation of necessitation, is itself a universal. If it is a law that H's are K's, then that is a matter of that same relation of necessitation holding between H-ness and K-ness. And the state of affairs of H-ness necessitating K-ness, also an instance of the relation of necessitation, is itself a universal (Armstrong 1983: 89–90). Hence, these two instances of the universal of necessitation are themselves universals, and even if one rejects Armstrong's view of laws as problematic, or perhaps as incoherent, the point still stands as long as there are or could be higher-order universals. If, for example, H is a higher-order universal that characterizes lower-order universals, including universal F, then the state of affairs of F-ness instantiating H-ness, an instance of the universal, H-ness, is itself a universal (notice that this state of affairs does not include any particular, so it is not a particular even granting the "victory of particularity" principle).

The general point is that it is not enough to distinguish between a universal and an instance of a universal to demonstrate that that instance is itself not a universal (and if it is a universal, it might not satisfy the principle that a non-zero distance is sufficient for non-identity). The same point applies to bundles of universals and instances of bundles of universals.

Notice that neither of these objections—the Complexes-But-No-Object Objection and the Duplication Objection—applies to Trope Bundle Theory. In the case of the first objection, for example, it is supposed that property Q is shared by objects a and b, but if properties are tropes, such sharing is not possible. Even though the members of each pair have one exactly similar trope, they do not share any tropes literally. (Although, as indicated in 1.2, it is not quite right to say that this objection does not apply to Trope Bundle Theory if there are enduring tropes.) The Duplication Objection also depends on the assumption that properties are universals. If properties are tropes and even if objects are bundles of tropes, then the Principle of the Identity of Indiscernibles will not be necessarily true, and it will also be true that even if electron e is a bundle of tropes, it could have had a duplicate. There can be *non-identical* objects that are indiscernible in the sense of having non-identical but exactly similar tropes, including both their non-relational and relational properties. On the other hand, the principle will be unproblematically true if the principle is read as saying that objects literally sharing all the same tropes are identical.

3. Trope Bundle Theory and regress objections

I now turn to an objection that is meant to apply to Trope Bundle Theory. The objection is that Trope Bundle Theory involves an infinite regress or at least an uneconomical regress. The gist of this objection is the following:

120   PART I: TROPES

If compresence tropes must themselves be compresent with the other tropes in the bundle that will require a further compresence trope, and this pattern will be repeated without limit.

In this section, I will identify two regress objections that basically fit this outline, consider various responses in the literature, and, then, offer a response that disarms the supposed regresses. I will not investigate responses that admit the regress but deny that it is vicious (but notice that if it is not vicious it still might be uneconomical).[29] All of the responses that I consider deny that there is an infinite regress.

3.1 Two regress arguments against Bundle Theory

The first infinite regress objection is directed against a certain compresence-based conception of a bundle. The second focuses more on compresence itself.

> *Regress Argument 1*: we begin with two assumptions: (1) an object is a bundle b of mutually compresent tropes, and, for every pair of tropes, t_1 and t_2, in the same bundle b, there is a compresence trope, say c_1, linking those tropes; and (2) every compresence trope linking tropes in a bundle is also in that bundle. From (1) and (2), we can infer that c_1 is in bundle b and that there is a compresence trope, c_2, linking t_1 and c_1 (as well as one linking t_2 and c_1). But then c_2 is also in the bundle and there must be a compresence trope linking c_2 to c_3, and so on. This is a vicious regress.[30]

(1) and (2) are independent assumptions, and it is not argued that (2) follows from (1) and the general principle that if two tropes are compresent, then there is a third compresence trope that is compresent with each. In this argument, it is not *assumed* that if two tropes are compresent, then there is a third compresence trope that is compresent with each. Also note that (2) would only follow from (1) and this general principle if we strengthened (1) by saying that an object is a *complete* bundle of mutually compresent tropes—which (1) does not say—such that any trope t that is compresent with a trope in a bundle is also in that bundle.

Let's now turn to a second regress argument.[31]

---

[29] The regress of Regress Argument 2 seems to be vicious. In effect, it says that the requirements for the compresence of any two tropes involve an infinite series of compresence relations, and are, hence, so stringent that they could never be fulfilled. For a discussion of the question of what makes a regress vicious, see (Maurin 2002: 98–104).

[30] We also infer there must be an infinite sequence of states of affairs, t_1's being linked by c_1 to t_2, t_1 being linked by c_2 to c_1, t_1 being linked by c_3 to c_2 and so on. Assuming that (2) is true, we must give up (1) and conclude that objects are not bundles of compresent tropes.

[31] Maurin seems to be describing just this kind of regress argument when she says that if distinct tropes are existentially independent entities, "then the difference between the case where they are and the case where they are not compresent would have to be accounted for—thus forcing us to a vicious regress" (2002: 142). Or again: "... we must be able to distinguish the case where compresence in fact does obtain from the case where it does not. And, to do so, postulating the existence of a compresence relation, c, holding between tropes a and b will not be enough. The existence of tropes a and b and the existence of compresence, c, does *not* give us the compresence of a and b. To get that we need to also connect a with c and b with c, and so

Regress Argument 2: for tropes t_1 and t_2 to be compresent, they must be linked by a compresence trope, say c_1. But the existence of tropes t_1, t_2, and c_1 is insufficient to make it the case that t_1 and t_2 are compresent since these tropes could each be parts of different, non-overlapping bundles. For t_1 and t_2 to be linked by compresence trope c_1, c_1 must be compresent with t_1 by way of a further compresence relation, say c_2 (and with t_2 by, say, c_3). However, the existence of t_1, c_1, and c_2 is insufficient to make it the case that t_1 and c_1 are compresent—since each of the latter could be parts of different bundles. For t_1 and c_1 to be compresent by way of compresence trope c_2, c_2 must be compresent with t_1 by way of a further compresence trope, say c_4, and so on. This is a vicious regress.

This regress argument focuses on a different aspect of Bundle Theory than does Regress Argument 1. Regress Argument 2 focuses on the notion of compresence whereas the latter focuses on the notion of a bundle. I will now consider a number of responses to these arguments that can be found in the literature, followed by my own response.

3.2 Compresence tropes not parts of bundles

One possible reply to the first regress argument is to reject (2), the assumption that bundles include the compresence tropes that link tropes in the bundle. Compresence tropes are *not* parts of bundles. Although non-compresence tropes in a bundle are linked by compresence tropes, the latter are not also in the bundle. If c_1 is *not* a part of any bundle, we *cannot* infer that since c_1 is a part of the same bundle with t_1, c_1 is linked by compresence relation c_2 with t_1 and so on. The conception of bundles operative in Regress Argument 1, which includes compresence tropes in the bundle, is, thus, rejected.[32]

Although it is not *obviously* true that bundles include compresence tropes, I believe it is true for two reasons, the first of which is the most important.[33] As I suggested earlier, we can resolve the problem of change for Bundle Theory if the latter is combined with

---

on... For it to be true that a is compresent with b, the next step in the regress must be the case. That is, it must be true that a is compresent with c and that b is compresent with c. But then again, this step, to be true, requires the truth of the following step in the regress, and so on *ad infinitum*" (Maurin 2002: 162). Chris Daly in (1994–5: 259) also seems to have this regress in mind: "But what is it for F and G to be compresent? It cannot be just that F, G, and a compresence relation C exist. All these entities might exist without it being the case that F stands in C to G... Moreover, introducing another compresence relation C', and claiming that F, G, and C stand in C' to each other, does not help... F, G, C, and C' could all exist at a world without F, G, and C standing in C' to each other."

[32] This response is not a challenge to Regress Argument 2. Whether or not compresence tropes are in or outside of bundles is irrelevant to the structure of that argument, which focuses on the conditions required for compresence.

[33] An inadequate response to this reply consists in the claim that it is *obviously true* that bundles include compresence tropes. One might cite a structurally analogous, Bradley-style argument in which a parallel assumption is obviously true:

> Suppose that every thing in the universe must be related to all other things in the universe. In particular, suppose that objects o and o' are related by some relation R. But then since R is in the universe, it is related by some relation R' to o. In that case, R' is related to R, etc.

four-dimensionalism, but that combination will work only if compresence tropes, understood as momentary tropes, are included in the bundles.[34] Second, and more tentatively, the compresent trope itself will be located in the same location as the tropes it unites, and co-location is a *prima facie* reason for thinking that that compresence trope is itself compresent with those tropes. This reason is only *prima facie* because there can be cases in which co-located tropes are not compresent, for example, cases in which two particles of different types coincide spatially. But in cases in which there is no reason to think there are two different objects that coincide this reason is quite strong. Also, it seems safe to assume that in most cases, co-location and compresence run together.

3.3 Compresence is not compresent

The second response is also directed at Regress Argument 1, but it has indirect implications for Regress Argument 2.[35] This response to Regress Argument 1 proceeds by reconceiving the relationship between compresence tropes and bundles. The conception of a bundle operative in Regress Argument 1 does not allow any tropes to be parts of a bundle that are not compresent with the other tropes in the bundle. Call this the "no-non-compresent-tropes" assumption. But suppose that compresence tropes are in bundles without themselves being compresent with the other tropes in their bundles.[36] An object is a maximal sum of compresent tropes *plus* any compresence tropes linking those compresent tropes, but those compresence tropes are not also compresent with the tropes in that bundle. We, thus, reject the assumption that if a trope is in the bundle, it is compresent with the other parts of the bundle. The bundle still includes all the tropes that are compresent with any tropes in the bundle, but also a trope that is not compresent with the other tropes in the bundle. The regress of Regress

---

The parallel assumption here is that if a relation R relates two items in the universe, then R is *in the universe*, which *is* plainly true. Similarly, it might be claimed that the assumption that any compresence relation that relates tropes in a bundle is itself a part of that bundle is also obviously true. In fact, the truth of that claim is not obvious. It is one thing to assume that if something exists it is in the universe, but quite another to assume that if two tropes are related by a relation of compresence that relation is a part of the same bundle of which those tropes are parts.

[34] If each bundle includes a *momentary* compresence relation-trope, temporally distinct bundles will be distinguishable. *These* bundles can serve as temporal parts even if they share all their other (enduring) trope parts. This gives us a reason to postulate that each bundle includes a compresence trope and to hold that if two tropes of bundle B are related by a relation of compresence, that relation is also in B.

[35] This response is not a *direct* challenge to Regress Argument 2. The claim that compresence tropes are parts of bundles plays no role in Regress Argument 2. However, for this response to Regress Argument 1 to work, it must be false that a compresence relation linking tropes must itself be compresent with those tropes. Otherwise, it is incoherent to propose, as this response does, that t_1 and t_2 are linked by compresence trope c_1, but c_1 is not linked by a compresence trope to t_1 (or to t_2). But Regress Argument 2 depends on the truth of just that assumption. Hence, this response to Regress Argument 1 would indirectly rebut Regress Argument 2 by rejecting the "compresence-requires-compresence" assumption. And, obviously, any attack on Regress Argument 2 that works by rejecting this assumption, if successful, will also support this response to Regress Argument 1.

[36] I took this view in (2001) but now reject it (while retaining the view that compresence tropes are momentary and parts of bundles).

Argument 1 is stopped. We cannot infer that c_1 is compresent with any other tropes in the bundle from the fact that c_1 is in the bundle. (There must be some basis for excluding *other* non-compresent tropes from the bundle. The relevant restriction is that the only non-compresent tropes to get in are those that ground inclusion of the other non-compresence tropes in the bundle. Only the "glue" tropes gain entrance as an exception to the compresence rule.) The first response puts the compresence tropes outside the bundle. This response puts them inside, buts without "compresence ties" to their fellow tropes.

This response to Regress Argument 1 will be convincing only if there is a reason for thinking that compresence does *not* require compresence. Maurin offers the best defense for thinking as much.

The existence of a compresence relation necessitates the existence of its terms since generally relations necessitate their terms.[37] From that it follows that "... no further addition of relations is needed to provide for it" (Maurin 2002: 163–6).

First-order compresence relations hold in the absence of any higher-order compresence relations between them and their trope-terms (2002: 163–6). Compresence relations necessitate the existence of their own terms, so there is no need for a compresence relation between that relation and its terms.[38] In fact, this argument is not convincing.[39] First, as Maurin herself worries, "although it is reasonable to suppose that a relation *must relate something*, it is perhaps not reasonable to suppose that any particular relation must relate some *specific individuals*" (2002: 165).[40] Second, the general claim upon which this argument rests—that relations necessitate their terms—can be shown to be false by reference to universals. If relations are universals, then they do not necessitate their specific terms. Suppose, for example, that a stands in the "next to" universal relation to b, and that the "next to" relation does not hold between any other things. Still, it is intuitively clear that the universal "next to" relation could have related different relata and not related a and b.[41]

---

[37] Maurin, *If Tropes*: "In being a relation-trope it is of its essence that it *does* connect the entities it relates" (2002: 165).

[38] And if there is no need, we should not postulate such a relation (Maurin 2002: 164): "it must, *given that it exists*, relate the entities it does in fact relate." If sound, this argument would allow us to claim, contrary to Regress Argument 1, that compresence relations are not compresent with their terms, although these compresence tropes are parts of the same bundles as their terms in accord with the response under discussion. Regress Argument 2 would also be refuted. That argument depends on its being a contingent matter whether or not any particular compresence relation relates the trope terms it does.

[39] Even if it is not true that relations necessitate the existence of their terms, it may still be true that the same relation could not change its terms or survive the demise of its relata. R could have had different relata, but given that R's relata are a and b, it could not survive the demise of a or b or go on to have different relata.

[40] This is no more convincing—Maurin imagines an objector protesting—than that the terms of a relation always necessitate the relation.

[41] In response, it might be suggested that even if it is not true that relations necessitate their relata, a more restricted form of this principle may be true: *trope* relations necessitate their relata. But why think that? (1) Perhaps there is some difference between tropes and universals that makes it reasonable to think that trope relations necessitate their terms, but not universal relations. In fact, there does not appear to be such a relevant

I will now consider two replies that appeal to supervenience or internal relations to cut short any possible infinite regress.

3.4 The supervenience response to the Regress Arguments

The third response applies to both Regress Arguments.

> Since compresence is an internal relation, it supervenes on its terms, and since that which supervenes is nothing over and above its supervenience base, compresence tropes are no ontic addition to the non-compresence tropes in the bundle.[42] Compresence relations are "nothing over and above" their terms, the "ground-level" tropes in the bundle.[43] Hence, there is no infinite regress.

The difficulty is that this argument falters at two points, as pointed out by various philosophers. First, that which supervenes is sometimes something over and above its supervenience base.[44] Second, compresence is *not* an internal

---

difference. For example, the capacity for simultaneous multiple locations typically associated with universals, but not with tropes, supports at best the claim that different instances of the same type of relation at the same time involve different relation-tropes. At this point, it might be argued that there is a further difference between tropes and universals that Maurin could cite in support of her claim that trope relations necessitate their terms (even though universal relations do not). She might argue, as does Lewis, that the same universal can exist in more than one possible world, but not the same trope. From that assumption it might be inferred that it is false that the *same* trope relation could have had different relata. After all, it might be argued that that would only be true if that same trope exists in other worlds with different relata, but no trope exists in more than one world. This reply, however, goes wrong in two ways. First, it is predicated on the assumption that modal realism is true, which is far from being uncontroversial. Second, even if modal realism is true, it can still be true that a trope relation *r* could have had different relata. This will be true as long as there exists a counterpart to *r* in another world with different relata. A trope is a particular, and just as the modal realist holds that a concrete particular is world-bound but may still be such that it is not necessary that it has just the properties it has (because there is a counterpart to that object in another world that lacks some of those properties), the same kind of thing may be true of tropes. (2) Alternately, one might argue that this restricted principle is supported by C. B. Martin's thesis of the non-transferability of tropes. If trope *t* characterizes object *O*, then *t* could not have existed without characterizing *O*, and if trope relation *r* relates object *O* and object *O'*, then *r* could not have existed without relating *O* and *O'*. But this principle applies to relations that relate objects (or are such that at least one of the relata is an object). It does not apply to all trope–trope relations. Hence, even if tropes are non-transferable with respect to objects, it does not follow that all trope relations necessitate their relata, even if some (for example, those between objects) do.

[42] Armstrong reasons from the fact that resemblance is an internal relation to the fact that resemblance supervenes on the resembling properties, and, therefore, "it is not distinct from what it supervenes on" (1989a: 56). Campbell says, "*supervenient* 'additions' *to ontology are pseudo-additions*" (1990: 37). Peter Simons in (1994: 556) says, "Internal relations do not constitute ontological additions and arrest infinite regresses. Supervenience is ontologically innocuous."

[43] Campbell characterizes internal relations as follows: "Were the relation to change ... the terms would cease to exist ... *Being intermediate in colour*, as a relation among colour patches, is internal in this sense" (1990: 111). Or, again: "Internal relations are generated by their terms in all possible worlds. It is logically necessary that if A is canary yellow and B is ultramarine, then A is lighter than B" (1990: 112). This characterization of an internal relation works well for tropes, given that tropes are simple and cannot change.

[44] For example, triangularity strongly supervenes on trilaterality, but it is at least arguable that being triangular is something over and above being trilateral. This point is made by Rodriguez-Pereyra (2002: 110) about supervenience when discussing a similar approach to Regress Arguments concerning resemblance: "... even if resemblances supervene upon the natures of particulars, they may still be distinct from what they supervene upon ... in no normal account of supervenience does supervenience entail identity." Daly makes a

relation.[45] For example, a trope *t*, which is compresent with a place-trope *p*, can move without ceasing to exist, although in moving it ceases to be compresent with that place-trope, which continues to exist.[46] Compresent tropes could have existed without having been compresent with each other, making compresence an external relation.

3.5 No higher-order compresence tropes

A fourth response applies to both Regress Arguments and grants "first-order" compresence relations, but it denies higher-order compresence relations, while accepting that there are truths about compresence at higher levels. These higher-level compresence truths do not correspond to higher-level compresence relations. This response is modeled on Armstrong's defense against a similar regress argument:

> The instantiation regress can be halted after one step. We have to allow the introduction of a fundamental tie or nexus: instantiation... Do we have to advance any further? I do not think that we do. For note that the alleged advance is now, as it was not at the first step, logically determined by the postulated state of affairs... As we go on expanding the regress, our statements remain true, but no new truth-maker, or ontological ground, is required for all these statements to be true (1989a: 109–10).[47]

The corresponding reply in the compresence case would run as follows:

> The particular trope, t_1, is compresent with some other trope, t_2. So the compresence of t_1 with t_2 is itself compresent with t_1. But here we have another token of compresence. So that token of compresence is itself compresent with t_1. And so on *ad infinitum*. However, the compresence regress can be halted after one step. We have to allow the introduction of a fundamental tie or nexus, compresence. Do we have to advance any further? I do not think that we do. For note that the alleged advance is now, as it was not at the first step, logically determined by the postulated state of affairs. As we go on expanding the regress, our statements remain true, but no new truthmaker, or ontological ground, is required for all these statements to be true.

---

similar point: "For *resemblance* could be an ontic addition that is necessarily incurred given just the existence of its relata. Consider a parallel. There is a necessary connection between murderers and murders such that, necessarily, if murderers exist so do murders. But this does not show that a murder is not an ontic addition to the existence of a murderer" (Daly 1994–5: 258).

[45] Maurin says, "Compresence is an *external* relation. This means that, merely given the existence of two distinct tropes we are not thereby given their compresence" (2002: 162). Or, again, she argues that since compresence is an external relation, "we cannot, therefore, characterize the relation of compresence as *supervenient* on the entities it relates and, consequently, we cannot characterize it as *no ontological addition* to the already present relata tropes" (2002: 133). Simons also makes this point (1994: 558).

[46] This is a slightly modified case from Campbell (1990: 131) who uses it to show compresence is not a "founded" relation. Simons argues that compresence is not always an internal relation between tropes, if it ever is (1994: 558–9).

[47] Armstrong is responding to the following regress argument: "The particular *a* instantiates property *F*... So this state of affairs, *a*'s instantiating *F*, is a token of the type *instantiation*... The state of affairs instantiates instantiation. But here we have another token of instantiation. So the state of affairs (that state of affairs instantiating instantiation) also instantiates instantiation. And so on ad infinitum" (1989a: 108).

The difficulty is that even if the original response works for instantiation, the analogue response does not work for compresence. Although it certainly seems that the state of affairs of a's instantiating F determines that that very same state of affairs instantiates instantiation, it does not seem at all obvious that the fact that t_1 is compresent with t_2 determines that the compresence of t_1 with t_2 is compresent with t_1. The compresence of t_1 and t_2 does not seem to logically guarantee that that compresence relation, call it c_1, is compresent with t_1 (and with t_2). What does seem to be logically determined, at best, is that the state of affairs "t_1's being compresent with t_2" is a token of compresence, but that does not guarantee that c_1 is compresent with t_1 (or with t_2). This supposed logical relation between states of affairs here is no help in eliminating either of the regresses, which are set at the level of the components of that state of affairs. What seems to be guaranteed in both the Armstrong case and the trope case, at best, is that the existence of a certain state of affairs guarantees certain higher-order truths about that state of affairs. That may be enough for Armstrong's purposes, but it is not enough for the trope theorist. What the trope theorist needs to be logically determined are certain same-level truths about the compresence components involved in t_1's being compresent with t_2, not certain higher-level truths about the state of affairs of t_1's being compresent with t_2.

3.6 A relation predicate without a relation

A fifth response, directed at Regress Arguments 1 and 2, rejects the assumption that tropes which fall under the predicate "...is compresent with..." must be linked by compresence relation-tropes.[48] There is no relation-trope corresponding to the predicate "...is compresent with..." even though that predicate has some true applications.[49] This response might be indirectly supported by reference to Lewis's claim that "doing away with all unanalyzed predication is an unattainable aim, and so an unreasonable aim. No theory is to be faulted for failing to achieve it" (Lewis 1983b: 353). It is an impossible task to give an analysis of *all* predications since any analysis will bring into play a *new* predication, itself requiring analysis. It might be suggested that some such sentences are primitive and true, sentences that express fundamental facts of compresence. These sentences are not reducible or explainable further by reference to compresence tropes.

Although this is certainly a response open to the trope theorist, it is not the optimal response, at least without supplementation. In particular, it seems to invite the following objection: if it is acceptable to posit primitively true predication, then we would be perhaps well-advised to make that proposal much earlier in the chain, say for predications of the form "a is F," at least where "F" is a fundamental predicate, and thereby

---

[48] Oliver in (1996: 37) says when discussing the predicates, "...is exactly similar to..." and "...is compresent with..." that "it is a brute fact that these predicates apply to some pairs of tropes and not others. In particular, one ought to avoid saying that when two tropes are exactly similar or compresent, there exists a relation-trope of exact similarity or of compresence holding between the two tropes."

[49] And, it is added, there can be no regress without compresence tropes.

save ourselves from positing any properties whatsoever. The proponent of this response must provide some reason for choosing just this stopping point, other than the question begging one that it saves his position from the regress argument. One wants to know why it is just this point at which predications go primitive. It would be better if we could offer a trope-based explanation of why it is true that "*t* is compresent with *t'* "—at least for some cases—if it is true, such that those explanations provide a principle reason for determining at which point predications go primitive (with the result that we do not violate the Lewisian imperative not to take up the impossible task of providing an analysis of every predication). I will suggest below just such a response, which avoids the regress while also avoiding the impossible task.

3.7 The no-relation response

A sixth response, related to the fifth, is modeled on Armstrong's no-relation "tie" view of "instantiation." Armstrong considers the following regress argument:

> If instantiation, *I*, is a relation, then it is a universal. A new relation of instantiation must then hold between *I* and whatever *I* relates, but then that further relation of instantiation will also require an even further relation of instantiation.

This regress is stopped, says Armstrong, if the two "factors" of particularity and universality "are too intimately together" to speak of a relation between them. The idea is that if *x* and *y* are inseparable, then they are not related, even if they are "tied" together. (Armstrong says that "size and shape are inseparable in particulars, yet they are not related" (1978a: 109).) In the case of instantiation, "the thisness and nature are incapable of existing apart" (1978a: 109). "Instantiation" is a "tie," not a relation, and, hence, not subject to a relation regress. Similarly, it might be suggested that the union of compresent tropes in an object is too intimate to speak of a relation between them, since the tropes of the same object could not have existed apart.

This "inseparability" argument, however, fails for two reasons. First, inseparability is not incompatible with all relations such as internal relations, including resemblance. The properties of being triangular and being trilateral are inseparable, but they bear a certain degree of resemblance to each other. Second, not all the properties of an object are inseparable. Although it is reasonable to think that certain determinable properties such as size and shape are inseparable, the same point does not apply to every pair of fully determinate properties of an object.[50] A fully determinate color of an object, for example, could have existed apart from the specific shape of the object. Third, there is a serious difficulty with the claim itself—that compresence is a tie but not a relation. As Devitt points out in discussing Armstrong's claim that "instantiation" is such a

---

[50] Maurin, for example, says, "from the fact that any colour-trope requires the existence of some extension-trope, it does not follow that *this* colour-rope requires the existence of *this* extension-trope" (2002: 151). Simons (1994: 557) says, "We may admit that any extension requires *some* color trope, but it does not follow that this extension trope E requires just this color trope C..."

tie—such that "F-ness is in a" is non-relational and inexplicable: "Do we have the remotest idea of what the words 'in' and 'have' mean here if they are not construed as relational predicates? Armstrong's Realism replaces the explanatory failings of relational Realism with a complete mystery" (Devitt 1997: 98). Similar comments would apply to treating compresence as a non-relation "tie."[51]

3.8 Compresence as self-relating

I will now introduce my own response. There is no regress because the compresence relation itself is a special kind of relation, a "self-relating" relation, one that can take itself as one or more of its own arguments. As we move up the supposed regress, we do not find ourselves with *new* compresence tropes, and, hence, there is no infinite regress at all.

How might this work? The supposed infinite regress for the bundle theorist involves an unending series of compresence tropes, $c_1, c_2, \ldots$, and c_n.[52] But notice that the series, $c_1, c_2, \ldots$, and c_n in each argument is infinite only on the assumption that each iteration in the series involves a new compresence trope, or more accurately, that there is no point in the series after which each "additional" compresence trope is identical to some previous compresence trope in the series. But if compresence is a "self-relating" relation, this assumption may be false. For example, there is no infinite series of distinct compresence tropes if each compresence relation, c_{1+n}, is identical to c_1—if at each iteration we are simply appealing to c_1 again.

> Tropes t_1 and t_2 in bundle b are linked by a compresence trope c_1 which is in b. c_1 is linked by a compresence trope to t_1, but that linking compresence trope, c_2, is just c_1 itself, which is both a relation and one of its own relata.

c_1 is linked by c_1 to t_1. It is related by itself to t_1. c_1 does double duty. What about further elements in the series? There are no "new" compresence tropes not identical to the "original" c_1. The series stops at c_1. This approach stops the regress in both Regress Arguments.[53]

This response is modeled on what the realist could say about instantiation. Consider the following regress argument.

> Suppose that instantiation is a relation and that the particular a instantiates$_1$ property F... So this state of affairs, a's instantiating$_1$ F, is a token of the type *instantiation*. The state of affairs, a's instantiating$_1$ F, instantiates$_2$ instantiation$_3$. But here we have

---

[51] Nevertheless, and contrary to Devitt, one might hold that if there were no explanatorily adequate alternatives, we might reluctantly opt for this more mysterious alternative. My objection to this is that there is an explanatorily adequate alternative to the inherently mysterious no-relation "tie" view, which I will now describe.
[52] Instead of the unending series of states of affairs facing the realist about universals.
[53] As a rejoinder to Regress Argument 1, this response retains the original conception of a bundle and the assumption that a compresence relation can link tropes only if it is itself compresent with those tropes.

another token of instantiation. So the state of affairs (that state of affairs instantiates$_2$ instantiation$_3$) also instantiates$_4$ instantiation$_5$.

The realist is not worried that there may be an infinite regress of "instantiation" relations because instantiation is a universal, if it is a relation. Each subscripted mention of instantiation picks out the same universal. Rather than saying "the state of affairs, a's instantiating$_1$ F, instantiates$_2$ instantiation$_3$" we should say, "the state of affairs, a's instantiating F, instantiates instantiation." There is no regress of instantiation universals since there is only one instantiation universal, if it is a universal (although there may be a regress of states of affairs, which is what the realist is really worried about and which is not helped by the fact that instantiation is a universal, if it is a relation). My claim is that the trope theorist can make a similar claim about compresence.[54]

To see how this works, let's first suppose that a bundle is wholly composed of tropes plus a compresence universal. In particular, suppose that bundle b includes only two tropes, t and t', and a compresence universal C. In addition, assume that t and t' are compresent as are t and C, and t' and C. Now suppose that whenever two entities are compresent there is a compresence relation C that is also compresent with that entity. In that case, t is compresent with C. But since compresence is a universal there is no reason to assume that the compresence relation holding between t and C is a relation other than C itself. The point is that there is no pressure under these assumptions to posit an infinite number of compresence relations if compresence itself is a universal and if compresence is a self-relating universal. I am suggesting that the same "self-relating" claim can be made about compresence even if compresence is a trope, not a universal. (I will address the worry that this line of response seems to make compresence out to be a universal and not a trope in Objection 2 below.)

Let's say that any *type* of relation that is capable of being one of its own relata is a relation that can be self-relating. Any token of such a type in which the relation itself, in fact, is one of its own relata is a "self-related" relation. Let's consider an example. Suppose that it is true that I hate hate. There are a number of things that might make this true, but not all of them involve a self-related relation in the intended sense. We can distinguish three variations: (1) I hate the hate trope that holds between Jones and Sally. The trope-relation that is one of the relata is a different trope from the trope-relation that has that trope as a relata; (2) I hate hate in general. I stand in a hate relation (a specific trope) to hate as a property type (say, a class of tropes); and (3) I hate this very hate trope itself. The trope-relation that is one of the relata is *not* a different trope from the trope-relation that has that trope as a relatum (self-hated hate). It is the third kind of case that involves a self-related trope-relation of the relevant type. The trope that is the relation must itself appear as one of its relata.

---

[54] Furthermore, there is no "states of affairs" regress, t_1's being linked by c_1 to t_2, t_1 being linked by c_2 to c_1, t_1 being linked by c_3 to c_2 and so on. Instead, on the t_1 side, we have a finite sequence, t_1's being linked by c_1 to t_2, t_1 being linked by c_1 to c_1, and similarly on the t_2 side, t_2's being linked by c_1 to t_1, t_2 being linked by c_1 to c_1.

If "hate" were a self-relating relation we could stop the following unlikely "hate regress."

A Hate Regress: Suppose every hate trope, h_1, must be directed against a hate trope, h_2. That means h_2 must also be directed against a hate trope, h_3, and so on.

If hate can be self-relating, this regress can be stopped. So consider the following series. I hate$_1$ hate$_2$. I hate$_2$ hate$_3$... and so on. If each hate trope involved is identical to h_1 then we do not have new hate tropes or new states of affairs at each point in the series, but only one, I hate$_1$ hate$_1$.

Consider the sentence "trope t_1 is compresent with compresence trope c_1 by way of compresence trope c_2." The proponent of the Regress Arguments takes this to say that t_1 stands in a compresence trope-relation c_2 to a compresence trope-relation c_1, such that c_1 and c_2 are not identical. But there are other possible readings. The regress can be stopped if what makes this sentence true is that the compresence trope-relation, c_1, that is the relatum is not different from the compresence trope-relation, c_2, that has that trope as a relatum. We can read this sentence as being made true by a self-related relation. What makes this sentence true is that trope t_1 is compresent with compresence trope c_1 by way of compresence trope c_1. We then don't have a regress of new compresence tropes nor do we have a regress of states of affairs. As for the latter, instead of the sequence ... t_1 is compresent with t_2 by way of c_1, t_1 is compresent with c_1 by way of c_2 (where c_1 is not identical to c_2) ... we have the following: t_1 is compresent with t_2 by way of c_1 and t_1 is compresent with c_1 by way of c_1.

3.8.1 Self-relating excluders

For this response to work, however, there must not be a reason for thinking that compresence cannot be a self-relating relation. We need to consider what I will call "self-relating-excluders." These are aspects of some relations that make it impossible for those relations to be self-relating. There seem to be three such excluders. The *first* self-relating-excluder involves what might be called "cross-category" relations. These are relations the terms of which must be from ontological categories under which the relation itself does not fall. Consider, for example, the relation "is taller than." The argument places of this relation must be filled with objects, not relations. Since relations cannot serve as arguments for this relation, neither can the relation itself. Or, consider the relation "is married to." This relation takes people as arguments, but the relation "being married to" is not a person. Is compresence a "cross-category" relation? In particular, does the compresence relation take only non-relation-tropes as terms? It does not. An object-bundle will include some relation-tropes. For example, relations between physical parts of the object will be in the bundle and compresent with other tropes in the bundle. Compresence, in virtue of being a relation, is not excluded from being a term in a compresence relation.

The *second* self-relating-excluder involves spatial relations. For certain relations, two (or more) things can stand to each other in that relation only if those things are spatially related in a certain way. In some such cases, the terms of that relation must stand to each other in spatial relations that cannot be satisfied if that relation itself were one of its own terms. For example, two things may be linked by a physical chain only if that chain is spatially between those two things. Let's see how this limitation on the "chain" relation blocks any resolution of the following fanciful Regress Argument by way of a self-relating strategy.

> Suppose that any two physical things must be linked by a physical chain. In particular, items a and b must be linked by a chain, say c. Since chain c is also a physical thing, a chain, c', must connect c to a. This pattern will repeat indefinitely, and we then must have an infinite number of chains.

A "self-relating" response would run as follows:

> Although a and b are connected by c, chain c is connected to a by way of chain c itself, not some further chain.

Clearly, this is not a coherent response. In order for two items to be connected by a chain, that chain must be spatially between those items. Chain c cannot be between itself and a.[55] Is there some spatial self-relating-excluder for compresence? First, the compresence "chain" need not be spatially between the compresent tropes it connects, so it is not required that it be spatially between itself and something else. Tropes that are compresent have the same location as each other and as the compresence trope that connects them, if they have locations, even if one of the linked tropes is itself a compresence trope.[56] Second, it is hard to see what other spatial constraint might both exclude self-related relations and be applicable to compresence.

The *third* self-relating-excluder involves causation. The terms of some relations must stand to each other in causal relations. Suppose that c and e stand to each other in relation R only if c causes e.[57] To illustrate, suppose that it is suggested that the "support" relation—as in "the dollar supports the yen"—is a self-relating relation such that the dollar supports support (just as it supports the yen). What makes this impossible is that it would require that a particular causal relation—the support relation—held between something and itself, but that is not possible. It is not possible that something cause that very instance of the causal relation (e stands in causing relation C to C).[58] Does this same self-relating-excluder apply to compresence? It

---

[55] A chain connecting two items must be spatially between those items and, hence, cannot be identical to either. Nothing can be spatially between itself and something else (short of some complicated time-travel scenario, perhaps).

[56] A compresence trope linking a non-compresence trope and a compresence trope (whether or not the latter is identical to the relating compresence trope) will not be spatially between those tropes.

[57] Might R be a self-relating relation? For that to be possible, it must be possible for c to cause that very R relation, including the causal relation between c and R.

[58] As opposed to e causing e, the impossibility of which is more debatable.

does not. The compresence relation is not a causal relation. If x is compresent with y, that does not require that x cause y, or the other way around.

3.8.2 Objection 1 It might be suggested that the challenge of this regress argument is to supply an infinite-regress-free and "compresence-free" condition for the compresence of any two compresent tropes. Regress Argument 2, in particular, begins with the fact that the existence of t_1, t_2 and compresence relations, including c_1, is insufficient for it being the case that t_1 and t_2 are compresent (the "insufficiency thesis"). Even if the self-relating strategy stops the infinite regress, it does not supply a "compresence-free" sufficient condition of the holding of compresence relations.[59]

In fact, we must concede that the "self-related" hypothesis does not supply a "compresence-free" sufficient condition for compresence.[60] But that is not really a problem for the "self-related" response. Regress Argument 2 does not go directly from the insufficiency thesis alone to the conclusion that t_1 and t_2 are not compresent. The insufficiency thesis alone is not meant to entail that there are no compresent tropes. For Regress Argument 2 to go through, it must turn out that what must be added to the existence of t_1, t_2, and c_1 to generate a sufficient condition for the compresence of t_1 and t_2 is unrealizable because it requires a vicious infinite regress. Under the "self-related" hypothesis, there is no infinite regress. The fact that we have not given perfectly general, "compresence-free" sufficient conditions is no argument by itself against compresence. Consider an analogy.

> c, e and the causation relation are not sufficient for its being true that c causes e. Now suppose that for a particular pair of events, c and e, to be causally connected, it must be true that x and y are causally connected along with other facts. But now suppose that causation is primitive. In particular, suppose that the causal connection between x and y cannot be reduced further. In that case, we cannot give a perfectly general, "causation-free" sufficient condition for c's causing e. That does not mean that c and e are not causally connected, but only that that fact is not fully reducible to non-causal facts.

---

[59] The self-relating response ultimately just *assumes* that some tropes are compresent without supplying a sufficient condition for compresence that does not assume that certain tropes are compresent.

[60] According to Regress Argument 2, t_1 is compresent by way of compresence trope c_1 with t_2 just in case t_1 is compresent with c_1 and t_2 is compresent with c_1. Under the self-related hypothesis, this means that t_1 is compresent with c_1 by way of c_1 and t_2 is compresent with c_1 by way of c_1. Focus on t_1's being compresent with c_1 by way of c_1. According to Regress Argument 2, that is true just in case t_1 is compresent with c_1 and c_1 is compresent with c_1. The self-related hypothesis says that that holds just in case:

t_1 is compresent with c_1 by way of c_1 and c_1 is compresent with c_1 by way of c_1.

At this point, the following starts to repeat:

t_1 is compresent with c_1 by way of c_1 and c_1 is compresent with c_1 by way of c_1.

There is no infinite regress here (the same holds if we focus on t_2), but there is also no perfectly general "compresence-free" sufficient condition for compresence.

The self-related hypothesis eliminates the infinite regress and that is enough to rebut Regress Argument 2. We have failed to give a non-circular *analysis* or reduction of compresence, but we have not tried to give an analysis or reduction at all.[61] Put another way, we can reject this objection's reading of Regress Argument 2 as requiring a "compresence-free" sufficient condition for compresence.[62]

3.8.3 Objection 2 For the trope theorist, unlike the proponent of universals, intuitive differences in aspects of reality correspond to numerically distinct tropes. He distinguishes the blueness of one object from that of another as well as the "5-feet-apartness" of x and y from the "5-feet-apartness" of z and y. However, this pattern does not continue in the case of compresence according to the "self-related" response. Suppose that compresence relation c_1 relates t_1 and t_2. Under the self-related response, the same two-place compresence relation-trope that relates t_1 and t_2 can be identical to the compresence relation-trope that relates t_1 and c_1. But one would expect the compresence *tropes* in these cases to be different since, intuitively, we are dealing with different aspects of reality.

In response, I would suggest that the compresence relation type should not be seen as a two-place relation under the self-related strategy, but one of variable-adicity, and that each complete bundle should be read as including only one compresence relation. If viewed as a two-place relation, this objection has force, but it does not under this alternative interpretation. To see this point, consider a simple example involving a complete bundle with only two "ground-level" tropes, t_1 and t_2, such that each stands in the compresence relation, c_1, to the other. Suppose that there is only one compresence relation, c_1, in the bundle. t_1, t_2, and c_1 stand to each other in a *three-place* compresence relation, which is just c_1.[63] So we don't posit the same two-place relation holding between two different pairs of tropes, which is what generates the worry expressed in the objection that the self-relating response is out of line with traditional Trope Theory. There is one compresence relation per bundle, but that relation varies in -adicity.[64]

---

[61] Indeed, there are reasons for thinking that compresence must be read as a primitive. Compresence will be primitive if we admit only tropes (and perhaps sets) and not locations as non-trope particulars into our ontology, which is typical of trope theorists. Without locations as non-trope particulars, we need place-tropes. Each spatio-temporal object-bundle will include a place-trope, compresent with the other tropes in the bundle. But if trope t is compresent with place-trope p that cannot mean that t is present at L and T and p is present at L' and T' and $L=L'$ and $T=T'$. That is because we have to make sense out of "t is present at L" on the assumption that L is not some further non-trope particular. "t is present at L" can only mean that t is compresent with the place-L-trope, which is just to say that t is compresent with p. We end up with circularity. To avoid circularity, compresence should be read as a primitive relation.

[62] Regress Argument 2 requires only that for tropes t and t' to be compresent there must be a compresent trope that is compresent with each. That condition is satisfied under the self-related hypothesis, without positing an infinite series.

[63] If there were three ground-level tropes, c_1 would be a four-place relation.

[64] The claim that compresence is a multigrade trope should be read not as applying to individual tropes but to the natural class of compresence tropes, which will include compresence tropes of varying -adicity.

3.8.4 Objection 3 Returning to Lewis's claim that it is an impossible task to give an analysis of *all* predications, it might be objected that the self-relating account presumes that every subject-predicate sentence can be analyzed in terms of further, distinct predications. In fact, that is not so. According to the "self-related" interpretation, tropes t_1 and t_2 are compresent just in case there is a compresence trope c_1 that is compresent with each, and that the latter is true just in case t_1 is compresent with c_1 by way of c_1 and t_2 is compresent with c_1 by way of c_1. t_1's is compresent with c_1 by way of c_1 just in case t_1 is compresent with c_1 and c_1 is compresent with c_1. That holds just in case,

(A) t_1 is compresent with c_1 by way of c_1 and c_1 is compresent by way of c_1 with c_1.

At this point, (A) starts to repeat. We are at a stopping point. What that means is that this analysis is consistent with Lewis's stricture. There comes a point at which the analysis invokes no *new* predications.

3.8.5 Objection 4 At this point, it might be objected that the "self-relating" response to the regress objections fails because it does not meet the explanatory challenge presented by such regress arguments. The challenge, it might be argued, is to explain why a given compresence relation holds between its relata. The "self-relating" approach to these regress arguments involves the following claims:

(1) t_1 is related by c_1 to t_2;
(2) t_1 is related to c_1 by c_2 ($=c_1$); and
(3) t_2 is related to c_1 by c_3 ($= c_1$).

Each of these claims faces, however, the above explanatory challenge. The explanation of (1) is given by (2) and (3). But what explains (2) and what explains (3)? The next part of the "self-relating" solution is to make further claims:

(4) t_1 is related to c_1 by c_4 ($= c_1$); and
(5) t_2 is related to c_1 by c_5 ($= c_1$).

Given the identities stated in claims (2)–(5), there is no regress. Claim (4) states the same relational fact as claim (2), and claim (5) states the same relational fact as claim (3). However, the objection goes, even if we grant that the regress is blocked, the cost of this solution is that the explanatory challenge has not been met. We wanted an explanation of why claim (2) is true: of why t_1 is related to c_1 by c_2 ($=c_1$). The truth of that claim is not explained by claim (4) because (2) and (4) state the same relational fact and nothing is the explanation of itself. (Note that meeting the explanatory challenge does not require a *compresence-free* sufficient condition for the holding of compresence relations.)[65]

---

[65] I owe this objection to a referee.

The first point to make in response to this objection is that the "self-relating" response *does* help to answer the explanatory challenge, at least in part, in the sense that without some way to stop the infinite regress, the explanatory challenge cannot be met. The "self-relating" response speaks to this challenge by stopping that regress. The second point involves combining the "self-relating" response with Lewis's point that we cannot require that all predications be analyzed—extended to this explanatory context. Recall Lewis's claim that "doing away with all unanalyzed predication is an unattainable aim, and so an unreasonable aim. No theory is to be faulted for failing to achieve it" (1983b: 353). It is an impossible task to give an analysis of *all* predications, since any analysis will bring into play a *new* predication, itself requiring analysis. And, since in this context "giving an explanation" of a sentence such as (2) would be to give an analysis of such a sentence, Lewis's point applies here too. In short, some such sentences are primitive and true for a trope theorist. Of course, as indicated earlier, we need some principled reason of claiming that this or that predication is not further analyzable. The "self-relating" response gives us such a principle for where to stop our analysis/explanation, with sentences such as (4) and (5). These predications require no further analysis/explanation and the demand for such an explanation is symptomatic of embracing the "unattainable aim."

4. What's next?

In the next chapter, I take up the topic of mental causation, a topic that might seem incongruous in the midst of a discussion of sparse properties and objects, a discussion that naturally takes place at a very general level of metaphysics. One might think that mental causation should be treated at a different level of metaphysics, but, in fact, mental causation is a fitting subject of inquiry for us in this context for two reasons. First, since sparse properties include higher-level properties, we need to see how a Trope Theory might handle such properties, especially with respect to the issue of their causal powers: mental properties can serve as a good test case. Second, since part of the task of Part 1 is to argue for the existence of tropes, we can strengthen that argument by showing how tropes, if they exist, help explain how mental causation is possible.

5
Tropes and mental causation

One way to argue in favor of a specific theory of properties is to demonstrate that it provides a basis for solving various philosophical problems that involve properties. For example, Trope Theory is shown to be more credible by the fact that tropes provide a basis for accounting for concrete particulars, specifically, by making a Bundle Theory of objects more plausible. In this chapter, I will argue that tropes help solve the problems of mental causation, thereby supplying some indirect support for the existence of tropes. As with the previous four chapters, I will remain neutral as to which conception of tropes should be adopted, the business of Part 2. The topic of mental properties is also fitting at this point in virtue of the fact that sparse properties are not confined to a minimal base: a theory of sparse properties must also take into account higher-level properties, which will likely include mental properties. Trope Theory, as we shall see, can be used to establish that mental properties have causal powers even given the completeness of physical causation (and related principles), a requirement for being a sparse property.

1. Mental causation

There are at least two problems of mental causation. The first concerns the possibility of mental causes of physical events in a causally closed physical world and the second concerns the possibility of mental causes being efficacious in virtue of their mental properties in such a world. I will consider the first problem in this section and the second problem in Section 2.

1.1 The problem of mental causation proper

The first problem (call this "the problem of mental causation proper") can be set up in various ways depending on the nature of causal relata. If causal relata are concrete events, the problem of mental causation proper concerns a challenge to the efficacy of any mental event with respect to any physical event. One well-known way to raise this problem is on the basis of an "overdetermination" argument. Mental causation is problematic given two appealing principles:

(1) *the completeness of physical causation:* every physical effect e, that has a cause at t, has a sufficient physical cause p at t,[1]; and
(2) *exclusion:* if p at t is a sufficient cause for e, then there are no causes of p at t that are distinct from p.

If e also has a wholly distinct mental cause m at t, we can reasonably rule out that either m or p is a cause of the other, given that m and p are simultaneous. We can also rule out that m and p are each partial causes, relative to each other. If p is a cause, it is a full cause, independently sufficient in conjunction with the circumstances, not including m, according to the completeness of physical causation. That leaves one other causal configuration: m and p overdetermine e. But here the exclusion principle comes into play, a principle that rests on the conviction that overdetermination is not, at the very least, widespread. If mental causation requires overdetermination, it requires that it be commonplace. That conflicts with our justified reluctance to posit extensive overdetermination in the world. Thus, this argument concludes, whenever physical effect e has a complete physical cause at t (which will be whenever e has a cause at t), then e does not have a mental cause at t.[2] If causal relata are property instances, then the same kind of overdetermination argument can be generated, with the conclusion that whenever a physical property instance e has a complete cause at t, then e does not have a mental property instance cause at t.

In what follows I will largely assume that causal relata are property instances, not concrete events. I have argued elsewhere that if causal relata are concrete events that will generate violations of the transitivity of causation, but not so if causal relata are property instances, either in the form of exemplifications of universals or tropes (1997).[3]

1.2 The token identity response

One response to this argument against mental causation—on the assumption that causal relata are events—is to claim that every mental event m that is a cause of a physical effect is itself identical to a physical event p ("token identity theory").

---

[1] This principle is meant to be compatible with physical indeterminism such that sufficiency means "sufficient for the actual chance of e."
[2] See, for example, (Kim 1993a: 360–1).
[3] Consider the following scenario on the assumption that causal relata are coarse-grained events.

The event (call this d) of Davidson's putting potassium salts into the fireplace occurs just as Jenny puts a lighted match into the fireplace. Following d there is a purple fire in the fireplace (call the purple fire c). The fire then causes Elvis's death (call the death e).

Assume that (d) putting potassium salts into the fireplace is a cause of (c) the purple fire. The fire is a cause of (e) the death. Putting potassium salts in the fireplace, then, is a cause of the death given transitivity. But that is not correct, since putting potassium salts into the fireplace has nothing to do with the death. On a coarse-grained view, there would appear to be a three-event chain running from d through c to e such that d causes c in virtue of c's being purple, and c causes e in virtue of c's having a certain high temperature. Since the "middle event" c is not required under this view to be such that the property of c that is relevant to c's being caused by d is the same property of c that is relevant to c's causing e, transitivity can fail. (This argument would still stand if the transitivity of causation were limited.)

Exclusion only applies to non-identical events. This strategy is familiar within a "Davidsonian" framework in which causal relata are individual, concrete occurrences exemplifying multiple properties. There is room in this framework to assert that every such multiply propertied mental cause of a physical event is identical to a physical event: that every physically efficacious mental event has some physical property/description.[4] One argues directly from the "overdetermination" argument to the token identity thesis, the idea being that we ought to infer that mental events are physical events given that there is mental causation in our causally closed physical world.

But what if causal relata are not concrete events, but property instances? Is the "token identity" response still available? There are two possible routes to a "token identity" response if causal relata are property instances. The first is a "top-down" strategy. Argue that there is some relation R between mental and physical property types that guarantees that every mental property instance is identical to a physical property instance. I will argue that this strategy fails given the most likely candidates for R. The second strategy is to mimic the Davidsonian line and argue directly from the "overdetermination" argument to the token identity thesis, in this case, a property instance identity thesis. I will adopt the latter strategy, but suggest that it works only if property instances are tropes.

1.2.1 The top-down approach to token identity There are two candidates for R that might give us the relevant token identity, identity and determination. Let's begin with identity. If mental property types are identical to physical property types, then a "token identity" response to the problem of mental causation property is immediately available. Every mental property instance is identical to a physical property instance (the "property instance identity" thesis). Even if every physical effect e, that has a cause at t, has a sufficient physical cause p at t, and even if p excludes any distinct causes of e at t, it will not follow that m, a mental property instance at t, is not a cause of e, since m may be identical to p. In fact, this type-type identity claim about mental and physical property types is not generally considered to be viable. This type-level identity thesis is inconsistent with the widely accepted principle that the same mental property can be realized by the instantiation of disparate physical properties or types.[5] Mental property types are not identical with any physical property types.[6] (In 2.4, I will mention some

---

[4] I am not offering an interpretation of Davidson here, but rather describing a view that tends to be associated with Davidson and is widely shared.

[5] Here I am endorsing the received views that mental properties are multiply realizable and that multiple realizability is inconsistent with type-type identity. Although I agree with both of these views, it should be noted that objections have been raised to these views. Examples include (Jackson et al. 1982) and (Hill 1991). I will not consider these various challenges in this work. If it turns out that these challenges are successful—which is far from clear at this point—then the advantage claimed for Trope Nominalism in this chapter—providing a basis for solving the problems of mental causation—will be illusory.

[6] A referee worries about a view that combines token-identity with type-non-identity. The worry is that that seems to entail, wrongly, that tokens (tropes) can have more powers than those associated with their

of the main reasons for rejecting a possible type-theoretic disjunctive move meant to save the type-type identity claim in light of multiple realizability—to the effect that mental types are identical to disjunctive property types, the disjuncts of which are physical types.)

The alternative relation between mental and physical property types that has been proposed as providing a basis for a property instance identity thesis is that of determination. This approach starts with the claim that although mental property types are not identical to physical property types, mental property types are determinables of the physical property types that realize them. It is, then, argued that this type-level determination relation ensures that mental property instances are identical to physical property instances. The idea is to argue that: (1) mental property types are determinables of the physical property types that realize them; and (2) this determination type-level relation entails that the corresponding property instances at the token level are identical.[7]

In the following section, I will examine this determination-based proposal. I will begin by trying to make some metaphysical sense of the claim that determinable property instances are identical to their corresponding determinate property instances. I will suggest that this claim makes metaphysical sense in a trope framework, not in a universals framework. However, I will argue that the mental/physical distinction is *not* a species of the determinable–determinate distinction. Hence, although good metaphysical sense can be made of a determination-based "token-identity" solution to the problem of mental causation proper, that solution does not apply to the problem of mental causation proper.

1.2.1.1 MAKING SENSE OF DETERMINATION-BASED TOKEN IDENTITY

The determinable–determinate distinction at least applies to predicates: the predicate "red" is a determinate of "color" and a determinable of the predicate "scarlet." The determination relation, say its proponents, also applies to properties: the property redness is determinate relative to color, but determinable relative to the property scarlet. Since properties are typically taken to be universals, that means that some universals are determinable relative to other universals and are less than fully determinate. What is the issue of determinable causation given that properties are universals? First, if causation is a relation between "property instances," then causal relata are exemplifications of universals by objects at times, and some causes will consist in the

---

types. The referee does not see how a token property can have more powers than its corresponding type: that would seem to be a good reason for not taking the token to be of that type. In response, I would say that I don't share the referee's concern. First, this combination does *not* entail that the token has more powers than *any* of its types. Second, it does seem possible for a token to have more causal powers than *some* of the types under which it falls. Consider the analogous case of objects and types. An object might fall under various types such that the object has more powers than those associated with *some* of the types under which it falls.

[7] As Cynthia and Graham Macdonald seem to suggest in their (1986: 39).

exemplification of a fully determinate universal by an object at a time *t* and other causes in the exemplification of a less-than-fully determinate universal. The key issue then becomes this: what is the causal status of the exemplification of a determinable universal (say "being red" by a chair) with respect to an effect *e*, given that the exemplification of a determinate of that determinable universal by that same object (say "being scarlet") caused *e*? Does the chair's being scarlet causally compete with the chair's being red? The thesis of interest is that there is no competition here since instances of determinable universals are identical to the instances of the corresponding determinate universals. There is no competition or exclusion since the chair's being red at *t* just is the chair's being scarlet at *t*, despite the distinctness of the properties.[8] We get property instance identity without property identity. Hence, if physical universals are determinates of mental universals, the completeness of physical causation and the massive failure of overdetermination are compatible with mental property instance causation.

This way of cashing out the property instance identity thesis, however, is deeply problematic since it conflicts with a plausible necessary condition for the identity of "exemplifications of universals." Exemplifications of universals by objects at a time are identical only if their constituent properties are identical (Kim 1993b: 9). On the plausible assumption that if *M* is the exemplification of a mental universal, then *M* has a mental constitutive universal, and that if *P* is the exemplification of a physical universal, *P* has a physical constitutive universal, *M* and *P* are identical only if the constituent mental universal of *M* is identical to the constituent physical universal of *P*. But many philosophers, as already indicated, hold that mental property multiple realizability precludes such type-level identities.[9] For example, since the mental state of pain can be realized in a variety of different physical states, say, P_1 and P_2, that type of state is not identical to P_1 nor is it identical to P_2.

---

[8] "No one would suppose, however, that an object's exemplification of a colour, say, red, requires, first, that it be an instance of the property of being red, and second, that it be a (distinct) instance of a second, related property, viz. that of being coloured. To be an exemplification of the former just is, in this case, to be an exemplification of the latter, despite the distinctness of the properties themselves. Does this mean that colour is causally inefficacious? Of course not; for any causally efficacious case in which a more determinate form of that property is exemplified is a case in which the exemplification of colour itself is efficacious, by the extensionality of the causal relation (think of the property of having weight and that of weighing 2.3 kg)" (Macdonald and Macdonald 1986: 39).

[9] In response to this situation, some philosophers have suggested that the identity of constituent universals is not required for exemption from the exclusion principle for non-identical Kimian events. More specifically, if one Kimian event *realizes* the other, some have claimed, those events are not causal competitors, even if their constituent universals are non-identical (where *p* realizes *m* just in case *M* is the property of having some property that satisfies requirements *H* and, this exemplification of *P*, *p*, satisfies *H*). Kim reasonably rejects this line: "we must, it would seem, still contend with two purported causes of a single event" (1993a: 361). On the other hand, Kim *does* recognize that trying to maintain a token identity response to the first problem of mental causation may require refinements of the property instance framework, "a revision of the standard property-exemplification account of events" (365).

Here's another possibility. Not all philosophers accept less-than-fully-determinate universals. D. M. Armstrong denies them: "all universals must be determinate" (1978b: 118). There are determinable predicates such as "colored," but no determinable properties. Still, there is a metaphysical basis for the application of determinable predicates: "to assert that a particular is red is to assert that the particular has some property, a property which is a member of a certain class of properties: the class of all the absolutely determinate shades of red" (1978b: 117). Nevertheless, strictly speaking, there are no determinable universals. "Being colored" is a determinable predicate relative to "being red" because the class of absolutely determinate colors includes the absolutely determinate reds as a proper subclass. From this view it perhaps follows that if mental predicates are determinable predicates, the statement "S's being in pain caused e" is true not because there is a mental universal "being in pain," the instantiation of which causes e, but because S exemplifies some fully determinate physical property which is a member of a certain class. There is, however, a heavy cost to this reading of determinable/mental causation: we save mental causation, but lose mental properties even though there are physical properties. If mental predicates are determinable predicates then there are no mental universals. There are no mental properties in that case since there are no determinable universals. We, thus, face a dilemma: either there are determinable universals that are distinct from determinate universals, and then the property instance identity thesis is problematic because exemplifications are identical only if their constituent properties are, or there are no determinable universals and there is a sense in which there is mental causation, but there are no mental properties.

The alternative is that causal relata, understood as property instances, are unshareable, spatio-temporal, particularized properties or tropes. The property instance identity thesis ran up against the requirement that the constituent mental and physical universals/types of identical exemplifications of a universal themselves be identical. But we face no such requirement with trope identity. Whereas a universal gives an exemplification of a universal its nature—the "type" is a constituent of the "token"—and the object its particularity, that is not so for tropes. Whereas an exemplification of a universal includes a constitutive *type-level* element precluding the token identity response because of the failure of the appropriate type-level identity between mental and physical property types/universals—a failure that is made clear by the multiple realizability of mental properties—mental/physical trope identity cannot be objected to on these grounds: tropes include no type-level element. They are not metaphysically hybrid as are exemplifications. Not unrelated to this point is the fact that within a trope metaphysics, *types* are classes of tropes rather than universals. The type "red" is a class of particular red tropes. If we adopt this reading of the property instance view of causal relata, there is room for a token identity response, even if mental types are *not* identical to physical types. The same property instance/trope will be a member of multiple classes, instancing more than one type. Since types are not constituents or components of the property instances, there is no basis for a requirement that identical tropes have identical constituent types. The trope view allows the option of making mental causation compatible with the completeness of physical causation and exclusion by asserting that mental trope *m* is identical to physical trope *p* where that one trope falls into more than one class of tropes, a mental type class and a physical type class.

This shift from universals to tropes, however, will not get us off the first horn of this dilemma if determinable tropes are posited as distinct from any determinate trope. In that event it is implausible to think that any determinable/mental property instance is identical to any determinate/physical property instance. Fortunately, further development of the trope-based option is possible, as follows.[10] First, postulate that all tropes are fully determinate and reject less-than-fully determinate tropes. Second, suppose that an object falls under a determinable predicate if and only if it is characterized by a fully determinate trope that is a member of a less-than-perfectly natural class of tropes (or alternately if one follows Campbell, is a member of a class of tropes, membership in which is a matter of less-than-exact resemblance). Third, suppose that every trope also falls into a perfectly natural class of tropes so that, for example, a trope of a specific shade of red falls into the perfectly natural class of tropes of that specific shade. Thus, there are no tropes that are in the red class, but not in a class of tropes of a more specific shade of red. Finally, suppose that the determinate–determinable distinction applies to classes of tropes and only derivatively to individual tropes: a class of tropes is fully determinate only if that class is perfectly natural (or, alternatively, the members of that class resemble each other exactly).

We can now make metaphysical sense of the property instance identity thesis. "The redness of the chair caused *e*" says of a particular fully determinate color trope that it caused *e*, but picks out that trope not by its membership in the class of tropes of a fully determinate shade of red. If property instances are tropes, then determinable causation statements pick out causes in virtue of their membership in these wider "determinable" classes. But since causation is extensional, the same trope-cause can be picked out in virtue of its membership in more determinate classes, subsets of the larger determinable class. Every "determinable" trope is identical to some "determinate" tropes: there are no less-than-fully determinate tropes, but each trope is both determinate and determinable in the sense that it falls into various appropriate resemblance classes.[11] Hence, even though there are no less-than-fully determinate tropes, we don't end up with eliminativism (if mental predicates are determinable predicates). Determinable causation, then, requires determinate causation. If a trope-cause is picked out in virtue of its membership in a determinable class, then that same trope falls into a fully determinate class. The color of the chair does not compete causally with the scarlet of the chair since these two property instances are one and the same, and, in fact, the efficacy of the

---

[10] Here I basically follow Keith Campbell in his (1990).
[11] For a denial of the claim that determinable and determinate tropes are identical, see Wilson (2008).

former requires the efficacy of the latter.[12] The same kind of property instance identity thesis can be extended to the mental–physical case if the mental–physical distinction encodes a determination relation.[13]

1.2.1.2 DETERMINATION AND THE MENTAL–PHYSICAL DISTINCTION

I will now argue that mental types are not determinables of physical types that realize them, no more than the former are identical to the latter. Hence, we cannot apply this reasoning to the mental–physical case.

Arguments for the thesis that mental property types are determinables of the physical types that realize them are not easy to find. Stephen Yablo comes closest to such an argument, but even his argument supports only one component of the determination relation, asymmetric necessitation. And, as we shall see, that component is insufficient to ground a property instance identity.

---

[12] The property instance identity thesis, as based on the determination relation, has some seemingly strange consequences. Suppose that Smith, who is 155 pounds, sits on and breaks a hammock that would break if anyone over 150 pounds were to sit on it. "Smith's weighing under 160 pounds caused the hammock to break" comes out true, since being 155 pounds is a determinate of being under 160 pounds. This certainly is an odd-sounding consequence. Nevertheless, it is no more than odd since similar consequences accompany any extensionalist reading of causal contexts, no matter what causal relata may be. For example, if Davidsonian events are the causal relata, then "the sitting down of Smith, who weighs under 160 pounds, caused the hammock to break" is true, although misleading. Consequences such as these are acceptable once we distinguish—following Davidson—between causes and the features we hit on for describing them, and, thus, between whether a causal statement is true—that one event/property instance caused another—and whether those events/property instances are picked out in a way which is informative about, for example, any relevant causal laws or appropriate explanatory framework (1980: 155). Davidson's point applies even if causal relata are tropes, given that causation is extensional. The hammock sentence is misleading, but true: misleading because it gives the wrong impression that being over 160 pounds would not have had the same effect, and/or that being under 150 pounds would have, but still true since just that particular weight trope of Smith, however described, did the causal work.

[13] It might seem that we could extend this type of view to a universals-based account of determinable causation and resolve our earlier dilemma if we took the view that "color" is the name of a class of universals, to which "scarlet" belongs, and then suggest that such class membership can be made a basis for indirect reference to a determinate universal—so that "color of the chair" picks out the scarlet universal exemplified by the chair by way of that determinate universal's membership in the class of "color" universals. We might then say that "the color of the chair caused e" and "the redness of the chair caused e" both say of the same property that it caused e. This way of extending the current approach fails, however, since in this framework "the color of the chair" refers to a universal as does "the redness of the chair," but universals cannot be causes. On the other hand, if we stick with "states of affairs" such as "the chair's having color" or "the chair's being red" then it is not clear that this line translates to the universals framework, since it seems wrong to say that "the chair's being red caused e" says of a particular fully determinate color universal that its exemplification by the chair caused e, but picks out that universal not by its membership in the class of "red" universals. An alternate view that might work is the following. Take the view that a property is either a universal or a set of universals. Those sets of universals, the members of which bear an inexact resemblance relationship to one another, are determinables. The constituents of a property exemplification are a universal, an object, and a time. Those properties that are sets of universals are always exemplified by one of their member universals being exemplified. So any exemplification of a determinable will be an exemplification of one of its determinates. Mental properties are then sets of universals rather than universals on the Macdonald thesis. I owe this point to Mark Heller.

For Yablo, the determination relation between properties is purely metaphysical, and the core of this relation is asymmetric necessitation.[14] Property P asymmetrically determines property M if and only if (i) necessarily, for all x, if x has P then x has M; and (ii) possibly, for some x, x has M but lacks P (1992: 252). Asymmetric necessitation, however, may not be enough for determination according to Yablo: "otherwise, for example, conjunctive properties determine their conjuncts and universally impossible properties are all-determining. For dialectical reasons, I try to remain as neutral as I can about where determination leaves off and 'mere' asymmetrical necessitation begins" (1992: 253, footnote 23). Further metaphysical components are likely to be necessary to yield the determination relation. Yablo argues that the supervenience and multiple realizability of the mental are best explained by positing a determination relation. Although asymmetric necessitation falls short of full determination, as Yablo concedes, still, if his argument is sound we are one step closer to the stronger conclusion. How does his argument go? Consider first supervenience. Supervenience consists in the fact that "necessarily, for every x and every mental property M of x, x has some physical property P such that necessarily all P's are M's." Supervenience, thus, supplies a necessitation relation from the physical to the mental. Now consider multiple realizability. Multiple realizability requires that "necessarily, for every mental property M, and every physical property P which necessitates M, possibly something possesses M but not P." Here we have a basis for an asymmetry of necessitation. Taken together, supervenience and multiple realizability make it a matter of necessity that something has a mental property if and only if it has a physical property by which that mental property is asymmetrically necessitated. If we say that P "super-realizes" M just in case M supervenes on P and P realizes M, then if P is a super-realizer of M, then M stands in a relation of asymmetric necessitation (one component of determination) to P. Super-realizers asymmetrically necessitate that which they realize and this gives us reason to think that "mental/physical relations are a species of determinable/determinate relations" (1992: 256). And, indeed, we would expect this kind of asymmetric necessitation if the mental is a determinable of the physical: if the physical determines the mental, then something has a mental property if and only if it has a physical determination of that mental property, since something has a determinable property if and only if it has some determinate falling thereunder (1992: 256). And if something has some such determinate physical property, then it will have that determinable mental property.

Asymmetric necessitation, however, as indicated, will not carry over to property instance identity or a genuine determination relation. To see why, consider two cases of asymmetric necessitation, the first based on conjunction and the second on disjunction. The conjunctive property of being P and Q asymmetrically necessitates the property of being P, but it is not true that an object o's being P and Q is identical to

---

[14] "...we should discount the traditional doctrine's conceptual component and reconceive determination in wholly metaphysical terms" (Yablo 1992: 253).

o's being P. Neither is it the case that the conjunctive property of being P and being Q is a determinate of the property of being P. Or, again, consider the disjunctive property of being P or being Q. This property is necessitated by the property of being P and this property necessitates that anything that has it will have one or the other of P and Q. Nevertheless, property instance identity does not follow. In the case of disjunctive properties, the property instance identity thesis would amount to this: o's being P is identical to o's being P or Q and that o's being Q is identical to o's being P or Q. But then this entails that in cases in which o is both P and Q, then o's being P is identical to o's being Q, which is false. This is entailed since each of these instances is identical to the disjunctive property instance and by the transitivity of identity. Asymmetric necessitation is not sufficient for property instance identity, nor is it sufficient for the determination relation.

Indeed, traditionally, more is imputed to the determination relation than asymmetric necessitation, and I want now to suggest that further necessary conditions for the determination relation make it clear that the super-realization relation, in the mental–physical case, embodies characteristics that distinguish that relation from determination. The super-realization relation, in the mental–physical case, even if it is a form of asymmetric necessitation, differs in important ways from the determination relation. Hence, even if determinate property instances do not compete causally with their corresponding determinable property instances (in virtue of property instance identity), determinable causation is simply irrelevant to the mental–physical case.

I will now briefly introduce some of the principles that govern the determination relation, the last four of which will be relevant to claim that determination does not apply in the mental–physical case.

The first principle worth noting is just that of (1) *Asymmetric Necessitation* as characterized by Yablo—determinates necessitate their determinables, but determinables don't necessitate any particular determinate. A second principle specifies that if something has a determinable it will have some determinate falling under that determinable. (2) *Downward Necessitation*: if $D_1, \ldots, D_n$ is a complete set of same-level determinates of Q, then if x has Q, then x has D_1 or $D_2, \ldots,$ or D_n. A third principle rules out certain kinds of conjunctive properties from being determinables relative to their conjuncts. (3) *Non-Conjunctive Determinates*: no determinate of Q is a conjunctive property of being P and of being P', such that P either is Q or a determinate of Q and P' is some property that does not necessitate Q.[15] This rules out, for example, our earlier case of the property of being P as a determinable of the conjunctive property of being P and of being Q. A fourth principle excludes arbitrary disjunctive properties from being determinables of their disjunct properties. (4) *Non-Disjunctive Determinables*: no determinable of Q is a disjunctive property of being P and of being P', such that either P is Q

---

[15] See (Searle 1959: 147).

or *P* is a determinable of *Q* and *P'* is some property that is not necessitated by *Q*. For example, being red or square is not a determinable of being red (Q), because being red, the first disjunct, is identical to the determinable itself. Or, being colored or square is not a determinable of being red (Q), since the first disjunct, being colored, is a determinable of being red (and being square is not necessitated by being red). A first approximation of the fifth principle dictates that an object can have at most one of a set of same-level determinates. (5) *Exclusion*: if $D_1, \ldots, D_n$ is a complete set of same-level determinates of *Q*, then if *x* has *Q*, then *x* has only one of the properties in this set. Thus if an object is colored it cannot be both red and blue, at least in the same areas. However, this formulation of the exclusion principle requires qualification. Consider, for example, that an object's color may instance distinct but overlapping not-fully-determinate shades of red if it falls into the area of overlap. The principle can be suitably revised by adding a clause that restricts its application to a complete set of same-level determinates of *Q* such that no pair of properties in the set shares a common determinate. This qualification takes account of our color case since the overlapping-not-fully-determinate shades of red will share a common determinate.[16]

A sixth principle dictates that determinates of a determinable can be ordered in a series such that differences between pairs of determinates can be compared with respect to the determinable. For example, in the case of color, its determinates can be so ordered: red is closer to orange than it is to yellow—a red object is more similar to an orange object with respect to color than to a yellow object. (6) *Ordering Principle*: if $D_1, \ldots, D_n$ is a complete set of same-level determinates of *Q*, then for any set of objects $o_1 \ldots o_n$ such that o_1 has $D_1 \ldots$ and o_n has D_n, these objects are orderable with respect to *Q* (or of some determinable of *Q*) in virtue of differences among these determinates. A seventh principle provides a sufficient condition for *P*'s *not* being a fully determinate *Q*—roughly, if there are further determinates falling under *P*. (7) *Non-Full-Determinancy Principle*: if *P* has a determinate *S* and there is a *Q* that is a determinable of *P* and *S*, *P* is not a fully determinate *Q*. "Blue" is a determinate of "color," but since there are determinates of "blue" and "color" (such as "azure"), "blue" is not a fully determinate "color." The final principle I will mention dictates that differences at the level of determinates are differences with respect to the common determinables of those determinates. (8) *Difference Principle*: distinct same-level determinates of a determinable *Q* differ with respect to *Q* (are different *Q*'s). For example,

---

[16] The exclusion principle might now seem to have a trivial ring—"exclusion applies unless it doesn't"—but, in fact, that would be a misreading of the modified principle. This principle would be trivial if it simply set aside all non-excluding property pairs through the additional clause. In that case there would be no room for counterexamples involving property pairs which ostensibly are same-level determinates, but are non-excluding. In fact, the additional clause does not automatically apply to all non-excluding property pairs, such as being green and being heavy (since these properties don't share a common determinate.) Hence, there remains room to come up with a property pair that consists in same-level determinates of a common determinable (but are non-excluding). It also follows that for any set of fully determinate determinates of a common determinable (if there are such), *x* has only one of the properties in this set.

"blue" and "red" are distinct same-level determinates of "color" and are thereby different colors.[17]

There are four objections, based on these last four necessary conditions, to the claim that the mental is determinable relative the physical.

Objection 1
The first objection is based on the exclusion principle—same-level determinates, which do not share a common determinate cannot characterize the same object. For example, no object can have two different masses.[18] Now consider the thesis that the physical super-realizers of mental properties are determinates of those mental properties. Suppose that P and P' are distinct super-realizers of "being in mental state M" of the same level of specification that do not share a common determinate. Now it follows that if P and P' are same-level determinates of being in M, the exclusion principle requires that P and P' cannot both characterize a person at the same time. But this is an objectionable result. There is nothing in the dual doctrines of supervenience and multiple realizability to guarantee this exclusion. Nothing in principle rules out the same person simultaneously instantiating distinct super-realizers of being in M, such as being in P and being in P'. The person may be in M in virtue of multiple super-realizers, even system-wide realizers. For example, suppose that the mental state at issue is "being in pain" and that there are two super-realizers of being in pain, "having one's C-fibers vibrate" and "having one's D-fibers vibrate," where the latter two properties manifest the same level of specificity. In effect, there can be a kind of non-causal overdetermination. Exclusion is not built into the nature of super-realizers (or, at least, the defenders of the thesis that the mental is determinable relative to the physical have given us no reason to think that this is true). This is the first disanalogy with determinates.[19]

---

[17] Walter describes this principle as follows: "Distinct determinates of a determinable F cannot be exactly the same with respect to F-ness. For instance, being crimson and being scarlet are distinct determinates of being red precisely because they differ with respect to redness" (2006: 229). Along the same lines, Funkhouser says, "Colors differ to the extent, and only to the extent, that they differ in hue, brightness, or saturation. As such, these are the three variables along which colors can be determined... How do we discover the determination dimensions of a given determinable, X? The easiest way is simply to inquire after the ways in which determinates under the determinable X can differ from one another with regard to their X-ness" (2006: 551).

[18] More precisely, given the possibility of trope piling, no object can have two different *maximal* masses. Notice, also, that the trope piling cases, even those involving imperfect piling, do not involve non-quantitative properties that are same-level determinates of the same determinable.

[19] A referee worries that this scenario is not really possible on the following grounds.

> Since a realizer is sufficient for the realized entity, then if a single realized state eventuated from two distinct realizers that would induce a form of systematic overdetermination. But there is no such systematic overdetermination in this domain, so either P or P' is not really an individual realizer of M, or it is not the case that M comes about in virtue of both of them (at a time).

This objection can be handled in the following way. The main concern of the objection is either that overdetermination of this sort is simply not possible, even one-off cases of overdetermination, or that although overdetermination is possible, systematic and widespread overdetermination is either very rare or not possible. As to the first way of taking the objection, I do not think that there are any good reasons for rejecting the possibility of one-off cases of overdetermination involving supervenience and realization. As for the second concern—that systematic and widespread overdetermination of this sort should not be posited—Objection 1 does not require that this form of overdetermination be systematic or widespread.

Objection 2
The second objection rests on the ordering requirement for same-level determinates. Determinates of a determinable are orderable relative to that same determinable in that differences between pairs of same-level determinates are comparable with respect to that determinable—so that, for example, the difference between determinates D_1 and D_2 with respect to a common determinable D may be greater than the difference between D_1 and D_3 with respect to D.[20]

A red object is more similar to an orange object with respect to color than to a yellow object. And this is a generalizable fact about same-level determinates.[21] Now we have noted that if the same mental property can be realized by disparate physical properties, mental properties are not identical with any non-disjunctive physical property. The latter implication is widely recognized, but there is a further implication: multiple realization does not guarantee, and perhaps makes it unlikely, that the physical realizers of mental properties will satisfy this orderability principle with respect to their would-be mental determinables. Super-realizing physical properties can be widely disparate physical properties such that their physical ordering may fail to correspond to the ordering of their supervening mental properties with respect to further determinables (less specific mental properties) of those mental properties. To see why this is so, consider three sets of super-realizers, P, P', and P'', such that each such set super-realizes a different type of pain, but such that all of them super-realize "being in pain." Within each set, say P, there is a wide variation of physical types (as dictated by multiple realizability). Consider one arbitrary physical type from each set, D_1, D_2, and D_3. For example, suppose that D_1 consists in C-fibers vibrating in humans, D_2 consists in the activation of some mechanical device in Martians, and D_3 consists in the activation of some components of the brains of dolphins. Suppose that physical type D_1 is more like D_3 than it is like D_2. The Martian states are silicone-based, but human states and dolphin states are carbon-based. That ordering of D_1, D_2, and D_3 will not necessarily correspond to the ordering of the supervening pains with respect to their painfulness. So whereas D_1 is more like D_3 than it is like D_2, *qua* physical properties, the specific pain properties which supervene on these states, may be ranked *qua* pain such that the D_1 is more like the D_2 than it is like the D_3 pain. The human pain may be more like the Martian pain than the human pain is like the dolphin pain. The comparable physical differences, if any, at the level of the physical realizers, do not necessarily correspond to comparable differences with respect to the would-be determinable "being in pain." If physical super-realizers were determinates of mental properties, we would expect

---

[20] This is not to say that there is only one dimension along which same-level determinates can be ordered. For example, in the case of colors, different intrinsic orderings are possible relative to hue, intensity, etc. There is no single ranking, but there is at least one dimension of intrinsic ordering.

[21] W. E. Johnson made a similar point: "...if a, b, c, are three determinates, there are cases in which we may say that the difference between a and c is greater than the difference between a and b; e.g. the difference between red and yellow is greater than the difference between red and orange. In this case the several determinates are conceived as necessarily assuming a certain serial order..." (1964: 181–2).

that physical orderings of those physical realizers would correspond to differences *qua* pains.

This claim is easier still to make if we combine supervenience and multiple realizability with functionalism. For functionalists, intrinsic features are irrelevant to the status of "being a pain," since the relevant states would retain their particular mental statuses even if those intrinsic features were absent or different without a change in any of the states' relational properties. If mental properties are extrinsic properties, any ranking according to intrinsic physical properties (the realizing properties) will not necessarily measure or gauge differences with respect to the relevant mental, realized properties. Multiple realizability, thus, (even combined with supervenience) is insufficient to make it likely that physical determines the mental. We need further reason to believe in the possibility of an ordering of the physical realizers that will correspond to the ordering generated at the level of mental properties.[22]

(Following "Objection 4," I will consider the question of whether or not the top-down strategy of ensuring that mental property instances are identical to physical property instances by appealing to a relation in certain respects analogous to the determinable–determinate relation can be salvaged, even supposing that physical realizers are not orderable with respect to mental states in the specified way. The same question will be raised about Objection 1 and the two objections that follow.)

Objection 3
The third objection to the thesis that super-realizers are determinates of that which they realize rests on the Non-Full Determinacy Principle:

> If P has a determinate S, then for any W that is a determinable of P and S, P is not a fully determinate W.

"Red" is a determinate of "color," but since there are determinates of "red" (such as "scarlet"), "red" is not a fully determinate "color." This is a sufficient condition for not being a fully determinate color. Now consider again the thesis that the physical super-realizers of mental properties are determinates of those mental properties. In particular, suppose that M is a fully determinate type of mental state. For example, make M a

---

[22] In response to this objection and the previous objection, a referee wonders what considerations are at issue when it is claimed that "nothing in principle rules out..." Perhaps, no *a priori* considerations rule out the configuration under discussion. However, as the referee suggests, it may be that the kind of necessitation at issue need not be knowable *a priori*. Thus, if the necessitation involved in the determinate–determination relation is metaphysical necessitation, that kind of necessitation needn't be *a priori* knowable. For example, in that case, it needn't be *a priori* knowable that being in P and being in P' exclude one another even if it is metaphysically necessary that they do. Here I would say that even if this is the best way to view the matter, still the burden of proof runs in the other direction. Those who claim that super-realizers are determinates of that which they realize need to give us some reason or evidence for thinking that they will always satisfy these principles that govern determination. This is especially true in light of the fact that the kinds of examples philosophers use in this area do not point in the direction of such exclusion. Hence, even if metaphysical necessity is at issue and that necessity can be discerned only *a posteriori*, still the likelihood seems to be quite low that same-level super-realizers of the same property, for example, always exclude each other.

precise state of searing pain such that there is no room for further specification of this mental state *qua* pain state. M is, of course, a determinate of the property "being in pain." Suppose that M and "being in pain" have a physical super-realizer, P. Suppose that P is a determinate of M and of "being in pain." Our principle then requires that M cannot be a fully determinate pain state. This is so since there are further determinates of that pain state and of "being in pain"—in the form of P. But, in fact, M is a fully determinate pain state by hypothesis. Thus, the physical super-realizers of mental properties are not determinates of that which they realize, since if that were true, M would not be a fully determinate pain property.

Objection 4
The fourth objection rests on the fact that same-level determinates of a determinable D should be different with respect to D (be different D's)—the Difference Principle. Let's consider a determinable mental property such as "being in pain." This determinable property will have various fully determinate pain properties that are determinates of it—for example, "having a searing pain of a certain intensity," etc. This determinate mental state will have various physical super-realizers, say P and P'. Suppose that P and P' are determinates of that searing pain property. Since the latter is a determinate of "pain," P and P' must each be determinates of "pain."[23] But if P and P' are determinates of "pain," then P and P' are pains and determinates of the same level. But then P and P', since they are different same-level determinates of pain, must differ with respect to pain (just as scarlet and crimson, different same-level determinates of "color," differ with respect to color, or, in short, are different colors). P and P' must be different pains, but our assumption is that P and P' are exactly the same kind of fully determinate pain—a searing pain of a certain intensity—and they do not differ with respect to pain. They are definitely not different kinds of pain.[24]

It is worth noting that the basis for this last objection is primarily the realization relation, since distinct realizers of the same fully determinate searing pain cannot be pains of different kinds (otherwise they are not both realizers of that fully determinate pain property). Indeed, each of these four objections is rooted in the nature of multiple realizability of mental properties. In the first objection, the important fact about the realization relation which makes for a disanalogy is that realizers are not necessarily mutually exclusive. In the second objection, the relevant aspect of that relation is the fact that physical realizers will not necessarily be orderable in terms of their physical differences in ways that correspond to differences with respect to the would-be determinable mental property. In the third objection, appeal is made to the

---

[23] Actually, as pointed out to me by Alastair Norcross, determination may be transitive only for a circumscribed set of cases: even though "being in a decade under one hundred" is a determinable of "being in one's 70s" and the latter is a determinable of "being 72," "being 72" may not be a determinate of "being in a decade under one hundred."

[24] See Walter (2006: 230) for another example that illustrates this argument. See also Funkhouser (2006). For a response to Objections 3 and 4, see Wilson (2009a).

fact that having multiple disparate physical realizers does not entail any lack of determinateness on the part of that which they realize. And, as indicated, the fourth objection trades on the fact that the physical realizers of the mental will not differ mentally at all, but they should if they are determinates of the requisite mental properties.

A possible reply
Finally, I will consider a reply to the argument of this section.[25] First, let's grant that asymmetric necessitation is insufficient to establish a property instance identity thesis—on the grounds that the instantiation of a conjunctive property (which asymmetrically necessitates the corresponding conjunct properties) is not identical to the instantiation of either conjunct property, and on the grounds that the instantiation of a disjunctive property is not identical to the instantiation of either disjunct property (which asymmetrically necessitate the disjunctive property). Still, perhaps the property instance identity thesis can be sustained without positing a full-fledged determination relation in the mental–physical case. This may be so if enough, but not all, of the necessary conditions for that relation are satisfied. In particular, if the only worrisome cases—worrisome with respect to property instance identity—are those of conjunctive properties and disjunctive properties we need not concern ourselves, since there is no reason to believe that the necessitation of the mental by the physical, that is brought to light by supervenience, is grounded in the conjunctive or disjunctive physical properties. We can safely assume that the mental–physical relation satisfies asymmetric necessitation, downward necessitation, and the non-conjunctive and non-disjunctive principles. Thus, it might be suggested, even if the mental–physical relation does not satisfy our last four principles of determination, that by itself does not guarantee failure of a property instance identity thesis—as long as the first four principles are satisfied. Call a relation which satisfies only the conjunction of the first four principles "quasi-determination": physical properties quasi-determine mental properties and this guarantees a property instance identity thesis. Hence, the objection goes, failure to satisfy the last four principles does not demonstrate the falsity of the property instance identity thesis. In order to reply to this objection we need to show specifically how quasi-determination might be satisfied but property instance identity fails.

Examples can be generated in which quasi-determination holds but property instance identity clearly fails. Consider a property Q such that instances of Q are deterministically caused by one of two possible alternate causes, in particular, instances of the non-disjunctive properties D_1 and D_2. Also suppose that instances of Q occur only if caused. In that case, conditions 1–4 are met: (1) property Q instances are (causally) necessitated by D_1 (and necessitated by D_2), but Q does not necessitate D_1; (2) Q necessitates that one or the other of D_1 and D_2 are realized; (3) D_1 is not a conjunctive property; and (4) Q is not a disjunctive property. Still, instances of Q are

---

[25] I owe this objection to David Papineau.

not identical to instances of D_1, on those occasions when the former is caused by the latter.

This case, it might be argued, proves irrelevant, since the supervenience of the mental/physical involves a form of necessitation stronger than causal necessitation. In fact, I don't think that that is so clear, but let's grant the objection for the sake of argument. Still, there are cases, involving stronger necessitation, that sidestep this worry.

Consider the property of being extended and the various fully determinate shades of color, but including being transparent. Quasi-determination holds between these properties: (1) being extended is necessitated by having a specific shade of color, say scarlet, but the necessitation does not run in the other direction; (2) scarletness is a member of a complete set of fully determinate properties (including being transparent) such that if x is extended, then x satisfies one of those properties; (3) being scarlet is not a conjunctive property; and (4) being extended is not a disjunctive property. Thus, being scarlet quasi-determines being extended.

The same holds for the properties of being extended and that of having a specific surface area a. Being extended is necessitated by having surface area a, but not the other way around. Having surface area a is a member of a set of fully determinate properties (specific surface areas), such that if x is extended then x has one of those properties. And, having surface area a is not a conjunctive property, and being extended, again, is not a disjunctive property. Thus, having surface area a also quasi-determines being extended. If quasi-determination sufficed for property instance identity, it would then follow that x's being extended is identical to x's being scarlet and that x's being extended is identical to x's having surface area s—and from that it should follow that x's being scarlet is identical to x's having surface area s. But the latter is clearly false.

The same property may be quasi-determined by distinct lower-level properties. Given the property instance identity thesis, now linked to quasi-determination, and the transitivity of identity, we end with absurd results. There are parallel mental/physical possible cases:

> Suppose that S and S' are same-level quasi-determinates of a mental property M in virtue of the fact that S and S' are super-realizers of M. For example, suppose that S and S' consist respectively in C-fiber-vibratingness and D-fiber-vibratingness, which, we can also suppose, are super-realizers of being in pain. As pointed out earlier, the dual doctrines of supervenience and multiple realizability do not rule out that the same person at the same time could realize more than one super-realizer of the same mental state. In this case, then, we can imagine, the same person a might simultaneously instantiate C-fiber-vibrations and D-fiber-vibrations. Now, if quasi-determination is sufficient for property instance identity (and super-realizers are quasi-determiners), then a's painfulness is identical to a's C-fiber-vibratingness and a's painfulness is identical to a's D-fiber-vibratingness. It should then be true that a's C-fiber-vibratingness is identical to a's D-fiber-vibratingness, but that is false.

If we prefer, we can set S and S' equal to distinct system-wide super-realizers of some mental state M. The consequences are the same.

This section began with the following argument against mental causation proper. For any physical property instance e that is caused, there is a physical property instance p, at an earlier time t, that is a complete cause of e, and e is not overdetermined. If there is also a mental property instance m at t, which is wholly distinct from p, but also causes e, then either physical causation is not complete or e is overdetermined. Hence, there are no mental causes at t of physical effect e. We examined two "top-down" strategies for circumventing this argument: deny that m and p are wholly distinct by affirming that m and p are identical property instances on the grounds that mental properties are either identical to or determinables of physical properties. Neither strategy is successful since mental property types are not identical to physical property types and because mental property types are not determinables of physical property types.[26]

1.2.2 Getting to a "token identity" thesis the old-fashioned (Davidsonian) way Let's now set aside a top-down strategy for deriving a token property instance identity thesis on the basis of a type-level identity claim or a type-level determination claim. The alternative

---

[26] With this "identity" strategy blocked, does the "determinationist" have left any other option? Yes, he could possibly deny that m and p are wholly distinct, while rejecting that m and p are identical. If the argument of this section is sound then this is, perhaps, the only alternative open to the determinationist. (The problem of causally relevant mental properties, also, cannot be solved by reference to a determination relation between mental and physical property types, since there is no such relation between these types. However, this problem may very well be solved by reference to a quasi-determination, asymmetric necessitation, which may be a relation that holds between mental and physical types.) The best example of this alternate "non-identity-determination" approach is advocated by Yablo. I will describe only that part of this approach that is aimed at mental causation proper. In a nutshell, Yablo argues that the token would-be competitors for being causes of e in our original argument (p and m—read now as events rather than property instances) are not wholly distinct—although they are non-identical—on the grounds that they themselves stand in a relation analogous to the determination relation for properties. Since p and m are not wholly distinct, they may both be causally relevant to e. This "determination" approach to mental causation proper is immune to the objections of this chapter, since it does not depend on the claim that mental properties are full-fledged determinables of physical properties (although Yablo's solution does depend on the claim that mental properties supervene on physical properties). In somewhat more detail, Yablo argues that every mental event m stands to some physical event p in a relation analogous to the determination relation based on the essences of these events. An event's essence consists in a certain selection of its essential properties and determination consists in one event's essence strictly including the essence of another event. Mental/physical supervenience, then, guarantees that if p realizes a mental event m, p's essence will include the mental properties in m's essence, but that p's essence will be physically richer than m's essence. Hence, p and m will be non-identical, but not wholly distinct. p and m will share their non-modal properties, but p's essence will strictly include m's essence, and, thus, these events will be non-identical but not wholly distinct (1992: 273, footnote 54). Yablo's approach to mental causation proper, then, differs from the approach examined in this chapter in two main ways. First, the determination relation relevant to mental causation holds between particulars—mental/physical events—not properties, and, second, this relation guarantees non-distinctness and non-identity of p and m. Hence, the claim of this chapter that mental properties are not determinables of physical properties is not directly relevant to Yablo's approach to the problem of mental causation proper. An evaluation of his alternative would require a close look at: (1) his assumption that events, rather than property instances, are the causal relata; (2) his account of event essences; and (3) his claim that the essences of the physical events that realize mental events include the essences of the latter. Whether or not this alternative strategy could work is a question I will not consider here.

strategy is to follow Davidson, and instead of starting at the type-level and trying to find some type-type relation that entails token identity, to argue directly for that token identity from the problem of mental causation proper. The problem of causation proper, as indicated, concerns how it is possible for there to be mental causes of physical effects given the completeness of physical causation and the exclusion principle. One response to this problem is to assert that mental property instances are identical to physical property instances. Is this viable?

This proposal is not viable, as we have seen, if property instances are exemplifications of universals. This way of cashing out the property instance identity thesis is problematic since it conflicts with a plausible necessary condition for the identity of "exemplifications of universals." Exemplifications of universals are identical only if their constituent properties are identical (Kim 1993b: 9). Since mental property types are not identical to physical property types, this proposal will not work.

On the other hand, this Davidson-style argument for property instance identity is viable if property instances are tropes. Assuming that causal relata are tropes, then one response to this argument is to claim that every mental trope m that is a cause of a physical effect is itself identical to physical trope p. Exclusion only applies to non-identical tropes. This conclusion is compatible with the non-identity of mental and physical types (given the multiple realizability of mental property types). The claim that a specific mental trope of mental type M is identical to a specific physical trope of physical type P is compatible with the non-identity of the mental type M and the physical type P.

2. The problem of causally relevant mental properties

However, as others have noted, even if a token identity response solves this first problem, the second problem of causally relevant mental properties remains. Let's see how that problem arises if causal relata are concrete events, not tropes. Suppose that every Davidsonian mental event is identical to a physical event. Still, Davidsonian causes are efficacious in virtue of some, but not all of their properties, opening the possibility that mental events may cause physical events in a causally closed physical world but *never* in virtue of their mental properties.[27] There are principles paralleling those above with just that apparent consequence: mental causation without mental property causal relevance (even granting that there are mental causes of physical effects):

(1) *the completeness of physical property causation*: for every physical effect e that has a cause at t, there are physical properties $P_i \ldots P_n$ that are instantiated at t that are causally sufficient for e; and

---

[27] For a discussion of this issue see, for example, (McLaughlin 1994).

(2) *property exclusion*: if the instantiation of $P_1 \ldots P_n$ at time t is causally sufficient for an event e, then no property distinct from $P_1 \ldots P_n$ instantiated at t is causally relevant to e.[28]

If mental properties are not physical properties, there are no causes at t of physical effect e that are efficacious in virtue of mental properties. Even if mental event m causes physical property effect e, m causes e only in virtue of m's physical properties, not its mental properties. (This problem also arises even if causal relata are tropes on the assumption that a trope may fall under more than one property type. I will say more about the second problem later on the assumption that causal relata are tropes.)

David Robb suggests one possible way around this kind of argument on the assumption that causal relata are concrete events. In his (1997), Robb takes the properties of Davidsonian event-causes to be *tropes* and proposes a *trope identity* solution to this second problem. Mental cause m, which is identical to a physical event p, causes physical event e in virtue of mental trope $m\star$, which is identical to a physical trope $p\star$. The property exclusion principle does not apply to $m\star$ since it only applies to properties that are not identical to physical properties (1997: 187). This solution is compatible with the non-identity of mental and physical types—given the multiple realizability of mental property types—if types are either universals or classes of tropes.

Robb's argument, which parallels and builds on Davidson's argument for a token event identity thesis, is just that if we adopt these *two* token identity claims—mental events are identical to physical events and mental tropes are identical to physical tropes—then we can solve both the problem of mental causation proper and the problem of causally relevant mental properties.

There are two difficulties with this proposal. The first concerns the assumption that causal relata are concrete events, not property instances. As indicated, I think this is not a viable account of causal relata since it leads to violations of causal transitivity. This difficulty can be avoided if we switch to the assumption that causal relata are tropes. Robb's proposal may, then, be adapted to the causal-relata-as-tropes framework as follows:

Every mental trope cause is identical to a physical trope and that trope is efficacious *in virtue of itself*, a property that is both mental and physical.

As particulars tropes can be causes, but as properties they can fulfill the "in virtue of" role. This alternative line of argument drops any "top-down" argument (such as a determination-based argument) for token identity, arguing that this token identity (causal relata are tropes and mental tropes are identical to physical tropes) is to be recommended because it solves the problem of mental causation proper and the problem of causally relevant properties. It is an elegant solution to both problems, it would seem.

---

[28] This formulation is adapted from (Robb 1997: 184).

Unfortunately, this proposed solution to the problem of causally relevant mental properties will not work. Even if causes are tropes and causally relevant properties are tropes, those tropes might turn out to be relevant in virtue of only some, but not others, of the *types* under which they fall. To see this, suppose that the crimson trope of a red light activates a device. The crimson trope may be relevant because of its precise shade rather than because it is some shade of red or other. A different shade of red would not lead to activation. If the cause is the crimson trope, that trope may be efficacious because of its particular shade rather than just its being some shade of red or other. To capture such facts, it could be argued that we attribute causal relevance to *types* and, contrary to Robb, there is room to worry about mental type relevance. There is room to worry about the causal relevance of mental types. In fact, the principles under consideration make this more than a worry if we substitute "types" for "properties":

(1) *the completeness of physical type causation*: for every physical effect e that has a cause at t, there are physical types $P_1 \ldots P_n$ that are instantiated at t that are causally sufficient for e; and

(2) *type exclusion*: if the instantiation of types $P_1 \ldots P_n$ at time t are causally sufficient for an event e, then no type distinct from $P_1 \ldots P_n$ instantiated at t is causally relevant to e.[29]

Since mental types are not identical to physical types (because of multiple realizability), even if mental tropes are identical to physical tropes, there are no causes of physical effects that are efficacious in virtue of mental property types.[30] (Or, for Robb, no mental types are relevant to causally relevant tropes of event-causes, if causes are not tropes.)[31]

---

[29] This formulation is adapted from (Robb 1997: 184).

[30] Notice that if Robb's account is combined with the claim that there is a determination relation between mental and physical types, then it would solve both problems on the reasonable assumption that determinables do not compete with their determinates for causal relevancy. But this must be ruled out, since mental properties are not determinables of their physical realizers.

[31] Robb tries to block this expansion of the second problem by denying that causally relevant properties—for Robb tropes—are ever causally relevant in virtue of falling under a type. Robb holds that otherwise we get a vicious regress (1997: 191). Robb stops this regress by disallowing causally relevant properties of causally relevant properties, types or otherwise. However, we can heed the ban on causally relevant properties of causally relevant properties by declaring that the causally relevant properties of trope-causes are types and that these types are not relevant in virtue of any higher-order properties. Second, Robb asserts that types are not the right sorts of thing to be causally relevant to effects. John Heil makes the same point in his (1999). But whether this is right depends heavily on one's theory of causation. On generalist theories, which I take to be on the right track, that is not so. Third, Robb argues that a "causally relevant property F simply does not have various aspects such that one can legitimately ask whether some but not others are responsible for F's being causally relevant." However, as Paul Noordhof points out in (1998: 223), "*complex* properties do have aspects concerning which one can ask 'Was that responsible?', namely, their constituents." And even tropes without constituent or higher-order tropes can still fall under multiple types, classes that are determined by a different degree of similarity required for membership. For an example, see (1998: 223).

2.1 Part–whole related types as exempt from exclusion

I will now propose a solution to the problem of causally relevant mental property types. To do this, I will continue to assume that causes are tropes in accord with the trope-based token identity solution to the problem of mental causation proper. The argument under consideration concludes that mental causes—tropes for us—are never efficacious in virtue of mental types. We cannot gain exemption from the type-exclusion principle by way of the identity of mental types to physical types. Multiple realizability rules that out. Nor can we appeal to a determination relation between mental and physical types in order to gain exemption. However, as I will now argue: (1) a part–whole relation between types is exemption-generating; and (2) mental and physical types are so related.

Before trying to argue for these two claims, two preliminary points must be made. The first is that one class is a subclass of another just in case the first is a part of the second. Here I follow David Lewis. Lewis argues that this thesis is supportable on a number of grounds, including that: (1) it conforms to common usage; and (2) the subclass–class and part–whole relations are formally analogous. On the latter point he notes that "just as a part of a part is itself a part, so too is a subclass of a subclass itself a subclass" and "just as a whole divides exhaustively into parts in many different ways, so a class divides exhaustively into subclasses in many different ways" (1991: 4–5). The second preliminary point simply reiterates my claim that types are classes of tropes. Throughout the following, I continue to hold that assumption, but notice that while I take types to be classes of tropes, I do not assume that all classes of tropes are types. Type-status will require further conditions, such as being natural.

Does the type-exclusion principle apply to part–whole related types? My answer will be "no." My strategy for approaching this question is to look at the justifications for this principle. This principle can then be seen not to apply to part–whole related types once we understand these justifications. The first justification is found at the level of token causation. This principle is aimed at excluding certain rare or non-existent patterns of causation, in particular, *token-level* overdetermination. Banning causal relevance for a type Y when there is a distinct type X that is instantiated and sufficient for a given effect blocks the possibility of the instantiation of Y as a causally sufficient, *overdetermining* cause of that effect.[32] The second justification is to block *non-causal* explanatory overdetermination where the efficacy of a cause with respect to an effect is *doubly* explained by non-identical types instantiated by that cause, but there is no causal overdetermination. Such independent explanations of the efficacy of the same cause are at best rare and the type-exclusion principle rules them out. Now let's consider the appropriate scope of the type-exclusion principle given each of these justifications.

---

[32] For example, Caston (1997: 316) seems to attempt just such a justification of a type-level exclusion principle on this basis.

158   PART I: TROPES

The ban-on-token-overdetermination justification certainly makes this principle apply to *wholly distinct* types (whose members are also wholly distinct), at least on my assumption that types are classes of tropes. To see this, suppose first that types M and P are made up of tropes m_1 and m_2 and of p_1 and p_2, respectively. In addition, suppose that every M trope is wholly distinct from every P trope. If M and P were each instantiated on the same occasion and each type was causally sufficient for the same type of effect, there would be token-level overdetermination. That is so because there would then be two independent, sufficient trope causes, say m_1 and p_2, of that effect. Our principle is meant to exclude this and it does: according to this principle, if P is relevant and sufficient to that effect, then M is not. But now consider whether this justification makes it appropriate to interpret the principle as applying to types that stand in the part–whole relation. In fact, it is not appropriate. Suppose that type P is a part of type M. It follows that P is a subclass of M on my assumptions that types are classes and that one class that is part of a second is a subclass of the second. Since P is a subclass of M, any member of P is a member of M. So every P trope is an M trope even though not necessarily every M trope is a P trope. Membership in one class does not mean non-membership in the other and, thus, it is *possible* that the *same* trope-cause falls into both classes. From this possibility, it follows that even if both types P and M are separately relevant and sufficient for the effect type and both are instantiated on the same occasion, that does not guarantee token overdetermination. This is so because each type may be instanced by the *same* trope-cause on that occasion. Thus, there is room for each type being independently sufficient on the same occasion, *without overdetermination*, something that is not possible with wholly distinct types (whose members are wholly distinct), if causal relata are tropes.[33] In so far as the type-exclusion principle is meant to rule out token overdetermination, it does not apply to types that stand in a part–whole relation to each other. However, this is not the only justification for this principle and we cannot say just yet, without qualification, that part–whole related types are exempt.

The second justification is that type-exclusion rules out non-identical types instantiated by the same cause c, where each is independently relevant to and sufficient for c's causing the same effect e: *explanatory* overdetermination without *causal* overdetermination. Type-exclusion is meant to exclude this possibility and it does. To determine whether this justification means that this principle applies to part–whole related types, a better understanding of what is objectionable about non-causal overdetermination is required. I would suggest that what is objectionable in non-causal overdetermination is

---

[33] The same point applies even if causal relata are Davidsonian events, if types are still taken to be classes of tropes. If types P and M stand in the part–whole relation, then it is possible that the same trope instances both types and that one trope characterizes a Davidsonian event. But even if mental and physical types do not stand in the part–whole relation, the argument to the irrelevance of mental types from the type-level exclusion principle (as based on the ban on token overdetermination) is still problematic. If our concern is with a ban on token overdetermination, then even if the instantiations of the wholly distinct types $P_1 \ldots P_n$ are sufficient for e, these types may all be instantiated by the same Davidsonian event.

that there are co-instantiated distinct types such that the relevancy of one (with respect to the same effect) is not identical to the relevancy of the other. In this respect, the type-exclusion principle is meant to guarantee the following:

> For any property type P that c instantiates such that the instantiation of P by c at t is sufficient for c to cause e and P is relevant to c's causing e, then for any property M instantiated by c at t that is sufficient/relevant to c's causing e, then the relevancy of M is identical to the relevancy of P.

The issue is whether guaranteeing the latter means that this principle should apply to part–whole related types. The answer would be "yes" if the identity of the relevancy of M and that of P was only possible when M and P were identical. In fact, that is not so. There is another way for the relevancy of M to be identical to the relevancy of P. The relevancy of P and M might *overlap*. Non-identical types might *share* relevancy. The principle says that if c's instantiation of type P is relevant/sufficient for c to cause e, then there is no other distinct type M instantiated by c relevant to c's causing e. If there can be overlapping relevancy, then this principle should be understood to continue with the phrase "such that the relevancy of P is not identical to the relevancy of M." In order to determine whether part–whole related types may share relevancy and, thus, fall outside the scope of this principle, we need to explore two issues: (1) under what conditions is there shared relevancy between distinct properties; and (2) are these conditions ever satisfied in the case of part–whole related types?

Jessica Wilson makes a point relevant to this first question. She says that if "each individual causal power associated with a supervenient property is *numerically identical* with a causal power associated with its base property," then overdetermination is avoided even if both properties are causally relevant to the same effect.[34] The same is true when there is more than one base property if the causal powers of the supervenient property are a subset of the causal powers of the base properties. Her point can be adapted to our discussion. What a property is causally relevant to will depend, in part, on its causal powers. *Shared relevancy* is possible with shared causal powers. If the causal powers of non-identical properties are numerically the same or the causal powers of one are a subset of the causal powers of the other, then they can share relevancy. This is so since a property type being relevant to c's causing e on occasion o will be a matter of the exercise of a causal power to produce e bestowed by that type. If the causal power to produce e bestowed by a type M on this occasion is identical to the causal power to produce e bestowed by a non-identical type P, then relevancy of M to c's causing e on this occasion is identical to the relevancy of P to c's causing e. In that event, there will be no non-causal explanatory overdetermination since the relevancy of M is identical to the relevancy of P. Those are conditions under which there is shared relevancy. Now we can consider the question of whether types that stand in the part–whole relation

---

[34] Wilson (1999: 41) says that overdetermination is not avoided if "mental properties have the *same*, but still numerically distinct, causal powers as their base properties."

meet these conditions. If so, then there will be occasions on which those types share relevancy and there is no non-causal overdetermination.

Let's specify some necessary conditions under which a class M of tropes has a causal power. Consider a class M of non-overlapping types $(P_1 \ldots P_n)$. Each P_i is a subclass and, hence, part of the class. First, the class M has a causal power to bring about e in circumstances C only if *every* such subtype P_i has a causal power to bring about e in C. For example, if not every red trope of whatever shade of red has the power to activate a "red detector" machine, then the type red does not have that power. Thus if P_1 has the power to bring about e, but P_2 does not, then the class M does not. Second, if there are other ways to divide up the class into non-overlapping types, such as $(Q_1 \ldots Q_n)$, then the class has a causal power only if each Q_i has such a power. Third, the power of the class as a whole to bring about e is just the set of exactly similar causal powers of each subtype to bring about e.

Do part–whole related types ever share causal power and possibly causal relevance? Suppose that type M has the causal power to produce e and subdivides exhaustively into non-overlapping part-types, $P_1 \ldots P_n$, where each P_i has the power to bring about e. Consider a particular occasion on which *both* M and P_1 are relevant to c's causing e, but no other P_i is instantiated and hence causally relevant on that occasion. Is the causal power that M has to bring about e *that is exercised on this occasion* (call that power "x") identical to the causal power to produce e that is exercised by P_1 (call that power "y")? The *exercised* causal power of M to produce e is certainly *not* identical to the causal power of one of the *other* P_i's since no other P_i's causal power is exercised on this occasion.[35] Might x still fail to be identical to y? The class $P_1 \ldots P_n$ has no causal power that is not a causal power of one of these P_i's. The causal powers of a class of types are the sets of exactly similar causal powers of its subtypes, when each subtype has such a causal power. If x were not identical to y, then x would not be in a set of causal powers that are exactly alike in being powers to produce e such that each is had by some P_i. Thus, x is identical to y. In short, since M is identical to $P_1 \ldots P_n$, M's causal power to produce e, which is exercised on this occasion, is identical to P_1's causal power to produce e, which is exercised on this occasion. The causal power of a type that is exercised on a particular occasion is identical to the causal power of its acting type-part on that occasion. Thus, the relevance of M to c's causing e on this occasion is identical to the relevance of P_1 to c's causing e on this occasion and there is no non-causal overdetermination.

2.2 Mental and physical types are part–whole related

That brings us to the question of whether mental and physical types are part–whole related. Recall that mental types are not identical to non-disjunctive physical types because of multiple realizability. What is the basis of this implication? It is that the

---

[35] Further, y is not identical to any e-causal power of any combination of P_i's, since no such combination is realized on this occasion.

members of any reasonable candidate class, $(P_1, \ldots, P_n)$, will be so physically disparate so as to disqualify $(P_1, \ldots, P_n)$ as a genuine physical type.[36] Call this the *disparity problem*.[37] However, what has not been noted is that the disparity problem, while ruling out that mental type M is identical to some physical type P, does not rule out that mental type M *includes* certain physical types as parts. That the disparity problem does not eliminate this possibility can be seen as follows:

> Suppose that X, a type, is identical to Y, a type, and that Y is made up of the subtypes A and B, where A does not overlap B and each is a physical type. Suppose also that there is sufficient similarity between A and B so that Y is a physical type. Also suppose that every X-trope is identical to an A-trope or to a B-trope. What is the relation between X and A? *Not* that X is identical to A, since there are instances of X that are not instances of A. X is identical to Y and Y is made of the subclasses A and B. Hence, the correct answer is that A is a part of X. But *now* let's change the case. Instead of supposing that A and B are sufficiently similar to each other in the right way for this class to qualify as a physical type, suppose that A and B are *not* sufficiently alike for this class to be a physical type, even though every X-trope is identical to an A-trope or to a B-trope. Type X is not identical to a particular physical type only because (A, B) does not form a physical type. However, since the relation between X and A is otherwise the same as in the case in which (A, B) forms a physical type, it is reasonable to conclude that X and A stand in a part–whole relation to each other in this case also.

From the fact that X is not identical to any physical type because the only reasonable candidate for that role, (A, B), is itself *not* a physical type, it does not follow that X does not stand in a part–whole relation to A or that X does not stand in a part–whole relation to B, where A and B are each physical types, even if it is false that X is identical to A and false that X is identical to B. A part–whole relation is compatible with the disparity problem. That leaves the question of whether it is plausible that mental types include physical types as parts. I believe it is, given certain credible suppositions.

Let's work with a general mental type, "being in pain." The first supposition is that every pain trope is a physical trope. This follows from our earlier claim that physically efficacious mental tropes are physical tropes (our solution to the first problem) when combined with the reasonable conjecture that every mental trope has or could have

---

[36] Teller (1984: 59) says in discussing long disjunctions of disparate physical properties: "Now what, I want to ask, makes it appropriate to call a property 'physical' when it is such a disparate and infinitely long disjunction of disjuncts...? Yes, it is a Boolean combination of physical properties, but I feel that to call it 'physical' threatens to be misleading. Which physical characteristics is it that all the things satisfying the individual disjuncts have in common?"

[37] As Robb puts this point: "But multiple realizability entails that these physical tropes do not themselves resemble one another in the way that members of a *physical* type must: they will be wildly dissimilar physically" (1997: 188). Or, as Jaegwon Kim puts the point: "Unless disjunctive physical kinds are embraced, we cannot reduce M to some P; that much is entailed by the multiple realizability of the mental" (1993a: 365).

physical effects. The second supposition is that for every pain trope there is some physical type P_i or other, such that that trope is a P_i trope and every P_i trope is a pain trope. This assumption is justified if there are local type-level species- or structure-relative mental–physical identities: for example, if "being in human pain" is identical to some physical type and the same is true of "being in (other-species) pain," or if multiple realizability reaches within species but there are structures such that "being in pain relative to structure s" is identical to "being in P_i." However, these local-type identities are not required for our second supposition. Even in their absence, it is likely still true that every pain trope is of some physical type P_i or other, such that every trope of that physical type is a pain trope (even if no mental type relative to a species or structure is identical to a physical type). Our third supposition is our earlier assumption that types are classes of tropes. Thus, the type "being in pain" is a class of tropes. But which class? Suppose that $(P_1, \ldots, P_n)$ is a list of physical types such that each P_i trope is a pain trope, and every pain trope falls under one of these types but no one pain trope falls under more than one. The answer, then, is the class of tropes falling under the types $(P_1, \ldots, P_n)$. What other class of tropes could "being in pain" be identical to? Thus the type "being in pain" is made up of the physical types $(P_1, \ldots, P_n)$. Still, that does *not* mean that "being in pain" is identical to a physical type. $(P_1, \ldots, P_n)$ is *not* a physical type—because the physical subclasses in it are too disparate. There is no physical type to which "being in pain" is identical, but since "being in pain" is identical to the class $(P_1, \ldots, P_n)$, it includes as proper parts the physical types that form subclasses (P_1, P_2, etc.) of this class. These physical types exhaustively and exclusively subdivide "being in pain."[38] The same will be true for any mental type M. There is no physical type to which M is identical, but there are physical types that M includes ("part–whole physicalism"), if types are classes of tropes.[39] Every M trope is identical to some P_i trope, and every such physical type subclass, P_i, is such that every P_i-trope is an M-trope.

Now we can return to non-causal overdetermination. Recall that the ban on non-causal overdetermination is aimed at ruling out distinct types instantiated by the same cause such that the relevancy of one *is not identical to* the relevancy of the other. The worry is that this ban is violated if both a mental and a physical type under which a

---

[38] Heil in (1999: 6) suggests that my approach to mental causation does not require that properties are tropes or that causal relata are tropes. The real work, he suggests, is done by the fact that mental predicates "encompass a range of properties that are similar, but not exactly similar." According to Heil, the same basic approach works, if a given mental predicate designates different physical universals in different creatures/at different times. The key is that "pain" designates varying universals on different occasions of use, but always a physical universal. The second problem is solved with a type-level identity solution: the mental predicate on any particular occasion will pick out a physical universal that is causally relevant. Even if Heil is right, there still might be a reason to prefer the trope version: the tropist might be able to say that there are general mental types (since types are classes of tropes and there may be an appropriate class for these general mental types), but the Universalist cannot say as much since there is no universal that corresponds to the predicate "pain in general."

[39] Perhaps something like this view is what Kim has in mind by his "multiple-type physicalism" (1993a: 364).

trope-cause falls are both relevant, with respect to the same effect. We can now see that that will not necessarily be the case. Since the causal power exercised by the mental type on a particular occasion, if any, is identical to the causal power exercised by its instantiated physical part-type on that same occasion, the relevancy of M will be identical to the relevancy of P_i. There will be no non-causal explanatory overdetermination in that event.[40] Hence, the argument under consideration, which is meant to show that mental types are never causally relevant to a physical effect, is unsound.

It is worth pointing out that there is a connection between our treatment of the first problem of mental causation and that of the second. A token identity claim solves the first problem and we share that much in common with the Davidsonian. However, we diverge from the Davidsonian over what causal relata are, tropes not concrete events, and this divergence has great significance. With tropes as causes, this token identity claim amounts to something quite different than it does for the Davidsonian. For the latter, his token identity claim is about mental and physical events, leaving open the relation between mental and physical properties except to say that they are sometimes instantiated by the same event. On the trope view, the token identity claim is about *properties*, mental and physical. Thus, when the tropist turns to the second problem of types he already has a leg up, unlike the Davidsonian, in having specified some substantial relation between mental and physical properties *before* getting to the problem of types. When turning to the second problem, he can build up an answer from the first answer by invoking the further assumption that types are classes of properties. Since mental causes are tropes (and physical tropes at that) and types are classes of tropes, that opens up the possibility that mental types have physical types as parts and a further argument establishes the latter.

In this section, I have argued that the overdetermination argument does not refute mental type causal relevance: there is no inconsistency in attributing relevancy to both mental and physical types with respect to the same physical effect, even with a ban on overdetermination and the completeness of physical causation. Physical and mental types may both exercise causal powers with respect to the same physical effect without overdetermination because mental types are composed of physical types.[41] What I have not yet shown is that mental types have causal powers. I turn to that issue now.

---

[40] The goal here is to leave room for the relevancy of mental types, which is threatened by the two principles, the Completeness of Physical Type Causation and Type Exclusion. Hence, the goal is not merely to avoid the overdetermination of causal efficacy while allowing for the explanatory overdetermination of the causal relevancy of types. Now there may be a further goal of showing that there is some sense in which mental types are *distinctively* relevant, but I am not sure that that goal is consistent with the Type Exclusion Principle.

[41] My approach is Yabloesque in that the goal is to identify some relation between non-identical types, that is, exemption-generating vis-à-vis type-exclusion. But there is another sense in which my approach is Yabloesque: if you are convinced that Yablo is right that mental types are determinables of physical types and that that shows that these types do not compete for causal influence, you still might be puzzled by the fact that determinables don't compete with determinates. You still might want a metaphysical account of that fact. Part–whole physicalism supplies such an account once it is recognized that the determinable–determinate

2.3 Causal powers of mental types

I approach this topic by further considering conditions under which a class of tropes as a whole has a causal power. I begin with a series of cases running from one in which a class C of tropes has a power to bring about *e* to one in which it does not. Not surprisingly, the causal powers of the class vary with the degree of similarity, among the members of C, with respect to potential causes/effects.

> *First Case*: consider the class of all mass tropes of a particular fully determinate magnitude *x*. Each is causally indistinguishable from the others. Every trope in the class C shares the same potential causes/effects, including, we can suppose, a power to cause *e* under certain circumstances.[42]

In this first case, it is clear that the class *as a whole* has a power to cause *e*. The type "mass of magnitude *x*" has a causal power to bring about *e*. Alternately stated, if one of these tropes caused an effect *e*, that would be explainable by the fact that this trope is a member of C or is of type C.

> *Last Case*: C is the class of all mass tropes of a particular determinate magnitude *x* and all color tropes of a particular determinate shade of color *s*. Assume that the subclass of mass and the subclass of color tropes share no potential causes/effects. (Assume also that these subclasses are also maximal: no trope that shares the same potential causes/effects as any member of one is not also a member of that subclass.)

In this case, C as a whole clearly lacks the power to bring about *e*. Even if the mass tropes have a power to cause *e*, this class C as a whole does not since the color tropes do

---

relation is an instance of the class–subclass relation account and it is that relation that grounds this non-competition, or so it can be argued as follows:

> Assume reasonably that all tropes are fully determinate and that falling under a determinable predicate is a matter of being characterized by a fully determinate trope that is a member of a class of tropes, membership in which is a matter of less-than-exact resemblance. With this assumption, it is best to construe the determinate–determinable distinction as applying to classes of tropes and only derivatively to individual tropes: a class of tropes is fully determinate only if the members of that class resemble each other exactly. If a trope-cause is picked out in virtue of its membership in a determinable class, that trope will also fall into a fully determinate class, a subclass of that larger class. Hence, a determinable property type is a class and its determinates are subclasses of that class that exhibit a higher degree of internal similarity. The color (type) of the chair does not compete causally with the scarlet (type) of the chair since these two property types stand in the part–whole relation.

If Yablo is right that mental types are determinables of physical types and don't causally compete, then that will be because determinables and determinates stand in the part–whole relation. However, even if Yablo is wrong, the spirit of Yablo's point remains secure. Even if mental types are not determinables of physical types, mental and physical types stand in a part–whole relation and that is enough to undercut the "overdetermination" argument against mental type causal relevance.

[42] For any two tropes, x and y, in C and for any trope t, if t could cause x (y) then t could cause y (x) in the same type of circumstance, and for any trope t, if x (y) could cause t, then y (x) could cause in the same type of circumstance.

not.[43] This is somewhat of a degenerate case in the series, from our point of view. Not all the trope members have a power to cause *e* and, hence, the main issue of the degree of causal similarity of the members of *C*, *independent of a power to cause e*, does not even arise. Clearly for a class of tropes as a whole to have a power to cause *e* each of its members must have such a power.

> *Next-to-Last Case*: *C* consists of two causally homogeneous and maximal subclasses of tropes. Between these two subclasses there are no common potential causes and only one common potential effect *e*.

This case brings us back to the main issue. *C* as a whole exhibits very low causal homogeneity, and the class *C* as a whole does *not* have a causal power to bring about *e*. If a member of the first subclass caused *e*, that cannot be explained by the fact that that trope is a member of class *C*, including the second subclass. Otherwise, we end up with exceedingly trivial explanations of the form "*c* caused *e* because it is one of the things that can cause *e*." This next-to-last case shows that there can be classes of tropes *all* the members of which have a particular power, but the class as a whole does not. The series suggests that: (a) if causal homogeneity is high, the class as a whole has the causal power at issue; but (b) if low, the class as a whole lacks the causal power at issue.

Where do mental types fit in this series? A mental type *M* is exhaustively composed of non-overlapping physical types, $P_1 \ldots P_n$, each of which is a class of tropes. If *M* is not to fall near the "last case" end, then it must be shown that there is some effect *e* (from a set of exactly similar effects) that each such physical subtype, P_i, has the power to cause. To show this we must work within some broad account of mental types. The one I choose is functionalism. Although heavily debated, functionalism remains very much a live contemporary program. I will be making use only of the claim that functionalism has successfully identified a necessary condition for being a mental trope of a certain type.

The functionalist begins with a psychological "theory," on the basis of which he defines mental terms. This theory incorporates all the causal facts appropriately included in a psychological theory about these mental states, but not all of the causal facts whatsoever about these mental properties. A Ramsey sentence is then constructed by replacing all the mental predicates in the theory with predicate variables, binding those variables with existential quantifiers. From the Ramsey sentence, definitions are generated which characterize each mental type in terms of potential causes and effects. These definitions will have the implication that all instances of a mental type share a set of the same potential causes/effects. In the language of tropes, that will mean that every physical trope that is a mental trope of a particular kind *M* shares some common

---

[43] A more extreme case would run as follows. At the other end of the spectrum, there is a class *C* of tropes such that its members are maximally causally inhomogeneous in that for any two tropes, *x* and *y*, in *C* there is no (type of) trope *t* that could cause both *x* and *y* and there is no (type of) trope *t* that both *x* and *y* could cause.

potential effects. Functionalism, thus, seems to guarantee that the class of M tropes does not fall near the "last case," a minimal requirement for having a causal power.

But there is an objection that must be considered:

> The functionalist account does say that tropes of the same mental type have some of the same potential effects, but not necessarily in the same circumstance. M tropes in different species have some potential effects in common in their respective species' environments, but not necessarily if swapped across species. But, the objection continues, to avoid "last case" status, M tropes must share some common effects in the *same* circumstances.

This objection, however, can be shown to be defective. The key to diagnosing this defect is a distinction made by Shoemaker (1984a: 261–86). Consider the following functional predicate derived from the psychological theory T vis-à-vis its Ramsey sentence:

$$(\exists F_1)\ldots(\exists F_n)[T(\ldots F_j x \ldots) \& F_j x]$$

where "F_j" replaces "is in pain" in the psychological theory. Now suppose that a particular individual A and a set of physical predicates $P_1 \ldots P_n$ such that if we replace the "F's" with "P's" and remove the initial quantifiers, the resulting physical predicate $[T(\ldots P_j x \ldots) \& P_j x]$ is true of A (1984a: 264). The physical predicate P_j might, for example, be "has C-fibers vibrating" and the physical predicate $[T(\ldots P_j x \ldots)]$ will be a determinate form of the property being physically constituted in such a way that P_j plays the causal role definitive of pain (1984: 265). Shoemaker designates P_j as a core realizer and $[T(\ldots P_j x \ldots) \& P_j x]$ as a total realizer of pain, and it is this distinction that undercuts the objection at hand. The total realizer is unconditionally sufficient for being in pain; the core realizer is not. The total realizer *includes* a determinate form of the property "being physically constituted in such a way that P_j plays the causal role definitive of pain." That means that different total realizers of pain will be causally indistinguishable with respect to the potential causes/effects specified in the psychological theory, even if swapped across species: "in no creature could a physical property which in us is a total realization of the property of being in pain be a realization of any other mental property, or fail to be a realization of that one" (1984a: 266). Thus, we need only restrict our physical subtypes to total realizers to handle the objection: a mental type M is exhaustively composed of non-overlapping physical types, $P_1 \ldots P_n$, each of which is a total realizer of M.

Although this objection can be answered, there is a further worry. Functionalism may establish *no more* than that mental types should not be grouped with the "last case," but not establish that they should be placed at the other end of the series. This worry rests on the fact that having a shared core of causal powers, as specified by the psychological theory, is only one factor relevant to the question of high causal homogeneity. High causal homogeneity also requires the cooperation of a second factor: the degree of causal variation, over and above this core, among the physical tropes playing these psychological roles. Even if the total realizers of M share a core of potential causes/effects, these realizers will differ causally, maybe even widely, since they will differ physically. If variation along this second dimension is great enough, we will not have a case at the high causal homogeneity end of the series. We might have a case in which there are a significant number of shared causal powers but a much greater number of unshared powers. Since functionalism cannot limit the extent of variation in this second factor, it cannot guarantee high causal homogeneity.

My response to this worry is not to take on this second factor directly. Instead, I will shift gears and suggest that a significant degree of similarity in potential causes/effects among the subtypes is itself sufficient for causal powers for the type. A significant degree of core causal similarity is enough for causal powers for a type despite further causal differences due to differences in the physical realizers. I will also suggest that mental types qualify as having causal powers under that condition. I begin by looking at a middle case in the series:

> *Middle Case*: Consider the class of red tropes. This class consists of a multitude of causally homogeneous subclasses made up of tropes of fully determinate shades of red. The subclasses share a significant number of potential causes/effects, but also differ in this respect.

In this case, it seems clear that the class of red tropes as a whole, the type "red," has certain causal powers. Indeed, this case and others like it show that there can be causal powers for a type even without high causal homogeneity. Two further points stand out. First, there must be some significant degree of causal similarity among the subclasses; otherwise it is not legitimate to ascribe causal powers to the class as a whole. Second, once that degree of causal similarity reaches a moderate level, it is to that degree true that the type has causal powers. It is not the ratio between shared versus differing causal powers among the subtypes that matters, but how extensive the shared causal powers are (the absolute level). Moderate causal homogeneity is associated with causal powers. Note also that there is no precise borderline between cases in which the class as a whole has causal powers and cases in which it does not.

Given that the type "red" has some causal powers, we are still left with the question of how the causal powers of this class as a whole are related to the causal powers of the subclasses of each determinate shade of red. I believe the answer is that the causal powers of the type "red" are those exactly similar causal powers shared by each of these subclasses. If all shades of red have powers exactly similar to e, f, and g, then the type "red" has those exactly similar causal powers. If every shade can activate a "red detector," then the type "red" has those exactly similar causal powers. For any causal power of a shade of red not matched by an exactly similar causal power belonging to each of the other shades of red, "red" lacks any such power. This is the basic function from the causal powers of the subclasses of determinate shades of red to the causal powers of the type "red."[44]

With this middle case in mind, we can return to the issue of causal powers for M as a whole. I would suggest that the basis for thinking that mental type M has causal powers (and what they are) is an analogy with this middle case. There are two aspects to this analogy,

> (1) There is a structural analogy between "red" and M. The type "red" is identical to a class of tropes that breaks down into mutually exclusive subclasses, each of which is a determinate type of color. The mental type "M" is identical to a class of tropes that breaks down into mutually exclusive physical subclasses, each of which is a physical type.
> (2) Just as the subclasses of red share a set of exactly similar causal powers, but also differ causally, the same is true of these various physical subtypes of M (at least if functionalism is right). In both cases there is a significant causal overlap among the relevant subtypes.

Given this dual similarity, it is reasonable that the questions of whether M has causal powers, and, if so, what they are, can also be answered on analogy with the "red" case. To the first question we can say that since the class "red" as a whole has causal powers, it is reasonable to infer that M does too, given the analogy, and to the second question, that since the causal powers of "red" are just those exactly similar causal powers shared by its subclasses, the same should be true for M. Since M breaks down into mutually exclusive physical types, we can say, on analogy with "red," that the causal powers of M as a whole are just those exactly similar causal powers shared by all such physical subclasses. Mental types have causal powers as a function of the causal powers of their parts, just like "red." And given functionalism, we have reason for thinking that there is a significant set of shared causal features. Thus it is reasonable to conclude that mental types have causal powers.

Notice that a full commitment to functionalism is not required for the argument of the last part of this chapter. We require only that every M trope has a significant core set of causal features and not the further functionalist claim that any property with those same causal potential causes/effects is an M property.[45]

---

[44] There will also be some cases in the middle in which it is indeterminate whether the class C has this causal power. For example, the class C of two diseases sharing half of their germ-causes and half of their consequences, including leg cramps. In that event, it is indeterminate whether C has the causal power to bring about leg cramps. Also, it is indeterminate whether appealing to membership in C can explain why a particular instance of one of these diseases causes a particular leg cramp.

[45] One further issue should be mentioned: should the class of tropes that is the type M include merely possible tropes, either physical or non-physical? There are two aspects to this issue. The first is whether there are merely possible tropes. I deny that there are. The second is, even if there are and even if they are included in the M class, their inclusion is compatible with the argument laid out thus far, although if we include merely possible non-physical tropes we can no longer say that mental types are exhaustively composed of physical subtypes. Still, if the only *actual* M tropes break down exhaustively into physical subtypes, then since the causal

2.4 Objections: The disjunctive strategy and part–whole physicalism

I now briefly consider some possible objections. The objections considered apply to another approach, the "disjunctive strategy," but might be thought also to apply to part–whole physicalism. The basic claim of the disjunctive strategy is that mental types are identical to disjunctive types. M is identical to a disjunctive property, $P_1 \vee P_2 \ldots P_n$, which may be an infinite disjunction of physical types. The main objections are directed at: (1) the very notion of disjunctive properties; and (2) the principle that for any two properties P and Q, there is a disjunctive property $P \vee Q$. The first three come from Armstrong and the last from Kim.

This first objection is based on the principle that objects, all of which are characterized by a property P, must literally share something in common, or in a trope framework, resemble each other in some significant way. This principle is violated by disjunctive properties.[46] Two objects characterized by a disjunctive property $P \vee Q$ may fail to be identical in any relevant respect or resemble each other significantly. This objection does not apply to part–whole physicalism since the latter identifies mental types with non-arbitrary classes of tropes that exhibit significant resemblance, with respect to the core causal features posited by functionalism.

The second objection is directed at the principle that if P and Q are properties so is $P \vee Q$, and, by extension to the principle that any combination of classes of tropes forms a type. Armstrong suggests that this principle of property closure under disjunction has the unacceptable epistemological implication that from that fact that a has P, it can be proven by *a priori* reasoning alone that a has an indefinite number of other properties such as $P \vee Q$. Fortunately, part–whole physicalism is not committed to the analogue principle that every class of tropes is a type and that if a is P, we can infer *a priori* that a falls under a further type made up of P and any arbitrary type Q. Part–whole physicalism does not sanction this inference because it does not assume that there is any such type composed of these arbitrary tropes.

---

power exercised by the mental type on any actual occasion is identical to the causal power exercised by its instantiated physical part-type on that same occasion, there will be no overdetermination, either causal or non-causal-explanatory, even if there are merely possible non-physical or physical M tropes. Even if M includes some merely possible non-physical/physical subtypes, there will be a shared causal power, shared even by such non-physical types, if functionalism accurately provides a necessary condition for being M. That is enough to ground a claim of causal power for the mental type M. Finally, even if we include merely possible non-physical tropes in the M class that is consistent with physicalism since that demands only that all *actual*, or perhaps all physically possible, M tropes be physical. On the other hand, we might treat "M" as a non-rigid designator that picks out a certain class of tropes in this world, but different classes in other worlds. In that case, since the causal power exercised by the trope class actually picked out by "M" in this world, on any actual occasion, is identical to the causal power exercised by its instantiated physical part-type on that same occasion, there will be no overdetermination. As to the argument of the last part, all of the tropes picked out non-rigidly by "M" will have the same shared causal powers if functionalism accurately provides a necessary condition for being M.

[46] For these first three objections, see (Armstrong 1978b: 19–23).

The third objection is that disjunctive properties violate the proper link between properties and causal powers. If *a* has *P*, but not *Q*, when *a* acts it does so in virtue of *P*, not *Q*, and its being either *P* v *Q* adds no power additional to that bestowed by *P* which undermines *the* claim that *P* v *Q* is a genuine property. Before determining if this objection applies to part–whole physicalism, consider again the case of red. Being red adds no additional powers to a crimson object beyond those bestowed by its being crimson. Still, red is a genuine type that is not identical to the type crimson. Red, however, can be distinguished from an arbitrary disjunction. The causal powers of red include a subset of those of crimson, specifically those causal powers matched by exactly similar causal powers of all shades of red. With the arbitrary disjunctive property being *P* v *Q*, there is no overlap in the causal powers of the disjuncts. Even though red adds no new power beyond that of crimson to this object, there is a story to be told as to how red remains a genuine type with causal powers. A similar story applies to the causal powers of mental types. Mental types retain causal powers under this approach.

A fourth objection is that disjunctive properties lead to spurious disjunctive causal explanations (Kim 1998: 108). Suppose that D_1 and D_2 are very different diseases, with one common symptom *s*, and that the evidence shows Jones to have either D_1 or D_2, but not which one. If there really are disjunctive properties, then the following is a legitimate causal explanation: Jones' having either D_1 or D_2 explains his having *s*. But this is not a legitimate explanation by way of a disjunctive cause, as Kim points out, but a disjunction of explanations.[47] Moving up to the level of causally relevant types, we can modify Kim's case. Suppose that we know that Jones has D_1 and we assert that his disease D_1 causes *s* because D_1 is of the type "being either D_1 or D_2." That also seems to be illegitimate. In fact, however, part–whole physicalism does not sanction it as legitimate. These diseases share only a single effect, and that puts this case near the end of our series, with the classes of tropes that lack any causal power. They share insufficient causal features.[48] Part–whole physicalism, combined with functionalism, makes the mental case differ from this modified Kim case on this scale of shared causal features.[49]

---

[47] This objection does not apply directly to part–whole physicalism since the latter does not posit causal explanations of specific events in terms of classes of tropes.

[48] A fifth objection, from Kim, is that disjunctions of heterogeneous properties generally fail to be nomic projectible properties. Consider the "law" that patients with either D_1 or D_2, very different diseases, will get *s*. This "law" cannot be confirmed by only numerous positive instances of people with D_1 and *s* with no negative instances because such observations say nothing about D_2. "So the disjunctive antecedent of the alleged law fails to be projectible" (1998: 109). First, note that projectibility is not a separate issue from causal homogeneity. As Kim points out, the unprojectibility of arbitrary disjunctive property is rooted in their causal heterogeneity. But part–whole physicalism, coupled with functionalism, is committed to a significant core of shared causal powers. And projectibility is a matter of degree; the more shared causal features, the more projectible. If *C* is a class of tropes composed of two subclasses that share potential causes *x*, *y*, and *z* and potential effects *a*, *b*, and *c*, then in so for as the evidence is confined to features linked as causes of those causes or effects of those effects, projection is possible, even if the sample includes only members of one of the two subclasses.

[49] In conversation, Mark Heller suggested that it might be objected that arbitrary classes of tropes have causal powers on this account under certain conditions. Suppose that (*P*, *Q*) is a class whose subclasses, *P* and *Q*, consist of intrinsically very different properties, and we construct a machine, with a light that goes on

2.5 Relation to a Subset-based Account of realization

In this final section, I will briefly discuss the relationship between my part–whole account of the relation between mental property types and the physical property types that realize them with Shoemaker's "causal powers subset" account of the realization relation. Shoemaker's approach to the realization relation between properties focuses on the causal powers of properties, or the causal powers that properties bestow on their possessors. The idea is that there is a relation between the causal powers of realized and realizer properties that is key to the realization relation. Consider Shoemaker's account of "same-subject" realization, in which the realized and realizer properties are instantiated in the same subject. Shoemaker offers the following Subset Account as a first approximation:

"Property P has property Q as a realizer just in case (1) the forward-looking causal features of property P are a subset of the forward-looking features of property Q, and (2) the backward-looking causal features of property P have as a subset the backward-looking features of property Q" (2007: 12).

Forward-looking causal features include how the instantiations of the property contribute to producing various effects and contribute to bestowing causal powers on its possessors, and backward-looking causal features include the types of states of affairs that can cause the instantiation of that property. The property red is realized by the property scarlet just in case, roughly, the effects of instantiations of red are a subset of the effects of the instantiations of scarlet and the causes of the instantiations of scarlet are a subset of the causes of the instantiations of red. According to the subset view property Q realizes property P only if the set of causal powers that constitutes Q is a subset of the causal powers that constitute Q. This approximation requires further refinements, but it is sufficient for my purpose here.[50] This view has several advantages. First,

---

whenever the machine is either in state P or Q, with no other effects. Does the class of P and Q as a whole thereby have a causal power? Consider a series of cases: (1) there is only one such machine; (2) there are many such machines and each reacts to P or Q with one and only type of effect that is different from one machine to the next; (3) same as (2), but the machines now react with multiple effects (the same effects for each); and (4) same as (3), but P and Q share also many causes with respect to each machine. In case (1), with so few causal features in common, the disjunct properties fail to form a class with a causal power. In case (2), more effects are shared. Moderate causal homogeneity should be read as requiring that there are some circumstances in which P and Q share a moderate number of causal features (including potential effects). Case (2) does not satisfy this condition. Case (3) partly addresses this issue. There are multiple effects for each machine. Still case (3) lacks common causes for P and Q. Case (4) makes up for this limitation. I would suggest that in case (4), P and Q really do form a class with a causal power. More generally, the account of this chapter does not automatically grant causal powers to just any class of tropes with some common causal features. Causal power for a class of tropes in part is determined extrinsically depending on the laws and circumstances. Even a class made up of intrinsically dissimilar tropes may under the right circumstances have a causal power. Nevertheless, an account of such powers should not make it too easy for a class to have a causal power.

[50] The subset account as described here is only an approximation since it makes even arbitrary conjunctive properties, such as the property of being red and square, realizers of each of their conjuncts. The forward-looking causal features of being red will be a subset of the forward-looking features of being red and square, and the backward looking causal features of being red will have as a subset the backward-looking causal features of being red and square (Shoemaker 2007: 13).

determinates turn out to be realizers of their determinables. The causal powers of determinables are a subset of the causal powers of each of their determinates. Second, there is no causal competition between realized properties and their realizer properties since the causal powers of the former are a subset of those of the latter; so when a causal power of the realizer property is exercised, either the realized property is in fact causally irrelevant (because no causal power of that property is involved) or the realized property is causally relevant (because the causal power that is exercised also belongs to that property too). Third, the subset model seems to fit the main case of realization in the literature, the realization of mental properties by physical properties.

What is the relation between my part–whole account and the Subset Account of realization? My account provides a *metaphysical explanation* for why the sets of causal powers of mental properties stand in the subset relation to the sets of causal powers of certain physical properties—the core of the realization relation, according to the Subset Account. The part–whole account explains why there is this subset relation: physical property types that realize mental property types are parts of the latter, and, as such, the associated causal powers of the latter form sets that are subsets of the sets of causal powers associated with the former. The part–whole account of the relation between mental properties and the physical properties that realize them, then, *adds* a level of explanation missing from the Subset Account of realization. Instead of simply postulating that the causal powers of realizer and realized properties stand in the appropriate subset relation, the part–whole account explains why there is that subset relation in the case of mental and physical properties.

3. What's next?

In Part 2, I take up the issue of choosing between the various conceptions of tropes that are on offer, and will argue for the Natural Class Trope Nominalist conception. In Chapter 6, I try to show that the tropes of Natural Class Trope Nominalism are superior to Campbellian tropes as well as to the tropes of Resemblance Trope Nominalism. I also respond to two objections to the effect that Natural Class tropes are more object-like than they are property-like. In Chapters 7 and 8 I defend Natural Class Trope Nominalism against certain classic objections as well as against some additional objections that might be taken to demonstrate the implausibility of this theory.

PART II
Natural Class Trope Nominalism

6
Why Natural Class tropes?

The burden of Chapter 2 was to establish the existence of tropes without specifying precisely what tropes are other than as properties and particulars, and, in some cases, enduring. That leaves the task of settling on a more specific conception of tropes. In the literature, as indicated earlier, there are three conceptions available:

1. *Standard Theory tropes (Campbell and Williams)* Their natures are identical to their particularity. Membership in natural classes of tropes and resemblance between tropes is determined by the nature of tropes, not the other way around.
2. *Natural Class Trope Nominalist tropes* Their natures are determined by their memberships in natural classes of tropes, and such membership is not determined by resemblance relations among tropes.
3. *Resemblance Trope Nominalist tropes* Their natures are determined by their resemblance relations to other tropes, as are their memberships in natural classes of tropes.

I will argue for the least popular of these options, the tropes of Natural Class Trope Nominalism. In (1), I will try to show that the tropes of Natural Class Trope Nominalism, "Natural Class tropes," are superior to the tropes of Standard Theory. My argument revolves around the charge made by Hochberg, Armstrong, Moreland, and others that Campbellian tropes collapse into exemplifications of universals (or, I would add, into non-Campbellian tropes).[1] I will sharpen that charge. I will also show why it does not apply to the tropes of Natural Class Trope Nominalism. In (2), I will present some reasons for preferring Natural Class tropes to the tropes of Resemblance Trope Nominalism. Finally, in (3), I address the following "collapse" objections against Natural Class tropes: (a) they cannot be distinguished from bare particulars; and (b) they cannot be distinguished from objects.

1. Trope simplicity

1.1 Standard theory/Campbellian tropes and the collapse-into-exemplifications objection

For many philosophers the most appealing form of Trope Theory is that of Keith Campbell, the best representative of the Standard Theory. The tropes of Campbellian

---

[1] (Armstrong 2005); (Hochberg 1988); (Moreland 2001). This type of charge also appears in (Brownstein 1973) and (Daly 1994–5).

Nominalism are both particulars and properties, and their natures are not determined by anything but the trope itself. A red trope is red not in virtue of its resemblance to other tropes or in virtue of its membership in various classes of tropes. Resemblance among Campbellian tropes is not further reducible, but it is determined by the natures of the resembling tropes. But the nature of a trope is identical to its particularity. Tropes do not include distinct particularity/individuating and nature-giving components.[2]

Campbellian tropes are, then, like universals in being properties, but they are not universals, and they are like objects in being particulars, but they are not objects. The redness trope of this chair is a property but not a universal, and the redness trope is neither the chair itself nor some spatial part of the chair as is, for example, one of the chair's legs. Campbellian tropes occupy a middle ground between universals and concrete objects. At the same time, Campbellian tropes are not exemplifications of universals, another resident of this middle ground, even though exemplifications are also particulars, not universals, and not objects.[3] Campbellian tropes are not reducible to exemplifications of universals. This brings us to an objection to the very foundations of Campbellian Trope Theory, the worry that they collapse into exemplifications of universals on closer examination. An exemplification of a universal consists in the having of a universal by a particular at a time, and two such exemplifications are identical only if their constituent universals are identical. An exemplification, thus, includes as a constituent not only particulars (the object and the time), but also a universal. Campbellian tropes, on the other hand, are supposed to lack any universal-constituent, being particulars all the way down, absent of any distinct nature-giving component that might be construed as a universal. Campbellian tropes, or at least basic ones, are supposed to lack constituents that are not tropes, making them clearly distinguishable from exemplifications of universals. Campbellian tropes do not include a nature-giving constituent and a non-identical particularity-given constituent. It has been charged, however, that Campbellian tropes have distinct particularity-given and nature-giving components. If so, that opens up the serious possibility that a Campbellian trope collapses into an exemplification of a universal (or, at best, into some form of non-Standard trope). I will argue that this charge of "non-simplicity" *does* hold against Campbellian tropes, giving us a reason to prefer an alternative conception of tropes.

(Although "simple" is normally used to mean "lacks parts," here "simple" will be used to mean lacks parts and lacks multiple, non-identical intrinsic "aspects." The latter

---

[2] What is most compelling about the Campbellian picture, in contrast to that of Natural Class Trope Nominalism and to that of Resemblance Trope Nominalism, is the assumption that the nature of a trope is not determined by anything other than the trope itself. In that respect, Campbellian tropes are like Armstrongian universals. This aspect of the theory makes it immune to certain kinds of objections. It has seemed to many philosophers that the nature of a property is basic and that resemblance and membership in natural classes are secondary. Consequently, the default condition for Trope Theory is and should be Campbell's theory. Unfortunately, as we shall see, this default condition must be abandoned.

[3] Exemplifications of universals are particulars, given Armstrong's "victory of particularity" principle.

conjunct is unnecessary if it is assumed that a property of something is a part of that thing. However, since some will find this assumption to be questionable and since it is at least an open question whether something that lacked parts might have more than one intrinsic property, I have included the second conjunct.)

1.1.1 Argument 1 against the simplicity of Campbellian tropes Here is a first pass at an argument that Campbellian tropes cannot be simple in this way since they figure in more than one fact.

> *Argument 1* If an entity, x, is involved in more than one fact such that each of these facts is grounded intrinsically in x, then x is not simple since x will have intrinsic "aspects" that are not identical to each other. Trope t_1 is numerically different from trope t_2 and trope t_1 resembles trope t_2 exactly. Each of these facts is grounded intrinsically in trope t_1 and trope t_2. Hence, there are "intrinsic aspects" of trope t_1 that are not identical to each other. Thus, tropes are not simple.[4]

A red trope, say, red_1, is intrinsically individual and red. "If it were the only entity in existence it would be both red and particular. It is because red_1 is red that it exactly resembles other reds and it is because it is a particular that it is individuated from other entities"[5] (Moreland 2001: 70–1). Hence, the "aspect" of red_1 that grounds red_1's exact resemblance relations—its nature—is not identical to the intrinsic "aspect" of red_1 that grounds its difference relations—its particularity. Since each trope has more than one intrinsic aspect, a trope is not simple but made up of a particularity-component and a non-identical nature-component. We end up with something very close to the exemplification of a universal by a particular.

As it stands, this argument requires some refinement. To see this, suppose that object a is exactly similar in color to object b and object a is similar in color to object b. Suppose that these relations are "grounded" in intrinsic aspects of each object, their colors. If so, the same color of a (and the same color of b) grounds the fact that a is exactly similar in color to b and the fact that a is similar in color to b. There might be some relations (here being exactly similar in color and being similar in color) that are so closely related that the principle requiring distinct aspects grounding those relations fails for them, but there clearly are relations that do require distinct aspects to ground them. I will call the latter relations "arbitrarily different relations."

Arbitrarily different relations are such that realization of one does not necessitate the realization of the other, nor does every variation with respect to one of the relations

---

[4] The particularity of a spatial point is an intrinsic feature of that point but not a point's spatial relation to another point. "If that point were the only entity to exist, it would be an individual point but it would not be spatially related to anything else" (2001: 70). He adds: "if a point is to the left of x but to the right of y, these two facts are not grounded in two different, intrinsic features of the point itself, but in two relations external to the point" (2001: 70).

[5] "Thus, the ground for these two facts about red_1 must be sought in its intrinsic being and not in external relations it sustains to other things" (2001: 70–1).

necessitate a variation with respect to the other. The realization of one of the relations or a change in one of the relations does not necessarily mean the realization of the other or a change with respect to the other relation. Consider an object a that is darker than object b but heavier than object b. These relations are arbitrarily different from each other, but each is grounded in intrinsic aspects of object a (and of b), its color and its mass. The same aspects of a and b could not ground both of these relations (assuming that conjunctive properties like "having mass m and color c" are out). Argument 1 can be recast in a way that involves a weaker principle.

> *Argument 1** Anything that stands in more than one arbitrarily different relation, each of which is grounded intrinsically in that entity, is not simple since that entity will have intrinsic "aspects" that are not identical to each other. Trope t_1 is numerically different from trope t_2 and trope t_1 resembles trope t_2 exactly. And, numerical difference and exact resemblance vary independently of each other for tropes (Armstrong 2005: 310). Each of these facts is grounded intrinsically in t_1. Hence, there are "intrinsic aspects" of trope t_1 that are not identical to each other. Thus, tropes are not simple.

That numerical difference and exact resemblance for tropes are arbitrarily different relations is confirmed by the fact that tropes can be numerically different but exactly similar or not exactly similar to each other, and tropes can be exactly similar but identical or numerically distinct from each other.[6] This is compatible with the fact that these relations are not completely independent: if tropes do not exactly resemble then they must be numerically different, and if they are not numerically different, then they must exactly resemble.[7]

---

[6] If nothing can resemble itself since resemblance only holds between distinct entities, then tropes that are exactly similar cannot be identical. In fact, I would deny that nothing can resemble itself.

[7] Some philosophers have proposed arguments like Argument 1, but with an explicit appeal to the notion of a truthmaker.
Consider the two true statements: "trope t is numerically different than trope t'" and "trope t is exactly similar to trope t'." Different truths, with various important exceptions, require different truthmakers (call this the "Different Truths–Different Truthmakers Principle"). Campbellian tropes, however, are supposed to be such that these two statements have the same truthmaker, just the tropes t and t' themselves. But this violates this principle. Since t and t' are Campbellian tropes, nothing external to t and t' is part of the truthmaker for either of these statements, and there must be some complexity involving t and t' that allows for different truthmakers for these statements. Given that they are not simple, it is reasonable to think that the truthmaker for the first statement is the particularity components of t and t' and the truthmaker for the second statement is the nature components of t and t' (Armstrong 2005: 310).
One might try to resist this version of the argument by reference to the fact that there are exceptions to the Different Truths–Different Truthmakers Principle (2005: 310). Consider the following two putative exceptions discussed by Rodriguez-Pereyra:

1. "a is crimson" and "a is red," (assuming crimson is a lowest determinate); and
2. "a exists" and "a is identical to a."

Suppose with Rodriguez-Pereyra that there is just one truthmaker for "a is crimson" and "a is red," a's being crimson, and that there is just one truthmaker for "a exists" and "a is identical to a," just a itself. Do these cases

Argument 1★ can be simplified by bringing the distinction between internal and external relations into play. The notion of an internal relation that I am employing is characterized by Armstrong as follows:

A relation is internal, as I shall use the term, when given certain terms with certain natures, the relation must hold between the terms. It holds in every possible world that contains these terms and where these terms have these natures (1989a: 43).

He illustrates this notion with the relation of "greater than" holding between numbers. Given the numbers 4 and 2 and their natures, it is necessitated that 4 is greater than 2. An external relation, on the other hand, is not natures-necessitated. "Being a mile apart" is generally an external relation (or, perhaps, it is an external relation only in many cases if space-time points have their locations essentially).[8] Two objects, a and b, may be a mile apart, but the existence of a and b and their natures does not guarantee that they are a mile apart. The following principle can, then, be substituted for the operative one concerning relations and aspects in Argument 1★:

If a and b are related by arbitrarily different internal relations then a and b are not simple.

To illustrate how to apply this principle, suppose that a is darker than b and a is cleaner than b. Both of these relations are internal relations and arbitrarily different than each other. Hence, a and b cannot be simple. Alternately stated, if we suppose that a and b are both simple (in the sense of lacking parts of any kind, spatial, temporal or non-spatial temporal and of lacking distinct intrinsic aspects), then we will *not* be able to suppose coherently that they stand to each other in both of these relations. We can apply this principle to Campbellian tropes.

(Argument 1★★) If a and b are related by arbitrarily different internal relations then a and b are not simple. Trope t_1 is numerically different from trope t_2 and trope t_1

---

raise a problem for the "truthmaker" argument against Campbellian tropes? No, because these two cases do not involve arbitrarily different relations or properties. This can be seen by noticing that there is at least a one-way necessitation relation within each pair of truths: "a is crimson" necessitates "a is red" and "a exists" necessitates "a is identical to a." But, in the case at hand, there is no such necessitation relation: "t and t' are numerically different" is not necessitated by nor does it necessitate "t and t' are exactly similar."

Another exception has to do with disjunctive properties. Consider the two truths, "a is F or H" and "a is F or G," and suppose that the sole truthmaker for both truths is a's being F. On the other hand, these relations do come out as arbitrarily different, as I have characterized that notion thus far, since neither necessitates the other and variations in one do not require variations in the other. Still, this case has a feature that is missing in the "different than"/"exactly similar" case. There is a further truth, "a is F," with a's being F as its truthmaker, that necessitates both "a is F or H" and "a is F or G," where the conjunction of the latter truths does not necessitate "a is F." It seems fair to say that these disjunctive properties are not arbitrarily different. I will therefore expand my characterization of arbitrarily different properties and relations to include those that have this feature. However, in the case at hand, "t and t' are numerically different" and "t and t' are exactly similar" are not necessitated by some third truth that has just t and t' as its sole truthmaker, where that third truth is not necessitated by the conjunction of "t and t' are numerically different" and "t and t' are exactly similar."

[8] A referee suggested this qualification concerning space-time points.

resembles trope t_2 exactly. Resemblance among Campbellian tropes and the difference relation are internal relations that are arbitrarily different than each other. Hence, t_1 and t_2 are not simple.

Since each Campbellian trope stands to some other trope in these two internal relations those tropes cannot be simple.[9]

1.1.2 Argument 2 against the simplicity of Campbellian tropes
Here is another, related argument against the simplicity of a Campbellian trope.[10]

> *Argument 2* The nature and particularity of a trope are intrinsically grounded in that trope. Given that the "natures" of a red trope and an orange trope are inexactly similar, then their "particularities" are inexactly similar since their particularities are identical to their natures. However, in fact, the "particularities" of these tropes are *exactly* similar. Hence, their particularities are not identical to their natures, and tropes are not simple.[11]

---

[9] A referee suggests that if this line of argument were effective, it could be used to show that electrons are not simple, since they may or may not exactly resemble other objects to which they are not identical. The referee takes this to show that this line of argument fails. In response, I would say that this kind of argument does show that electrons are in some sense not "simple," at least in that they involve a particularity aspect and a nature aspect, although how that gets spelled out is wide open, including the possibility that electrons are bundles of non-Campbellian tropes. The argument would not show that electrons have spatial parts.

[10] Here is a similar argument from Moreland against the simplicity of Campbellian tropes: "Consider two red tropes. *Qua* red tropes they stand to each other in an internal exact similarity relation grounded in their natures. But *qua* particulars they are spatially related to each other in [an] external primitive spatial relation. But the particularity and nature of a trope are identical to each other... by the transitivity of identity, the particularities of the two tropes stand in an internal exact similarity relation to each other and the two red natures are externally related to each other. But this seems unintelligible" (2001: 64). It is unintelligible that the tropes' "particularities" ("natures") are involved in/ground facts about a trope's exact similarity to (spatial relations to) other tropes. Presumably, Moreland would *also* hold that it is unintelligible that the tropes' "natures" are involved in/ground facts about their "difference" relations. However, it should also be noted that these claims of "unintelligibility" seem to me too strong, but also unnecessary for Moreland's argument. Consider the claim that it is unintelligible that tropes' natures stand in spatial relations and other external relations to each other. As the case of universals bears out, that seems wrong. It is at least intelligible to claim that universals stand to each other in external relations such as (non-derivative) spatial relations or contingent relations of law, such that those same universals could exist without standing to each other in those law relations. And if it is intelligible for universals, it should also be intelligible for tropes. The other two claims of "intelligibility" seem equally too strong.

[11] Here is a related argument for the non-identity of a trope's "particularity" and its "nature":

> Suppose that two tropes are such that their natures are not similar to *any* degree to each other. If the particularity and nature of a trope are identical, it will follow that the particularities of these tropes are not at all similar to each other. Presumably, however, the particularities of any two tropes will be similar to some degree to each other.

A trope theorist might respond by insisting that some particularities are not at all alike. But this response is even less intuitively persuasive than the claim that some particularities are more similar to each other than are other particularities similar to each other.

The "particularities" of tropes always stand to each other in relations of exact similarity, and not of inexact similarity as they would sometimes if the particularities of tropes were identical to their natures.[12]

One might respond to this argument by biting the bullet by claiming without argument that only *some* particularities are exactly alike; others are inexactly alike. The particularities of the red and orange tropes *are* merely inexactly similar, but the particularities of two red tropes of the same shade are exactly alike. This response, however, is counterintuitive. Presumably, the particularity of any particular is exactly like the particularity of any other particular, just as the universality of any universal will be indistinguishable from the universality of any other universal.

Alternately, one might try to provide some reason for claiming that some, but not all, particularities are exactly alike. Specifically, one might argue that particularity is a determinable and various properties such as being crimson and being wine red are determinates of that determinable. If that is so, it might then be argued that not all particularities are exactly alike just as not all rednesses, also a determinable, are alike whereas some are. The difficulty with this response is that particularity is not a determinable of being crimson and being wine red. To see this, consider the following principle that applies to the determination relation. If D_1, D_2, and D_3 are same-level determinates of Q, then if D_1 is more similar to D_2 than it is to D_3, then D_1 is more similar to D_2 *qua* Q than it is to D_3 *qua* Q. For example, since yellowness is more similar to orangeness than it is to redness, yellowness is more similar to orangeness *qua* color than it is to redness *qua* color. Determinates of a determinable are orderable in terms of similarity and that order "translates up" to the determinable level, but there is no such "translating up" for particularity. For example, a yellowness trope is not *more similar qua particularity* to an orangeness trope than that yellowness trope is to a redness trope *qua* particularity. Furthermore, even if we granted that a yellowness trope is somehow *more similar qua particularity* to an orangeness trope than it is to a redness trope, there is an additional consequence that is unacceptable based on the following principle that applies to determinables and their determinates. If D_1, D_2, and D_3 are same-level

---

[12] Moreland presents another argument against the simplicity of Campbellian tropes from the assumptions that two red tropes *qua* red stand to each other in an internal exact similarity relation grounded in their natures, but *qua* particulars they are spatially related to each other in an external primitive spatial relation, and that the particularity and nature of a trope are identical to each other. He says that it follows "that the two simple entities stand to each other in internal and external relations due to the same metaphysical feature of the relata. But how can this be?" (2001: 64). The first point to note about this last claim—that entities cannot stand to each other in internal and external relations due to the same metaphysical feature—will not be relevant to Argument 1 since in that argument we don't clearly have an external relation contrasted with an internal relation. Although "exact similarity" is assumed by Campbell to be an internal relation, it does not seem clear that "different from" is an external relation. The second, and more important point, is that this claim—that entities cannot stand to each other in internal and external relations due to the same metaphysical feature—is open to counterexample. x may stand in a causal relation to y in virtue of x's F-ness and x may stand in an internal relation of similarity to y in virtue of x's F-ness. There is no barrier to entities that "stand to each other in internal and external relations due to the same metaphysical feature of the relata."

determinates of Q, then for any set of objects o_1, o_2, and o_3 such that o_1 has D_1, o_2 has D_2, and o_3 has D_3, then if D_1 is more similar to D_2 *qua* Q than it is to D_3 *qua* Q then o_1 is more similar to o_2 with respect to Q than o_1 is to o_3 with respect to Q. But that means, in our example, a yellow object will be more similar in particularity to an orange object than that yellow object is to a red object. But that is clearly not so. The nature of a trope is not a determinate of its particularity.

As with Argument 1, Argument 2 can be reformulated in terms of internal relations, but in this case, reformulated in terms of internal relations relativized to a respect R. To illustrate the idea consider two such relativized internal relations, being similar with respect to color and being similar with respect to cleanliness. If objects o and o' are simple, then o and o' cannot be exactly similar with respect to color but inexactly similar with respect to cleanliness. Now we can reformulate Argument 2 as follows:

> *Argument 2★* Suppose that being similar exactly or inexactly with respect to N is an internal relation and that being similar exactly or inexactly with respect to P is an arbitrarily different internal relation. If a and b are inexactly similar with respect to N, then if a and b are simple, a and b must also be inexactly similar with respect to P if similar at all with respect to P. A red trope t and an orange trope t' are inexactly similar with respect to color, an internal relation for Campbellian tropes. However, t and t' are exactly similar with respect to their particularity, also an internal relation for Campbellian tropes. Hence, t and t' are not simple.

Another possible response to Argument 2 is to suggest that it wrongly assumes that particularities are similar to each other to some degree or other, but, in fact, particularities are neither exactly similar nor inexactly similar to each other. In other words, this response claims the argument makes a category mistake. The problem with this response is that even if we accept that particularities are incommensurable, since properties such as being red and being orange are commensurable, the argument could be reformulated with this new assumption. In short, if the particularities of tropes are not commensurable but their natures are, then it would seem to follow that the nature of a trope is not identical to its particularity.

1.1.3 Arguments 1★★ and 2★ work against Campbellian tropes On Campbell's Trope Theory, what makes an individual whiteness trope a trope of that type is an intrinsic matter. Its "whiteness" nature is not determined by or grounded in its class memberships or resemblance relations. A Campbellian trope's nature wholly determines its relations of resemblance to other tropes and its membership in "natural" classes of tropes, not the other way around. Resemblance relations as well as difference relations among Campbellian tropes are internal relations. Hence, Argument 1★ applies to such tropes. Argument 2★ also works against Campbellian tropes since for any such trope, t, it is possible that there is another trope, t', such that t and t' are inexactly similar with respect to their natures.

At this point, it might be objected that Campbell does *not* say that a trope's nature is identical to its particularity. More specifically, it might be thought that when Campbell says that a trope's particularity (or in his earlier view (1981), a trope's location) and its nature are not really distinct, he did not mean to be claiming that a trope's nature is identical to its particularity (or on his earlier view, location). He meant only to say that a trope's nature and its particularity, although not identical, are somehow unified in a particularized property, which is neither just a particularizing feature nor just a characterizing nature. In fact, this reading of Campbell is not accurate. First, note that Campbell does accept the implication that if x and y are not "distinct in reality" then x and y are identical. He acknowledges this implication in discussing Moreland's critique of his (1981) view. According to that view, a trope's place and a trope's nature were not genuinely distinct: "the distinctions we can make between color, shape and size are distinctions in thought to which correspond no distinctions in reality" (1981: 486). He, then, accepts the implication that if a trope's place and nature (here a green trope) are not "genuinely distinct," they are identical: "For if it is individuated by its place that means it must have a place, and if it is simple, this place must not be something genuinely distinct from its colour. Thus a shape, a colour... collapse into identity" (1990: 68). He goes on to posit a new view: "a colour trope and a spatial quasi-trope are distinct entities" (1990: 68). The key point is that Campbell accepts the implication from "not genuinely distinct" to "collapse into identity." Second, in (1990) Campbell treats a trope's nature and its particularity in the same way he treated a trope's nature and its place in his earlier work, as not genuinely distinct: "... all tropes are particulars, and each of them has a nature, this does not involve conceding that a trope is after all complex (a union of particularity with a nature-providing property). The distinction is perhaps a 'formal' one, as Scotus used the term" (1990: 56). Or again, in discussing an act of "hyper-abstraction" applied to a green trope, "we can, by an act of selective attention, ignore the nature—that they are green—and focus on the particularity..." but "hyper-abstraction does not imply distinctness... of particularity from nature" (1990: 89–90). Thus, Campbell affirms that there is no distinction in reality between a trope's nature and its particularity, and that they are, thus, identical.

Notwithstanding Campbell's commitment to this identity claim, it might be asked whether or not this identity thesis is really required under the Standard Theory. Does distinguishing tropes from exemplifications of universals really require that tropes be simple—require the identity of a trope's nature and a trope's particularity, even if the complexity of exemplifications and the simplicity of Campbellian tropes is sufficient for this distinction? Why can't Campbellian tropes be distinguished from exemplifications merely by not including either objects or universals as constituents? The distinction between Campbellian tropes and exemplifications of universals might arguably remain even if tropes are not simple, since the particularizing aspect of a trope is not an object but a "thin" trope, and the nature aspect of a trope is not a universal but a particular. In response, I would suggest that although there very well may be such a conception of tropes, that conception takes us out of the realm of Campbellian tropes or leads to an infinite regress. For example, one might conceive of tropes as follows. A trope's nature is part of or a constituent of the trope, just as a universal is a constituent of a state of affairs for Armstrong; however, a trope's nature consists in the resemblance classes or natural classes of which it is a member. A trope includes as constituents a particular (a "thin" trope), the relation of class membership and constituent resemblance/natural classes, the latter of which is the trope's nature. "Thick" tropes are not simple, but tropes are not exemplifications of a universal. The difficulty is that such a conception of tropes makes the Standard conception of tropes collapse into either one or the other of the other two conceptions. In response, one might ask why the proponent of the Standard Theory could not simply maintain that complex tropes involve a particular (a "thin" trope) and a non-universal intrinsic nature in such a way that we distinguish the particularity of a trope from its nature, without making that nature either universal *or relational*—without a collapse into one of the alternative conceptions of tropes. Here I would suggest that this option is not viable because it leads to an infinite regress. Consider the trope's nature under this alternative. It is a non-universal, and, hence, a particular. But now we can apply the above arguments to *that* component of the trope, with the consequence that that component include another thin trope and nature component that is itself a particular. And so on.

1.1.4 Arguments 1** and 2* do not work against Natural Class tropes To see why not, we need to return to the notion of an internal relation. An internal relation is a relation that is necessitated by the existence and nature of its relata (again, using Armstrong's characterization). External relations, such as the relation of being a mile apart, are not necessitated in this way. However, Armstrong notes that "one could take 'nature' so widely that being a mile from *b* was counted as part of the nature of *a*. With nature so defined one would have an—uninteresting—case of an internal relation." Or, take the relation of being a sibling of. That relation will be internal on the assumption that the parental origins of people are part of their natures. Let's call the latter class of "uninteresting" internal relations that are necessitated by their relata and the relations of their relata, "relational" internal relations. R is a relational internal relation just in case R is an internal relation, but the holding of that relation necessitates the existence of something that is neither one of its relata nor one of the proper parts of its relata.[13] What is important to note is that Arguments 1** and 2* fail for such "relational" internal relations. That failure will help us demonstrate that the tropes of Natural Class

---

[13] This definition, however, requires further qualifications. The holding of any relation entails every necessary fact. For example, the holding of the one mile from relation between *a* and *b* entails that $7 + 5 = 12$, which arguably involves the existence of numbers. Hence, the holding of the one-mile-from relation between *a* and *b* entails the existence of things distinct from *a* and *b*, with the consequence that every internal relation qualifies as a relational internal relation. One should, thus, restrict the definition to the entailment of contingent existents. I owe this point to a referee. Second, since every trope *t* necessitates the existence of a singleton class, a contingent existence, a further qualification is necessary to avoid the implication that all internal relations between tropes are relational. One must restrict the necessitated contingent existents to those that are not necessitated by either relatum alone.

Trope Nominalism are immune to Arguments 1★★ and 2★. Arguments 1★★ and 2★ must be qualified in a way that makes them inapplicable to Natural Class tropes.

Arguments 1★★ and 2★ do not work on "relational" internal relations. This can be shown by way of a case involving simple, spatio-temporal points. Consider two simple points that stand to each other in the "different than" relation, but are also 5 feet apart. The distance relation is certainly not a non-relational internal relation. However, it can be interpreted as a "relational" internal relation if the "positional" nature of each point is included in their "natures." In that case, the 5-feet-apart relation between them is necessitated by the relata. However, clearly, this does not demonstrate that these points are not simple. Even if being 5 feet apart is an "internal" relation in the "relational" sense, that does not show that these points are not simple. "A point is as simple as you can get" (Campbell 1990: 70).[14] Consider an analogue to Argument 1★★:

> Point 1 is numerically different from point 2 and point 1 is 5 feet apart from point 2 exactly. The 5-feet-apart relation is an internal relation (albeit a "relational" internal relation) as is the difference relation. Hence, point 1 and point 2 are not simple.

Clearly, this argument fails to show that these points are not simple. (Campbell makes a similar point (1990: 70).) The mistake is in allowing "relational" internal relations into the mix. If at least one of the arbitrarily different relations cited in the argument is merely a "relational" internal relation, then the argument fails. The same conclusion applies to Argument 2★ since the following analogue to that argument fails:

> Again, call the position of a point in a coordinate system its "nature." Consider two points with inexactly similar "natures" (two points that are close together). Now, if the "natures" and "particularities" of each of these points were identical, that would mean that their particularities should also be inexactly similar, but their particularities are exactly similar. Hence, the "nature" and "particularity" of each point are not identical and points are not simple.

But clearly this does not show that these points are not simple since their "natures" are not intrinsically grounded in each point. The mistake is in allowing "relational" internal relations into the mix.[15]

Arguments 1★★ and 2★ against simplicity are sound only if the internal relations involved do not include "relational" internal relations. These arguments work only if the "different than" relation and the resemblance relation between properties are not grounded in relations of the relata. If tropes are Campbellian, both of these relations between tropes are internal in the "non-relational" sense. In particular, resemblance

---

[14] Or, at least, physical theories are compatible with the simplicity of points: "We find that physical theories require almost nothing of the points intrinsically. They require only that the set of space-time points has a certain structure. This structure consists in the holding of spatiotemporal relations between the points, but is indifferent to what the points are like in themselves" (Sider 2006: 10).

[15] This point still holds if the positions of these points are essential to them.

among Campbellian tropes is necessitated by the non-relational natures of the resembling tropes. However, we can now see that Argument 1★★ does not work against Natural Class Trope Nominalism tropes because the resemblance relation between such tropes is a "relational" internal relation. The resemblance of Natural Class Trope Nominalism tropes depends upon the relations of such tropes. What it is for tropes to resemble each other for Natural Class Trope Nominalism is for those tropes to be co-members of a common natural class. That means that resemblance among tropes is not a non-relational internal relation. For Campbell, trope–trope resemblance is determined by the non-relational nature of those tropes, but for Natural Class Trope Nominalism trope–trope resemblance is determined not by their non-relational natures since they lack any such nature, but by their co-membership in a natural class. There is still a trivial sense in which resemblance is an internal relation since the "natures" of the tropes in some sense necessitate their resemblance relations, but in that sense the "internal" character of the resemblance relation among Natural Class tropes is irrelevant to Argument 1★★.[16] For similar reasons, Argument 1★ does not apply to Natural Class tropes. A trope's nature is determined solely by its *membership in certain natural classes of tropes*, and these class memberships are not grounded intrinsically in the trope. Arguments 2 and 2★ also fail to apply to Natural Class tropes. Since the nature of a Natural Class trope is not intrinsically had by the trope, then these arguments will not work and non-simplicity will not follow.

1.1.5 Campbell's "distinction by abstraction" response At this point, I will consider a response, as outlined by Campbell, to arguments such as Argument 1:

"Although the idea ... is that all tropes are particulars, and each of them has a nature, this does not involve conceding that a trope is after all complex (a union of particularity with a nature-providing property). The distinction is perhaps a 'formal' one, as Scotus used the term. It is a matter of the level of abstraction at which an item is being considered. To illustrate: let us grant that red, orange, yellow and brown are *warm* colours. Then a particular instance of orange will be a case of warm colour, as well as a case of orange. But this does not imply that it is a union of two features, warmth and orangehood. To recognize the case of orange as warm is not to find a new feature in it, but to treat it more abstractly, less specifically, than in recognising it as a case of orange.

In parallel fashion, to recognize that a particular case of orange is a particular nature, hence a case of particularity, does not include a duality of being, but two levels of abstraction in considering the case. The particularity of particulars is what I call a hyper-abstract, incapable of distinct and independent existence" (1990: 56–7).

According to this response, then, in considering the numerical relationships of a trope we are considering the trope on one "level" of abstraction, but in considering a trope's exact resemblance relationships we treat the trope on a different level of abstraction.

---

[16] Furthermore, even if the nature-determining class memberships are essential to each trope that does not make Argument 1★★ any more applicable to Natural Class Tropes.

These characteristics of a trope—its nature and particularity—can be separated in the mind "by an act of partial consideration," but in reality they are identical. The nature–particular distinction, in the case of tropes, is a "distinction by abstraction," one that does not imply that a trope is a union of two constituents, despite the fact that a trope can stand in independently variable relationships of numerical identity and exact resemblance.

How should "abstraction" be understood here? There seem to be two relevant senses: (1) abstraction as selectively attending to one feature A of x rather than attending to another, non-identical feature of x, say B; and (2) abstraction as treating x "less specifically." In fact, neither interpretation of "abstraction" helps the trope theorist. On interpretation (1), a "distinction by abstraction" requires that A and B be *non-identical* "aspects" of x. Appealing to that notion will not help the Standard Trope theorist show that tropes are simple.

On the second interpretation, which seems to fit with the way Campbell puts the point, abstraction consists in treating something "less specifically." How might we understand the latter notion? Two possibilities come to mind. The first is to cash out the notion of treating something "less specifically" in terms of the determinate–determinable relation, and the second, in terms of the species–genus relationship. To illustrate the first case, one might think of the color of an object, for example, not as crimson, but as falling under a less determinate predicate such as "red." An example of the second case might involve thinking of a specific dog not as falling under a species, "wolf," but as falling under a genus, "canine." Neither of these interpretations, however, will help the trope theorist defend trope simplicity. The species–genus interpretation obviously fails. A species can be defined in terms of a genus plus some further property or properties, a differentia, that distinguish the species from other members of the genus. But crimsonness, for example, is not the conjunction of particularity and some further property. Crimsonness is not a species of particularity. In addition, as indicated in 1.1.2, "crimsonness" is not a determinate of "particularity" since that would lead to violations of the principle that if D_1, D_2, and D_3 are same-level determinates of Q, then if D_1 is more similar to D_2 than it is to D_3, then D_1 is more similar to D_2 *qua* Q than it is to D_3 *qua* Q.

2. Natural Class Trope Nominalism tropes compared to the tropes of Resemblance Trope Nominalism

Arguments 1 and 2 and their variants provide a basis for preferring Natural Class tropes to the tropes of Campbellian Trope Nominalism, since those arguments work against the latter but not against the former. However, these arguments do not give us a reason to prefer Natural Class Trope Nominalism to Resemblance Trope Nominalism. Argument 1** does not work against Resemblance Trope Nominalist tropes because the resemblance relation between tropes is not a non-relational internal relation given

Resemblance Trope Nominalism. A non-relational internal relation between *a* and *b* is a relation that is necessitated by the combination of the non-relational natures and existence of *a* and *b*. But according to Resemblance Trope Nominalism, no trope possesses a non-relational nature. Similarly, Argument 1★ does not apply to the tropes of Resemblance Trope Nominalism. According to the latter, a trope's nature is determined solely by its resemblance relations to other tropes and is not grounded intrinsically in that trope. Argument 2 also fails to apply to Resemblance Trope Nominalist tropes for the same reason. We, therefore, need some additional reason to opt for Natural Class tropes over the tropes of Resemblance Trope Nominalism. I will offer three reasons, the first being the most important.

2.1 Resemblance is nature-based under Natural Class Trope Nominalism

The first reason is that Natural Class tropes fit better with a fundamental aspect of the resemblance relation between properties: resemblance among properties is nature-based. The following passage in Armstrong nicely captures the latter aspect of resemblance, although he is discussing object–object resemblance: "Do not things resemble each other, to the extent that they do, because of what they are in themselves, in their own nature, rather than that they are of that nature because they resemble?" (Armstrong 1989a: 49). This point applies to property–property resemblance. Property–property resemblance is nature-based, grounded in the natures of the resembling properties rather than the other way around. Orange and red are alike because of what they are like rather than what they are like being explainable by their similarity to each other and to other properties. This is a powerful intuition about property–property resemblance that an adequate account of properties should preserve, if possible. Resemblance Trope Nominalism does not preserve this intuition. According to this view, a trope's nature is determined by its resemblance relations, not the other way around. Natural Class Trope Nominalism, on the other hand, has the resources for preserving this intuition.

To show this, I need to sketch out a conception of a Natural Class trope's nature. A trope is *not* identical to its nature, nor is its nature a part of or a component of any trope. The nature of a trope is the set of all the natural classes of which it is a member. A trope is not identical to such a set, so it is not identical to its nature. A trope is a member of each "natural" part of its nature. For example, suppose that trope t is a member of only two natural classes *T* and *T'*. In that case, the nature of *t* is the class of *T* and *T'*. *T* and *T'* are subclasses of the nature of *t*. Since a class is a part of whatever class it is a subclass of, *t* is a member of those parts of its nature. Speaking loosely, a trope is "part of" or "participates" in its nature or is a member of its nature.[17] A trope is not

---

[17] One should not read "participates in a nature" to mean that a trope is strictly speaking a part of a nature or even part of a part of a nature.

identical to a nature, but it is "of a certain nature."[18] Under this conception, tropes may be simple. Here is a loose analogy. The "nature" of a simple point in a coordinate system is the position that point has in that coordinate system. That a point could have a "nature" in that limited sense is consistent with the simplicity of the point. The nature of a trope is its "position" in the realm of types. The nature of a trope *is identical to the natural classes it is a member of.* So the nature of trope t is determined by its class membership, but the trope's nature is not a constituent of the trope. The nature of a trope is just the set of natural types it falls under, but those types are not constituents of the trope. A red trope is a trope that is a member of the red trope class. What makes it true that trope t is an F-ness property is t's membership in a natural class of F-ness tropes.[19] And that class is part of that trope's nature, but that nature is not a component of the trope. (Under this conception, tropes are distinguishable from exemplifications of universals since the latter include their "natures" as components.)[20] Under this conception, it comes out as true that trope–trope resemblance is grounded in the natures of tropes, not the other way around. Natural Class tropes t and t' are similar just

---

[18] A referee worries that entities whose natures are relational cannot be the substance of the world. There are four parts to my answer to this worry. First, even if their natures are relational, tropes themselves are not necessarily relations or relational properties (except in the case in which there is a relation at issue or the property involved is a relational property). Second, on this account, the nature of a trope is not a relation, but a natural class or natural classes. Those classes are not relational. Third, the only relation that plays some foundational role is the class membership relationship, which seems unproblematic. Fourth, even if this objection had merit, Natural Class Trope Nominalism would be no worse off than certain other views that make relations fundamental such as Dispositionalism or Resemblance Object Nominalism.

[19] But, then, as a referee worries, what makes it the case that one class of tropes ends up constituting one type rather than another? It is not that there are different types of naturalness, say, red-naturalness and green-naturalness. In fact, the answer is exceedingly simple: type T, one class, C, of tropes, is not type T', also a class, C', of tropes because C and C' are not identical. If the question so what makes the first type, blueness, the answer is that it just is. This is similar to the response that the Standard Trope theorist gives and the answer that the Universalist gives to analogous questions. In virtue of what is a Standard charge trope a charge trope? The answer is "its being what it is" (Campbell 1990: 30). Similarly, a Universalist gives the same answer to the question "in virtue of what is the charge universal a charge universal?" The answer is "its being what it is."

[20] Under a *second conception*, a Natural Class trope's nature is part of or a constituent of the trope, just as a universal is a constituent of a state of affairs for Armstrong. A trope includes as constituents a particular (a "thin" trope), the relation of class membership and constituent natural classes, the trope's nature. A trope (a "thick" trope), then, is the having of a membership relationship to *all* the natural classes of which that trope is a member by a "thin" trope. A "thick" trope's nature consists in just those constituent natural classes. Trope t is identical to trope t' iff the "thin" trope of t, p, and the "thin" trope of t', p', are members of all the same natural classes and the "thin" trope of t is identical to the "thin" trope of t'. "Thick" tropes are not simple, but tropes are not exemplifications of a universal. Even if a "thin" trope could be said to "exemplify" its natural class constituent that would not be a matter of the exemplification of a *universal* since these natural classes are not universals. Universals are not classes of any kind. In addition, the "thin" trope, on this view, does *not* stand in an *exemplification relation* to the natural classes. It stands in the *membership relation*. There are advantages for each conception, but nothing decisive. For example, the first conception fits better with our belief that a property of an object is located where the object is located. Properties of objects are localized in the way that objects are. But if the second conception is adopted, we have to worry that one intuitive characterization of tropes as local "ways particulars are" is lost. We would have to say that the redness of an object is located where all the objects that are red are located. On the first conception, the intrinsic tropes possessed by an object are local to the object so this worry is not so pressing. On the other hand, the second conception fits better with our belief that a property includes, in some sense, its own nature. In the following, I will use the first conception.

in case their natures are identical or overlap. t and t' are exactly similar just in case their natures are identical, where their natures consist in the sets of natural classes each of which is a member. t and t' are inexactly similar just in case their natures merely partially overlap.[21]

2.2 Resemblance axioms explainable without modal realism

The second reason to prefer Natural Class Trope Nominalism to Resemblance Trope Nominalism is that the former must either take the logical properties of resemblance as primitive or, if it can explain those logical properties, it can do so only if it is combined with modal realism. On the other hand, Natural Class Trope Nominalism can explain those properties and do so without such a commitment. That gives us a second reason to prefer the latter to the former.

2.2.1 The Natural Class Trope Nominalist account of the axioms of resemblance
What are the axioms of resemblance and how does Natural Class Trope Nominalism explain them? The following are the main logical features of resemblance:

(A) Resemblance is reflexive, symmetrical, but not transitive.
(B) Exact resemblance is reflexive, symmetrical, and transitive.

The Natural Class Trope Nominalist explanation of the axioms of resemblance is quite similar to Armstrong's (1989a: 102).

Assume that the nature of a trope consists in all the natural classes of which it is a member and that resemblance between tropes is a matter of the overlap of their natures, with exact resemblance being perfect overlap of their natures, the identity of their natures. (1) *Reflexivity of Resemblance and the Reflexivity of Exact Resemblance* If objects a and b are identical, then a and b share all of their tropes. Hence, the natures of the tropes of a will overlap perfectly with the natures of the tropes of b and vice versa. If tropes t and t' are identical, then their natures overlap perfectly and t and t' resemble each other exactly. So a resembles b and b resembles a and a exactly resembles b and b exactly resembles a. (2) *Symmetry of Resemblance and Exact Resemblance* Object a resembles b just in case there is a trope t_1 of object a that resembles trope t_2 of object b. Trope t_1 resembles trope t_2 just in case their natures overlap, that is, the set of natural classes that constitutes t_1's nature overlaps the set of classes that constitutes t_2's nature. But then the set of classes that constitutes t_2's nature overlaps the set of classes that

---

[21] A referee suggests that if the natures of tropes of the same type are identical, that introduces a universal aspect. There is one thing, the type (the natural class), and it is literally shared by everything with the property since everything with the property will have a trope with the numerically same nature reflecting membership in this class. In response, I would point out that this instance of sharing does not introduce a universal. Even though there is something literally shared across different but exactly similar tropes and across different objects, this is not sufficient for the existence of a universal. The thing that is shared, a class of particular tropes, is itself a particular. This class satisfies our earlier characterization of a particular—a perfect copy of that class is possible.

constitutes t_1's nature, which means that t_2 of b resembles t_1 of a, so that b resembles a. Furthermore, if a exactly resembles b, then each of the tropes of a exactly resembles a trope of b and each of the tropes of b exactly resembles a trope of a. In that case, for every trope of a (and for every trope of b) there is a trope of b (a trope of a) that have the same natures. Hence, b exactly resembles a. (3) *Transitivity of Exact Resemblance* If object a exactly resembles b, then a and b have exactly similar tropes. Trope t_1 and t_2 are exactly similar just in case their natures overlap perfectly, that is, their natures are identical. So consider arbitrary trope, t_1, of a, and the trope, t_2, of b that are exactly similar. The nature of t_1 and the nature of t_2 are identical. Now consider a trope of c, t_3, which is exactly similar to t_2. The nature of t_2 is identical to the nature of t_3. Since identity is transitive, that means the nature of t_1 is identical to the nature of t_3, and, hence, t_1 and t_3 are exactly similar. This exercise can be repeated for all the tropes of a, b, and c, and it will turn out that for each trope of a there is a trope of c that has the same nature and for each trope of c there is a trope of a that has the same nature, so a and c are exactly similar. (4) *Non-Transitivity of Inexact Resemblance* Even if a inexactly resembles b, and b inexactly resembles c, a may not inexactly resemble c. There are two cases to consider. In the first, suppose that a and b share some exactly resembling tropes, say, t and t', but none of the remaining tropes of a (or b) are exactly or inexactly similar to tropes of b (or a). Also, suppose that the same is true of b and c. Tropes t and t' are exactly similar just in case they are members of all the same natural classes. Now even if a and b have a pair of exactly similar tropes, t and t', and b and c do too, say, t'' and t''', it does not follow that a and c do too. It still may be the case that there is no trope of a that is exactly or inexactly similar to any trope of c. In the second case, a and b share some inexactly resembling tropes, say, t and t', where t and t' are members of some but not all of the same natural classes. And suppose that b and c do too. Again, it does not follow that a has a trope that exactly or inexactly resembles a trope of c (tropes that are members of some of the same natural classes but not all of the same natural classes).

On the other hand, Resemblance Trope Nominalism will either fail to explain the logical properties of resemblance or the explanation it offers will involve a commitment to modal realism. Why think that? Consider the reflexivity of resemblance. How might the Resemblance Trope Nominalist derive the proposition that everything (objects, tropes, etc.) resembles itself? For the Resemblance Trope Nominalist, resemblance between objects is a matter of possessing similar tropes. So the Resemblance Trope Nominalist needs to demonstrate that the tropes of an object resemble themselves: tropes resemble themselves. The most promising strategy to derive the latter, available to the Resemblance Trope Nominalist, starts with the following two possible axioms, plausibly attributable to Resemblance Trope Nominalism. These are analogues of axioms proposed by Rodriguez-Pereyra for Resemblance Object Nominalism. I try to mirror Rodriguez-Pereyra's derivation of reflexivity within the framework of Resemblance Object Nominalism.

1. If trope t resembles a trope t', then resembling t', among other tropes, makes t some type of trope, say, T.
2. Resembling T-tropes is what makes a trope a T-trope.

From these two axioms, it follows that any trope that resembles some other trope resembles itself. Suppose that t and t' resemble each other. By the first axiom, it follows that t is a trope of some type, T. According to (2), t is a T-type trope *because it resembles T-type tropes*, but since t is one of the T type tropes, then t resembles itself (Rodriguez-Pereyra 2002: 74). In short, t resembles itself, if it resembles *other* tropes.

But what about the "unique trope" case—an actual trope, t, which resembles no other actual tropes? One might think that it can be derived that t resembles itself from axiom 2 *alone* even though t is "unique" (here I am mimicking what Rodriguez-Pereyra says about the parallel case involving objects).

What if t is the only T-type trope? The reflexivity of resemblance is derived from axiom 2—if t did not resemble itself, then resembling T-type tropes would not be what made it a T-type trope (2002: 74).

According to this derivation, if t is a unique trope *of some type T*, then t resembles itself. But notice that if t is a unique trope but "type-less," then this derivation will not go through. If t is "type-less" then we cannot by this route prove that it resembles itself. So we need to be able to show that these axioms guarantee that there could be no such "type-less" trope. Without such a demonstration we will not have derived the general proposition that if t is a trope then t resembles itself.

How might it be derived from these axioms that there is some type T such that t is of that type? Can we *derive* the fact that there is a type T such that t is a T-type trope from axioms 1 and 2? Do these axioms guarantee *that* claim? To get that result we must make use of axiom 1. If modal realism is true then there will be other tropes that t resembles, in which case axiom 1 will guarantee that there is some type T such that t is a T-type trope. What if modal realism is false?[22] Axiom 1 can, then, be applied to t to guarantee that there is some type T such that t is a T-type trope only if t resembles itself, that is, only if resemblance is *assumed* to be reflexive. Hence, if we don't assume that resemblance is reflexive or assume that there is some T such that t is a T-type trope, we can show that a "unique" trope t resembles itself only if we can appeal to modal realism. Only then, on the basis of these axioms, can we infer that t resembles itself

---

[22] This argument will fail if the Resemblance Trope Nominalist does not really require modal realism at this point. Perhaps, mere possibilia constructed from actualia, say, in combination with a counterpart theory for properties, will be enough, given that actualists can countenance mere possibilia. In fact, I am doubtful that this is a viable option since I suspect that the relata of the resemblance relation must be real even if not actual in so far as that relation plays a foundational role under Resemblance Trope Nominalism. (I make use of actualist accounts of modality and a counterpart theory of properties in subsequent chapters so as to provide a basis for responding to certain key objections to this Natural Class Trope Nominalism, but not to provide an account of what it is for a trope to be of a certain type.) In any case, the details of the proposal would need to be further specified for a full evaluation.

without circularity. Natural Class Trope Nominalism, on the other hand, can derive the logical properties of resemblance, including reflexivity, without circularity and without modal realism.

Furthermore, even if the reflexivity of resemblance is taken to be a primitive and it is suggested that our unique t is a T-type trope in virtue of resembling itself, there is a further problem with this "self-resembling" treatment of the unique trope case. Assume that if t is unique, the ground for t's being a particular type, T, of trope is that t resembles itself and not any other tropes, including merely possible tropes. In that case, it is far from clear how the Resemblance Trope Nominalism answers the question "what makes t a T-type trope?" is fundamentally different than the answer given by the Campbellian. The latter says that t's being a T-type trope is a primitive matter, not further reducible. The former says that if t is unique, then t's being a T-type trope is a matter of t's resembling itself. For both theories, under these assumptions, t's being a T-type trope is not determined by anything other than t itself. If resemblance is primitively reflexive, t's resemblance to itself requires only the existence of t. It is hard to see much of a difference between Resemblance Trope Nominalism and Standard Trope Nominalism: in both cases, if the reflexivity of resemblance is primitive, then the truthmaker for a unique trope t's having a specific nature is just t itself. Furthermore, if self-resemblance is sufficient for being a T-type trope for any type that a trope t falls under, it is presumably necessary too. In that case, it is not clear why even in the non-unique cases the Resemblance Trope Nominalist needs to appeal to other tropes, and, then, in those cases too, as with the Standard account, the ground for t's being a T-type trope is just t itself, given that resemblance is reflexive and that it is primitively so. Natural Class Trope Nominalism, on the other hand, can account for the nature of a unique trope t by identifying it with its singleton class.

3. Collapse objections to Natural Class tropes

I will now discuss two "collapse" objections, specifically directed against Natural Class tropes, according to which Natural Class tropes collapse into some other ontological category that is incompatible with being a property. As per the first (3.1), Natural Class tropes are not distinguishable from traditional bare particulars, making them extremely un-property-like. According to the second, (3.2), they are not distinguishable from objects, bare or not, also making them un-property-like. These are important objections that, if cogent, demonstrate that the notion of a particularized *property* is incoherent, as that notion is deployed by Natural Class Trope Nominalism.

3.1 Bare particulars

Traditionally, bare particulars are invoked as individuators by some substratum theorists. On the assumption that properties are universals, some substratum theorists say that objects include both a bare particular and universals, and the object's bare particular instantiates its universals. Bare particulars serve as individuators for objects, if properties are universals, making for numerical difference between objects that are qualitatively exactly similar. The bare particular-constituent of an object is not a further universal, and, indeed, it could not be, but still play this individuating role. The bare particulars that play this individuating role are not properties and *in themselves* they do not have any properties. Whatever tropes are, tropes are *not* supposed to be bare particulars in this traditional sense for at least the reason that tropes *are* properties, whether or not tropes *have* properties.[23]

But, according to the objection under consideration, Natural Class tropes cannot be distinguished from bare particulars in the traditional sense, and, hence, Natural Class tropes fail to be properties. If successful, this objection presents a foundational problem with the notion of a Natural Class trope. Here is how the objection goes:

Under Natural Class Trope Nominalism, properties are particulars that have no specific nature independently of their class memberships. "In themselves" Natural Class tropes are nature-free, both in the sense of not having any property or being a property, but still they are particulars. But that is what bare particulars are in the traditional sense (Armstrong 1978b: 87).

In short, Natural Class Trope Nominalism makes tropes bare, in themselves, independently of their class memberships, but since they are particulars, that makes them bare particulars. In order to respond to this objection, it is necessary to show that there are significant differences between Natural Class tropes and bare particulars in the traditional sense. I will suggest four such differences.

Let's divide bareness into its two components, not having properties and not being a property. Traditionally, bare particulars are contrasted both with concrete particulars and with universals *qua* properties. Unlike concrete objects, bare particulars do not have properties, and unlike universals, bare particulars are not properties. It is important to note that not having higher-order properties is not sufficient for being bare. Even if there are universals that do not have any higher-order properties, they are not bare: there is no such thing as a bare universal.

The first important difference is that the bare particulars of traditional theory are bare in not being properties, without qualification or *simpliciter*, but Natural Class tropes are not so. Traditional bare particulars, *even when they are not considered in themselves* but as the things that instantiate properties, are not properties. On the other hand, even if we grant the claim that Natural Class tropes are bare—not being any specific property—when *considered in abstraction* from their natural class memberships, if Natural Class Trope Nominalism is right, tropes are specific properties in so far as they are members of natural classes. And, since they *are* members of such classes, they are properties, not bare particulars. Although a given trope has no nature when considered independently of its class memberships, a trope is of a certain nature since it is a member of various natural classes. Hence, even if there was some sense—the abstraction sense or the

---

[23] For the Campbellian, this is an easy distinction to make. Campbellian tropes are not bare. Campbellian tropes are natures and are so intrinsically, but bare particulars are not natures.

"in-themselves" sense—in which Natural Class tropes are bare particulars, there is also a sense in which they are not (when not considered in abstraction from their class memberships). The bare particulars of traditional theory, on the other hand, are not properties considered from any perspective, no matter what we fail to abstract away from.

Second, the tropes of Natural Class Trope Nominalism are members of natural classes like "crimson," but the bare particulars of traditional theory cannot be members of *any* natural classes.[24] Consider that the only possible candidate for a "natural" class of which traditional bare particulars could be members would be a class made up of only traditional bare particulars. But would that class constitute a natural class? It would not. A class of traditional bare particulars is not a natural class even if it is maximal. That is borne out by the fact that no such class would be associated with any particular property and would not cut nature at its joints in a way that would provide the basis for similarity of nature among objects. This difference between Natural Class tropes and traditional bare particulars is important, because it indicates that traditional bare particulars are not properties or even concrete objects. The primitive membership of Natural Class tropes in natural classes such as the redness class distinguishes them from traditional bare particulars. The natural classes that Natural Class tropes are members of are associated with bases for cutting nature at its joints and for similarity among objects. Even the biggest class of traditional bare particulars is not a natural class.

In response to this second claimed difference between traditional bare particulars and Natural Class tropes, one might reject the claim that the maximal class of bare particulars is not a natural class on the grounds that that class *is* associated with a particular property, the property of "having no properties." This property is possessed by every bare particular. But this response must fail. The proponent of traditional bare particulars is at pains to deny that there is such a property so as to avoid the implication that the notion of a bare particular is incoherent, since there can be nothing that both has no properties and has the property of "having no properties" (Sider 2006: 394). (It is worth noting that Sider defends bare particulars against this charge of incoherence by arguing that the predicate, "having no properties," does not correspond to a sparse property, but at best an abundant property. "A thing can have no sparse properties without having a sparse property of **having no properties**" (2006: 394).) Alternately, one might reject this second claimed difference on the grounds that the class of bare particulars does cut nature at its joints, since the distinction between the class of bare particulars and the class of properties (whether properties are universals or natural classes) is a vital metaphysical distinction, one that is not gerrymandered or anthropocentric. In fact, I can concede that there is a sense in which traditional bare particulars would mark a metaphysical joint in nature, if they existed, but still affirm

---

[24] One might ask how different Natural Class tropes get sorted into different classes if they are nature-free "prior" to such memberships, but that is a different worry.

that since bare particulars could not ground similarity of nature among objects, the class of bare particulars would fail to be a natural class.[25]

But suppose that we were to grant that bare particulars are members of natural classes for the sake of argument. Still, there are two further differences between Natural Class tropes and traditional bare particulars having to do with membership in natural classes that are maximal. These differences do not speak against the membership of traditional bare particulars in natural classes, but against the property-like character of bare particulars and for the property-like character of Natural Class tropes. The first difference has to do with membership in perfectly natural maximal classes. According to Natural Class Trope Nominalism, there are tropes that are members of different perfectly natural classes that are maximal. For example, there is a red trope that is a member of the perfectly natural class of "crimson" tropes but not a member of the perfectly natural class of 3-gram mass tropes. There is a trope t and a trope t' such that t is a member of a perfectly maximal class C of which t' is not a member. There are trope–trope differences, in some cases, with respect to membership in perfectly natural classes that are maximal. But if bare particulars, as traditionally conceived, were members of perfectly natural classes that are maximal—which we have just rejected—they would all be members of the *same* perfectly natural such class. If traditional bare particular b is a member of the perfectly natural class C that is maximal, then so is any other traditional bare particular b'. There is a selectivity vis-à-vis natural classes in the case of Natural Class Trope Nominalist tropes that one does not find for traditional bare particulars. And it is this selectivity that makes Natural Class tropes property-like and traditional bare particulars not property-like even if we were to grant that bare particulars are members of a natural class.

At this point, it might be objected that this talk of "selectivity" and the associated differences between the selectivity of natural classes in the case of Natural Class tropes and the lack of the selectivity of traditional bare particulars doesn't address the real concern about Natural Class tropes, which is that tropes without intrinsic natures are no more fit to somehow "naturally" be sorted into distinct natural classes than are collections of traditional bare particulars. What is the basis for this selectivity, if different tropes are, in themselves, just barely numerically different? Insisting that there is such selectivity doesn't address this deeper concern. How can different Natural Class tropes get sorted into different classes if they are nature-free "prior" to such memberships? For example, in virtue of what does one bunch of "bare" tropes constitute a type such as the class of red tropes?[26]

First, Natural Class Trope Nominalism is no worse off than is Natural Class Object Nominalism in this respect (and one might add, than is Resemblance Object Nominalism). One *might* think otherwise if one thought the following about Natural Class

---

[25] I owe both of these responses to the second claimed difference between Natural Class tropes and bare particulars to a referee.

[26] A referee presses this objection.

Object Nominalism: one can see how objects, having the rich natures that they have independently of their membership in natural classes (and one can add, under Resemblance Object Nominalism, independently of resemblance classes), might be suited to be sorted into different natural classes (or different resemblance classes). By way of contrast, one might think that tropes on Natural Class Trope Nominalism do not have any natures independent of their membership in a natural class and, hence, lack the same nature-basis for sorting into different natural classes.[27] In fact, I don't think this is the right way to understand Natural Class Object Nominalism. I would suggest that both Natural Class Object Nominalism and Resemblance Object Nominalism are not generally understood to posit a nature for an object independent of its natural class memberships or resemblance relations. For example, consider what Rodriguez-Pereyra, a proponent of Resemblance Object Nominalism, says of any attempt to combine Resemblance Nominalism with the view that objects have natures independent of their resemblance relations: "invoking particularized natures betrays the spirit of Resemblance Nominalism. For if that a and b resemble each other is determined by their natures, then their natures are not determined by their resembling each other, and so what is doing the work is their natures, not their resembling each other. Indeed, if in the case of one-instance properties what grounds the attributions of the property to the instance is its nature, why appeal to resemblances in cases of multiple-instances properties?... in this respect endowing particulars with particularized natures, means abandoning Resemblance Nominalism" (2002: 88–9). The same point can be made about combining Natural Class Object Nominalism with particularized natures. Hence, since *neither* Natural Class Object Nominalism nor Resemblance Object Nominalism invokes a class-independent/resemblance-independent nature, they are on a par with Natural Class Trope Nominalism with respect to the objection under discussion. Thus, for those who are sympathetic to either of Natural Class Object Nominalism or Resemblance Object Nominalism in this respect, then this objection will carry less weight: if the "blobs" of Natural Class Object Nominalism and Resemblance Object Nominalism sort themselves into different natural classes without having a nature prior to such class membership/resemblance relations, then why not Natural Class tropes?

Notwithstanding this comparative point, what should be said about the absence of a "basis" for the "selectivity" of Natural Class tropes? In a theory of properties, there will always be certain facts that are primitive and non-reducible. If one always objected to the presence of such primitive facts—if one took the position that there should be no such primitive facts in the theory of properties—then no theory of properties would be acceptable. Now it might be argued that there is something special about the fact at hand—the selectivity of Natural Class tropes with respect to membership in various natural classes—such that this issue is somehow more pressing than just the issue of some primitiveness in every theory of properties. But I don't see this. There is just this

---

[27] A referee suggests this contrast.

greater selectivity and that is a non-reducible fact. If this means that it is misleading to call these tropes "bare particulars," so be it. In any case, Natural Class Trope Nominalism seems no worse off than the Universalist position. Is it any less perplexing how one universal gets to be a redness universal and another gets to be a blueness universal? In both cases we have a primitive fact. So in virtue of what does this selectivity of Natural Class tropes hold? The answer is: in virtue of itself. In virtue of it being the case that these tropes are selectively sorted in these ways. This is similar to the claim that a charge universal is a charge universal in virtue of nothing other than its being a charge universal. Metaphysical explanation comes to an end.

The second difference along these lines also has to do with membership in maximal natural classes of varying degrees of naturalness. A Natural Class trope will ordinarily be a member of multiple maximal natural classes of varying degrees of naturalness. For example, a fully determinate crimson trope will be a member of the maximal class of fully determinate crimson tropes, which will be a perfectly natural class. But a fully determinate crimson trope will also be a member of the maximal class of red tropes, which is a less-than-perfectly natural class. If a bare particular were a member of any maximal natural class, it would be a member of at most one—that of all bare particulars (if there were such a natural class, which I denied above). For a traditional bare particular b—if it is granted that there is a maximal natural class C of which it is a member—there will be only one such class. Any would-be maximal class of bare particulars C' that b is supposed also to be a member of could be distinguished from C only if C' were more or less natural than C, but there is little sense to that idea. A bare particular, hence, does not display this feature of properties: a fully determinate property (and even a less-than-fully determinate property) can be an instance of multiple property types, whereas even if we allowed that bare particulars were "instances" of some type, they would be instances of only one type. Crimson is an instance of the type redness and the type color whereas bare particulars could, at best, be members of a single maximal natural class, if they could be members of any such class (which they cannot).

In response to this last supposed difference between traditional bare particulars and Natural Class tropes, it might be argued that bare particulars are members of at least one maximal less-than-perfectly natural class: the class of bare particulars and ordinary objects. In fact, not only is this class not a perfectly natural class, it is not a less-than-perfectly natural class either—since it is not a natural class at all. This class is too highly gerrymandered to count as a natural class, including highly varied entities—such as writing desks and blackbirds, thereby constituting just the sort of class that philosophers have agreed is non-natural.

3.1.1 Bare particulars do not have properties There is, however, a related objection that can be raised to Natural Class tropes, having to do with the other component of being a bare particular, the failure to *have* any properties. The standard objection to the *traditional* bare particulars is not based on the fact that they are not properties, but that they *have* no properties. The idea is that there can be no entities that do not have properties. Since bare particulars would lack properties if they existed, they cannot exist. But it appears that Natural Class tropes are half-bare in the sense that they do not have properties *in themselves*, and, so, they cannot exist either, even if they are not fully bare. My response to this objection is twofold. First, I reject the claim that nothing that failed to have properties could exist. Properties are, in fact, one exception to this principle. It is logically possible that properties lack properties. Indeed, the position of Elementarism is that properties never have properties and this position seems to me to be one that cannot be automatically ruled out. Second, Sider has argued that there are actual bare particulars, so they are not impossible. He cites the example of space-time points. "We find that physical theories require almost nothing of the points intrinsically. They require only that the set of space-time points has a certain structure. This structure consists in the holding of spatiotemporal relations between the points, but is indifferent to what the points are like in themselves... I suggest, then, that a natural and economic theory of points of space-time is that each one is a partless, truly bare particular that stands in a network of spatiotemporal relations" (2006: 10). Whether or not Sider is right to claim that there are such space-time points, it certainly seems right to think that there could be such points, and that is all that is needed to refute the claim that nothing without properties could exist.

3.2 Natural Class Trope Nominalist tropes collapse into objects

Even if Natural Class tropes can be distinguished from traditional bare particulars given the resources of Natural Class Trope Nominalism, it might be objected that Natural Class tropes are still too much like objects to be properties. The argument for this objection rests on the similarity between Natural Class *Object* Nominalism and Natural Class *Trope* Nominalism. The tropes of the latter, it might be argued, play the same role that objects do within Natural Class Object Nominalism. In particular, just as a Natural Class *Object* Nominalist holds that for a thing to be of a certain type is for it to be a member of a certain natural class of objects, a Natural Class Trope Nominalist holds that for a trope to be of a certain type is for it to be a member of a certain natural class of tropes. The only difference, the objector argues, is that Natural Class tropes are, so to speak, just "smaller" versions of the objects of Natural Class Object Nominalism, rather than properties. In fact, I do not think that this objection is cogent. There are differences between Natural Class tropes and the objects of Natural Class Object Nominalism that make the former more property-like than the latter.

One reason for thinking that Natural Class tropes are more property-like than object-like emerges when we compare the role of natural class membership in Natural Class Trope Nominalism with the role of membership in Natural Class *Object* Nominalism. What is grounded by natural class membership is importantly different between these two theories. A Natural Class *Object* Nominalist holds that for a thing to be white is for it to be a member of a certain natural class of objects. Membership in a natural class F does *not* make it true for the object theorist that the object o *is* a property, only that *o has* property *F*, or at least that it is true that "*o* has property *F*." For the trope theorist, on the other hand, membership in a natural class makes it true that the tropes themselves *are* qualities of a certain type. Membership in the natural class of white tropes makes it the case that a particular trope *is* a whiteness property. Closely related to this point is that for the Natural Class Object Nominalist, there will be much more variation in the natural classes that *o* is a member of than there will be in the natural classes that a trope *t* is a member of. The greater selectivity of the tropes of Natural Class Trope Nominalism with respect to the maximal natural classes that they may be members of, as compared to the objects of Natural Class Object Nominalism, is another indicator of the property-like character of Natural Class tropes as compared to the objects of Natural Class Object Nominalism.

Second, and related to this first difference, is another difference that comes to light when we look more closely at what the intrinsic similarity of properties amounts to and how that contrasts with object similarity. Consider two intrinsically similar objects. These objects are similar only in virtue of the properties they *have*. For example, two objects that are similar in color are so in virtue of the color properties that they have. Properties, on the other hand, may be intrinsically similar not in virtue of (higher-order) properties of themselves. For the Natural Class Trope Nominalist, membership in the same natural class grounds the similarity of the properties and that similarity is not a matter of higher-order properties of those tropes. Two color tropes may be similar in virtue of their natures, not in virtue of any higher-order tropes that they may have. In that sense, vis-à-vis similarity relations, Natural Class tropes behave like properties, not like objects.[28]

There is a third possible reason for thinking that Natural Class tropes are property-like given the following difference between objects and properties: "Properties are properties *of* individuals. Relations are relations *holding between* individuals. But individuals are not individuals *of* their properties. Nor do individuals hold between the

---

[28] At this point it might be objected that the tropes of Natural Class Trope Nominalism are not properties for the following reason:

> One feature of properties is that for each object there are many properties, each *distinguishable* from the others. However, the Natural Class tropes of a single object would be *indistinguishable* from one another independently of their memberships in natural classes. Natural Class Trope Nominalism is inconsistent with the ordinary fact about properties, that each object possesses many of them that are distinguishable from each other.

Armstrong makes an objection like this to "Stoutian particulars" when that view is combined with immanent realism: "This would make the different Stoutian properties of a thing, in abstraction from their universal properties, indistinguishable from each other, which seems absurd" (1978a: 87). If one substitutes "their membership in natural classes" for "universal properties" one gets the current objection. In fact, this objection fails. The consistency of Natural Class Trope Nominalism with this ordinary fact does *not* require that properties as described by that theory be distinguishable *independently of the full apparatus of the theory*, independently of their class memberships. What is important is that this ordinary fact be consistent with the output of the theory. A consequence of Natural Class Trope Nominalism is that each object has multiple distinguishable properties, since an object's various properties will be members of different natural classes. That is enough to do justice to this ordinary fact.

relations which relate them" (Armstrong 1989b: 44). Even if properties can also themselves have (higher-order) properties, objects cannot be had by objects or by properties. I would suggest that there is nothing standing in the way of thinking of Natural Class tropes as satisfying this asymmetry. Think of it this way. What is important here is not the Natural Class conception of tropes, but the notion of a trope in general. The idea of a trope can be generated by considering how tropes and universals differ, leaving in place what they have in common. Where tropes and universals differ (universals cannot have duplicates but tropes can) does not, however, have anything much to do with this asymmetry. Hence, if universals are property-like in this respect, then there is no reason to think that tropes cannot be. And there is nothing in the conception of a Natural Class trope to undermine this difference between objects and properties.

Similarly, there is a fourth reason for thinking that Natural Class tropes are property-like that will carry weight with those philosophers who accept a numerical account of the difference between universals and objects. The idea is that even if the numerical difference does not track the universal–particular distinction, it may track the property–object distinction: properties, but not objects, set up numerical constraints on the constituents of "facts" of which they are constituents. Properties can only ever occur in facts with n constituents, but objects can occur in facts with any number of constituents. The possession of -adicity is characteristic of properties but not objects. An object and a Natural Class trope can, then, be distinguished in virtue of the fact that the latter, but not the former, possess -adicity. For example, it is reasonable to think that a Natural Class trope from the red class will be a one-place property.[29]

This application of such numerical differences, however, brings us to the worry that some properties, such as "forming a circle" are multigrade (MacBride 2005: 572).[30] In response, I would argue that if properties are tropes, we can accommodate the phenomenon of multigrade "properties" within a trope framework without abandoning the underlying thesis that properties are unigrade. The trope theorist distinguishes between particular properties and property types, the former being tropes and the latter, classes of tropes. That leaves it open to claim that multigrade "collective predicates" at best correspond to property types, classes of tropes, within which there is -adicity variation. The members of the class of " ... carried the boat" tropes may vary in -adicity, even though no specific " ... carried the boat" trope does. Property types may be multigrade, but particular properties, tropes, are not.[31]

---

[29] This difference concerning -adicity might help explain why tropes can be possessed by objects but objects cannot be possessed by tropes: the -adicity of the latter and the lack of -adicity by the former.
[30] If this line of objection holds, then the unigrade–multigrade distinction cannot be used to set up a workable distinction between universals and particulars.
[31] This response will not go through, however, if there are higher-order tropes, both properties and relations, with varying numbers of argument places, that the same lower-order trope figures in.

4. What's next?

In Chapter 7, I turn to certain key objections to Natural Class Trope Nominalism. The first two objections are that Natural Class Trope Nominalism seems to rule out the possibility that a property might have had: (1) fewer instances than it has; and (2) more instances than it has. The third objection is that Natural Class Trope Nominalism seems to make all properties causally irrelevant. I will suggest that these objections can be answered by adopting a counterpart theory of properties without adopting modal realism.

7

The classic objections to Natural Class Trope Nominalism

Natural Class Trope Nominalism does not currently enjoy a "live option" status among philosophers who work on the "problem of universals." In fact, I do not know of any other contemporary adherents to this view. In this chapter, I focus on the basis for this disfavor in the form of the three "classic" objections to Natural Class Trope Nominalism. The first objection, which I call the "One-Over-Fewer" objection, is that Natural Class Trope Nominalism seems to rule out the genuine possibility that a property might have had fewer instances than it has. Had even a single member of the class of red tropes not existed, then if "being red" is a matter of being a member of just that class, then nothing would have been red. The second objection, which I will call the "One Over More" objection, is that Natural Class Trope Nominalism seems to entail wrongly that there could not have been one more red trope. The third objection, the "Causation" objection, is that Natural Class Trope Nominalism seems to make all properties causally irrelevant by requiring the causal relevancy of non-local tropes for the causal relevancy of any tropes local to a causal sequence. All three of these objections can be answered, I will argue, by adopting a counterpart theory of properties.[1]

1. The One-Over-Fewer objection

I begin with the One-Over-Fewer objection:

> A class has its membership essentially and could not have had different members. The class of all actual red tropes would not have existed had even just one actual red trope not existed. If the type "redness" is identical with that class, then it would seem

---

[1] At this point, one might raise a worry about priority, as a referee does—the concern that entities get sorted into natural classes in virtue of having the natures they do, not vice versa. In response, I would suggest that this intuition does have force in the context of thinking about objects—natural classes of objects are grounded in the properties of objects—and that that intuition is preserved here, but that it may be wrongly transferred to properties. Furthermore, even if we do have such an intuition at the level of properties, every metaphysical theory of properties will require abandoning *some* intuition of this sort (for example, Resemblance Object Nominalism requires that we abandon our intuition that the overall resemblance between objects is grounded in their properties).

to follow that "redness" would not have been instantiated and nothing would have been red had even just a single actual red trope not existed. But the latter is false.

In short, the fragility of the class of actual red tropes—it could not exist with fewer members—does not correspond to any similar fragility possessed by the property type "redness." This is the most important objection to Natural Class Trope Nominalism, and it is this objection that I believe is most responsible for the lack of support for this view. How might the Natural Class Trope Nominalist respond? I begin with three inadequate responses.

1.1 Three responses that don't work

One might defend Natural Class Trope Nominalism by claiming that it is no worse off than its rivals with respect to this objection or some analogous objection. Consider, for example, realism and the following objection that at least *sounds* like the One-Over-Fewer objection.

> The redness universal of this ball could not have existed in the absence of the redness universal of any other red objects since the redness of this ball is identical with the redness of these various other objects. Had the redness of any of these other objects not existed (the universal "redness" had not existed) then the redness of this ball would not have existed.

With respect to this objection, we need to ask, first, whether it has any plausibility, as it stands, as an objection to Realism, and, second, whether it is really analogous to the One-Over-Fewer objection to Natural Class Trope Nominalism. As to the first question, it is clear that this objection lacks any plausibility as an objection to Realism. As stated, this objection amounts to the claim that if the universal "redness" had not existed, the universal "redness" would not have existed. Certainly that is true, but the Realist will agree. However, this objection is not particularly similar to the One-Over-Fewer objection. A closer approximation to an analogue would run as follows.

> Had this ball not exemplified redness, then nothing would have exemplified redness.

Had there been one fewer instance of the universal "redness," there would have been no instances of "redness." That certainly is similar to the One-Over-Fewer objection, but it fails to have any plausibility as an objection against Realism. Nothing in the Realist position makes it have this consequence. The universal "redness" could have been one over not-so-many objects. Nor does this kind of objection work against Campbell's Trope Theory. For Campbell, the nature of the redness of the ball is not determined by that redness's membership in the class of rednesses or by its resemblance to the members of the class of rednesses. The redness of the ball could have existed, and been the nature it is, even if the redness tropes of these other objects had not existed. Each redness trope might still have existed and been a redness trope in the absence of other members of the class of actual red tropes.

A second possible response involves modifying Natural Class Trope Nominalism. According to the One-Over-Fewer objection, since the class of redness tropes would not have existed had one of the actual redness tropes not existed, the type "redness" would not have existed either, and, hence, the type "redness" would not have been instantiated by anything. In response, why not drop any reference to property types? In particular, don't identify the "redness" type with the class of redness tropes or anything else. Although a particular trope's nature is determined by its membership in various natural classes, no natural class is identified with any property type. The One-Over-Fewer objection cannot, then, get started. Unfortunately, this response fails. First, the trope nominalist cannot avoid providing an account of property types since property types play legitimate metaphysical roles including the roles of causally relevant property types and, perhaps, as relata for laws of nature.[2] Second, something close to the One-Over-Fewer objection can still be formulated. Since a trope *t*'s nature is still determined by its membership in various classes including, say, C, had C not existed (because one of its actual members had not existed), then *t* would have had a different nature. But that consequence is very close to the one embodied in the One-Over-Fewer objection, and it is no more acceptable.

A third response involves adopting modal realism and identifying property types not with natural classes of actual tropes, but with natural classes of actual as well as merely possible tropes. Redness is the natural class of all actual and all merely possible red tropes. The fact that there could have been fewer red tropes is, then, easily accommodated. That possibility is grounded in the existence of a possible world in which there are fewer red tropes than exist in the actual world. What makes those tropes red is their membership in a crossworld natural class of red tropes including the red tropes of the actual world. This response depends on a commitment to modal realism, which is certainly controversial. Given that controversy, it is perhaps best not to adopt this response, especially if there is an alternative response without this commitment. I will now suggest that there is.

1.2 A response based on a counterpart theory of properties

My response to the One-Over-Fewer objection involves combining Natural Class Trope Nominalism with a counterpart theory for properties. I will begin by giving an alternate formulation of the One-Over-Fewer objection, and note a structurally similar objection, considered by Lewis, to the claim that persons and their actual bodies are identical (Lewis 1983a). Second, I will outline Lewis's counterpart-based response to the latter objection. Third, I will suggest that this response can be adapted to the One-Over-Fewer objection by expanding counterpart theory to include properties. Consider an alternate formulation of the One-Over-Fewer objection:

---

[2] Natural classes of actual tropes play those roles for the Natural Class Trope Nominalist.

Since there are red tropes that might not have existed, (A) the type "redness" and the class of actual red tropes are such that they might not have been identical. But if "redness" is identical to the class of actual red tropes, by Leibniz's law, it follows that (B) the class of actual red tropes and the class of actual red tropes are such that they might not have been identical, which is absurd. Hence, the type "redness" is not identical to the class of all actual red tropes.

Now notice a structurally similar objection to the claim that persons are identical to their bodies[3]:

Since I could have switched bodies yesterday (1) I and my body are such that (without any duplication of either) they might not have been identical today. But then if I am identical to my body, by Leibniz's law, it follows that (2) my body and my body are such that (without any duplication of either) they might not have been identical today, which is absurd. Hence, I am not identical to my body (Lewis 1983a: 50).[4]

In both cases, an identity claim is challenged because it seems to imply a statement of the form "x and x are such that they might not have been identical" when it is conjoined with an uncontroversial possibility. Let's now consider Lewis's counterpart-based response to this objection to person–body identity theory.

1.2.1 Counterpart theory I will begin with some basics of his counterpart theory. For Lewis, an object o might have had a property it does not have just in case o has a counterpart with that property in some other world. The counterpart to o in that other world is not o itself. The counterpart relation is a relation of similarity, not the relation of identity. Crossworld identity for objects is rejected. o's counterpart must resemble o closely enough in important respects and more closely than do the other things in that world. However, the same object may have different counterparts in the same world depending upon *which* counterpart relation is at stake in any particular context. And that depends on "the relative importances we attach to various different respects of similarity and dissimilarity..." (1983a: 50). When these weightings are varied, different counterpart relations result (1983a: 51). If, in one context, respect R is ranked more important than R' in determining similarity, then in that context the R-counterpart relation may be at issue rather than the R'-counterpart relation. Depending on which term we use to denote an individual in a modal claim, that term may signal different counterpart relations as relevant to the truth-value of that modal claim. Using counterpart theory, Lewis argues that the objection to the person–body identity thesis fails. When (1) and (2) are properly understood, through sensitivity to

---

[3] Lewis has in mind cases in which the person occupied the same body from the time when it and the person began to the time when it and the person ended.

[4] Lewis includes the phrase "without any duplication of either" in order to avoid the irrelevancy that I and my body both might have been twins.

the different counterpart relations that are invoked by different terms "I" and "my body" in these statements, (2) does not follow from (1).[5] Although "I" and "my body" denote the same thing, "I" invokes personhood and the personal counterpart relation and "my body" invokes bodyhood and the bodily counterpart relation. The consequence is that although (1) is true and (2) is false, (2) does not follow from (1). (1) says that there is a possible world in which I have personal and bodily counterparts that are not identical, which is true.[6] (2), on the other hand, says something false but not something that follows from (1): there is a possible world with a unique bodily counterpart, X, of my body and a unique bodily counterpart, Y, of my body such that X and Y are not identical.[7]

1.2.2 Type and class counterparts There is a structurally similar response to the One-Over-Fewer objection to the claim that "redness" is identical to the natural class of red tropes, if counterpart-theoretic semantics is extended to properties.[8] First, posit a "type" counterpart relation and a "class" counterpart relation for property types.[9] Second, suggest that (A) should be read as the truth that there is a world in which there is a type counterpart to the type "redness" but no class counterpart to the class of actual red tropes, but claim that (B) should be read as the falsehood that there is a world in which there is a class counterpart, X, to the class of red tropes and a class counterpart, Y, to the class of red tropes such that X and Y are not identical. Third, point out that (B) does not follow from (A).

Or, to put the point another way, consider that the One-Over-Fewer objection says, in effect, that the following statements form an inconsistent set:

1'. The class C could not have existed had x, a member of C, not existed.
2'. The type T could have existed had x not existed.
3'. T is identical to C.

Our response can be read as positing different counterpart relations in evaluating 1' and 2', eliminating the apparent inconsistency. The terms "class C" and "type T" bring into play different counterpart relations, although they pick out one and the same thing. The "type" counterpart relation grounds the possibility of the instantiation of "being a T-type trope" in the absence of x, a member of C, since there is a world in

---

[5] Depending on which term is used we have a different way of following the fortunes of that thing in other worlds (Lewis 1983a: 54).

[6] More specifically, the proper translation, for Lewis, of (1) is the following: there are a world W, and a unique personal counterpart X in W of me, and a unique bodily counterpart Y in W of my body, such that X and Y are not identical today.

[7] There are a world W, and a unique bodily counterpart X in W of my body, and a unique bodily counterpart Y in W of my body, such that X and Y are not identical today (Lewis 1983a: 57).

[8] This endorsement of a counterpart theory for properties has the consequence of anti-essentialism for properties. What is essential to a property will vary with different contexts.

[9] And, to grant as much as possible to the objection, assume that the class "counterpart" relation is just class identity.

which there is a "type" counterpart to *C* but no counterpart to x.[10] The "class" counterpart relation, however, rules out the possibility of class *C* existing in the absence of *x* because there is no world with a "class" counterpart to *C* that does not include a counterpart to *x*. Although (3) is true (being a *T*-type trope is just being a member of *C*), (1') and (2') are both true.[11] In short, Natural Class Trope Nominalism in combination with property counterpart theory is immune to the One-Over-Fewer objection.[12]

1.3 Further development of the counterpart response

As indicated, the form of Natural Class Trope Nominalism being defended here assumes that modal realism is false. After all, if modal realism were true, then the Natural Class Trope Nominalist would, presumably, identify property types with natural classes of both actual and merely possible tropes. But the version defended here does not. This raises an issue for the property counterpart theoretic response to the One-Over-Fewer objection. The issue is whether this use of property counterpart theory commits us to modal realism. In effect, we need to show that there are actualist

---

[10] A referee suggests that it isn't completely obvious that there would be a case in which there is a world in which there is a "type" counterpart to *C*, but no counterpart to *x*. Why wouldn't any of the tropes in *C*'s type counterpart serve as a counterpart for *x*? In order to make this more obvious, suppose that the only difference between the actual world and a possible world *w* is that a certain rose is white rather than red, where "*x*" is the redness trope of that specific rose in the actual world. There might be a type counterpart to "redness" as well as counterparts for all the other specific redness tropes from the actual world, but given the absence of a "redness" trope at the location of the rose, there is no counterpart to *x*.

[11] Although we have assumed for the sake of argument that the class "counterpart" relation is just class identity, there are alternate assumptions worth considering. Another possibility is that this counterpart relation is compatible with different members but requires the same number of members. Still another is that it is compatible with a different number of members. If the same number of members is required (but not necessarily the same members), then a smaller class of tropes (smaller than the class of actual red tropes) in another world fails to be a class counterpart but might still be a type counterpart to the property type "redness." If the class counterpart relation is such that there can be classes with fewer members than the class to which they are counterparts, then there are classes that could have existed with fewer members and the members of such classes are not essential to those classes. But then the objection does not get off the ground since it depends upon the assumption that a class's membership is essential to it.

[12] A referee suggests that if the trope theorist can appeal to counterpart theory as a way of accommodating the classic objections to Natural Class Nominalism without endorsing modal realism, it might be possible for the Natural Class Object Nominalist to do the same thing. Since actualists have ways of accommodating possibilia, as combinatorial or other constructions from actualia, perhaps an actualist could implement the spirit of the modal realist's strategy for distinguishing coextensive properties, for example, by taking property classes to contain actual and possible entities, compatible with rejecting modal realism. In response, I would suggest that although the Natural Class Object Nominalist might be able to use this strategy for dealing with some problems—for example, accounting for the possibility that there could have been fewer or more red objects—it would seem that there are some objections to Natural Class Object Nominalism that cannot be handled along these lines, such as the problem of distinguishing coextensive properties, *P* and *Q*. In order to respond to the latter problem, Natural Class Object Nominalism must distinguish between the two classes involved, the class of *P* objects and the class of *Q* objects. These classes must differ in their membership. But the things that make up those classes must in some sense exist even if they are not actual. My worry is that whereas modal realism gives us existence for the mere possibilia, actualism does not. Actualism, in principle, can supply the grounds for what could have been the case for property *P*, but I don't see how it has the resources to solve, for example, the problem of distinguishing coextensive properties.

theories of modality that are compatible with this combination of Natural Class Trope Nominalism and property counterpart theory. That is what I will attempt to do at this point. There is also a more specific task of showing how the property counterpart theoretic response to the One-Over-Fewer objection gets worked out within an actualist account of modality. We need to show how to understand counterpart relations as similarity relations, within the context of actualism, given the Natural Class Trope Nominalism account of similarity. In order to answer these questions, I will briefly show how Natural Class Trope Nominalism can be combined with two actualist theories of modality, combinatorialism and linguistic ersatzism.

1.3.1 Combinatorialism For combinatorialists, possible worlds are built out of elements from the one concrete world, including actual objects and properties. For example, for Armstrong (under his first approximation), the one concrete world divides into first-order states of affairs, the constituents of which are simple individuals and simple universals that are mutually logically independent (1989b).[13] The simple individuals are "thin particulars" that differ from each other in being numerically distinct, but not otherwise, and are always bound together with universals in states of affairs. The having of a universal by a thin particular or the holding of a relation between thin particulars is a state of affairs. *Possible states of affairs* are any combinations (conforming to the form of an atomic state of affairs) of these actual individuals and simple, instantiated properties (1989b: 48). It is true that "it is possible that *a* is *F*" just in case *a* is an actual thin particular, *F* is a simple, instantiated universal, and *a*'s being *F* has the form of a state of affairs, even if there is no such actual state of affairs. "It is this world which is to supply the actual elements of combinations" (Armstrong 1986: 575). Within certain constraints, a *possible world* is any conjunction of possible atomic states of affairs (Armstrong 1989b: 48). A Natural Class trope version of this view replaces universals with actual tropes and natural classes of actual tropes.[14] The result is that possible worlds are built up from actual elements but including actual tropes and classes of actual tropes.[15] Natural Class Trope Nominalism by itself appears to be compatible with this actualist theory since Natural Class Trope Nominalism merely calls for a change in how the properties of combinatorialism are characterized and not much beyond that. Still, we need to see what happens when property counterpart theory is brought into play.[16]

---

[13] For our purposes here, Armstrong's first and simplest approximation will do, when modified along trope nominalist lines and to include a property counterpart relation.

[14] It is the individual constituents and states of affairs themselves, *in the actual world*, that serve, in their various ways, as the sole truthmakers for the modal truths (Armstrong 1997: 151).

[15] Although for Armstrong these actual properties and relations are universals, he allows that combinatorialism is compatible with nominalism (1989b: 37).

[16] Armstrong makes limited use of counterpart relations for individuals: "... when we say that some actual thing, such as Descartes, might have been, in his own nature, different than he actually was ... it is not *strictly* Descartes that we are envisaging. It can only be one of Descartes' 'counterparts' ... " (1997: 169).

Since the property counterpart relation between crossworld property types is a similarity relation, we must look at Natural Class Trope Nominalism's account of property type resemblance. Two property types are similar just in case either they are subclasses of a common natural class or they overlap. The property types "crimson" and "scarlet" are similar because, although disjoint, they are subclasses of a common natural class, "red." The property types greenish-blue and bluish-purplish are similar because there is an area of overlap (although they are also similar because they are subclasses of a common natural class). What, then, will it mean to read the counterpart relation between crossworld types in terms of the subclass or overlap relation? Consider type overlap across worlds first. Suppose that T in the actual world and T' in another possible world, w, overlap. The tropes in the overlap area will have to exist in both worlds. That is so since the form of Natural Class Trope Nominalism defended here assumes that the membership of a type that is instantiated at a world w is restricted to tropes that exist in w. The type "red" is the class of all actual red tropes, including no merely possible tropes.[17] Hence, type overlap across worlds requires trope identity across worlds. The same is required for type similarity across worlds based on those classes being subclasses of a common natural class. Suppose that T in the actual world and T' in another possible world are similar in virtue of being subclasses of a common natural class, N. Since N is instantiated in the actual world, then all of its members are tropes that exist in the actual world, and since N is instantiated in w, all of its members are tropes that exist in w. Hence, for a counterpart relation between types given the Natural Class Trope Nominalist account of type similarity, there must be trope identity across worlds, it would appear. For the trope combinatorialist, that is not a problem. There is crossworld trope identity for the trope combinatorialist since the trope components of any possible world are actual tropes. Crossworld type counterparts can be read as a matter of being subclasses of a common type or of class overlap. So how then does the property-theoretic response to the One-Over-Fewer objection, specifically, get spelled out in this framework? Suppose, for example, that a combinatorially constructed possible world w includes a class C- with all the same members as the natural class C of all actual red tropes except for one, such that there is one fewer red trope in w than in the actual world. C- may be a type counterpart of C if there is no other class in w that is more similar to C and C- is similar enough where the similarity of these classes of tropes across the actual world and a possible world is a matter of their being subclasses of a common natural class in the actual world. The trope combinatorialist can say that our two classes, C and C-, satisfy this condition. C- is

"There can be combinatorially constructed Descartes counterparts, and these can properly be *said* to be Descartes himself." (1997: 169).

[17] This assumption does not rule out that a type T's being instantiated, say, in the actual world while also including tropes that exist in other worlds, as long as those tropes also exist in the actual world. T cannot have any members which are not actual tropes and T' cannot have any members that do not exist in w. For example, T cannot consist of some tropes in w (that are not actual tropes) and some tropes from the actual world that are not tropes that exist in w (which would make possible overlap without any tropes existing in both worlds).

a subclass of *C* and the latter is a subclass of itself.[18] Or, if we reject the notion of a class being a subclass of itself we can appeal to the overlap between these two classes. The class most similar to *C* in *w* is *C-*, since the latter is *just like the former* only lacking one member.[19]

1.3.2 Linguistic ersatzism For the "ersatzist" theorist too there is only one concrete world. All properties and objects are in this one concrete world, assuming no uninstantiated properties. For the *linguistic ersatzist*, possible worlds, including the "actual world," are maximal-consistent descriptions of the one concrete world. The "actual world" is one such description, albeit the only one that is completely accurate. The one and only concrete world is not itself a "possible world" since it is not itself a description. On linguistic ersatzism (in particular, on Mark Heller's version), these world-descriptions are sets of sets.[20] Each of these member sets is an ordered pair representing properties assigned to locations. The first member of each such pair is an ordered set of numbers representing a particular point in space-time and the second member, in the property place, a set of numbers playing the role of existentially bound variables ranging over properties.[21] Although there is no transworld identity for *represented* objects and properties of any world, both may have counterparts in another world. It is possible for a property *P* in the concrete world to lack a property or relation

---

[18] One might ask what the connection is between understanding similarity of types in terms of subclasses and understanding similarity of types in terms of having tropes that are members of a common natural class. In so far as two types are similar in virtue of being subclasses of a common natural class—for example, the property type "crimson" and "scarlet" are subclasses of a common natural class, "red"—every member of these classes, "crimson" and "scarlet," is a member of a common natural class, "red." And, if all the members of two classes are members of a common natural class, then those classes will be subclasses of that common natural class. In addition, in so far as two types, *C* and *C'*, are similar in virtue of overlapping, at least one member of *C* and one member of *C'* will be co-members of a common natural class.

[19] A referee raises the following objection to this approach to the One-Over-Fewer objection. If the member tropes of *C* don't have any natures in themselves, but only as being members of *C*, then why think that natural class *C* and *C-* would be similar? The natures of tropes *qua* members of *C-* could be very different from the nature of tropes *qua* members of *C* on a relational account of natures. The referee proposes the following analogy to make this point. Suppose that dots have no intrinsic nature but get their nature relationally, by being part of a given shape. Suppose that three dots form a triangle and so have a nature such as to constitute a "2-D shape." A subclass of these dots entering into a line shape would have an entirely different "relational" nature. If tropes have relational natures, then they might also be very dissimilar, depending on what natural class they were part of. In response, I would suggest that given that *C* is a natural class—and for the sake of discussion suppose that *C* is a perfectly natural class—that means that the members of *C* exactly resemble each other. Also, any subclass, such as *C-* will also be a perfectly natural class. It follows that the tropes of *C-* are exactly similar to each other and that the tropes of *C-* are exactly similar to the of the "remainder" tropes of *C*, those tropes of *C* minus the tropes of *C-*. Hence, in this case, it is not the case that the natures of tropes *qua* members of *C-* could be very different from the nature of tropes *qua* members of *C* on *this* relational account of natures in terms of natural classes. The same kind of reasoning applies to an example in which *C* is a natural class but not a perfectly natural class: the tropes of *C-* will not be "very different" from the tropes of *C* including the remainder tropes of *C*.

[20] Talk about possibility is reconstructed in terms of actual elements from the concrete world, in particular, linguistic elements.

[21] When different member sets of a single world contain the same number in their property places, it is stipulated that that number represents the same property.

that P actually has just in case there is a possible world—a set of sets—that represents a property P' that is a counterpart to P, such that P' lacks counterparts to that property or relation.[22] Now let's modify this ersatzist picture to bring it in line with Trope Nominalism. Heller's theory involves universals—they are the properties represented in the property place of these member sets, but we need a trope-based substitute. One possibility is to treat the property number as representing a natural class of tropes and to include an additional number to represent the individual trope. That would give us sets of triples of <location tuple, natural class number, individual trope number>. Following Heller, we can stipulate that different member sets of a single world that contain the same number in their natural class place (and in their individual trope place) represent the same natural class (individual trope). Across worlds (across sets of sets), the individual trope numbers are treated via counterpart theory. We assume no crossworld trope identity.

Our response to the One-Over-Fewer objection, in the context of linguistic ersatzism, is that there is a world w (set of sets) that includes a representation of a "type" counterpart to C ("redness"), C-, which is represented as lacking one member of C but as otherwise no different than C, although w lacks a representation of a "class" counterpart to C.

But now we seem to have a difficulty, one that we did not have with trope combinatorialism. According to the story we told about combinatorialism, the type counterpart relation is a matter of being subclasses of the same class or overlap, each of which required trope identity across worlds. In the case of linguistic ersatzism, however, crossworld trope identity is denied. There is no transworld identity for *represented* objects and properties of any world, including even universals if there are universals, but certainly tropes. Does that mean that there is no basis for a type counterpart relation and, ultimately, for our property-counterpart theoretic response to the One-Over-Fewer objection? What could be the basis for the type counterpart relation on the assumption that there is no crossworld trope identity?

The answer to this last question has to do with the fact that the similarity relations (and hence counterpart relations) of represented properties across worlds for the linguistic ersatzist are derivative. Crossworld represented properties are only ever similar to each other in virtue of similarities between the sets of sets that *are* those possible worlds.[23] Consider, for example, a variation on Heller's case of two worlds

---

[22] For example, as Heller says, "positive charge could have existed even if I had never written about it, if and only if positive charge has a counterpart that exists in a (close enough) world in which I (or rather my counterpart) do not write about that counterpart" (1998: 301).

[23] How should our response to the objection to Natural Class Trope Nominalism be formulated on this theory of modality? In some cases, a property type—a class C of actual tropes for trope-class nominalism—will not have all its properties/relations essentially. That will be so if there is a possible world W in which a non-identical class C- is represented that is similar enough to C (the class of all actual red tropes) to be its type counterpart, even if not its class counterpart. If we suppose that C- has fewer members than does C and there is no other class in W that is more similar to C and C- is similar enough, we may suppose that C- is a type counterpart to C. Hence, even if C- is not a class counterpart to C, if there is an object y represented in W that

that are exactly similar in every respect—with the same sets as members—but with one difference: in one world a trope number nineteen is associated with a given location but the other has twenty-five associated with that location. "Clearly, these two sets, considered as sets, would count as very similar in many contexts. Likewise, considered at a higher level of interpretation, considered as representations of property distributions, these two representations would often count as very similar. Independent of any question of which properties are being distributed, the patterns of property distribution are very similar, and there are surely many contexts in which we would therefore count the two worlds as very similar. In such contexts, we would say that the property numbered seven in the one world plays almost exactly the same role as the property numbered seven in the other world, and we would even say that the property numbered nineteen in the one world plays almost exactly the same role in the other world" (Heller 1998: 302). But these sets of sets are all elements of the one concrete world.[24] Hence, the similarity relations that ground the counterpart relation between the represented properties of different worlds hold only among actual elements (sets of sets) of the one concrete world or universe.[25] The ultimate relata of the similarity/counterpart relations are all elements of the one concrete world, actual properties of sets of sets (or for the trope-based linguistic ersatzist, actual tropes of sets of sets). There are no non-derivative counterpart relations between represented tropes of different worlds. At the most basic level, then, the trope-based linguistic ersatzist is not comparing tropes or classes of tropes across worlds, but tropes or classes of tropes (of sets) in this one universe. Hence, even if there is no identity of represented

---

is a counterpart to a red object x from the actual world and that object y is characterized by a trope from C-, then "being red" could still have been instantiated and something (e.g. x) would still have been red even if some other particular red object z had not been red. Returning to the alternate formulation we can say that (A) translates as the following: there is a world W in which there is represented a unique type counterpart X in W of "being red," but no unique class counterpart Y represented in W of the class of actual red tropes such that X and Y are identical. The proper translation of (B) becomes: there are a world W, and a unique class counterpart X represented in W of the class of actual red tropes, and a unique class counterpart Y represented in W of the class of actual red tropes, such that X is not identical to Y. Under these translations, (A) is true, (B) is false, but (B) does not follow from (A).

[24] If one seeks to make this trope-based ersatzist position consistent with Armstrongian naturalism, which does not allow anything to exist outside of space and time, then one must give some sense to the notion that the relevant sets are concrete—existing in space and time. Here I would follow Armstrong's suggestion that "in the case of sets whose members are spatio-temporal entities, the sets are located wherever their members are located" (1989b: 10). Under that assumption, which seems reasonable, "a set theory limited to spatio-temporal objects does not challenge Naturalism. Such a limitation will give the Naturalist what he needs. He may have to deny that there is literally such an object as the null class. But that seems a negotiable degree of scepticism" (1989b: 11). What must the Hellerian linguistic ersatzist do to guarantee satisfaction of this limitation? On the Heller version of linguistic ersatzism, possible worlds are sets of sets such that each member set is an ordered pair, the first member of which is an ordered set of numbers representing a particular point in spacetime and the second member, in the property place, a set of numbers playing the role of existentially bound variables ranging over properties. To remain within the confines of naturalism, given Armstrong's thesis that a set theory limited to spatio-temporal objects does not challenge naturalism, an account of numbers that remains within those naturalistic confines must be supplied.

[25] They hold presumably between properties of these sets and not directly between the properties represented by these different "worlds."

tropes across worlds for the trope-linguistic ersatzist, counterpart relations between property types of different worlds are not dependent on the identity of tropes across such worlds, but are derivative on relations of similarity between elements of the one concrete world, in this case linguistic elements. One consequence, then, of combining Natural Class Trope Nominalism with linguistic ersatzism and property counterpart theory is that we must give different accounts of the similarity of types within the one concrete world and the similarity of "types" across possible worlds, including the actual world. Within the one concrete world, we retain the original conception of type similarity: subclasses of a common type-class or overlap. However, with respect to possible worlds, things are different. Here we are talking about "represented types." Represented types in different possible worlds are not similar to each other (and, hence, counterparts of each other) in virtue of being subclasses of a common type-class or of overlap. That is because there is no crossworld identity of represented tropes. Rather, as indicated, the similarity of represented types across worlds is derivative on the similarity of classes of tropes all the members of which exist in the one concrete world.[26]

1.3.2.1 THE INVERSION PROBLEM

We must now deal with an objection to this marriage between linguistic ersatzism and Natural Class Trope Nominalism. A trope-based linguistic ersatzist strategy appears to have a problem with property inversion. Consider a world w_1 with a certain distribution of reds and greens. It seems possible that everything that is green in that world could have been red and everything red in that world could have been green, a green–red color inversion. Such an inversion seems to be intuitively possible. But that possibility seems to require that there is *another* world, w_2, that is just like w_1 save that everything that is red at w_1 is green at w_2, and vice versa. But the difficulty is that it is hard to see how the ersatzist strategy can account for there being two possibilities here since the Heller-style representations of w_1 and w_2 are identical (and, hence, these worlds are identical). The representations are identical since the property numbers in the member sets are distributed in the same way. Recall that the property numbers are

---

[26] A referee raises the following worry about property counterpart theory in general. Counterpart relations between objects presuppose that properties are held fixed, but what is supposed to play the role of such fixed points in judging whether distinct properties are similar? The answer to this question will vary somewhat depending on whether property counterpart theory is combined with ersatzism or combinatorialism. In the first case, we need to remember that comparisons between worlds ultimately consist in a comparison between only things that exist in the actual world. Here is how Heller puts the point: "We compare one representation with another to see how similar they are, and these representations actually exist... Because the similarity comparison is between actually existing objects, there is no need to suppose that the respects in which the various individuals or properties are similar are themselves properties that exist in more than one world" (1998: 306). In short, the "fixed properties" are properties of things in the actual world. If property counterpart theory is combined with combinatorialism, the answer to this question is similar. Since the similarity between objects and properties in different worlds ultimately consists in comparisons between things that are composed out of objects and properties that are actual, the properties that serve as fixed points for purposes of such comparisons are properties that are instantiated in the actual world.

not names of specific properties but are existentially bound variables. A Ramsey-style description of w_1 will exactly match the Ramsey-style description of w_2, and "for representation worlds, the description is all there is to the world" (Heller 1998: 300). Moreover, and more importantly to our purposes here, even if we could get around this problem, there seems to be no basis for a type counterpart relation between the distinct red classes at each world, given that the class of red tropes at w_1 has a spatio-temporally perfect counterpart in the class of "greens" at w_2.

In order to answer this objection, we need first to consider Heller's response to the inversion objection on his assumption that properties are universals. Heller seeks to represent that the relevant properties (in his example, "dis" and "dat") of one world, w, have exchanged places such that these properties are represented as playing each other's roles. It is not required for the representation of this exchange that there be a world not identical to w, which is the inverse of w. "What I need is a world w^* in which a counterpart to dis plays dat's w role and a counterpart to dat plays dis's w role; and there is such a world; it is w itself. World w contains two properties, the roles of which are similar enough so that each can be the counterpart of the other" (1998: 304). If w is the actual world, it is the actual world itself that grounds the possibility of inversion. ("Similarity of role" is ultimately a matter of similarity of roles as determined by the properties of the sets of sets that make up the world w.) Inversion, then, does not require *two different* worlds either in the form of two different representations or as corresponding to a single representation. The same representation (world) serves as w_1 and w_2, the inverse worlds, once it is understood that w_1 and w_2 may be *the same world*.

The tropist can adopt the same response. Suppose, again, that the property number represents a natural class of tropes and that there is a further number representing the individual trope, where different member sets of a single world that contain the same number in their natural class place (and in their individual trope place) represent the same natural class (individual trope). To represent the possibility that two natural classes, say RED and GREEN, of tropes of one world, w, have exchanged places, we need a world, but not necessarily a different world than w, in which a counterpart to RED plays GREEN's w role and a counterpart to GREEN plays RED's w role. That world is w itself on the assumption that the roles of RED and GREEN are similar enough so that each can be the counterpart of the other. (For the trope theorist, similarity of roles means similarity of the tropes of the sets of sets, and similarity of tropes for the Natural Class trope theorist is a matter of joint membership in a natural class.)

The second part of the objection is that there seems to be no basis for a type counterpart relation between the distinct red classes at each world, given that the class of red tropes at w_1 has a spatio-temporally *perfect* counterpart in the class of "greens" at w_2. This objection is not resolved by appealing to the fact that these worlds may be one and the same. A further aspect of Heller's ersatzism must come into play, that the counterpart relation is context-relative. One can then follow Heller in claiming that in contexts in which the possibility of inversion is genuine, the relevant counterpart relation, or rather the similarity relations that ground that relation, is such that the role of RED in *w* is *too much* like the role of RED in *w* to count as a counterpart of RED in *w*. In those "inversion is possible" contexts, RED in *w* is *not* a counterpart to RED in *w*, but GREEN in *w is* a counterpart of RED in *w*. The relevant context requires *less than exact similarity* of role for the type counterpart relation in question. This answer to inversion, also, involves dropping the requirement that *x*'s counterpart must resemble *x* more closely than do the other things in that world no matter what counterpart relation is at stake.

2. The One-Over-More objection

I now turn to an objection that is similar to the One-Over-Fewer objection. This objection, the "One-Over-More" objection, trades on the possibility that one more, say, red trope might have existed. Here, the difficulty is not that in that case the class of actual red tropes would not have existed. It would have. The difficulty is twofold. First, had there been an additional "red" trope, *r*, it would not have been a member of the actual class of red tropes, and, hence, would not have been a "redness" trope. Second, although the class of all actual red tropes would still have existed, that class would not have been maximal. And, since, being maximal is required for being a type, the type "red," which is identical to the maximal class of actual red tropes, would not have existed and would not have been instantiated. Nothing would have been red.

My answer to this objection will be the same as my answer to the One-Over-Fewer objection. What makes it true that had there been one more red trope, "redness" would still have been instantiated is that there is a possible world with one more red trope that is a member of a natural class that is a type counterpart to the natural class of actual red tropes. Furthermore, even if there had been one more trope, that trope, *r*, would have been a member of a natural class that is a type counterpart to the natural class of actual red tropes.

Does this line of response work within a linguistic ersatzist or trope combinatorialist theory of modality?

2.1 Linguistic ersatzism

Let's start with linguistic ersatzism. Natural Class Trope Nominalism, combined with the latter, can easily handle the One-Over-More objection. Why think that? It is because there is no special problem created by "addition." There will be "worlds," sets of sets, which represent the world as including more red tropes. That is so since the version of linguistic ersatzism under discussion does not use names of actual tropes in the construction of worlds, which would exclude names of tropes of alien kinds (alien property types that have no instances in the actual world or just additional tropes of a non-alien kind). Tropes are picked out by way of existential bound variables. "What makes Ramsification useful is that it allows us to pick out properties in other worlds by description, rather than by name. Adopting Ramsification, we can now say that there is a property above and beyond any of the actual properties" (Heller 1998: 300).[27] Linguistic ersatzism can ground the possibility of more red tropes. That means that we are, then, free to give the same property-counterpart theoretic answer to the One-Over-More objection as we gave to the One-Over-Fewer objection in the context of linguistic ersatzism.

2.2 Combinatorialism

Things are more complicated with trope combinatorialism. "Addition" presents special problems for this theory. I will consider and answer three worries.

Consider the following difficulty. Even if a class, C-, found at a world with one fewer red trope, can still count as a type counterpart of C, it is hard to see how $C+$, found at a world with one more red trope, could ever count as a type counterpart of C. $C+$ will face a competitor for type counterparthood with C, namely $C+$-, which is $C+$ minus the added trope, and which would automatically seem a perfect counterpart of C. In fact, this objection can be answered by saying a bit more about *type* counterpart relations. Specifically, it should be noted that only types can stand to each other in a type counterpart relation. Hence, even before considerations of similarity come into play the candidate classes must within their respective worlds satisfy conditions for being types. One such condition is that each class is a *maximal* natural class within its world. As a consequence of this constraint, although $C+$- in w might be a perfect counterpart for C of the actual world, relative to some counterpart relations, it will not be relative to the *type* counterpart relation. Only types can be type counterparts, but had $C+$ existed, C would not have been a type since types are *maximal* natural classes. Had $C+$ existed, $C+$- would not have been a maximal natural class. *Type* counterparts in other worlds to the type C in the actual world must first be *types* in those worlds.

The second and more basic worry is that $C+$ does not seem to be constructible if we are limited to elements of the actual world since $C+$ would seem to require as a member a trope that does not exist in the actual world. $C+$ does not appear to be

---

[27] A referee asks what description is at issue in the Ramsification, given that tropes have no nature independent of being a member in certain natural classes, not all of which by assumption exist at the world in question? In response, the first point to make is that under linguistic ersatzism, "worlds" are just sets of sets, so even the "actual world," understood as a set of sets, does not include, for example, the class of red tropes. The "worlds" are representations. So there is nothing special about the fact that $C+$ does not exist in the relevant "world in question," since C does not exist in the "actual world," which is a set theoretic representation of the one concrete world in which C does exist. Second, the member sets of these sets of sets are sets of numbers in which the property number places are interpreted as existentially bound variables. Two or more numbers in property places in a single world that match are interpreted as representing the same property and if the numbers do not match as different properties. A set of sets that is a world represents a complete description of a distribution of properties. "Although a world completely represents a distribution, it says nothing about which properties are distributed" (Heller 1998: 299). The representations will also include a separate representation of the nomological role of these properties, if those nomological roles are not reducible to those distributions. The description at issue in the Ramsification picks out properties in other worlds by way of a "distributive" description without "saying what property it is" (1998: 299). These "distributive" descriptions are available no matter what one's metaphysical account of properties might be, say, as universals or tropes.

available by way of recombining actual tropes. A third worry rests on how we are to make sense out of there being a counterpart relation between C and $C+$ given the resources of Natural Class Trope Nominalism and combinatorialism. What is the basis for the similarity of C and $C+$ that makes possible a counterpart relation? The similarity of these classes, C and $C+$, cannot be grounded on the principle that two types are similar if they are subclasses of a common natural class, all the members of which exist in the actual world, since $C+$ is not a subclass of any natural class in the actual world. This third worry, if it can be resolved, will be resolvable by reference to class overlap, the alternative basis for type similarity. But how is class overlap supposed to work between C and $C+$?

In order to handle this basic problem and the issue of the similarity of these classes, we must answer two preliminary questions: (1) how does the combinatorialist accommodate "alien" individuals and properties? and (2) how can this strategy be extended to the trope combinatorialism?

I will suggest that *if* the Armstrongian combinatorialist strategy for handling alien individuals and properties is sound and can be so extended to trope combinatorialism, then the trope combinatorialist can rely on this alternative grounding for similarity between, and a counterpart relation between, the types involved in the addition case. Armstrong seeks to accommodate the dual possibilities that there could be fully determinate simple universals that are not in fact instantiated and fully determinate individuals that do not in fact exist. Here I will focus on his attempted accommodation in (1997). Starting with all the simple universals and particulars that reality contains—but leaving out of account that these are all the constituents—he notes that "between each of these entities the internal relation . . . of *difference* holds" (1997: 167).

> We can go on to form the notion of a further such entity which is different from, other than, *each* of the original entities. We can specify further whether this entity is a particular or a universal, and if the latter the number of 'places' this universal has. Relative to the original assemblage, this new entity is an alien. Our conception of it is in a way combinatorially formed: using the original assemblage and the relation of difference (1997: 167).

The truthmaker for the modal truth that alien properties and individuals are possible is the actual individuals, universals, and relations of mutual difference, all found in the actual world (1997: 167). Armstrong notes that this approach does not work if particulars have haecceities, unique inner essences, other than their repeatable properties. In that case, the alien individual must be supposed to have a fully determinate haecceity (for Armstrong, only fully determinate individuals and properties exist or could exist), but then the alien individuals must be conceived to have some definite haecceity, "different from, and not obtainable combinatorially from, actual haecceities" (1989b: 59–60). Armstrong rejects this form of haecceitism, which he calls "strong haecceitism," but accepts "weak haecceitism," which is not committed to thinking of "haecceity as a unique inner nature or essence possessed by each particular, something property-like" (1997: 108): "individuals *qua* individuals (abstracting away from their properties and relations) are merely, barely, numerically different from each other" (Armstrong 1989b: 60).[28] This approach also fails, for the same reason, if each property has "its own nature, whatness or *quidditas* so that to encounter one is emphatically not to have encountered all" (Armstrong 1997: 168). Armstrong rejects "strong" quiddities, but does accept "weak" quiddities to the effect that "every universal that had the same -adicity was, if simple, merely numerically different than every other universal of that same -adicity" (1997: 168).[29]

Let's now transpose this strategy onto a Natural Class trope combinatorialist framework. We begin by considering all the actual simple tropes that reality contains—but leaving out of account that these are all the tropes—and note that between each of these tropes the internal relation of difference holds. We then form the notion of a further such entity, t, different from each of the original tropes, and specify that this further entity is a trope and the number of "places" that this trope has. Relative to the original collection, this new trope, t, is an alien. However, we need to go further than Armstrong since we want t to be an alien trope of a certain type, say "red." To do this, we can, first, consider a particular natural class C of actual tropes of the same number of places (the red tropes). Each of these entities stands to each other in a relation of being co-members of a natural class of a certain degree of naturalness. Although t is different from *each* of the actual red tropes, we can stipulate that t is a co-member of a further natural class, of the same degree of naturalness as C, made up of t and all and only the actual red tropes. Call that class "$C+$." Relative to the assemblage of all the tropes and classes of tropes of the actual world, $C+$ is an alien class. Our conception of $C+$ is "in a way" combinatorially formed: using the original assemblage of tropes, classes of actual tropes, the relation of difference, and the property of being a natural class to a specified degree (with respect to the latter we go beyond what Armstrong avails himself to in the actual world). The "truthmakers" for $C+$ are found in the actual world.

As indicated, any similarity between C and $C+$ is not grounded in their each being subclasses of a common class made up solely of actual tropes. We must bring into play the alternative basis for similarity of classes, class overlap. In this regard, as a first gloss, we might claim that C and $C+$ are similar because C is a subclass of $C+$. But that is not quite right. $C+$ does not exist. We need to shift our attention to the truthmakers for the truth that $C+$ is possible, or more specifically, to the class made of just those things. Call that "truthmaker" class X. X includes the truthmakers for the possibility of $C+$,

---

[28] "This concept of otherness is derivable from actuals. When applied to further, alien, individuals, it encompasses the whole of their nature *qua* individuals. Nothing is missing, as it would be missing if Haecceitism were true" (Armstrong 1989b: 60). "And since the relations of difference are internal, the ultimate truthmaker is no more than the plurality of existing constituents" (1997: 167).

[29] "But within an -adicity equivalence class... the difference between different members would be no more than the difference between particulars considered merely as particulars" (Armstrong 1997: 168).

whatever those things are. Among these "truthmakers" are all the members of the class of actual red tropes, C (X will also include the relation of difference and the relation of being co-members of a natural class of a certain degree). The important point is that C is a subclass of X. We can now say that the merely possible class, $C+$, is similar to the actual class C if C overlaps a class made up of the truthmakers for the possibility of $C+$.[30] *This* is the ontological basis for a counterpart relation between those classes.[31]

It is also worth noting that Armstrong's worry about quiddities is not an issue here. Even if each trope possessed a quidditas, that does not generate a problem. Two tropes can have exactly similar quiddities, and tropes that are members of the same perfectly natural class will, if they have quiddities at all. The possibility envisioned in the One-Over-More objection that we are trying to take account of does not involve the possibility of an alien quiddity that was not exactly similar to any existing quiddity. (In this context, there is no reason to rule out a kind of strong quidditism for tropes such that tropes of the same -adicity, which are *not* members of all the same perfectly natural classes, are more than merely, barely, numerically different from each other for a natural class trope nominalist.) We are trying to allow for an alien red trope, but not an alien type of trope at this point.[32]

3. Digression: The Actual Single Instance case

There is another objection to Natural Class Trope Nominalism that is somewhat similar to the One-Over-Fewer objection except for an important difference. In the One-Over-Fewer objection, we begin with a property type that has numerous actual instances and, then, consider the counterfactual possibility that there had been fewer instances, even to the point of a single instance. In the Actual Single Instance objection, we begin with a property type that has just one instance. Suppose, for example, that crimson is a superdeterminate (a determinate that is not also a determinable) but that there is only one actual crimson trope, c. But, according to this objection, it would seem that Natural Class Trope Nominalism would require a perfectly natural class of actual crimson tropes that includes more than one trope for c to be of the "crimson" nature.

---

[30] A referee suggests that a theory that requires such an elaborate apparatus—including property counterpart theory, actualism, similarity based in overlap of truthmakers for possibilities, etc.—to defend itself against a simple objection, the One–Over-More objection, isn't really worth defending. In response, I would suggest that this objection would carry weight only if the most important components of this "apparatus" lacked independent motivation, in which case the defense against the objection might very well seem overly complicated and even *ad hoc*. In fact, however, key components of this apparatus are independently defensible—specifically, property counterpart theory and actualism—taking some of the sting out of this objection. Furthermore, one can avoid some of this apparatus by adopting the linguistic ersatzist defense against the One-Over-More objection.

[31] A real mountain is similar to a gold mountain because the real mountain includes constituents that are among the class of truthmakers for the possibility of a gold mountain.

[32] I take the point from Friesen (2005), who corrects my earlier thinking on this issue.

In fact, Natural Class Trope Nominalism requires no such thing. Natural Class Trope Nominalism requires that there be a perfectly natural class of which c is a member, and there is such a class, the singleton class with c as a member, $\{c\}$. There is no claim that the perfectly natural class of which c is a member has more than one member. The "actual single instance" case may be a problem for some forms of Resemblance Trope Nominalism that require that there are other actual tropes that c resembles exactly, but it is not a problem of Natural Class Trope Nominalism.

Still, there may be some difficulty accepting the notion that c's nature is this singleton class. Here I think that there are a number of things to say. First, this unease may just be an expression of the general unease with the notion that a trope's nature is determined at all by its class memberships, that is, with the main claim of Natural Class Trope Nominalism and not so much with the "actual single instance" case. In fact, we should set aside such "intuitive" unease if Natural Class Trope Nominalism is otherwise the best account of properties. Second, this unease may be based on the intuition that in the "actual single instance" case, Natural Class Trope Nominalism makes the nature of the single instance trope depend on something very close to the trope itself, its singleton class. In response, I would say that in all cases, not just the "actual single instance" case, Natural Class Trope Nominalism has the trope itself play a role in determining its own nature.[33] After all, even if the maximal perfectly natural class of which c is a member has numerous other members, it will still include c and it will still determine c's nature. So, there is nothing special about the "single instance case" in assigning some role to the trope itself in determining its own nature. Furthermore, even if c is the sole member of the maximal perfectly natural class of which it is a member, c will still be a member of other, maximal but less than perfectly natural classes, which have numerous members, and those other classes also contribute to c's nature. So, it is *not* the case that c's nature is determined solely by the singleton class of which c is a member.

But perhaps we should also consider a more extreme case. Suppose that there is only one instance of color in the actual world, a single crimson trope, c. c is a member of only one natural class, the singleton class, $\{c\}$. In that case, c's nature is limited to just that singleton class. Is this a problem? One might think it is a problem if one thinks that

---

[33] At this point, it might be objected (following the comments of a referee) that if Natural Class Trope Nominalism has the trope itself play a role in determining its own nature, then either the trope has its own nature independently of its class memberships—making membership in a natural class otiose contrary to Natural Class Trope Nominalism—or it does not have a nature independent of its class memberships, making it hard to see what determines which classes the trope is a member of or how the trope itself plays a role in determining which classes it is a member of. In response, I would make two points. First, in saying that the trope itself plays some role in determining its own nature, I mean to say merely that since the natural classes of which a trope is a member constitute that trope's nature there is a sense in which that trope is part of its own nature. That does not require that a trope have a nature independent of its class memberships. Second, to the question as to what determines or what is the basis of a trope's membership in this or that natural class, as indicated earlier, that is a primitive, non-reducible matter—and certainly not grounded in a trope's class-independent nature which it lacks.

what makes c a crimson trope and what makes it a red trope cannot be the same thing, and, in particular, there must be a natural class of crimson tropes that is not identical to the natural class of red tropes. In response, I think the Natural Class Trope Nominalist should reject the assumption that what makes c a crimson trope and what makes it a red trope must be different classes. Even though it is true that c is both a crimson trope and a red trope, those truths can be grounded in membership in the same class in the extreme case we are discussing. I will expand on this problem and this answer in the next chapter.

4. The causation objection

There is a further, well-known objection, outlined by Armstrong, that has also contributed to the low estimation of Natural Class Trope Nominalism by metaphysicians. The gist of this objection is that Natural Class Trope Nominalism is not compatible with the existence of causally relevant properties. More specifically, Natural Class Trope Nominalism is claimed to be inconsistent with causes' being efficacious in virtue of having tropes of a certain type. In this section, I will suggest that this objection is closely related to the One-Over-Fewer/More objections, and, as with those objections, the combination of Natural Class Trope Nominalism with property counterpart theory supplies the basis for a response. I will begin with Armstrong's statement of this objection as directed toward the *object*-based version of "natural class" nominalism rather than to Natural Class Trope Nominalism.

For an object class nominalist, for a thing to be of a certain type is nothing more than for it to be a member of a certain class. For x to be of the type "tree" is for x to be a member of the class of trees. "The idea is that the 'property' of being an electron is constituted by being a member of the class of electrons" (Armstrong 1989a: 9). A *natural* class nominalist holds that for a thing to be of a certain type is for it to be a member of a certain *natural* class, where the notion of a natural class is taken as primitive. "The class of all white things forms a natural class, a class with a reasonable degree of naturalness. That is all that can be said about what makes a white thing white" (1989a: 18). For a thing to be white is for it to be a member of this natural class. Membership in this class is *not* based on resemblance between these objects. Resemblance ultimately rests on natural class membership. The causal-irrelevancy objection begins with the assumption that when a thing acts causally, it acts in virtue of its properties. For example, if a thing acts in virtue of the fact that it has a mass of 4 kilograms, then it is efficacious in virtue of possessing that property. But for an object-based natural class nominalist, what it is for that object to have a mass of 4 kilograms is for it to be a member of a natural class of objects, all of which have that mass. But "if a class analysis of what it is to be four kilograms in mass is correct, then the whole class of tokens should be relevant" (1989a: 28). The difficulty is that the other 4-kilogram things in the universe seem to be irrelevant. "But in fact, though, the only thing relevant is the thing that actually acts. This suggests that any class account of properties is unsatisfactory" (1989a: 28).

The causal-irrelevancy objection can be extended to Natural Class Trope Nominalism. According to the latter, a trope's being of a certain sort is a matter of its *membership in a certain natural class of tropes*. A trope's nature is determined by its membership in such natural classes. The trope itself, independently of such membership, has no (is not a) nature and is not of a particular type. It would seem, then, that when a thing acts in virtue of having a trope of a certain sort, that thing's efficacy will require the relevancy of that trope's membership in at least one natural class, and, thus, the relevancy of the *other* members of that class, but it is highly implausible to assign relevancy to those other, perhaps far-flung tropes. The consequence is that nothing ever acts in virtue of having a trope of a certain type, contrary to our assumption.

What is the structure of this objection? Armstrong himself does not fill in the details, so it will be necessary to speculate. Let's begin by replacing Armstrong's apparent assumption, at least when he is discussing this objection, that objects are causes, with the more widely held view that causes are events. Let's further suppose that event x causes e in virtue of x's having a trope t of type T, where T is a natural class of actual tropes, C. The causal argument starts with the irrelevancy of the non-t members of T to x's causing e. These other members of T might very well be scattered around the universe at great spatial or temporal distances from the causal action. Some of these tropes might come into existence only *after* the causal sequence at issue has run its course. It is hard to see how these distant or future tropes could impinge on the efficacy of x with respect to e. Call this the "Irrelevancy Thesis." This is certainly a very appealing thesis. The objection concludes with the irrelevancy of t's being a T-type trope to x's causing e.[34] How are we supposed to get from the Irrelevancy Thesis to that conclusion?

I believe this inference is meant to go as follows. From the fact that the non-t members of C, the type T, are irrelevant, it follows that the causal sequence would have occurred even in their absence. More precisely:

(A) Even if t had not been a member of C, solely in virtue of the absence of some of the other non-t members of C (other things being as similar as possible, including x's having t), x would still have caused e.

Since being a T-type trope is just being a member of C, from (A) it follows that

(B) even if t had not been a T-type trope, solely in virtue of the absence of some of the other non-t members of C (other things being as similar as possible, including x's having t), x would still have caused e.

---

[34] A referee suggests that if tropes have only relational natures, and causation occurs in virtue of the nature of tropes, then it would seem that the Irrelevancy Thesis is false. In fact, even given these assumptions, the Irrelevancy Thesis, which concerns the relevancy of far-flung tropes, will still be true because it is true that had those far-flung tropes not existed, the causal sequence in question would still have unfolded.

From (B) we infer that *t*'s being a *T*-type trope is irrelevant to *x*'s causing *e* in virtue of *t*.

This objection does not apply to Campbellian tropes. The key claim, which is supposed to sustain the inference from (A) to (B), is that being a *T*-type trope is just being a member of *C*. The Campbellian rejects this claim. For Campbell, there is no pressure to think that had some of the non-*t* members of *C* not existed, then *t* would not have been a *T*-type trope. Had there been one fewer red trope, but *t* had still existed, *t* would still have been a red trope and there still would have existed a property type "red" in the form of a class of red tropes. But "red" would have picked out a different class of tropes than it does in the actual world.

I want to suggest that the Natural Class Trope Nominalist is not forced to accept the inference from (A) to (B) as long as he is willing to bring on board property counterpart theory. (B) follows from (A) only if the worlds that make (A) true also make (B) true. For the latter to be the case, the antecedent of (B) must also be true in the worlds that make (A) true. The claim that the antecedent-of-(A) worlds make the antecedent-of-(B) true is supposed to follow if being a *T*-type trope is just being a member of *C*. In fact, the natural class trope nominalist is *not* forced to agree. It does not follow from the fact that being a *T*-type trope is just a matter of being a member of *C* that the worlds that make the antecedent of (A) true make the antecedent of (B) true.

The reason for thinking that trope-class nominalism *is* committed to the inference from (A) to (B) is the Natural Class Trope Nominalist claim that being a *T*-type trope just is a matter of being a member of *C*. From that it would seem to follow that the worlds that make (A) true make the antecedent of (B) true. Why think that? From the fact that being a *T*-type trope is just to be a member of *C*, it would seem to follow that if *any* of the members of *C* had not existed, *nothing* would have been a *T*-type trope. From this apparent entailment, it is a short step to the conclusion that if *any* of the non-*t* members of *C* had not existed, no trope would have been a *T*-type trope. Hence, it seems natural to think that if "being a *T*-type trope" is just "being a member of *C*," then if *any* of the non-*t* members of *C* had not existed and *other things had been as similar as possible*, *nothing*, including *t*, would have been a *T*-type trope (the antecedent of (B) would have been true). But we know from the Irrelevancy Thesis that if any of the non-*t* members of *C* had not existed but *t* had, the causal sequence at issue would still have run its course. Natural Class Trope Nominalism, thus, *seems* to entail that the worlds that make (A) true also make (B) true. Hence, it appears that the Irrelevancy Thesis, in combination with the assumption that "being a *T*-type trope" is just "being a member of *C*," implies that being a trope of type *T* is causally irrelevant to *x*'s causing *e*.

In fact, the Natural Class Trope Nominalist can deny this apparent entailment from (A) to (B) by denying that it follows from the fact that being a *T*-type trope is just to be a member of *C*, that had *any* of the members of *C* not existed, *nothing* (including *t*) would have been a *T*-type trope. In that case, satisfaction of the antecedent of (A) does not guarantee satisfaction of the antecedent of (B). We have already seen how it is possible for the proponent of Natural Class Trope Nominalism to deny the latter entailment. The trick is to combine Natural Class Trope Nominalism with property counterpart theory. When so combined, Natural Class Trope Nominalism is compatible with its being false that if *some* of the members of *C* had not existed, nothing would have been a *T*-type trope. Given property counterpart theory, the fact that to be a *T*-type trope is just to be a member of *C* is compatible with the possibility that *T* could be instantiated in the absence of some of the members of *C*. As indicated earlier, we can reasonably assume that there is a "type" counterpart relation that differs from a "class" counterpart relation. That opens up the possibility of worlds in which there is a type counterpart to *T* but no class counterpart to *T*. There are worlds in which "being a *T*-type trope" fails to have a "class" counterpart but has a "type" counterpart. In particular, Natural Class Trope Nominalism in combination with property counterpart theory allows that the number of tropes falling under a type—understood as a class of actual tropes—is *not* essential to that type by way of a type counterpart relation. It does not follow that if some of the non-*t* members of *C* had not existed and other things had been as similar as possible (the antecedent of (A)), *t* would not have been a *T*-type trope (the antecedent of (B)).[35] The inference from (A) to (B) depends on the latter entailment, but Natural Class Trope Nominalism is not, if combined with property counterpart theory, committed to it.[36]

In short, the proponent of Natural Class Trope Nominalism could agree that the non-*t* members of *T* are causally irrelevant to *x*'s causing *e*, but disagree that that makes *t*'s being a *T*-type trope irrelevant to *x*'s causing *e*. It would only automatically follow from Natural Class Trope Nominalism that *t*'s being a *T*-type trope is causally irrele-

---

[35] This response to the causal-irrelevancy objection can be redescribed in the context of Heller's linguistic ersatzism so as to make clear that it does not require modal realism. On Heller's linguistic ersatzism, possible worlds or world descriptions are sets of sets. Each of these member sets is an ordered pair. Each of these member sets represents properties assigned to locations. The first member of each such pair is an ordered set of numbers representing a particular point in space-time and the second member, in the property place, a set of numbers playing the role of existentially bound variables ranging over properties. When different member sets of a single world contain the same number in their property places, it is stipulated that that number represents the same property. There is no transworld identity, but represented objects and properties of one world may have counterparts in another world. If property types are classes of tropes, the same number in the property places in a single world represents a non-identical but exactly similar trope. It is possible for some property *P* in the concrete world to lack a property or relation that it actually has. That will be so just in case there is a possible world that represents a property *P'* that is a counterpart to *P*, such that *P'* lacks counterparts to that property or relation. The reply to the causal-irrelevancy objection outlined above takes much the same form but with possible worlds interpreted as sets of sets. In the relevant worlds that make the antecedent of (A) true, a counterpart to *t* is represented that causes a represented counterpart to *e* despite the fact that there is no representation of "being a member of *C*" or of a class counterpart to "being a member of *C*" in those worlds. However, the represented *C'* that includes a counterpart to *t* may be a type counterpart to the represented *C* of the actual world and the represented "being a member of *C'*" may be a type counterpart of "being a *T*-type trope."

[36] The objection under consideration might be interpreted along different lines as follows. Causation is a wholly local matter, but if Natural Class Trope Nominalism is true, then causation is not a wholly local matter. In fact, I reject the claim that causation is a wholly local matter, even though I think that the "local" component of causation deserves careful attention (see my 1997a). Nonetheless, there is a "generalist" component to causation—involving type–type relations—as is made clear in neo-Humean theories and even Counterfactual theories, the latter of which implicate laws in causation by implicating them in the truth conditions for counterfactuals.

vant from the fact that the non-*t* members of *T* are irrelevant if it automatically followed that had some of the non-*t* members of *T* not existed, then *t* would not have been a *T*-type trope, but that does not automatically follow. The kind of case that shows the irrelevancy of the non-*t* members of *T*—a close world in which some or all of the non-*t* members have no counterparts—is not necessarily a case that shows that being a *T*-type trope is irrelevant, since *t* or its counterpart in that world may very well be a member of a class of tropes that is a type counterpart to T.[37]

5. Summary and what's next

The three classic objections to Natural Class Trope Nominalism can, thus, be resolved once the latter is combined with an actualist theory of modality and a counterpart theory of properties. However an actualist-counterpart theory of modality deals with counterpart properties, and the problems of alien entities and properties can be adapted to the framework of Natural Class Trope Nominalism to answer these objections. This makes Natural Class Trope Nominalism vulnerable if some such actualist account of modality is not eventually worked out, but what I have tried to dispel is the notion that Natural Class Trope Nominalism has some special problem with the possibilities of fewer or more tropes (and the related causation issue). These are problems that must be addressed by actualist-counterpart theories of modality. In the next chapter, I will develop and respond to the charge that Natural Class Trope Nominalism is inconsistent with certain aspects of the determination relation between properties.

---

[37] One might object to Natural Class Trope Nominalism on the grounds that it is natural to think that entities are members of sets in virtue of their shared properties or in virtue of resembling each other and not vice versa. In response, I would suggest that this line of thought is appropriate to concrete particulars, which get to be members of natural classes in virtue of the properties that they *have* and not the other way around, but I would suggest that this natural line of thought should *not* be extended to properties themselves. I do not think that we have clear intuitions one way or the other about properties in this respect, and, in addition, I would suggest that it would be a mistake to carry over this intuition from objects to properties. While this intuition clearly applies to objects, it is not so clear that properties enter into natural classes in virtue of their higher-order properties, if they even have any.

8

The determination objections

A philosophical account of properties should be compatible with various general characteristics of properties, including various relations between properties. In this chapter, I consider the question of whether or not Natural Class Trope Nominalism is consistent with the fact that some properties stand to each other in the determination relation. I will begin by restating two principles that govern the determination relation in the terms of Natural Class Trope Nominalism. What will become clear is that there is a *prima facie* case to be made that Natural Class Trope Nominalism is *not* consistent with the determination relation. More specifically, it appears that the following three central features of the determination relation are not compatible with Natural Class Trope Nominalism: (a) determinates necessitate their determinables; (b) determinables do not necessitate any particular determinate; and (c) necessarily, if something has a determinable it will have a determinate falling under that determinable. As it will turn out, Natural Class Trope Nominalism can answer these objections, if it is combined with property counterpart theory.

1. Some principles of determination

The determination relation is a relation between property types. The property type "red" is a determinable of the property type "crimson." The same property, except for fully determinate properties ("superdeterminates"), can be a determinate relative to one property but a determinable relative to another. "Crimson" is a determinate of "red," but it is also a determinable of a specific shade of crimson. For the Natural Class Trope Nominalist, I would suggest, the determination relation should be read as applying non-derivatively to classes of tropes and only derivatively to individual tropes. A class of natural tropes, C', is a determinate of another class of natural tropes, C, only if: (1) both C and C' are property types; (2) C' is a subclass of C; and (3) C' is more natural than is C.[1] An object is characterized by a determinable property such as "red" if and only if it is characterized by a trope that is a member of the maximal natural class of

---

[1] That this is only a necessary condition on determination is demonstrated by the fact that it also applies to properties that do not stand in the determination relation such as "red or round" and "red."

red tropes.[2] An object is characterized by a superdeterminate property, say, "crimson" if and only if it is characterized by a trope that is a member of a class of tropes that is perfectly natural. Strictly speaking, individual tropes do not stand in the determination relation to individual tropes and the determinable/determination classification applies only indirectly to individual tropes by way of their memberships in various classes of tropes. An individual trope is "determinable" only relative to its membership in a determinable class and "determinate" only relative to its membership in a determinate class. Indeed, we should suppose that every trope is a member of a class of perfectly natural tropes even if it also belongs to less-than-perfectly natural classes. An object can be characterized by a determinable property type and a determinate property type in virtue of being characterized by the same trope.[3] For example, an object o will be crimson and red in virtue of the same trope, which is a member of a superdeterminate class of "crimson" tropes and a determinable class of "red" tropes. Now let's consider two of the principles that govern the determination relation and how those principles might be understood in the context of Natural Class Trope Nominalism.

(1) *Asymmetric Necessitation* Determinates necessitate their determinables, but determinables don't necessitate any particular determinate. Necessarily, something that possesses a determinate of a determinable also possesses that determinable. Nothing could be crimson but not red. However, even if Q is a determinable of P, something can have Q without having P. Something can be red without being crimson. Possession of a determinable does not necessitate possession of any particular determinate of that determinable.

Let's translate Asymmetric Necessitation into the language of Natural Class Trope Nominalism. As indicated, a class of natural tropes, C', is a determinate of another class of natural tropes, C, only if: (1) both C and C' are property types; (2) C' is a subclass of C; and (3) C' is more natural than is C. Necessarily, if x possesses a trope from a

---

[2] As noted by a referee, naturalness tracks objective similarity and the bestowing of powers, so it might seem that if a determinable is associated with a distinctive set of powers that provides a basis for exact similarity with respect to those powers, then that determinable is as natural as its corresponding determinates. In fact, however, even granting this point about exact similarity with respect to those powers, the determinable will be less natural than its determinates on the assumption that if C' is a determinate of C, then C' is a subclass of C. For example, the class of red tropes is more varied than the class of crimson tropes. There is a greater degree of similarity between the least similar crimson tropes than between the least similar red tropes, on the assumption that the red trope class includes as a subclass the crimson trope class as well as other classes. The claim that crimsonness tropes form a more natural class than do redness tropes would perhaps not be true if every crimson trope were not also a redness trope and some redness tropes were not also tropes of some more determinate shade of red.

[3] One concern about identifying determinable and determinate tropes, mentioned by a referee, is that, as a consequence of this identification, a token property can end up having more powers than are associated with its type. The referee suggests that whereas a token property might have fewer powers than are associated with its type, a token property cannot have more powers than its corresponding type. If so, that would seem to be a good reason for not taking the token to be of that type. In fact, I do not share this concern. What seems right about this point is that a token property cannot have powers that go beyond the powers associated with all of its types even if it can have powers that go beyond the powers associated with some of its types. An analogy might help. An object can have powers that go beyond the powers associated with some of the types it instantiates although not beyond the powers associated with all of the types it instantiates.

subclass, P, of Q, where Q is less-than-perfectly natural, then o possesses a trope from Q. In that case, if Q is a determinable of P, then x possesses a determinable, Q, of P. But, it is not necessarily the case that if x possesses a trope from Q, it possesses a trope from any particular subclass of Q including P.

(2) *Downward Necessitation* Necessarily, if x has a determinable Q, then it has some determinate of Q and, if $P_1, \ldots, P_n$ is a complete set of same-level determinates of Q, then if x has Q, then x has P_1 or $P_2, \ldots,$ or P_n. Necessarily, if something is red, it will be some specific shade of red. And, if crimson, apple red, ..., wine red are a complete set of same-level determinates of color, then it will have one of these determinates, setting aside possible problem cases from quantum mechanics. Translated into the Natural Class Trope Nominalist framework, Downward Necessitation says that necessarily, if x possesses a trope, t, from Q and Q is a determinable of some of its subclasses, then x possesses a trope from at least one subclass of Q that is a determinate of Q. It also says that if x possesses a trope from Q and if $P_1 \ldots P_2$ are exclusive subclasses of Q, which are exhaustive of Q, each of which is a determinate of Q, then x possesses a trope from P_1 or $P_2, \ldots,$ or P_n.

2. The determination objections to Natural Class Trope Nominalism

There are, however, reasons to think that Natural Class Trope Nominalism may not be compatible with the Asymmetric Determination and Downward Necessitation features of the determination relation. More specifically, Natural Class Trope Nominalism seems to be compatible with it being false that determinates necessitate their determinables, and compatible with it being false that determinables do not necessitate any particular determinate of a determinable. In addition, Natural Class Trope Nominalism appears to be compatible with a false version of Downward Necessitation.

Objection 1 Suppose that red is the natural class R of actual red tropes and that crimson is a subclass, C, of R. If none of the non-crimson red tropes had existed, then R would not have existed, and if R had not existed, but C had, the crimson tropes would not have been red tropes. But this violates the principle that necessarily something has a determinate of P only if it has P. Since the class of actual crimson tropes could have existed without the remaining members of the wider class of actual red tropes, given that redness just is this wider class, then it would seem to follow that there could have been non-red crimson tropes. Thus, it appears that the Natural Class Trope Nominalism is compatible with it being false that determinates necessitate their determinables, the first part of the Asymmetric Necessitation Principle.

Objection 2 Suppose that the only red tropes are crimson. Call that crimson-only class "R." Call the (improper) crimson subclass of R that has all the same crimson tropes as members "C." Since the membership of a class is essential to it, then necessarily, if something is a member of R, then it is a member of the C class. Translated back into the language of properties, that would mean that necessarily, if something is red it is crimson, given Natural Class Trope Nominalism and assuming that only red tropes are crimson. But the latter is inconsistent with the principle that determinables don't necessitate any particular determinate. According to this objection, Natural Class Trope Nominalism is committed to the proposition that in cases in which a determinable is represented in the actual world by only one superdeterminate, then necessarily, nothing that possesses that determinable possesses any superdeterminate other than that one. Necessarily, if something is red, it must be crimson, if the only actual shade of red is crimson.

Objection 3 Suppose that there is a missing shade of red, crimson. All of the other shades of red are realized. Now consider the class of actual red tropes, R. This class includes subclasses that correspond to various shades of red, $C_1 \ldots C_n$, except the missing shade of red, crimson. Since the property type of "redness" just is the class of actual red tropes, it would seem that if o, which is not in fact red, had been red, then it would, according to Natural Class Trope Nominalism, have been one of these actual shades of red and not the missing shade of red. In that case, the Natural Class Trope Nominalist seems to be committed to the following falsehood. Necessarily, if something is red it will have one of the actual shades of red and not this missing shade. But something could have been red, but not one of these actual reds. It could have had the missing shade of red. In short, under certain circumstances, Natural Class Trope Nominalism is committed to a false version of the principle that necessarily, if something has a determinable, it will have a determinate falling under that determinable.

2.1 Response to Objection 1

According to this first objection, Natural Class Trope Nominalism entails the absurdity that something could have been crimson without being red. More generally, it allows for the possibility of something having a determinate of a determinable, but not the determinable. On Natural Class Trope Nominalism, something is crimson just in case it has a trope from the maximal natural class of crimson tropes, C, and it is red just in case it has a trope from the maximal natural class of red tropes, R. C is a subclass of R. But had none of the non-crimson tropes existed, then the class R would not have existed, and, it would seem, according to Natural Class Trope Nominalism, nothing would have been an instance of the property type "red," including any of the crimson tropes that would have existed. Since it is possible that none of the non-crimson red tropes had existed, but the crimson tropes still had existed, then it is possible that something could have been crimson but not red.

How might the Natural Class Trope Nominalist respond to Objection 1? The first response I will consider runs as follows. As we shall see, it does not work.

> The Natural Class Trope Nominalist can guarantee that determinates necessitate their determinables by reference to the subclass relation. Suppose that C is a subclass of R. Given that the membership of a class is essential to it, if C and R both exist,

then necessarily, C is a subclass of R. If both C and R exist, then so do their members, and nothing then could be characterized by a member of C but not by a member of R, if both C and R exist. There is no world in which o is crimson but not red, if both crimson and red are instantiated in that world.

This response fails for the following reason. This response does not capture the *relevant* necessitation feature of determination. This response is aimed at guaranteeing, at best, that at any world, if something is crimson and *if red exists at that world*, then it is red at that world. (Of course, it may not guarantee even that much.) The necessitation feature of interest, however, is stronger: in any world, if something is crimson then it is red. This feature is supposed to take us from the instantiation of crimson to the instantiation of red, not from the instantiation of crimson and the instantiation of red to their joint instantiation by the same object. We must consider a different approach.[4]

The key idea operating behind Objection 1 is that without all the members of the class of actual red tropes, the property type "redness," which just is that class, would not have existed, and, hence, "red" would not have been instantiated. In fact, the trope nominalist who adopts property counterpart theory can resist this idea and the implication that had there only been crimson tropes, but no non-crimson red tropes, those crimson tropes would not have been red tropes. The property-counterpart theorist can argue that the closest possible world w in which there is a type counterpart to C, C', but no type counterparts to any of the other shades of red, then C' is itself a type counterpart to R and the only such counterpart. In short, C' is a type counterpart twice over, both to red and to crimson. In w, there is a class of tropes that is similar enough and more similar to C than any other class in w and C' is maximal, but there are no counterparts for the other shades of red. But also in w, the "crimson" tropes are more similar to the red tropes than any other tropes in that world—C' is more similar to R than any other class in w, and C' is similar enough to R. In that world, C' will also be maximal since it includes all the "crimson" tropes of w. In w, the class of "crimson" tropes is the type counterpart to red. The type counterpart to C and the type counterpart to R are identical in this world and, thus, it is possible that the red tropes that existed included all and only the crimson tropes of the actual world.[5]

2.1.1 Variation on Objection 1 and response But now let's consider the possibility that the red tropes that existed included all the red tropes of the actual world plus one more crimson trope (R+). According to a variation on Objection 1, Natural Class Trope

---

[4] Also, even if nothing could be characterized by a member of C, but not by a member of R, if both C and R exist, it does not follow that nothing could have been crimson without being red. If one more crimson trope had existed, then that additional crimson trope would not have been a member of any subclass of R and, hence, it would seem, not a red trope under Natural Class Trope Nominalism. The classes C and R would still have existed and the former would have been a subclass of the latter.

[5] This response borrows from our earlier response to the One-Over-Fewer objection, but it goes beyond the latter response so as to guarantee that the type counterpart to red coincides with the type counterpart to crimson in w.

Nominalism must say that the additional "crimson" trope would not have been red since it would not have been a member of a subclass of R. In response, I would suggest that property-counterpart theory provides a basis for accommodating this possibility. It is possible that there existed all the red tropes plus one more crimson trope since there is a possible world with a type counterpart to C, C+ (which includes one additional trope than does C), while R+ is itself a type counterpart to R. R+ is similar enough to R and more similar than any other class in that world (and, we can suppose, it is a maximal natural class). R+ is C+ along with the type counterparts to the other shades of red. This class of "red-plus-one-crimson" tropes is the type counterpart to red. The type counterpart to C is a subclass of the type counterpart to R in this world. Since that is true, on property counterpart theory, it is possible that the red tropes that existed included all the red tropes of the actual world plus an additional crimson trope.[6] More generally, the following principle seems to be true (assume that C is a subclass/determinate of R in the actual world):

> (X) In any world w, if C has a type counterpart, C', in w, then R has a type counterpart, R', in w and C' is either identical to or a subclass of R' in w.

The idea here is that if C is a determinate of R, then there is a connection between the type counterpart to C in another world, w, and the type counterpart to R in that same world.

But we need to say more about principle (X) in the context of linguistic ersatzism and combinatorialism. The principle as stated posits a subclass relation between type counterparts. In fact, when we look more deeply into the metaphysics of this principle, we find it difficult to make sense of this subclass relation under combinatorialism and linguistic ersatzism. Consider, again, our response to the variation on Objection 1, the case which focuses on the possibility that the red tropes that existed included all the red tropes of the actual world plus one more crimson trope. We said that a property-counterpart theorist can accommodate this possibility by positing a possible world in which C+ is counterpart to C, R+ is a type counterpart to R and C+ is a subclass of R+. The difficulty is that within trope combinatorialism, neither of the alien classes, C+ or R+, exist. Hence, C+ is not a subclass of R+. And, within linguistic ersatzism, although the sets that represent the classes C+ and R+ exist, those classes do not exist.

---

[6] Another variation runs as follows. It is possible that the red tropes that existed included all the crimson tropes of the actual world plus one more crimson trope, but none of the non-crimson red tropes (C+ but not R). A property counterpart theorist can accommodate this possibility while remaining within the scope of Natural Class Trope Nominalism: it is possible that there existed all the crimson tropes plus one, but no other red tropes since there is a possible world with a type counterpart to C, C+. C+ is similar enough to C and more similar than any other type-class in that world (although C in w is more similar, it is not a type-class since it is not maximal in w). In addition, C+ is itself a reasonable candidate for being a type counterpart to R. C+ is similar enough to R and more similar than any other class in that world (and, we can suppose, it is a maximal natural class). The type counterpart to C and the type counterpart to R are identical in this world, and, thus, it is possible that the red tropes that existed included all and only the crimson tropes of the actual world plus an additional crimson trope.

Hence, they do not stand in a subclass relation to each other. Principle X must be modified given linguistic ersatzism and combinatorialism.

How should (X) be formulated or modified within combinatorialism? In our response to the variation on Objection 1, *C'* is *C+*, which is the class of actual crimson tropes plus an additional crimson trope. *C'* "includes" (as does *R'*) an "alien" crimson trope. But then there is no subclass relation between *C'* and *R'* since neither class exists. The resolution of this issue requires a combinatorialist solution to the problem of the possibility of alien properties. As indicated in the last chapter, I assume that the combinatorialist can supply truthmakers for the possibility of alien properties. On that assumption, I would suggest a two-step approach to principle (X). First, identify the combinatorialist truthmakers for the possibility of each alien classes, *C'* and *R'*. Second, add a further clause to principle (X): in any world *w*, if *C* has a type counterpart in *w*, *C'*, then *R* has a type counterpart in *w*, *R'*, and *C'* is either identical to or a subclass of *R'* in *w*, or the class of truthmakers for the possibility of *C'* is identical to or a subclass of the class of truthmakers for the possibility of *R'*.

What is the linguistic ersatzist analogue to (X)? A first approximation of what Principle X says under linguistic ersatzism is the following:

> If the represented class *C'* in *w* is similar enough to the represented class *C* and more similar than any other represented class in *w* so as to be a type counterpart to *C*, then there is a represented class *R'* in *w* that is similar enough to the represented class *R* and more similar than any other represented class in *w* so as to be a type counterpart to *R*, and the represented class *C'* is identical to or is a subclass of the represented class *R'*.

The difficulty is that since the represented classes, *C+* and *R+*, do not exist, neither stands in a subclass relation to the other. This is a species of a more general problem faced by linguistic ersatzism, the problem of relations between merely possible represented entities. Consider, for example, the claim that there is a possible world in which the merely possible objects, *a* and *b*, are next to each other. Since *a* and *b* do not exist (although their representations do), that is not made true by the fact that *a* and *b* are next to each other. What makes that true is that there is a possible world *according to which a* and *b* are next to each other. In that sense, possible worlds are like stories and, as such, we should focus on what is true according to the story. Accordingly, we need to modify the last part of our restatement of Principle X within linguistic ersatzism. Instead of saying that "the represented class *C'* is identical to or a subclass of the represented class *R'*" we should say that "*w* represents class *C'* to be identical to or a subclass of class *R'*."

2.2 Response to Objection 2

According to the second objection, Natural Class Trope Nominalism allows for the possibility that nothing could have been red without being crimson. More generally, Natural Class Trope Nominalism entails that if anything that actually possesses a certain determinable, *D*, possesses one specific determinate of *D*, then necessarily, anything possessing that determinable possesses that determinate. For example, suppose that the only reds in the world are crimsons. On Natural Class Trope Nominalism, there could have been no trope *t* that was a red trope that was not a crimson trope, since the nature of a trope is determined by its class membership. And, that means that, under these conditions, nothing could have been red without being crimson. The second objection makes it out that Natural Class Trope Nominalism cannot *guarantee* that determinables never necessitate any particular determinate. In the case described, it appears that given Natural Class Trope Nominalism, it is necessary that if something is red, then it is crimson (since the only red tropes are crimson). To respond to this worry, we must again resort to property counterparts.

Given property counterpart theory, the membership of a class that is identical to a property type according to Natural Class Trope Nominalism is not essential to that type even if it is essential to that class. In particular, property counterpart theory provides truthmakers for certain modal truths to the effect that a property type could have had tokens of a determinate of that type even if there are no tokens of that determinate in the actual world. In the case at hand, it can be reasonably suggested that there are worlds with type counterparts to *R*, but with member tropes that are not members of any class in that world that is a type counterpart to *C*, crimson. There is a world in which there is a type counterpart to *R* in *w* that includes both "crimson" and non-crimson red tropes, even though there are no non-crimson red tropes in the actual world. This makes it true that there could have been red tropes that were not crimson tropes, even if all actual red tropes are crimson and Natural Class Trope Nominalism is true.

This gives us a basis for responding to a variation on this objection mentioned by Manley.

> Suppose that in the actual world everything that is colored is red. Still, if someone in that world says "*Redness* and *coloredness* need not be co-extensive properties" that will be true. "But if the two words in italics refer to the same class, this sentence ... is false" (2002: 94, footnote 20).

Again, we can give a counterpart-theoretic response. The sentence in question is true because there is a world in which there is a colored-type counterpart to that class that is not identical to the class counterpart of that same class, such that the former includes member tropes that are not members of any class in that world that is a redness type counterpart to that class. The type counterpart relations differ depending upon whether the type is "redness" or "coloredness."[7]

---

[7] A referee expresses the concern that we may have no right to suppose that there is a viable notion of type similarity, in that the members at issue have no nature independent of membership in specific classes. Here I would suggest that there are viable notions of type similarity at stake depending upon whether one is operating with the linguistic ersatzist framework (where type similarity is cashed out in terms of the represented roles of the properties) or with combinatorialism (where type similarity is spelled out in terms of the subclass and overlap relations).

2.3 Response to Objection 3

According to the third objection, Natural Class Trope Nominalism is committed to a false version of an otherwise true principle. The principle is that necessarily, if something has a determinable, it will have a determinate of that determinable. The defective version of this principle is the following: necessarily, if something has a determinable of a property, it will have one of the actually tokened determinates of that determinable. If there is a missing shade of red, then the class of actual red tropes, R, does not include a red trope of that shade. Since the membership of a class is essential to it, it would seem that nothing could be red without being one of those actual shades. Natural Class Trope Nominalism would seem to be committed to the claim that necessarily, if something is red, it will have one of the actual reds, whereas something could have been red but not one of *these* reds, but the missing shade of red. This objection is closely related to Objection 2 and the One-Over-More objection. Part of the difficulty raised by the latter objection is that had there been an additional "red" trope of a shade of red that is instantiated in the actual world, r, it would not have been a "redness" trope since it would not have been a member of the actual class of red tropes given Natural Class Trope Nominalism. Call this the issue of "minimally alien tropes." I answered that objection by saying that what makes it true that had there been one more "red" trope, it would have been red, is that there is a possible world with a trope from the missing shade that is a member of a natural class that is a type counterpart to the natural class of actual red tropes. Can we rely on this answer to the One-Over-More objection to deal with the current objection?

Objection 3 adds certain complications not found in the One-Over-More objection. First, the additional trope would not be exactly like any actual trope. This is the issue of "moderately alien tropes." Second, Objection 3 brings into play two property types, "red" and "crimson" and their relations, whereas the One-Over-More objection does not require that more than one property type be referenced. Still, to respond to this objection, we can, again, resort to property counterpart theory. There is a world with a type counterpart to the class of actual colors that includes this missing shade of red. That is what makes it possible for something to be red but not one of the actual shades of red. How will this answer fit with linguistic ersatzism and combinatorialism?

Let's start with linguistic ersatzism. There is no special problem created by the "addition" of a property that only inexactly resembles some actual trope over and above the problem generated by the possibility of a new trope that is exactly like some actual trope (the One-Over-More objection). There will be "worlds," sets of sets, representing the world as including additional tropes that are inexactly like some actual trope. These "worlds" are no harder to come by than "worlds" that represent the world as including more tropes exactly like some actual trope. In such "worlds," there will be type counterparts to "red."

However, we need to take a bit more time with combinatorialism. Recall how we handled the possibility of the mere "addition" of a new red trope, exactly similar to an actual red trope. We began with all the actual simple tropes and the difference relation, and we, then, formed the notion of a further trope, t, different from each of the original tropes, and specified the number of "places" that this trope has. We, then, considered the maximal natural class C of actual red tropes of the same number of places, each of which stands to each other in a relation of being co-members of a natural class of a certain degree of naturalness. Although t is different from *each* of the actual red tropes, we can stipulate that t is a co-member of a further natural class, $C+$, of the same degree of naturalness as C, made up of t and all and only the actual red tropes. We then focused on the class of truthmakers, X, for the truth that $C+$ is possible. Among these "truthmakers" are all the members of the class of actual red tropes, C. C is a subclass of X. The merely possible class, $C+$, is similar to the actual class C, since C overlaps a class made up of the truthmakers for the possibility of $C+$. The story for the possibility of an additional trope, the missing shade of red, which is merely inexactly similar to some actual tropes, will start the same as above with the difference relation along with all the actual red tropes. We will, then, form the notion of a trope, r', different from each of the original red tropes, but possessing the same number of "places." We then further triangulate r' by reference to tropes directly adjacent to the missing shade of red, say r and r'': r, r', and r'' form a natural class that is more natural than any other combination of at least two not-exactly similar tropes from the actual class of red tropes and r', and r and r' do not form a perfectly natural class and neither do r' and r''.

3. Variation on Objection 2

I want now to consider a variation on Objection 2. According to this objection, it is not possible for the distinct properties of crimsonness and redness to be identical properties, but if properties are classes of tropes, then since it is possible that all the redness tropes are crimson tropes, it is possible for redness and crimsonness to be identical:

> Consider a possible world in which the only red things are crimson. In that world the class of redness tropes is identical to the crimson tropes, although in the actual world the class of redness tropes is not identical to the class of crimson tropes. If property types are classes of tropes, then it follows that although redness is not identical to crimsonness, it is possible for those properties to be identical. But if P and Q are distinct properties, then they are necessarily distinct. "Consider a possible world where all objects are red. Here the class of colored tropes and the class of red tropes coincide exactly... these [redness and coloredness] collapse into the same property. But they are necessarily distinct properties..." (Manley 2002: 83).

I think the best response to this objection for the trope theorist is to deny that if P and Q are not identical property types, then necessarily, P and Q are not identical property types. Even if redness is not identical to crimsonness, it could have been identical to crimsonness. And, in fact, given the application of counterpart theory to properties, that is what one would expect: P and Q may have counterparts in another world, relative to different counterpart relations, that are identical, and, hence, P and Q could have been identical. Thus, the counterpart theorist can make room for the following: crimson and redness might have been identical. There is a possible world in which there is a crimson counterpart and a redness counterpart to that class that are identical.[8]

It might be objected that this just shows that counterpart theory should not be applied to properties, because distinct properties are necessarily distinct. Why might one think that if P and Q are distinct, then they are necessarily distinct? Manley offers the following line of reasoning. We certainly think that the distinct properties of being spherical and being red could not have been identical. There is no world in which these properties are identical. "But there is something (prohibitively) odd about saying that *redness* just happens to be the very same property as *being spherical*. For the same reason, we cannot allow that *redness* could ever be the very same property as *coloredness*" (Manley 2002: 83). In fact, although it does seem extremely odd to say that redness is identical to being spherical, the same is not true of redness and crimsonness. Suppose, for example, that in the actual world sphericalness and redness and crimsonness are coextensive. It would be extremely odd to answer the question, "What is it to be spherical in the actual world?" with "It is to be red." However, it would not be odd to answer the question, "What is it to be colored in the actual world?" with "It is to be red." We have a *difference in our intuitions with respect to these questions*. So it does seem that we do leave room for some contingent identity in the case of properties, although there are limits on how that contingency works out. No one has the intuition that redness could have been sphericalness. However, we need to guard against generalizing from this and similar cases to the claim that for all properties, there is no contingent identity. Even though it is true that for many properties, P and Q, if property P and property Q are not identical it may not be true that P and Q could have been identical, it does not follow that is true for all properties. There is an "intuitive ban on the possible identity of distinct properties," but it is a mistake to think this applies to all property pairs. And, notice, that there is no reason to think that Trope Theory combined with a counterpart theory for properties implies that redness could have been identical to sphericalness. Any class of tropes that might be similar enough to the class of actual sphericalness tropes to count as a counterpart of "sphericalness" will not be similar enough to the class of actual redness tropes to count as a counterpart of "redness" and vice versa.[9]

---

[8] One might object to the notion of contingent identity, but in the context of counterpart theory that merely involves the possibility of diverging counterparts in the same world under different counterpart relations.

[9] A referee worries that given that tropes have no intrinsic nature under Natural Class Trope Nominalism, there is nothing to bar the class of "sphericalness" tropes from counting as a counterpart of the "redness" type—if, say, the two classes had the same number of members. The answer to this worry varies depending

It is also worth pointing out that a Universalist who rejects determinable universals and accepts the Principle of Instantiation—the principle that dictates that there are no uninstantiated properties—may agree. To see this, suppose that the predicate "is colored" does not pick out a universal but a disjunction of universals, each of which is a fully determinate color. Also suppose that there are no uninstantiated universals (no universals that are not instantiated in the actual world). Finally, suppose that as a matter of fact it is not the case that the only redness in the actual world is crimson. In that case, "being red" does not pick out a universal but a disjunction of universals, and the property being red is not identical to the property of being crimson. Still there is a possible world in which the only redness is crimsonness. In that world, "being red" does pick out a universal, crimsonness, not a disjunction of universals. Hence, although the property of being red is not identical to the property of being crimson (since "being red" does not pick out a universal in the actual world), it could have been identical to crimsonness. But note also that the Universalism does not imply that redness could have been identical to sphericalness.

4. Utterly alien tropes

This is a good point to bring up another objection based on the possibility of the "extremely alien tropes," tropes that are not even inexactly similar to any actual tropes, except perhaps with respect to their particularity, to trope combinatorialism, and see how it is related to Natural Class Trope Nominalism. Let's first recall Armstrong's response to the possibility of alien simple universals, universals that are not identical to or partly identical to any instantiated universal (and, hence, not similar to the latter). Armstrong's response seeks to accommodate the possibility that there could be fully determinate simple universals that are not in fact instantiated. Starting with all the simple universals that reality contains, he notes that "between each of these entities the internal relation... of *difference* holds" (1997: 167).

> We can go on to form the notion of a further such entity which is different from, other than, *each* of the original entities. We can specify further whether this entity is

---

upon whether one has a combinatorialist or linguistic ersatzist approach to modality. Let's start with the latter. Under linguistic ersatzism, "worlds" are just sets of sets, representations, and the member sets of these sets of sets are sets of numbers in which the property number places are interpreted as existentially bound variables. Two or more numbers in property places in a single world that match are interpreted as representing the same property and if the numbers do not match as different properties. A set of sets that is a world represents a complete description of a distribution of properties. The representations will also include a separate representation of the nomological role of these properties, if those nomological roles are not reducible to those distributions. Comparisons of properties across worlds are made in terms of the distributive (and perhaps nomologial) role of the properties. The idea would be that the "role" of what we are calling "sphericalness" in one world would not match up very well to the "role" of "redness" in the other world. Now consider combinatorialism and recall that similarity across worlds involves two classes being subclasses of a common natural class or class overlap. In our example, presumably neither of these conditions will be satisfied with respect to the "redness" tropes and the "sphericalness" tropes.

a particular or a universal, and if the latter the number of 'places' this universal has. Relative to the original assemblage, this new entity is an alien. Our conception of it is in a way combinatorially formed: using the original assemblage and the relation of difference (1997: 167).

Recall, also, that Armstrong says that this approach will fail if each property has "its own nature, whatness or *quidditas* so that to encounter one is emphatically not to have encountered all" (1997: 168). Armstrong rejects such "strong" quiddities. It is clear that any account of properties that posits "strong quiddities" in the context of a combinatorialist theory of modality will face Armstrong's worry. So one question for Natural Class Trope Nominalism is the following: does each trope have its own quidditas? In fact, I will not take a position directly on this question here. Instead, I will argue that if Natural Class Trope Nominalism has a problem with properties with strong quiddities, that problem is a shared one that does not arise from the particular account of tropes offered by Natural Class Trope Nominalism. More precisely, the view that takes a trope's nature to be a matter of class membership does not as such generate a quidditas-based problem for combinatorialism. All of the objections considered in this chapter so far are tied to the fact that for Natural Class Trope Nominalism, a trope's nature is determined by its membership in natural classes of actual tropes. That seems to generate difficulties by tying the nature of tropes too closely to such actual classes. But the problem of completely alien tropes is unrelated to this aspect of Natural Class Trope Nominalism. Natural Class Trope Nominalism will face a problem with completely alien tropes only if it endorses both quiddities and combinatorialism. Even if a trope's nature is determined by such actual classes and even if class membership is essential to a class and even if we do not have available property counterpart theory, the possibility of completely alien tropes does not raise a problem for Natural Class Trope Nominalism *per se*. Consider for example the One-Over-More objection. That objection cannot be generated on the basis of the possibility of additional, but completely alien, tropes. Suppose it is possible that there exists a completely alien trope z. Given that z would not instance any actual property type, we do not have to figure out how z could have existed and been, say, a red trope without having been a member of the class of actual red tropes. The point is that for the Natural Class Trope Nominalist this issue is not any more pressing than it is for the proponent of universals who also adopts combinatorialism. Hence, although this is a serious issue for combinatorialism it does not cut any more against the Natural Class Trope Nominalist combinatorialism than it does against Realist combinatorialism. So I will leave it to one side as a shared problem. Now it would be possible for the proponent of Natural Class Trope Nominalism to follow Armstrong down this path and deny that tropes have quiddities. In fact, Natural Class Trope Nominalism seems to come close to saying just that. However, I will not attempt to resolve this issue for trope combinatorialism. The reason is that it is a shared problem with a universals-based combinatorialism and it seems likely that for any solution one camp adopts, there will be an analogue solution for the other camp. So this issue is not "decisive" when it comes to comparing tropes and, at least, Armstrongian universals.

5. Defense of counterpart theory

In this and last chapter, I have defended Natural Class Trope Nominalism against objections by advocating that this theory be combined with property counterpart theory. In this final section, I will briefly mention three independent reasons for favoring property counterpart theory. The first is that there are philosophical purposes, independent of defending nominalism, that are well served by a counterpart theoretic approach to properties, and that lends independent credibility to the claim that property types have counterparts, whether or not they are natural classes of tropes. I have in mind the philosophical use Mark Heller makes of property counterparts in giving an account of possible worlds that avoids modal realism. This work is a good demonstration of the independent merits of property counterpart theory.[10]

The second reason, offered by Heller, for favoring property counterpart theory is based on the fact that not all of a property's properties are essential to it, and which of its properties are essential and which are accidental varies with the context. Redness could have been instantiated even if the Empire State Building had not existed. The property of having 5 grams of mass could have existed even if the color of my notebook had been different. But what counts as essential and what counts as accidental to a property varies with the context. There are contexts in which we grant that "positive charge could have existed even if the laws of nature were radically different." But because there are other contexts in which laws of nature are important to us, we sometimes make judgments like "there could not have been even a single isolated incident in which two positively charged particles attracted one another... The fact that we are sometimes led to pass the judgment that there could be isolated incidents of positive attracting positive and sometimes to pass the opposite judgment is some evidence for a context-sensitive counterpart account of properties" (Heller 1998: 303). "If a property's essential properties were grounded in transworld identity, there would be no room for this sort of context relativity, since identity not relative" (1998: 304).

The third reason is more specific to the idea that the modal aspects of property-types-as-classes-of-tropes might be governed by counterpart relations that vary with context. Principles of re-identification for classes of ordinary particulars are context-dependent and tend to be paired with corresponding modal principles that similarly

---

[10] The best way to avoid modal realism is to give an alternative account of modality. Linguistic Ersatzism is one of the main alternatives, but its viability depends in part on being able to handle the problem of alien properties. Adopting a counterpart theory for properties, as Heller persuasively argues, supplies Linguistic Ersatzism with that ability.

vary with context. For example, in some contexts, re-identification of the Department Study Group from a few years ago with a group existing today requires that the groups have the same members, but in other contexts, a difference in membership is allowed. Judgments about what is possible for the Department Study are also guided by similarly varying principles. In some contexts, the Group could have existed with fewer members, but in others, that is not possible. This suggests that in considering classes of particulars, including classes of tropes, there are at work multiple counterpart relations, depending upon context.[11]

---

[11] A referee raises the following question. In the case of counterpart theory, for objects the counterpart relations typically reflect different properties of the objects, with different properties being relevant for different counterpart relations. But if properties themselves are counterpart-theoretic, what is it, exactly, that the different counterpart relations are picking up on? I would suggest, in response, that in the case of Linguistic Ersatzism, the different counterpart relations are picking up on different aspects of the roles of the properties that are represented in the "worlds," and in the case of Combinatorialism what is being picked up on are different degrees of overlap or how many natural classes the classes at issue are common subclasses of.

Bibliography

Adams, R. M. (1979). "Primitive Thisness and Primitive Identity." *Journal of Philosophy*. 76: 5–26.
Armstrong, D. M. (1978a). *Universals and Scientific Realism*. i: *Nominalism and Realism*. Cambridge: Cambridge University Press.
——(1978b). *Universals and Scientific Realism*. ii: *A Theory of Universals*. Cambridge: Cambridge University Press.
——(1980a). "Identity Through Time," in P. van Inwagen (ed.), *Time and Cause*. Dordrecht: D. Reidel Publishing Company, 68–78.
——(1980b). "Against 'Ostrich Nominalism'." *Pacific Philosophical Quarterly*. 61: 440–9.
——(1983). *What Is a Law of Nature?* Cambridge: Cambridge University Press.
——(1986). "The Nature of Possibility." *The Canadian Journal of Philosophy*. 16: 575–94.
——(1989a). *Universals: An Opinionated Introduction*. Boulder: Westview.
——(1989b). *A Combinatorial Theory of Possibility*. New York: Cambridge.
——(1997). *A World of States of Affairs*. New York: Cambridge.
——(2005). "Four Disputes about Properties." *Synthese*. 144: 309–20.
Ayer, A. J. (1954). *Philosophical Essays*. London: MacMillan.
Bacon, J. (1995). *Universals and Property Instances: The Alphabet of Being*. Oxford: Blackwell.
Bacon, J., Campbell, K. and Reinhardt, L. (eds). (1993). *Ontology, Causality, and Mind: Essays in Honour of D. M. Armstrong*. Cambridge: Cambridge University Press.
Black, M. (1952). "The Identity of Indiscernibles." *Mind*. 61: 153–64.
Braddon-Mitchell, D. and Miller, K. (2006). "The Physics of Extended Simples." *Analysis*. 66: 222–6.
Brownstein, D. (1973). *Aspects of the Problem of Universals*. University of Kansas.
Campbell, K. (1981). "*The Metaphysic of Abstract Particulars*." *Midwest Studies in Philosophy*. 6 (1): 477–88.
——(1990). *Abstract Particulars*. Oxford: Blackwell.
Caston, V. (1997). "Epiphenomenalisms, Ancient and Modern." *The Philosophical Review*. 106: 309–63.
Casullo, A. (1988). "A Fourth Version of the Bundle Theory." *Philosophical Studies*. 54: 125–39.
Clapp, L. (2001). "Disjunctive Properties: Multiple Realizations." *Journal of Philosophy*. 98: 111–36.
Daly, C. (1994–5). "Tropes." *Proceedings of the Aristotelian Society*. 94: 253–61.
Davidson, D. (1980). "Causal Relations," in his essays on *Actions and Events*. Oxford: Oxford University Press, 105–21.
Devitt, M. (1997). "'Ostrich Nominalism' or 'Mirage Realism'," in A. Mellor, and A. Oliver, 1997, 93–100.
Dunn, M. (1990). "Relevant Predication 2: Intrinsic Properties and Internal Relations." *Philosophical Studies*. 60: 177–206.

Ehring, D. (1996). "Mental Causation, Determinables and Property Instances." *Nous*. 30: 461–80.
——(1997a). *Causation and Persistence: A Theory of Causation*. New York: Oxford University Press.
——(1997b). "Lewis, Temporary Intrinsics, and Momentary Tropes." *Analysis*. 57: 254–8.
——(1998). "Trope Persistence and Temporary External Relations." *The Australasian Journal of Philosophy*. 76: 473–9.
——(1999). "Tropeless in Seattle: The Cure for Insomnia." *Analysis*. 59: 19–24.
——(2001). "Temporal Parts and Bundle Theory." *Philosophical Studies*. 104: 163–8.
——(2002a). "Spatial Relations Between Universals." *The Australasian Journal of Philosophy*. 80: 17–23.
——(2002b). "The Causal Argument Against Natural Class Trope Nominalism." *Philosophical Studies*. 107: 179–90.
——(2003). "Part–Whole Physicalism and Mental Causation." *Synthese*. 136: 359–88.
——(2004a). "Property Counterparts and Natural Class Trope Nominalism." *The Australasian Journal of Philosophy*. 82: 436–54.
——(2004b). "Distinguishing Universals From Particulars." *Analysis*. 64: 326–32.
——(2009). "Causal Relata." *Oxford Handbook on Causation*. (Eds) H. Beebee, C. Hitchcock, and P. Menzies. Oxford: Oxford University Press, 387–413.
Ellis, B. (2001). *Scientific Essentialism*. Cambridge: Cambridge University Press.
Friesen, L. (2005). "Armstrong on Aliens." *The Canadian Graduate Journal of Philosophical Analysis*. 1: 47–68.
Funkhouser, E. (2006). "The Determinable–Determinate Relation." *Nous*. 40: 548–69.
Gendler, T. and Hawthorne, J. (eds) (2002). *Conceivability and Possibility*. Oxford: Oxford University Press.
Gilmore, C. (2003). "In Defence of Spatially Related Universals." *The Australasian Journal of Philosophy*. 81: 420–8.
Hacking, I. (1975). "The Identity of Indiscernibles." *Journal of Philosophy*. 72: 249–56.
Harre, R. and Madden, E. H. (1975). *Causal Powers: A Theory of Natural Necessity*. Oxford: Basil Blackwell.
Hawley, K. (2001). *How Things Persist*. Oxford: Oxford University Press.
Hawthorne, J. (2001). "Causal Structuralism." *Philosophical Perspectives*. 15: 361–78.
Heil, J. (1999). "Part, Wholes, and Causal Relevance." (Read at the APA Pacific Division Meeting, 1999).
——(2003). *From an Ontological Point of View*. New York: Oxford University Press.
Heller, M. (1998). "Property Counterparts in Ersatz Worlds." *Journal of Philosophy*. 95: 293–316.
Hill, C. (1991). *Sensations: A Defense of Type Materialism*. Cambridge: Cambridge University Press.
Hochberg, H. (1988). "A Refutation of Moderate Nominalism." *The Australasian Journal of Philosophy*. 66: 188–207.
Humberstone, L. (1996). "Intrinsic/Extrinsic." *Synthese*. 108: 205–67.
Jackson, F. (1977). "Statements About Universals." *Mind*. 76: 427–9.
——(1994). "Metaphysics by Possible Cases." *The Monist*. 77, number 1, January.
Jackson, F., Pargetter, R. and Prior, E. (1982). "Functionalism and Type–Type Identity Theories." *Philosophical Studies*. 42: 209–25.

Johnson, W. E. (1964). *Logic.* New York: Dover.
Kim, J. (1993a). "Postscripts on Mental Causation," in his *Supervenience and Mind: Selected Philosophical Essays.* New York: Cambridge University Press, 358–67.
——(1993b). "Causation, Nomic Subsumption, and the Concept of Event," in his *Supervenience and Mind: Selected Philosophical Essays.* Cambridge: Cambridge University Press, 3–21.
——(1998). *Mind in a Physical World.* Cambridge: MIT Press.
Kripke, S. "Time and Identity," unpublished lectures.
Landesman, C. (1971). "Introduction: The Problem of Universals," in his *The Problem of Universals.* New York: Basic Books, 3–20.
Lewis, D. (1983a). "Counterparts of Persons and Their Bodies," in his *Philosophical Papers Volume I.* New York: Oxford, 47–54.
——(1983b). "New Work for a Theory of Universals." *The Australasian Journal of Philosophy.* 61: 343–77.
——(1986a). "Causation," in his *Philosophical Papers Volume II.* Oxford: Oxford University Press, 159–213.
——(1986b). *On the Plurality of Worlds.* Oxford: Blackwell.
——(1986c). "Introduction," in his *Philosophical Papers Volume II.* Oxford: Oxford University Press, ix–xvii.
——(1991). *Parts of Classes.* Oxford: Blackwell.
——(1994). "Humean Supervenience Debugged." *Mind.* 103: 473–90.
MacBride, F. (1998). "Where are Particulars and Universals?" *Dialectica.* 52: 203–27.
——(2005). "The Particular–Universal Distinction: A Dogma of Metaphysics?" *Mind.* 114: 565–614.
Macdonald, C. and Macdonald, G. (1986). "Mental Causation and Explanation of Action," in L. Stevenson, R. Squires, and J. Haldane (eds), *Mind, Causation and Action.* Oxford: Basil Blackwell, 35–48.
McDaniel, K. (2007). "Extended Simples." *Philosophical Studies.* 133: 131–41.
Mackie, J. L. (1974). *The Cement of the Universe.* Oxford: Oxford University Press.
McLaughlin, B. (1994). "Epiphenomenalism," in Samuel Guttenplan (ed.), *A Companion to the Philosophy of Mind: Blackwell Companions to Philosophy*, volume 5. Oxford: Blackwell, 277–88.
Manley, D. (2002). "Properties and Resemblance Classes." *Nous.* 36: 75–96.
Martin, C. B. (1980). "Substance Substantiated." *The Australasian Journal of Philosophy.* 58: 3–10.
——(1993). "Power for Realists," in J. Bacon, K. Campbell, and L. Reinhardt (eds), *Ontology, Causality, and Mind: Essays in Honour of D. M. Armstrong.* Cambridge: Cambridge University Press, 175–86.
Maudlin, T. (2007). *The Metaphysics within Physics.* Oxford: Oxford University Press.
Maurin, A. (2002). *If Tropes.* Dordrecht: Kluwer.
Mellor, H. and Oliver, A. (1997). *Properties.* Oxford: Oxford University Press.
Moore, G. E. (1922a). *Philosophical Studies.* K. Paul, London: Trench, Trubner & Co.
——(1922b). "The Conception of Intrinsic Value," in Moore 1922a, 253–75.
Moreland, J. P. (2001). *Universals.* Canada: McGill-Queen's University Press.
Noordhof, P. (1998). "Do Tropes Resolve the Problem of Mental Causation?" *The Philosophical Quarterly.* 48: 221–6.
O'Leary-Hawthorne, J. and Cover, J. A. (1998). "A World of Universals." *Philosophical Studies.* 91: 205–19.

Oliver, A. (1996). "The Metaphysics of Properties." *Mind*. 105: 1–80.
Papineau, D. (1993). *Philosophical Naturalism*. Oxford: Blackwell.
Parsons, J. (2000). "Must a Four-dimensionalist Believe in Temporal Parts?" *The Monist*. 83: 399–418.
——(2004). "Distributional Properties," in F. Jackson and G. Priest (eds), *Lewisian Themes: The Philosophy of David K. Lewis*. Oxford: Oxford University Press, 173–80.
Price, H. H. (1953). *Thinking and Experience*. London: Hutchinson's University Library.
Ramsey, F. P. (1925). "Universals." *Mind*. 34: 401–17, reprinted in Ramsey 1990, 8–30.
——(1990). *Philosophical Papers*, (ed.) D. H. Mellor. Cambridge: Cambridge University Press.
Robb, R. (1997). "The Properties of Mental Causation." *The Philosophical Quarterly*. 47: 178–94.
——(2001). "Reply to Noordhof on Mental Causation." *The Philosophical Quarterly*. 51: 90–4.
——(2005). "Qualitative Unity and the Bundle Theory." *The Monist*. 88: 466–92.
Robinson, D. (1989). "Matter, Motion, and Humean Supervenience." *The Australasian Journal of Philosophy*. 67: 394–409.
Rodriguez-Pereyra, G. (2002). *Resemblance Nominalism: A Solution to the Problem of Universals*. Oxford: Oxford University Press.
——(2004). "The Bundle Theory is Compatible with Distinct but Indiscernible Particulars." *Analysis*. 64: 72–81.
Schaffer, J. (2001). "The Individuation of Tropes." *The Australasian Journal of Philosophy*. 79: 247–57.
——(2003). "The Problem of Free Mass: Must Properties Cluster." *Philosophy and Phenomenological Research*. 66: 125–38.
——(2004). "Two Conceptions of Sparse Properties." *Pacific Philosophical Quarterly*. 2004: 92–102.
——(2005). "Quiddistic Knowledge." *Philosophical Studies*. 123: 1–32.
Searle, J. (1959). "Determinables and the Notion of Resemblance." *Proceedings of the Aristotelian Society*. Supplementary volume 33: 141–58.
Shoemaker, S. (1984a). "Some Varieties of Functionalism," in his *Identity, Cause, and Mind: Philosophical Essays*. Cambridge: Cambridge University Press, 261–86.
——(1984b). "Causality and Properties," in his *Identity, Cause, and Mind: Philosophical Essays*. Cambridge: Cambridge University Press, 206–33.
——(1998). "Realization and Mental Causation." *The Proceedings of the Twentieth World Congress in Philosophy*. 20th World Congress of Philosophy: Boston.
——(2007). *Physical Realization*. Oxford: Oxford University Press.
Sider, T. (1993). "Intrinsic Properties." *Philosophical Studies*. 83: 1–27.
——(2000). "Recent Work on Identity Over Time." *Philosophical Books*. 41: 81–9.
——(2001). *Four Dimensionalism: An Ontology of Persistence and Time*. Oxford: Oxford University Press.
——(2006). "Bare Particulars." *Philosophical Perspectives*. 20: 387–97.
——(2007). "Parthood." *Philosophical Review*. 116: 51–91.
Simons, P. (1994). "Particulars in Particular Clothing: Three Trope Theories of Substance." *Philosophy and Phenomenological Research*. 54: 553–75.
——(2004). "Extended Simples: A Third Way Between Atoms and Gunk." *The Monist*. 87: 371–84.

Sosa, E. (2007). "Experimental Philosophy and Philosophical Intuitionax." *Philosophical Studies*. 132: 99–107.

Stout, G. F. (1921–3). "The Nature of Universals and Propositions." *Proceedings of the British Academy*. 10: 157–72.

——(1923). "Are the Characteristics of Particular Things Universal or Particular? II." *Aristotelian Society*. 3: 114–22.

Teller, P. (1984). "Comments on Kim's Paper." *The Southern Journal of Philosophy*, XXII (1984). Supplement: Spindell Conference, 1983, 57–62.

Tooley, M. (1987). *Causation: A Realist Approach*. Oxford: Clarendon Press.

——(1988). "In Defense of the Existence of States of Motion." *Philosophical Topics*. 16: 225–54.

van Cleve, J. (1985). "Three Versions of the Bundle Theory." *Philosophical Studies*. 47: 95–107.

van Inwagen, P. (1986). "Two Concepts of Possible Worlds." *Midwest Studies in Philosophy*. 9: 185–213.

Walter, S. (2006). "Determinates, Determinables, and Causal Relevance." *The Canadian Journal of Philosophy*. 37: 217–43.

Williams, D. C. (1953a). "On the Elements of Being I." *Review of Metaphysics*. 7: 3–18.

——(1953b). "On the Elements of Being II." *Review of Metaphysics*. 7: 171–92.

——(1986). "Universals and Existents." *The Australasian Journal of Philosophy*. 64: 1–14.

Wilson, J. (1999). "How Superduper Does a Physicalist Supervenience Need To Be?" *The Philosophical Quarterly*. 49: 33–52.

——(2008). "Trope Determination and Contingent Characterization," unpublished paper.

——(2009a). "Determination, Realization and Mental Causation." *Philosophical Studies*. 145: 149–69.

——(2009b). "Resemblance-based Resources for Reductive Singularism." *The Monist*. 92: 153–90.

Wolterstorff, N. (1960). "Qualities." *The Philosophical Review*. 69: 183–200.

——(1970). *On Universals*. Chicago: University of Chicago.

Yablo, S. (1992). "Mental Causation." *The Philosophical Review*. 101: 245–80.

Zimmerman, D. (1997). "Distinct Indiscernibles and the Bundle Theory." *Mind*. 106: 305–9.

——(1998). "Temporal Parts and Supervenient Causation: The Incompatibility of Two Humean Doctrines." *The Australasian Journal of Philosophy*. 76: 265–88.

Index

-adicity 36, 38–40, 219, 219n.29
Against Standard Trope Nominalism 10, *see also* Standard Trope Theory
A Little More Red 84
Aristotle 13, 19, 25, 28, 40–1, 43, 91
Armstrong, David M. 7, 7n.11, 8n.12, 11, 11n.20, 20, 30–2, 34n.24, 37, 38n.29, 85–6, 94n.37, 99, 108, 108n.10, 119, 124n.42, 125–8, 125n.47, 141, 169, 179, 184, 190, 209, 209–10n, 213n.24, 218–20, 222–3, 239–40
asymmetric necessitation 145, 228–9
atomic states of affairs 20–1
Avogadro's number 26

"being identical with x" 33–4, 34n.24–5
Bi-Located Response 110–11, 115–16
Blob Theory 11
Braddon-Mitchell, D. 27
Bundle Theory 12–13, 12n, 47, 77, 97–111, 105n.8, 110n.16, 116, 118, 120–2, 121n.33, 122n.34, 128
    objection 1 132, 134–5
    objection 2 133
    objection 3 134

Cambridge changes 92–3, 96
Campbell, Keith 8–10, 8n.15, 14–15, 32n.21, 46–7, 49, 76n.1, 91–8, 93n, 124n.43, 125n.46, 142, 175–87, 176n.2, 193, 194n.23, 204, 224
Campbell's objections
    possibility 1 93–4
    possibility 2 94–5, 94n.38
canceling out hypothesis 51–2
cases
    1 25–7, 29n.19
    2 27, 29
    3 27, 42
    4 28, 42
Categorical Primitivism 10, 37–40, 37n.28, 40n.30
category mistake 112, 112n.19
causal-exemplification theory 65
causal powers subset 171–2, 171n.50
causal relata 47–8, 136–41, 157–9, 158n.33, 163–4, 167–8, 168n.44, 170
causation 3, 15, 44, 48, 56–9, 56n.13, 59n.19, 62, 65–8
    neo-Humean theory of 63, 63n.23
    reductive theory of 62, 67, 67n.28

combinatorialism 209–10, 209n.13, 211n.18, 212, 216–20, 232–3, 235–6, 237–8n.9, 239
completeness account 21–3
Complexes-But-No-Object Objection 119
compresence 12–14, 12n.26–7, 98, 103–4, 106–7, 120–6, 123n.38–9, 125n.45, 128–34, 131–2n, 133n
counterfactual theory 63–4, 81, 206–7
counterpart theory 11, 15, 78, 80–1, 83, 85, 99, 203n.1, 207–12, 207n.8, 208n, 209n.16, 214, 214n.26, 215–18, 225–6, 225n.36, 226n.37, 234, 237, 237n.8, 240, 241n.11
Cover, J. A. 99, 99n.2, 107, 109–11, 109–10n.14
crossworld trope identity 81, 83, 205–6, 210, 212, 212–13n.23

Davidson, D. 138n.4, 154–5
"Davidsonian" framework 138, 153–5, 158n.33, 163
determinable-determinate distinction 139–42, 140n.8, 143n, 146–7, 147n.17
determination
    objection 1 229
    objection 2 229–30
    objection 3 230
    objections response 1 230–3, 231n.4
    objections response 3 235–63
determination objections
    some principles of 227–9, 228n.2–3
    utterly alien tropes 238–40
    variation on Objection 2 236–8
Devitt, M. 127–8
Difference Principle 150
disjunctive strategy 169, 170n.48
Distance-as-Three-Placed view 114n.26
doctrine of Humean Supervenience 58–63, 58n.16, 59n.17, 67
Downward Necessitation 229
Dunn, M. 33
duplication Objection 107–8, 119

empty possibilities 78
Exact Similarity Formulation 32, 40–4
exemplifications 23, 23n.11, 55, 140–1
extended simples 25–7

four-dimensionalism 53, 55, 57, 66–8, 100–3, 106, 122
functionalism 149, 165–70, 168–9n.45

Gilmore, Cody 29

Hacking, I. 109n.12
haecceitism 218–19, 219n.28
Hawley, K. 21, 21n.60, 67, 67n.29
Heil, J. 162n.38
Heller, Mark 170–1n.49, 211–15, 212n.22, 225n.36, 240

Identity of Indiscernibles Principle 32–4, 36–7, 108–9
immaculate property replacement 5, 50–2, 51n.6, 54–6
imperfect piling 90
incomplete-complete distinction 24
Indeterministic Sphere Case 57–8, 61–2, 65–6, *see also* sphere case
inexact resemblance 8
inexact similarity 30
instantiation 19–21, 24–5, 105, 126–9, 151, 209, 210n.16, 238
intrinsic instantaneous velocity 59–61, 59n.20, 60–1n
Irrelevancy Thesis 223, 223n.34

Johnson, W. E. 148n.21

Kim, J. 140n.9, 169–70, 170n.47–8
Kimian events 140n.9

Lewis, David 2–3, 13, 46, 67–71, 69n.30, 71n.33, 126–7, 134–5, 157, 205–6, 206–7n
linguistic argument 49
linguistic ersatzism 211–17, 213n.24, 217n.27, 225n.36, 232–3, 235, 237–8n.9
localism 112–13, 113n.20–1, 115–16

MacBride, Fraser 19, 19n.1, 20n.3, 21, 21n.6, 24n.12, 29n.18
McDaniel, K. 26n.13–16
Manley, D. 234, 237
Maudlin, T. 56–7n.15
Maurin, A. 120–1n.31, 123, 123–4n, 125n.45, 127n.50
mental causation
 first case 164
 last case 164
 mental property problems 154–72, 163n.40
 middle case 167–8
 next-to-last case 165–7, 165n.43
 objections 169–70
 proper 136–7
 token identity response 137–47, 137n.3
 tropes 10, 14, 135–6, 148–54
mental/physical determinability
 objection 1 147, 147n.19, 150
 objection 2 148–9, 148n.20, 149n.22, 150

objection 3 149–51
objection 4 150–1, 150n.23
reply to objections 151–3, 153n.26
mereological sums 6, 12, 14, 26, 98–9, 106, 110n.15, 117
Miller, K. 27
minimality 3–4
modal realism 6–7, 9, 11, 15, 124, 192–3, 192n.22, 205, 208–9, 240n.10
modification 1 28–9
modification 2 29–30
monistic causal/nomic role view 35–6
Moore, G. E. 34
Moreland, J. P. 180n.10, 181n.12, 183
multigrade 20, 21n.6, 24
multi-locators 25–6, 26n.14, 30, 78
multiple realizability 144, 148–50

Natural Class Object Nominalism 6–7, 7n.9–10, 11, 196–7, 199–200
Natural Class Trope Nominalism 1–2, 9–11, 9n.18, 15, 44, 44n.35, 76, 172
 Argument 1 (Campbellian tropes) 177–80, 177n.4, 178–80n, 182, 184–8, 184n.13, 185n.14, 186n.16
 Argument 2 (Campbellian tropes) 180–2, 180n.10–11, 181n.12, 184–8, 184n.13, 185n.14
 causation objection 222–6
 collapse objections 193–201, 200n.28
 determination objections 229–39, 231n.4, 237–8n.9
 determination relation 227–9, 228n.3
 distinction by abstraction response 186–7
 inversion problem 214–16
 One-Over-Fewer objection 203–14, 208n.12, 211n.19, 212–13n.23, 214n.26, 220, 222
 One-Over-More objection 216–20, 220n.30, 222
 Resemblance Trope Nominalism 187–93, 189n, 190n, 192n.22
 singleton class 221–2, 221n.33
 standard theory 175–7
 three conceptions 175
neo-Humean theory of causation 63, 63n.23
Non-Full Determinacy Principle 149–50
nonsalient qualitative change 5, 51–2, 52–3n.8
non-supervenient relations 68
Norcross, Alastair 150n.23
no-relation response 127–8

objection (duplication) 107–8, 119
objections (Bundle Theory)
 1 132, 134–5
 2 133
 3 134

objections (determination)
  1 229
  2 229–30
  3 230
objections (mental/physical determinability)
  1 147, 147n.19, 150
  2 148–50, 148n.20, 149n.22
  3 149–51
  4 150–1, 150n.23
  reply 151–3, 153n.26
objections response (determination)
  1 230–3, 231n.4
  3 235–6
Object Principle 77
objects 11–12, 11–12n.22, 41, 55, 65, 67–73, 70n.32, 106, 116
Occam's Razor 46
O'Leary-Hawthorne, J. 99, 99n.2, 107, 109–11, 109–10n.14
Oliver, A. 126n.48
one-category Universalism 46
One-Over-Fewer objection 15, 203–14, 208n.12, 211n.19, 212–13n.23, 214n.26, 216, 220, 222
One Over Many problem 4
One Over Many Times problem 4–5
One-Over-More objection 15, 216–20, 220n.30, 222, 235, 239

pain 140–1, 147–50, 152, 161–2
Parsons, Josh 26, 96n.42
particulars 19, 24–7, 29–31, 43, 45
  bare 1, 15, 175, 193–6, 198–9
  concrete 47, 194
PCI 117–18
perceptual argument 49
physical causation 137–40, 138–9n.5–6, 153–7, 160–3, 170
physical-object identity 52
Planck squares 27
Pointhood universals 115–16
possibility 1 (Campbell's objections) 93–4
possibility 2 (Campbell's objections) 94–5, 94n.38
Primitivist Principle 75–6, 78, 81, 81n.17, 86–91, 87n.25, 91n.32
probabilistic theory 64–5
properties
  abundant 2–3
  counterpart theory 11, 15, 203n.1, 208, 210–12, 214, 217, 234, 240
  immaculate property replacement 50–1
  impure relational 108n.11
  inherent/non-relational 32–3, 33n.22
  interior 33
  intrinsic 33–4, 61
  mental 4

  nature of 36
  non-intrinsic 40
  non-relational 108
  persistence 5, 48–51, 51n.7, 53–8, 65, 75
  qualitative 33
  qualitative-intrinsic 34
  relational 110, 110n.17
  second-order 61
  sliding 84
  sparse 2–5, 4n.4, 5–6n.5
  structural 49
  swapping 84
  theories of 5–6
  time-indexed 70–4, 70n.31, 71n.34, 72n.36
  type persistence 50, 54
  types 14–15, 205, 210, 227
  universal-particular 35, 78
  universals/not universals 32, 34, 139
Pure Universalism 111, 111n.18, 115–16

qualitative persistence 45
qualitative similarity 55, 55n.11
quasi-determination 151–2
quiddities 38, 220, 239

Ramsey, F. P. 215–17, 217n.27
"Ramsey Lawbook" 35
Ramsey sentence 165
realism 38, 128, 204, 239
Regress Arguments
  1 120–30, 120n.30
  2 120n.29, 121, 121n.32, 122n.35, 124–30, 132–3, 132n.60, 133n.62
Regress Objection 13, 119–20
resemblance, axioms of 190–2
Resemblance Object Nominalism 6, 6n.6–7, 7n.10, 11, 46, 191, 196–7
Resemblance Trope Nominalism 9, 172, 187–93, 189n, 190n, 192n.22, 221
Resemblance Trope Theory 15
Robb, R. 49, 155–6, 156n, 161n.37
Robinson, D. 61
Rodriguez-Pereyra, G. 116–18, 117n.27, 124–5n.44, 178–9n.7, 191–2, 197
R-relation 53, 56, 101–2
Russell, Bertrand 20

Schaffer, J. 3, 3–4n, 76n.2, 78–81, 80n.14, 81n.17, 83, 83n.19, 88–91, 88n.27, 91n.32
self-relating-excluders 130
self-relating response 135
Shoemaker, Sydney 166, 171
Sider, T. 195, 199
similarity accounts 30
Simons, P. 26–7
Socrates 34

space indexing 114–15
space-time 26, 43, 53, 55, 100–1, 106, 115, 199
spanners 25–6, 26n.15
spatially extended simple particulars 25–6
spatial parts 114, 114n
spatial relations 111
Spatio-Temporal Principle 14, 55, 75–81, 77–9n, 81n.17, 83n.19, 86–91, 87n.25, 91n.31
spectrums 95–6, 95n.39
sphere case 56, 56–7n.15, 61, 66–7
Stage Theory 14, 53, 53n.9, 55, 66–7, 100–2, 105–6
Standard Trope Theory 2, 8–10, 175, 183–4
Stout, G. F. 11n.19
Substance-Attribute Theory 11
super-realizers 147–50
supervenience 144, 149, 152
Swapping Across Locations 78–9
Swapping Across Objects 79, 79n

Teller, P. 161n.36
Temporal Parts Theory 14, 102
temporal relativization proposal 71
temporary external relations 113
temporary intrinsics 13, 69–70
thick particulars 11
thin particulars 11–12, 11n.21, 209
three-dimensionalism 53–4, 69
time-located tropes 71
time-traveling 27–9, 41–2, 78
Tooley, M. 59–60, 60–1n.22
top-down approach 138
Trope Bundle Theory 1, 13–14, 47, 50, 97–101, 103, 107–8, 119
tropes
  enduring 66–8, 66n.27, 71, 73–5, 73n.38, 104
  enduring, objection 68–75
  individuation 75
  momentary distance 72–3, 105, 105n.9, 122
  Nominalism 1–2, 13, 19, 46
  piling 86–91, 88n.27, 90n.30, 94

pyramiding 87–8, 87n.26, 91
response 113, 113n.22–3
stacking 87
swapping 80–5, 84n.20
trope sliding 82–4
  A Little More Red 84
  All Red 84
  Almost All Red 84
  case 1 82, 82n.18
  case 2 82–3
  case 3 83
  case 179 82–4, 83n.19
  One-Quarter Red 84
trope sliding/swapping, case 180 82–4, 82n.18
truthmakers 4, 178, 209, 219–20, 236

unigrade 20–2, 21n.5, 24
unigrade-multigrade distinction 24, 201n.30
Universalism
  one-category 46
  Pure 111, 111n.18, 115–16
universal-particular distinction 9–10, 19, 21, 21n.7, 25, 27, 31, 36, 39, 43–4, 91
universals 7–8, 11–13, 19, 21–32, 21n.6, 22n, 34, 37–45, 40n.31, 49, 52–5, 84–5, 85n.21, 91, 97, 99, 103, 107, 111–12, 115, 117–19, 139–42, 176, 194, 198, 201, 209, 238
Universals-based Bundle Theory 14, 47, 99–101, 104–5, 107–10, 116

Walter, S. 147, 150
Williams, D. C. 10, 19, 32–6, 32n.21, 39, 41n.32, 44n.35, 47, 49, 89
Wilson, Jessica 48n.2, 159, 159n.34
Wolterstorff, N. 49
Worm-Bundle Theory 100–1, 101n.5, 105
Worm Theory 53, 53n.9, 55, 66–7, 100, 100n.4, 102, 105

Yablo, Stephen 143–5, 153n.26, 163–4n.41

Zimmerman, D. 60, 60n.21

The manufacturer's authorised representative in the EU for product safety is
Oxford University Press España S.A. of el Parque Empresarial San Fernando de
Henares, Avenida de Castilla, 2 – 28830 Madrid (www.oup.es/en or product.
safety@oup.com). OUP España S.A. also acts as importer into Spain of products
made by the manufacturer.

www.ingramcontent.com/pod-product-compliance
Ingram Content Group UK Ltd.
Pitfield, Milton Keynes, MK11 3LW, UK
UKHW022231230426
12048UKWH00016BA/1181